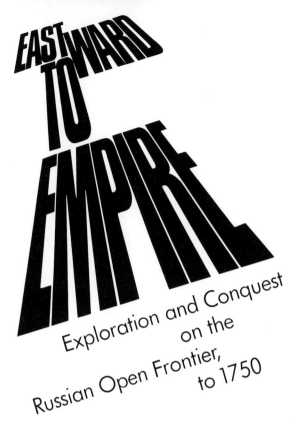

EASTWARD TO EMPIRE

Exploration and Conquest
on the
Russian Open Frontier,
to 1750

George V. Lantzeff and Richard A. Pierce

McGILL–QUEEN'S UNIVERSITY PRESS
MONTREAL AND LONDON 1973

© McGill-Queen's University Press 1973
International Standard Book Number 0 7735 0133 9
Library of Congress Catalog Number 72-82244
Legal Deposit Third quarter 1973

Design by Pat Gagnon
Printed in the United States of America by Edwards Brothers Inc.

This book has been published with the help of a grant
from the Social Science Research Council of Canada
using funds provided by the Canada Council.

Contents

MAPS *1*

PREFACE *17*

1 RUSSIAN EXPANSION IN KIEVAN TIMES

The Kievan State and the Eastern Frontier *21*
The Rise of Novgorod as a Colonial Power *22*
Expansion of the Volga Principalities at the Expense of Novgorod *24*
Suzdal Encroachment on Bulgar Territories *27*
Continuing Strife between Suzdal and Novgorod *27*
Suzdal against the Bulgars and Mordva *29*
Summary *30*

2 RUSSIAN EXPANSION UNDER MONGOL RULE

The Rulers of Novgorod *31*
The Rise of Tver and Moscow *32*
The Novgorodian Colonies *34*
Novgorod and the Early Moscow Princes *35*
The Novgorodian Ushkuiniki *36*
Moscow and the Perm Lands *37*
Novgorod and the Dvina Region *38*
Moscow Contests the Dvina Region *39*
Annexation of Novgorod and Its Territories by Moscow *45*
Annexation of Viatka *47*
Moscow Presses beyond the Urals *48*
Summary *49*

3 LIBERATION AND ADVANCE

Decline of the Golden Horde *51*
Breakup of the Horde *52*
Tatars in Russian Service *54*
Muscovite Policy toward the Crimean Tatars and the Nogais *55*
Ivan III and Kazan *55*
Relations with Poland-Lithuania *56*
Moscow Achieves Liberation *57*
New Trouble with Kazan *59*

Diplomatic Revolution in the Steppe   *60*
Struggle with Crimea   *61*
Vasilii III and Kazan   *62*
Crimea Profits from a Change of Tsars   *63*
Ivan IV and Kazan   *64*
The Conquest of Kazan   *66*
The Kazan Territories   *67*
Fortification of Conquered Territories   *68*
The Annexation of Astrakhan   *69*
The Fruits of Conquest   *69*
Defence Lines Against Crimea   *70*
Summary   *72*

4   THE RISE OF THE COSSACK HOSTS

'Russian Cossacks'   *74*
The Cossack Hosts   *77*
Summary   *79*

5   THE STROGANOVS AND THEIR FRONTIER MARK

Origins of the Stroganov Family   *81*
Anika Stroganov   *82*
The Charters of 1558 and 1564: a Fiefdom on the Kama   *84*
Grant of the Chusovaia Valley (1568)   *86*
Clashes with the Natives   *86*
Raiders from the Siberian Khanate (1573)   *88*
Authorization to Invade Siberia (1574)   *89*
Relations with Foreigners: a Sixteenth-Century Project for a Northern Sea
   Route to China   *90*
Summary   *91*

6   THE EXPEDITION OF ERMAK, THE RUSSIAN CORTEZ

Organizing the Expedition   *94*
Crossing the Urals   *95*
The Advance from Tiumen   *96*
Capture of Isker (Sibir)   *98*
Disintegration of the Tatar Khanate   *99*
The Stroganovs Appease Ivan IV   *101*
Native Resistance   *102*
The Death of Ermak   *105*
Evacuation of Siberia   *106*
Summary   *106*

7 THE FRONTIER POLICIES OF BORIS GODUNOV

Fortifying the Frontier *109*
Re-establishment in Western Siberia: Tiumen (1586), Tobolsk (1587) *112*
Tara (1594) and the End of Kuchum *114*
Improvement of Communications *119*
The Destruction of the Pelym Principality *120*
Verkhotur'e (1598) and Turinsk (1600) Secure the Road to the Irtysh *121*
Operations on the Lower Ob: Berezov (1593) *121*
Founding of Mangazeia (1601) *122*
Operations on the Upper Ob: Surgut (1594), Narym (1598), Ketsk (1602) *123*
The Tatars and Kirgiz of the Tom River Country: Tomsk (1604), Kuznetsk
    (1618) *124*
Summary *124*

8 FROM THE OB TO THE PACIFIC

The Advance to the Enisei: Turukhansk (1607) *127*
Native Rebellions *129*
Mangazeians Explore the Lower Lena *132*
Eniseisk Men Explore the Upper Lena *133*
Rivalry Between Mangazeian and Eniseisk Men on the Lena *135*
Tobolsk and Tomsk Men on the Lena *136*
Moskvitin Reaches the Pacific (1639) *137*
Continued Rivalry on the Lena *138*
Moscow Centres Control of the Lena at Iakutsk *138*
Summary *139*

9 THE CONQUEST OF BURIATIA AND TRANSBAIKALIA

Expeditions from Eniseisk under Kozlov, Savvin, Alekseev (Tiumenets),
    and Perfil'ev *141*
Dubenskii Founds Krasnoiarsk (1627) *143*
Beketov's Expedition (1628) *144*
Khripunov's Expedition (1629) *145*
Pacification by Perfil'ev: Bratsk (1631) *146*
Reconnoitring Transbaikalia: Perfil'ev's Expedition (1638–1640) *148*
Ivanov Discovers Lake Baikal (1643) *148*
Kolesnikov Founds Verkhne-Angarsk (1646) *149*
Pokhabov Visits the Eastern Khalka Mongols *150*
Galkin Founds Barguzin (1648) *151*
Beketov on the Amur. Nerchinsk (1653) *153*
Summary *154*

10   THE SEIZURE AND LOSS OF THE AMUR

Poiarkov's Expedition down the Amur to the Sea of Okhotsk   *155*
Alternative Routes to the Amur: the Vitim, the Aldan, and the Olekma   *159*
Khabarov's First Expedition to the Amur (1649–1650)   *159*
Khabarov's Second Expedition to the Amur (1650–1653)   *162*
A Rush to the Amur   *165*
Khabarov Ousted by Zinov'ev   *166*
The Baikov Mission to China (1653)   *167*
Stepanov Clashes with the Chinese (1655–1658)   *167*
The Amur a No Man's Land (1658–1672)   *170*
Russia Returns to the Amur   *171*
The Spafarii Embassy to China (1675–1677)   *172*
China Ousts the Russians from Albazin (1685)   *173*
The Golovin Embassy   *176*
The Mission of Veniukov and Favorov to Peking (1686)   *176*
Golovin's Journey Across Siberia   *177*
Korovin's Mission to Mongolia   *178*
Negotiating the Treaty of Nerchinsk   *179*
Significance of the Amur to Russia   *180*
Summary   *182*

11   TO ARCTIC SHORES

Early Voyages along the Arctic Coast   *183*
Perfir'ev and Rebrov Descend the Lena and Explore the Iana and the Indigirka   *184*
Buza Explores the Iana, the Indigirka and the Olenek   *185*
Posnik Ivanov goes Overland to the Iana and the Indigirka   *187*
Zyrian Traverses the Indigirka, Uiandina and Alazeia   *188*
Stadukhin Reaches the Kolyma (1644)   *188*
The First Voyage through the Straits Between Asia and America   *190*
Dezhnev Founds Anadyrsk (1649)   *191*
Summary   *193*

12   THE CONQUEST OF KAMCHATKA AND CHUKOTKA

First Information Concerning Kamchatka   *195*
Atlasov's Expeditions to Kamchatka   *196*
Disorders, and the End of Atlasov   *200*
Antsyferov and Kozyrevskii Reconnoitre the Kuriles (1711)   *203*
Continued Disorders   *204*
The El'chin Expedition   *208*
Evreinov and Luzhin Map the Kuriles (1721)   *208*

Further Disorder   *209*
Bering's First Expedition   *210*
The Shestakov Expedition   *211*
The Kamchadal Rebellion of 1731   *212*
Pavlutskii's Expedition against the Chukchi   *214*
Major Merlin Restores Order (1733–39)   *214*
Bering's Second Expedition   *215*
The Pacification of Kamchatka   *217*
The Subjugation of the Koriaks   *217*
The Subjugation of the Chukchi   *218*
Summary   *219*

13   CONCLUSIONS
Diversity of Russian Eastward Expansion   *221*
Causes   *223*
Effects   *227*
Achievements and Aims   *229*

APPENDIX   A Note on Ethnic Groups Mentioned in this Work   *231*

NOTES   *233*

GLOSSARY   *253*

BIBLIOGRAPHY   *255*

INDEX   *261*

Maps

1 Kievan Russia, to 1054   *1*

2 Russian Eastward Expansion, to 1237   *2*

3 The Moscow State, 1425–1533   *3*

4 Moscow and the Eastern Frontier, 1533–1605   *4*

5 The Occupation of the Ob-Irtysh and Enisei Basins   *5*

6 Principal Explorations, 1610–1632   *6*

7 The Occupation of the Lena Basin   *7*

8 Routes of Poiarkov and Khabarov   *8*

9 The Occupation of the Baikal-Amur Region   *9*

10 Explorations, 1633–1639   *10*

11 The Occupation of Northeastern Siberia   *11*

12 Atlasov's Expedition on Kamchatka   *12*

13 Voyages of Bering and Chirikov 1728, 1741   *13*

14 The Exploration and Conquest of Siberia   *14*

15 The Peoples of Siberia   *15*

1. KIEVAN RUSSIA, to 1054

------ Routes of the Varangians (Vikings)

2. RUSSIAN EASTWARD EXPANSION, to 1237

EASTWARD EXPANSION, TO 1237

LAPPS
SAMOYEDS
Archangel'sk
IUGRA
PERM
URAL MTS
NOVGOROD LANDS
Üstiug
Beloozero
VIATKA
Novgorod
LANDS
CHEREMIS
Riga
Pskov
Rostov
Tver Suzdal
Vladimir
BALTIC SEA
TEUTONIC KNIGHTS
Moscow
Lithuania Polotsk
Smolensk
VOLGA BULGARS
Riazan
Poland
Turov
Novgorod-Severskii
POLOVTSY
Vladimir-Volynskii
Chernigov
Galich
Kiev Pereiaslavl
Hungary

Bulgaria
BLACK SEA
CASPIAN SEA
BYZANTINE EMPIRE Constantinople
TURKS

- - - - - - - Borders of Russia at beginning of 13th century
.... Borders of Russian principalities

3. THE MOSCOW STATE, 1425–1533

MOSCOW STATE,
1425-1533

Norway

Sweden

ZYRIANS

VOGULS

PERMIANS

BALTIC SEA

Teutonic Order

Riga

Novgorod   Vologda   CHEREMIS   Viatka

Tver   Kostroma   KAZAN

Nizh.   Kazan
Novgorod
Moscow   KHANATE
Kasimov   (from 1437)

Vilno   Polotsk

Prussia   Smolensk

Grand   Briansk   MORDVA

Duchy   Gomel   Ryl'sk   NOGAI
HORDE

Poland   of   Putivl'

Lithuania   ASTRAKHAN
KHANATE
(from 1463)

CRIMEAN   Astrakhan

KHANATE

Kaffa

Bakhchisarai   CHERKESS

BLACK   SEA   CASPIAN SEA

DANUBE

Miles

-·--·--·- Borders of the Moscow State
▭▭▭ Lands annexed by Moscow, 1462-1533
---------- Boundary of Lithuania, 1462

3

4. MOSCOW AND THE EASTERN FRONTIER, 1533–1604

EASTERN FRONTIER, 1533-1604

----- Line of 1571
---•-- Expedition of Ermak, 1581-82

4

5. THE OCCUPATION OF THE OB-IRTYSH AND ENISEI BASINS

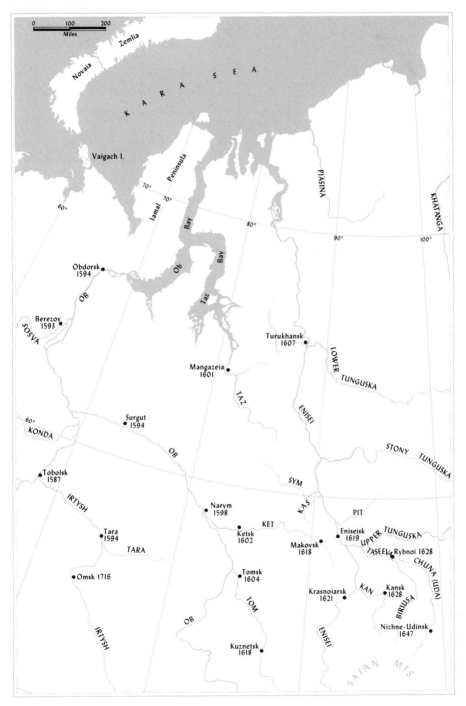

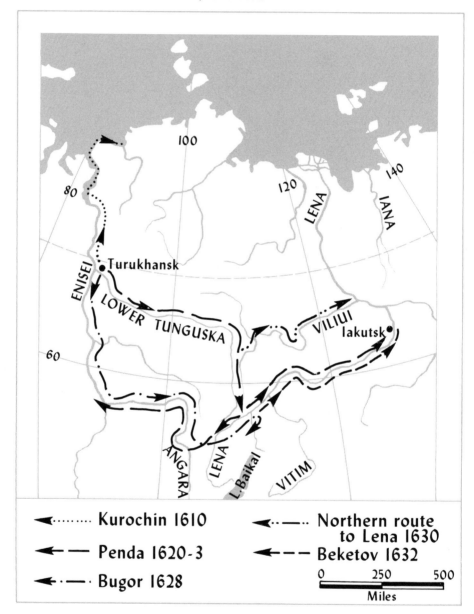

7. THE OCCUPATION OF THE LENA BASIN

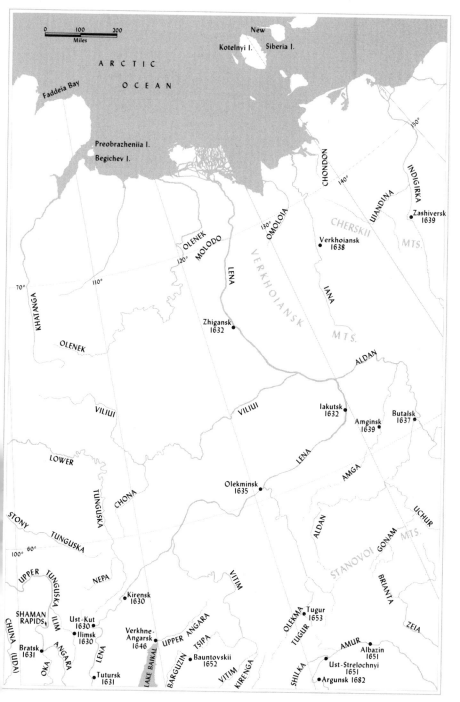

0   100   200
Miles

New
Kotelnyi I.   Siberia I.

A R C T I C

Faddeia Bay

O C E A N

Preobrazheniia I.

Begichev I.

CHONDON

150°

INDIGIRKA

140°

UIANDINA

Zashiversk
1639

OMOLOIA

130°

CHERSKII

Verkhoiansk
1638

MTS.

OLENEK

MOLODO

120°

LENA

VERKHOIANSK

IANA

70°

110°

KHATANGA

Zhigansk
1632

MTS.

OLENEK

ALDAN

VILIUI

VILIUI

Iakutsk
1632

Butalsk
1637

Amginsk
1639

LOWER

LENA

AMGA

Olekminsk
1635

TUNGUSKA

CHONA

STONY

ALDAN

UCHUR

TUNGUSKA

GONAM

MTS.

100°   60°

UPPER

TUNGUSKA

NEPA

VITIM

STANOVOI

BRIANTA

ZEIA

Kirensk
1630

SHAMAN
RAPIDS

Ust-Kut
1630

ILIM

Verkhne-
Angarsk
1646

UPPER

ANGARA

TSIPA

OLEKMA

Tugur
1653

CHUNA
(UDA)

Ilimsk
1630

ANGARA

AMUR

Albazin
1651

Bratsk
1631

OKA

LENA

BARGUZIN

Bauntovskii
1652

VITIM

KIRENGA

TUGUR

Ust-Strelochnyi
1651

SHILKA

Tutursk
1631

LAKE BAIKAL

Argunsk 1682

7

120

140

Iakutsk

Olekminsk   LENA

130   60   Okhotsk

OLEKMA

ALDAN

MAIA

UL'IA

OKHOTSK SEA

GONAM

UCHUR

Albazin

ZEIA

AMUR

SELEMDZHA

BUREIA

AMUR

50

SUNGARI

USSURI

← Poiarkov 1643-6

←⋯ Khabarov 1649

0   250

Miles

9. THE OCCUPATION OF THE BAIKAL-AMUR REGION

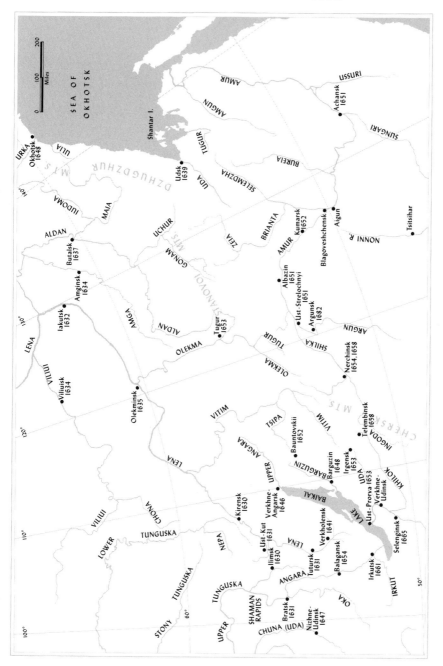

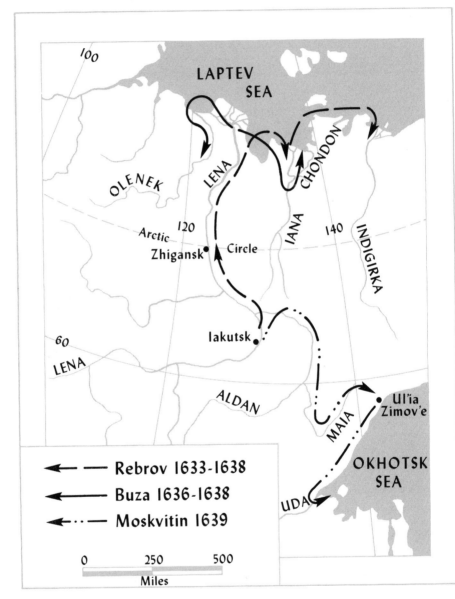

LAPTEV
SEA

OLENEK

LENA

CHONDON

Arctic   Circle

120

IANA   140

INDIGIRKA

Zhigansk

60

LENA

Iakutsk

ALDAN

MAIA

Ul'ia
Zimov'e

OKHOTSK
SEA

UDA

← — — Rebrov 1633-1638
←——— Buza 1636-1638
←··— Moskvitin 1639

0   250   500
Miles

11. THE OCCUPATION OF NORTHEASTERN SIBERIA

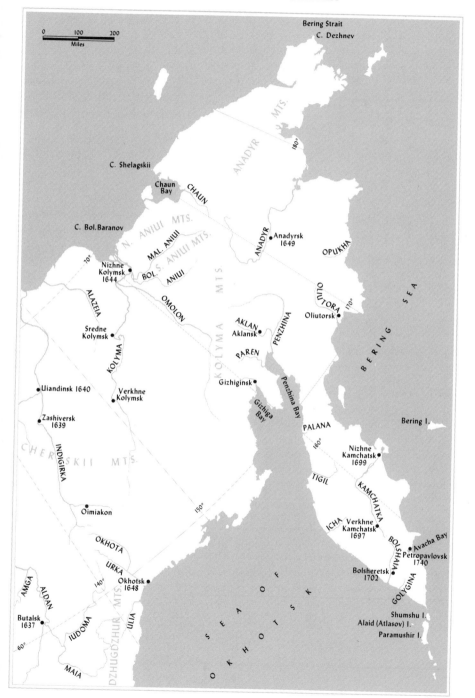

Bering Strait
C. Dezhnev

0   100   200
Miles

C. Shelagskii

Chaun Bay
CHAUN

ANADYR MTS.

180°

C. Bol. Baranov

N. ANIUI MTS.
MAL. ANIUI
BOL. S. ANIUI MTS.
ANIUI

ANADYR

Anadyrsk
1649

OPUKHA

70°

Nizhne Kolymsk
1644

OMOLON

KOLYMA MTS.

OLIUTORA

170°

BERING SEA

Oliutorsk

ALAZEIA

Sredne Kolymsk

AKLAN
Aklansk

PENZHINA

BERING

PAREN

KOLYMA

Uiandinsk 1640

Verkhne Kolymsk

Gizhiginsk

Penzhina Bay

Bering I.

Zashiversk
1639

CHERSKII MTS.

INDIGIRKA

Gizhiga Bay

PALANA

160°

Nizhne Kamchatsk
1699

TIGIL

Oimiakon

150°

ICHA

KAMCHATKA

Verkhne Kamchatsk
1697

BOLSHAIA

Avacha Bay
Petropavlovsk
1740

OKHOTA

URKA

140°

Okhotsk
1648

S E A   O F

Bolsheretsk
1702

GOLYGINA

AMGA

ALDAN

IUDOMA

ULIA

DZHUGDZHUR MTS.

Butalsk
1637

60°

O K H O T S K

Shumshu I.
Alaid (Atlasov) I.
Paramushir I.

MAIA

11

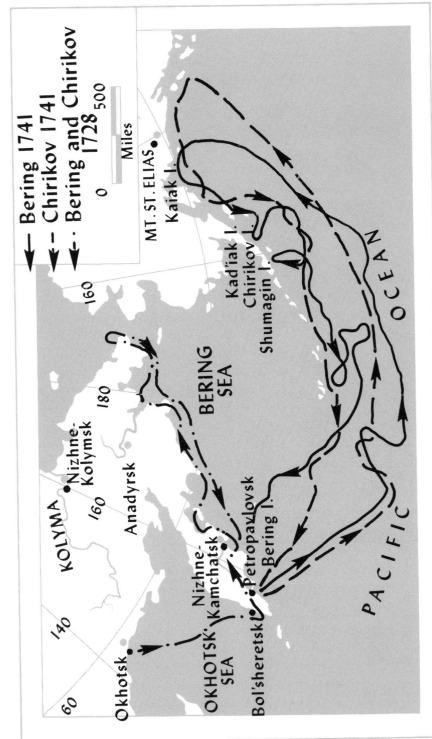

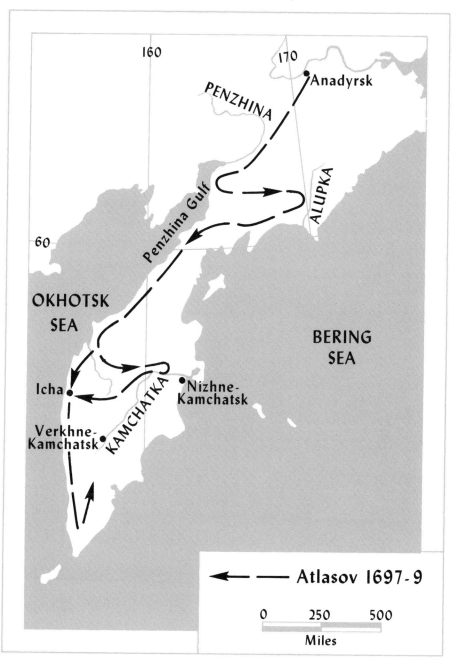

160

170

Anadyrsk

PENZHINA

ALUPKA

Penzhina Gulf

60

OKHOTSK
SEA

BERING
SEA

Icha

Nizhne-
Kamchatsk

KAMCHATKA

Verkhne-
Kamchatsk

←——— Atlasov 1697-9

0   250   500

Miles

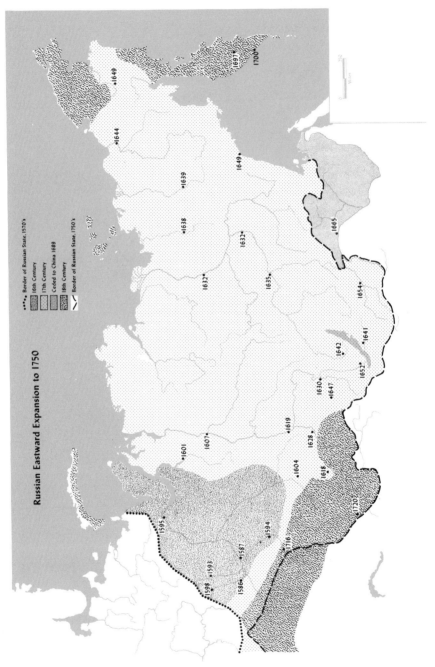

Russian Eastward Expansion to 1750

Border of Russian State, 1570's
16th Century
17th Century
Ceded to China 1689
18th Century
Border of Russian State, 1750's

14

15. THE PEOPLES OF SIBERIA

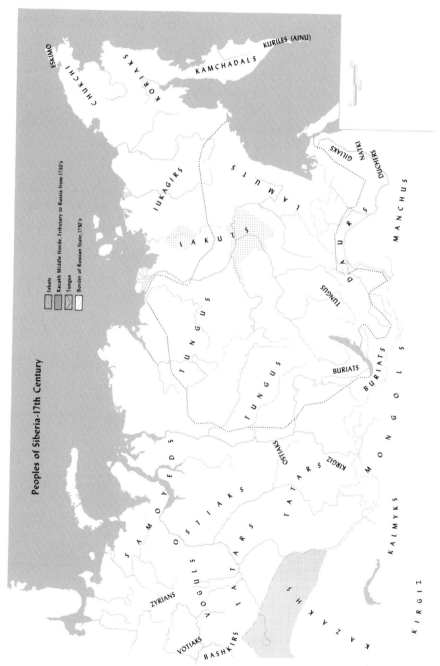

Peoples of Siberia-17th Century

Iakuts
Kazakh Middle Horde. Tributary to Russia from 1730's
Tungus
Border of Russian State, 1750's

ESKIMO
CHUKCHI
KORIAKS
KAMCHADALS
KURILES (AINU)
IUKAGIRS
LAMUTS
IAKUTS
GILIAKS
NIVKHI
DUCHERS
MANCHUS
DAURS
TUNGUS
TUNGUS
TUNGUS
BURIATS
BURIATS
MONGOLS
KIRGIZ
OSTIAKS
TATARS
TATARS
KALMYKS
SAMOYEDS
OSTIAKS
VOGULS
TATARS
BASHKIRS
VOTIAKS
ZYRIANS
KAZAKHS
KIRGIZ

Preface

Of the several frontiers of the Russian state, the best known is that to the west, facing Europe. Although shifting back and forth, it can be easily traced even in the early days of Russian history. It ran from such and such a town to such and such a hill, from there to a certain river, and from there on, always following definite landmarks. Along this frontier the Russians faced territorially organized states with relatively dense sedentary populations.

The northern, eastern, and southern frontiers of Russia are less well known. Here the conditions were entirely different as compared with the western frontier. In the north, east, and south, the Russians faced tribes and nations that were either semi-sedentary and scattered in small groups over a vast area, or were nomadic, sometimes very large but constantly shifting their grazing grounds. This frontier was not fixed. It lacked sharp demarcation between the Russians and their neighbours; there was an abundant no man's land between them which either side could claim, and along such a frontier either side could easily infiltrate the territory of the other. It was on this uncertain, flexible, and fluid periphery that Russia made its greatest territorial gains and acquired a body of experience in dealing with alien, less advanced peoples which has been drawn upon by the Russian state and which has affected Russian attitudes ever since.

There were two main currents of expansion on this 'open' frontier. One went north and east, but chiefly eastward. Another went east and south, but chiefly southward. Each had a pattern of its own. The outstanding characteristic of the eastward expansion was its economic motive, primarily the quest for furs. Indeed, no search for any single commodity has ever resulted in the acquisition of as huge an area as the one acquired by Russia in this quest. The southward expansion was marked by a quest for security, with the economic factor a later stimulus. This expansion was therefore characterized to a greater extent by diplomatic and military activity. It involved a long struggle with nomads, first for the safety of the Russian population from predatory raids, and later for the opening and maintaining of trade with central Asia. Both types of expansion proceeded simultaneously, but because of the differences in the pattern of these two currents, they should be treated separately. Following the terminology of Professor George Vernadsky, the first type may be referred to as a 'forest' expansion, although it culminated in sea voyages. The second type might be called a 'steppe' or 'prairie' expansion, although it involved also operations in deserts and mountains. This book will take up the initial phases of both, but will then be devoted to the eastward, or forest, expansion.

The concept for this work originated with the late George V. Lantzeff, Professor of Russian history at the University of California, Berkeley. A product of what a Soviet historian has called 'the California school' of Russian history that formed around Professor Robert J. Kerner, Lantzeff became one of the few specialists outside the USSR in the study of Russian eastward expansion. His dissertation, published as *Siberia in the Seventeenth Century: A Study of the Colonial Administration* (Berkeley, 1943), remains a fundamental, though little-known, work. His course on Russian expansion was virtually unique in its content and approach. During the few years of his university teaching career, he imbued a number of students, of whom the present writer was one, with similar interests. About 1950 Lantzeff began work on a survey of the history of Russian eastward expansion which would sum up his thoughts and research and help to fill the need for a systematic, documented survey in English on the subject. Unfortunately, when he died in 1955 he had completed only the first few chapters. From there on, the account consisted of fragments, notes, and outlines.

Because of the value of what Lantzeff had begun and the continuing need for such a work, I have undertaken to retrieve as much of his study as possible from the limbo of unfinished manuscripts. Chapters One to Seven, presented here, are substantially as he wrote them, except for certain alterations necessary within the context of the entire work or in order to include the results of recent research. The later chapters follow the original plan, but contain a larger proportion of introduced material. The book thus deals with the early Russian penetration of northeastern Europe, the struggle between Novgorod and Moscow for this region, the prospects and problems opened by liberation from Tatar rule, the beginnings of southward expansion, and the march to the east. Some of Lantzeff's own insights are introduced: he shows how the elimination of the Nogai Horde provided a vacuum later filled by the cossacks; he indicates the importance of the 'frontier mark' of the Stroganovs; and he introduces Tsar Boris Godunov in the new guise of an empire builder. The advance into Siberia is carried to its culmination in the conquest and loss of the Amur valley and in the conquest of Chukotka and Kamchatka, whence, in the middle of the eighteenth century, the frontier shifted to North America.

Unfortunately, there was not enough in Lantzeff's papers to permit inclusion of several matters to which he attached particular importance, namely, the development of the 'defence lines' in the southern steppe, the threat of Kalmyk incursions in the seventeenth century—which he termed 'the second Mongol invasion'—or 'the closing of the Ural gate' by the establishment of Orenburg in the first half of the eighteenth century. However, the contest for the steppe region has in any case been dealt with in detail by Boris Nolde, A. A. Novosel'skii, and others. The movement into the southern Ural region has been taken up in a study by one of Lantzeff's former students, Alton S. Donnelly, in *The Russian conquest of Bashkiria, 1552–1740: A Case Study in Imperialism* (New Haven and London, 1968).

The present study, of Russian expansion to the north, the beginnings of expansion to the south, and the movement eastward through Siberia, is based on published materials, both primary and secondary, used to a greater or lesser degree by other scholars, but drawn here into a single comprehensive account. Others have treated parts of this expansion, but not its entirety. G. F. Müller (*Opisanie Sibirskago tsarstva . . .*, [St. Petersburg, 1750], reprinted in part as *Istoriia Sibiri*, 2 vols. [Moscow-Leningrad, 1937–41]) and Johann E. Fischer (*Sibirische Geschichte . . .*, 2 vols. [St. Petersburg, 1768]) both wrote extensive accounts of Siberian expansion, but though mines of information for the scholar, their works are too detailed for use as surveys. In the 1920s, V. I. Ogorodnikov undertook a history of Russian expansion in Siberia, which might at least partially have filled this need, but died before he could complete it. Boris Nolde intended to describe the whole of Russian expansion, including that into Siberia, to 1917, but died before he was able to treat more than the conquest of Kazan, the Urals, and the southern steppes. Yuri Semyonov's lively and informative *The Conquest of Siberia, An Epic of Human Passions* (London, 1944, a translation of the German edition of 1937; revised and republished as *Siberia, Its Conquest and Development*, London, 1963), is popularized and undocumented. The recent collective work, *Istoriia Sibiri*, 5 vols. (Leningrad, 1968–69) devotes only one chapter to the Russian conquest. No extensive scholarly treatment of the subject exists in English, although it has been summarized in many books and articles.

Because this book is concerned primarily with the advancing frontier line as carried eastward by exploration and conquest, it must therefore omit the equally significant aspects of Russian expansion behind the line of advance. This is done deliberately, since others have already adequately covered many of these matters. Thus, Robert J. Kerner's *The Urge to the Sea* (Berkeley and Los Angeles, 1946) summarizes the role of rivers and portages underlying the advance and the subsequent development of Siberia. Raymond H. Fisher's *The Russian Fur Trade, 1550–1700* (Berkeley and Los Angeles, 1943) concerns the most valuable commodity of Siberia, and Lantzeff's earlier book describes the administration. The important new book by James R. Gibson, *Feeding the Russian Fur Trade: Provisionment of the Okhotsk Seaboard and the Kamchatka Peninsula, 1639–1856* (Madison, Milwaukee and London, 1969), although focused on the Far East, reveals problems of food supply and transport which existed throughout Siberia. Clifford M. Foust's *Muscovite and Mandarin: Russia's Trade with China and Its Setting, 1727–1805* (Chapel Hill, 1969) deals with the vital China trade. Mark Mancall's *Russia and China, Their Diplomatic Relations to 1728* (Cambridge, Mass., 1971) is concerned with frontier diplomacy. Many other specialized works dealing with colonization, agriculture, town growth, and other developments behind the advancing line of the 'open frontier' have appeared in recent years in the USSR, and it is to be hoped that more Western scholars will turn their attention to these subjects. This volume, which will take up in some detail the initial penetration of these regions, is intended as an aid to such research.

A modified form of the Library of Congress system for transliterating the Russian alphabet has been used in this work. Thus: Afanasii, Ermak Erofei, Fedor, Iaroslav, Enisei, Iugra, Iakutsk, Iukagirs, iurt, Kirgiz, Saian. Exceptions are made in cases where the names of persons or places, or certain terms are in more or less common western usage in another form, e.g. Alexander, Daniel, Michael, Stephen, Tobolsk, Ob, Kazan, Tver, cossack, or where strict renderings would be clumsy or misleading, e.g. Buriatia, Bashkiria, streltsy, Semeon, Samoyed. For uniformity, Turkish and Mongolian terms are transliterated as they occur in Russian documents and historical works.

I would like to extend thanks to Professors Oleg Maslenikov and Wolfram Eberhard of the University of California, Berkeley, Raymond H. Fisher of the University of California, Los Angeles, Alton S. Donnelly of the State University of New York, Binghamton, and other friends for helpful suggestions; to Mr. John Flambard, of Berkeley, and to Professor Henry W. Castner and Mr. Ross Hough of the Cartographic Laboratory of the Queen's University Department of Geography for the maps; to Mr. W. A. E. Peterkin and Ms. Joan Harcourt for their editorial work; and to the Guggenheim Foundation, the Canada Council, and the Social Science Research Council of Canada for grants which have facilitated research and publication.

Richard A. Pierce
QUEEN'S UNIVERSITY
KINGSTON, CANADA

Chapter 1

Russian Expansion in Kievan Times[1]

The Russian people began to expand eastward soon after they formed a state. While it is difficult to separate legend from fact, it can safely be said that in the ninth century certain Scandinavian adventurers descended from the north and drew some of the Slavic tribes along the river route from the Baltic to the Black Sea into a hegemony which became known as Kiev Rus', after Kiev, its chief town. Even then, the chieftains of the Russian tribes continued for some time to move about freely, concerned mainly with spoils, tribute, and trade. In a sense, the whole region remained for a long time a frontier, with land for the taking around every river bend, if it could be wrested from neighbouring Slavic or Finnic tribesmen or from a resistant Nature.

THE KIEVAN STATE AND THE EASTERN FRONTIER

The first organized Russian state was formed in the reign of Sviatoslav (962–972). By wars and alliances, this prince brought under at least nominal rule a vast, thinly populated region extending from the Baltic to the Black Sea. The confluence of the Volga and Kama rivers, to the east, was inhabited by the Bulgars, a Turkic people, and the southeastern steppes by the Khazars, another Turkic people who had formed a strong state in the seventh century, barring alike the westward movement of other nomadic tribes and the eastward strivings of the Slavs. Sviatoslav sought to break up the Khazar state. He finally succeeded, but by so doing wrecked the dam which had held back the nomads of Asia. Another Turkic group, the Pechenegs (Patzinaks), then invaded the steppes and began to attack Russian villages. In 967 Sviatoslav aided the Byzantines against the Bulgarians, but later turned on his allies. How little he was bound to his patrimony is shown by his aspiration to move the centre of his realm to Bulgaria. He was soundly defeated, however, and in 971 had to sue for peace. While returning to his homeland he was killed by Pechenegs at the Dnepr rapids.

After a period of civil war, Sviatoslav's son Vladimir (980–1015) came to power. He and his son Iaroslav, surnamed The Wise (1019–54), were strong rulers able to hold back the invaders, but upon Iaroslav's death many squabbles arose among his sons, and civil strife permitted incessant incursions by Turkic tribesmen into southern Russia. They did not often attack fortified towns, but carried away thousands of villagers into captivity.

In the mid-eleventh century, yet another group of Turkic tribesmen, the Polovtsy (sometimes known as the Cumans or Kypchaks), moved into the Black Sea steppes. Some of the Pechenegs they pushed into the Balkans, others they incorporated within their own host. Like the Pechenegs, the Polovtsy made frequent raids on the southern Russian settlements to capture slaves.

The Kievan princes tried to stop these predatory raids by various means, in which can be seen the pattern followed in later centuries. They fortified towns and built strong-points and outposts in the steppe; they formed alliances with some tribes against others; they married their daughters to pagan nomad chieftains; they established military colonies composed in part of friendly Turks; and they made punitive expeditions deep into the steppe. The famous poem of an unknown Russian medieval author, *The Campaign of the Host of Igor,* has perpetuated the memory of one of these expeditions, made in 1184, which came to a disastrous end.

The nomad forays had a bad effect on the young Russian state. Trade was insecure, and the southern lands were devastated. The nomads barred any southward movement, and declining trade and a desire to escape the strife of the princes seem to have caused a flow of population away from Kiev toward the northeast. Many moved into the less populated forest area along the upper Volga and Oka rivers, then inhabited largely by Finnic peoples, the Muroma, Ves', and Meria. Many of these tribes accepted Christianity and intermarried with the Russians. The assimilation of these peoples led to the formation of a Finno-Slavic mixed group which, from a linguistic and cultural point of view, was to become the Great Russian branch of the Eastern Slavs. The principalities of Rostov and Suzdal took shape in the Volga region and grew in power as their energetic and enterprising princes encouraged further colonization in order to obtain new subjects, soldiers, and taxpayers.

Still farther north, the city of Novgorod replaced Kiev as the chief Russian trading centre. Novgorod developed an intensive commerce with its Baltic neighbours and eventually became a junior member of the Hanseatic League. It was Novgorod that was to initiate the first great eastward movement of Russia.[2]

THE RISE OF NOVGOROD AS A COLONIAL POWER

The principal export items from Novgorod in this period were, first of all, furs, then honey (for sugar), and wax (for candles). After the regions near Novgorod were exhausted, the search for items for export brought the Novgorodians into what was later to be the northeastern corner of European Russia, a vast region stretching from Lake Onega to the Ural Mountains, and from the northern tributaries of the Volga to the Arctic Ocean. In the forests in the valleys of the great rivers flowing into the Arctic, the Novgorodians obtained the pelts of sables, ermine, foxes, and other animals, some by hunting and trapping, but mostly through barter with the local Finnic tribes or as tribute from these tribes.[3] Along the Arctic coast they obtained salt, fish, and walrus ivory.

It is difficult to determine when the men of Novgorod first appeared in this region; the chronicles note a Novgorodian expedition 'to the Iron Gates' in 1032.[4] The location of these Iron Gates is disputed, but there seems to be no doubt that this place was at least as far east as the valley of the Pechora River, and possibly farther.[5] Under the date 1079, the chronicles narrate that the Novgorodian Prince Gleb Sviatoslavich was killed in the 'Country beyond the Portage' [*za Volokom;* later Zavoloch'e],[6] most likely while collecting tribute. This territory extended east of Lakes Onega and Beloozero and embraced the valley of the Northern Dvina. In 1096 the chronicles describe the Novgorodian barter trade with the Iugra,[7] a Finnic tribe which inhabited the region east of the Pechora River and both slopes of the northern part of the Ural Mountains. The story mentions high mountains descending into the sea, probably the Urals. According to Karamzin, in 1113 the Novgorodians paid the Prince of Kiev a 'Pechora tribute',[8] apparently a share of their spoils from this river. Under the year 1114, the chronicle mentions a story about the 'older men' who used to go beyond the Iugra and Samoyeds into the 'land of midnight'.[9] All these scattered bits of information indicate that toward the beginning of the twelfth century the Novgorodians were familiar with northeastern Russia as far as the Urals and perhaps with the lower Ob region of Siberia. The early activities of the Novgorodians in the northeast of Russia were in the nature of raids but gradually permanent colonies appeared. By the middle of the twelfth century, about thirty administrative posts had been established by the Novgorodians in the territory 'beyond the Portage' where the revenues were collected regularly enough to provide tithe for the Bishop of Novgorod. These places are enumerated in the charter of Prince Gleb Ol'govich,[10] who ruled Novgorod in 1137–38, and most of them can be located on the map with the aid of the study by E. K. Ogorodnikov.[11] They were distributed east of Lake Onega, along the Onega River, the middle and lower Northern Dvina, the tributaries of the latter (the Emtsa, the Vaga, and the Sukhona), the Pinega River and the Pinega portage, as well as on the sea coast, probably in the vicinity of the mouth of the Northern Dvina.[12]

Within this territory a sort of colonial administration was established. The monastery of the Archangel Michael, situated at the mouth of the Northern Dvina on the site of the present city of Arkhangel'sk, has preserved a document issued to its Abbot by the Bishop of Novgorod sometime between 1110 and 1165. In this document a blessing is pronounced on the governors (*posadniki*) of the Dvina, on the boyars (nobles) of the Dvina, on the Elder of merchants, as well as on all the merchants and peasants.[13] The Dvina Chronicle notes that 'since the early days' the people of the Dvina were ruled by Novgorodian city officials to whom they paid tribute (*dan'*) and taxes (*obroki*). The officials appointed boyars from the city to collect these revenues and to attend to administration (*rasprava*). These boyars resided in Ukhoto-Ostrov, Matigory (both at the mouth of the Dvina), and in other districts (*volosti*) and they received for guidance (*v oberezhenie*) instructions from the Novgorodian highest officials (*posadniki*), as well as from the Bishop of Novgorod.[14]

EXPANSION OF THE VOLGA PRINCIPALITIES AT THE EXPENSE OF NOVGOROD

In the twelfth century the northeastern possessions of Novgorod became exposed to a threat from the principalities that rose within the river quadrilateral formed by the Volga, Oka, and Moskva rivers, particularly the Rostov-Suzdal principality. The effectiveness of this threat depended on factors of geographic location. Along the rivers enclosing the quadrilateral passed the well-known Baltic–Volga–Caspian trade route. The Novgorodians used this route both for trading purposes and for bringing food supplies to their city from the Oka region. The Volga princes within the quadrilateral held a strategic position from which they could block the river grain traffic at will and thereby cause food shortage and even famine at Novgorod. Besides, through the northern tributaries of the Volga, they could invade the Novgorodian colonial possessions and intercept communications between Novgorod and its colonies.[15]

Until the twelfth century the Novgorodians were not particularly affected by the developments in the Volga region. The danger came with the rise of the Rostov principality, which not only comprised territories within the Volga-Oka quadrilateral but also included the land along the Sheksna River (a northern tributary of the Volga) and the town of Beloozero, situated close to the very road from Novgorod to the Northern Dvina. At the time of Rurik, the semi-legendary founder of the ruling dynasty (862?–870?), the towns of Rostov and Beloozero were themselves Novgorodian colonies and dependencies,[16] but under his successors they became detached from Novgorod and were governed from Kiev. As long as the Rostov principality was a sort of Kievan province, remote from Kiev but involved in the politics of Kiev, its proximity to Novgorod's lifelines caused no inconvenience to the Novgorodians, who were not disturbed in their business and colonizing activities.

The situation changed entirely when the Rostov principality, including Beloozero, became a part of the hereditary holdings of the descendants of Vladimir Monomakh (Prince of Kiev, 1113–25). Vladimir's son, Prince Iurii Dolgorukii (Prince of Kiev, 1115–57), having received Rostov from his father, determined to preserve it in his own family and to make it the strongest principality in Russia. He was the first to formulate the local Rostov-Suzdal policy directed toward the domination of the Novgorodian route along the Volga and penetration into the Novgorodian colony 'beyond the Portage'.[17]

Iurii was a source of constant trouble to the Novgorodians. Twice he seized Torzhok (Novyi Torg) on the Tvertsa River, thereby shutting off the eastern trade of Novgorod and the importation of grain. Repeatedly he sent his men to intercept the colonial tribute on its way to Novgorod.[18] His prolonged struggle, from 1147 to 1154, with Iziaslav of Kiev, in the words of the latter, was caused by the fact that 'Iurii of Rostov oppressed Novgorod, took away its tributes, and caused grievances to the Novgorodians on their trade routes.'[19]

Faced with the aggressive policies of Iurii, the Novgorodians resisted his encroachments whenever they felt they might have some chance of success. In 1134 they invaded the Suzdal principality but were defeated. They had better luck in 1149 when, as a part of a Kievan army, they devastated both banks of the Volga as far as Iaroslavl' in a raid in which seven thousand Rostov-Suzdal men were led into captivity.[20] More often the Novgorodians had to appease the powerful Suzdal prince by accepting his sons (Rostislav or Mstislav) as rulers of Novgorod.

The 'Suzdal orientation' of Iurii prepared the ground for his son Andrei Bogoliubskii. Andrei followed his father's practice of naming his sons, nephews, or allies as Novgorodian princes.[21] In 1160 he announced his intentions in a message to the Novgorodians: 'Let it be known that I shall seek Novgorod by good means or evil.'[22] Acting in agreement with the Grand Prince of Kiev, Andrei succeeded, in 1161, in replacing a prince in Novgorod and establishing there his protégé, Sviatoslav Rostislavich. Six years later, the latter quarrelled with the Novgorodians and was forced to leave the city. Andrei gave him military aid, but the attempt to restore Sviatoslav by force failed, although Sviatoslav's army burned the towns of Torzhok and Velikie Luki and devastated

Novgorodian territory. Meanwhile, the Novgorodians secured for themselves a prince from Kiev. There followed a violent contest between Grand Prince Mstislav of Kiev and Andrei over the domination of Novgorod, which ended in the capture and looting of Kiev (1169) by Andrei's armies. Mstislav was expelled, and Andrei assumed the title of Grand Prince. Contrary to long historical tradition, but true to his 'Suzdal orientation,' instead of moving to Kiev, Andrei remained in the Suzdal princiaplity, choosing the town of Vladimir as his capital.[23] Then Andrei turned against Novgorod.

The 'Country beyond the Portage', otherwise the region of the Northern Dvina, was viewed longingly by the men of Suzdal, who occasionally attacked Novgorodian tribute collectors. In about 1169 a secession movement developed among the Dvinans, who refused a pay tribute to Novgorod and recognized Andrei as their prince. The Novgorodians sent a punitive expedition of five hundred men against the rebels. Andrei's troops, operating from Beloozero, tried to intercept the Novgorodians. The latter emerged victorious from the battle and succeeded in collecting the tribute not only from the people of the Dvina but from the Suzdal peasant colonists as well. This failure aroused Andrei to greater efforts against Novgorod. In the winter of 1169, under the command of Andrei's son, Mstislav, who earlier in the same year had helped to expel his namesake, Grand Prince Mstislav, from Kiev, a huge Suzdal army, reinforced by Murom, Riazan, Smolensk, and Polotsk troops, invaded the territory of Novgorod. According to the chronicle, seventy-two princes participated in the invasion. The country around Novgorod was ravaged, but the Novgorodians bravely defended the city. The besieging army, suffering from disease and lack of food, was finally forced into a disastrous retreat in which many men died from hunger or were captured by the Novgorodians. Although the frontal attack against the Novgorodians ended in a fiasco, in 1170 Andrei forced them to accede to some of his demands by cutting off the grain supplies and causing a terrible famine in Novgorod.[24]

The assassination of Andrei by his own boyars in 1175 relieved Novgorod of this dangerous neighbour. Andrei had transferred the political centre of Russia from the Dnepr valley to the Volga–Oka region, had maintained a firm hold over the upper and middle Volga, and had tried to dominate Novgorod and to encroach on its colonies. The possession of Novgorod meant access to the Baltic trade based on exports from the Novgorodian colonies. The parallel between Andrei's Novgorodian policies and his operations against the Volga Bulgar state, which blocked access to the Asiatic markets, suggests that he may have conceived of an empire to be founded on the river route connecting the Baltic and Caspian seas.

SUZDAL ENCROACHMENT ON BULGAR TERRITORIES.

The Bulgar state during the eighth to the fourteenth centuries occupied the territory of the lower Kama and the middle Volga rivers. Near the mouth of the Kama, about ten Bulgar towns were situated, the most important among them being Briakhimov (or Bulgar the Great). This town, according to archaeological research, must have had a population of about fifty thousand. The Bulgars explored the territories north and east very much in the same manner as did the Novgorodians in northeastern Russia, crossing the path of the latter in the Perm region. Through the eastern tributaries of the Kama they traded across the Urals.[25] Arab sources describe Bulgar barter with the Siberian natives, whom they call 'Iura' (Iugra), the same name used by the Novgorodians.[26] In their brisk commerce with Asiatic merchants who came by way of the Volga, the Bulgars offered furs from the forest regions as well as slaves obtained from the Russian princes, who sold their war prisoners. The possession, or at least control, of the wealthy commercial Bulgar state would mean to the Rostov-Suzdal princes very much the same as possession of Novgorod with its colonies. Therefore, it is not surprising that the attention of the Suzdal princes became divided between Novgorod and the Bulgars.

From the beginning of the twelfth century, the chronicles record a series of predatory Suzdal incursions into the land of the Bulgars. In 1120 Iurii Dologorukii sailed down the Volga and, after defeating the Bulgars, returned with numerous prisoners.[27] Andrei alternately fought and traded with the Bulgars, from whom he obtained white stone for his churches. In 1164 he led a large expedition that destroyed three small frontier towns and captured the main town of Briakhimov. The Suzdal troops again appeared in Bulgar territory in 1172, seized six villages and a town, and brought back spoils and captives.[28] The successor of Andrei, his brother Prince Vsevolod Iur'evich, continued Andrei's imperialistic policies. In 1184 he attacked the Bulgars with his own Suzdal and Beloozero forces and with the armies of the Riazan and Murom princes. The Bulgars suffered heavy losses and begged for peace. During the same expedition the Russians raided the territory of the Mordva, a Finno-Ugrian people living east of the Oka. In 1186 Vsevolod sent another expedition on a large scale against the Bulgars, and his generals (*voevody*) again devastated the Bulgar land, destroying towns and villages and carrying away many prisoners.[29]

CONTINUING STRIFE BETWEEN SUZDAL AND NOVGOROD

While pursuing an aggressive policy against the Bulgars, Vsevolod kept a watchful eye on Novgorod. In 1178 and 1181 he seized and plundered

Torzhok; in 1178 he also looted Volok-Lamskii; and many times he intercepted Novgorodian merchants, confiscating their goods.[30] In vain the Novgorodians tried to find support from other princes. Vsevolod forced Novgorod to appeal to him when they needed a prince and sent to Novgorod his nephews and sons.[31] The position of the Novgorodians was particularly difficult because during this time they struggled with their western and northern neighbours and, in addition, had troubles in their own colonies.

The discontent and restlessness among the Dvina colonists, which in 1169 had led to their refusal to pay tribute to Novgorod and to their recognition of Andrei of Suzdal as their master and protector, apparently did not subside with the years. Under the year 1187, the chronicles record a general massacre of the Novgorodian tribute collectors who operated 'beyond the Portage' and in the valley of the Pechora, where they collected tribute from the Pechora and Iugra tribes. Altogether a hundred men (*kmety* or, in one variant, *dobroimenitye*, that is, men of substance) were killed.[32] Six years later, in 1193, perhaps in retaliation for this massacre, Novgorod sent a very large force to the Iugra, where, after an initial success, it was almost completely annihilated. In 1194 only eighty men returned to Novgorod. Some of them were accused of treason; three of these were killed, and others saved their lives by payment of heavy fines.[33] The circumstances of this disaster seem to indicate a clash between the interests of the state and those of the private businessmen who traded with the Iugra and had business connections with the local princes. The government tributes unfavourably affected the trade, and the resentful merchants 'held councils with the natives against their own brethren'.[34] It is worth noting that during the negotiations preceding the destruction of the Novgorodian army, the Iugra chief said to the Novgorodian commander, 'we are gathering silver, sables and other furs. Do not destroy your subjects (*smerdy*) and your own tribute.' The words of the chief seem to indicate that the Iugra people were subjects of Novgorod at this time.[35]

In 1196 the Novgorodian colonies suffered once more from the aggression of the Volga princes. The Novgorodians quarrelled with Iaroslav, son of Grand Prince Vsevolod, whom they had previously accepted in Novgorod under pressure from his father. Iaroslav left Novgorod and established himself at Torzhok. From there he blocked the Novgorodian Volga route and gathered tribute from the 'Country beyond the Portage' as well as from the Novgorodian peasants up the Msta River. Meanwhile, his father seized the Novgorodian merchants 'beyond the Portage',[36] apparently in a raid into the territory of the Northern Dvina.

Following the death of Grand Prince Vsevolod in 1212, the Novgorodians ceased to feel the heavy pressure of Rostov-Suzdal. They even took part in the civil wars which raged among the sons of Vsevolod for the title of Grand Prince of Vladimir. Having won the battle of Lipitsa (1216), the Novgorodians were instrumental in placing their favourite in Vladimir.[37] He soon died, however, and Iurii Vsevolodovich, who became Grand Prince (1219–36), renewed the Suzdal policies, at various times sending his brothers to rule Novgorod. The Novgorodians were willing to accept the Suzdal princes, whose armies protected them against Germans, Lithuanians, and Finns.[38]

SUZDAL AGAINST THE BULGARS AND MORDVA.

The new Grand Prince, Iurii, sent expeditions against the Bulgars and the Mordva people. The Bulgars thought to take advantage of the temporary weakness of the Suzdal state and in 1218 captured and looted the frontier town of Ustiug,[39] and then attempted to descend the Unzha (a tributary of the Volga west of the Vetluga River), but were repelled by the Suzdal colonists of this region.[40] In 1220 Iurii, whose position as Grand Prince was secure by this time, invaded the land of the Bulgars with a large army led by several princes. A part of his forces went to the sources of the Kama, but the main army, using the mouth of the Oka as a base, went down the Volga and landed near the fortified town of Oshel, which it stormed, captured, and destroyed. The other force, descending the Kama from the north, devastating its banks, burning and plundering many villages, came to the Volga and joined the main body. The Bulgars had to sue for peace on Iurii's terms.[41] Following this expedition, Iurii, in 1221, built a fortified town, Nizhnii Novgorod, in the Mordva terrritory at the junction of the Volga and Oka rivers.[42] The founding of Nizhnii Novgorod (Novgorod on the Lower Volga), a city with a name suggestive of the commercial role that was expected of it,[43] was a landmark in the Suzdal expansion. It was a frontier outpost leading to new acquisitions and effectively guarding the water route from the Bulgars to the tribes of the Mordva who paid a fur tribute to the Bulgars. While weakening the Bulgars, it opened the field for the exploitation of the Mordva, and it was against them that Iurii concentrated his efforts.

In 1226 Iurii sent two of his brothers against the Mordva, and they captured a number of villages and returned with spoils. This raid was followed by another in 1228. Once more the fields of the Mordva were burned, their cattle slaughtered, and the people either captured or scattered in the woods. In 1229 the Mordva attempted to attack Nizhnii Novgorod, but were defeated by the garrison. The advance on the Mordva continued, and in 1232 the armies of the princes of Suzdal, Riazan, and Murom again devastated their land.[44]

SUMMARY

The first centuries of the Russian state thus saw several significant developments. While the congeries of principalities under Kievan rule was beset by internal strife and pressure from nomads in the southern steppes, three currents of expansion flowed outward into the ill-defined open frontier to the south and east. One of these was directed toward the southern steppe, where, from time immemorial, Asiatic peoples had roamed into Europe through the great gate between the Caspian Sea and the Ural Mountains. A second current of expansion accompanied the decline of Kiev. The Russian people began moving away from Kiev toward the northeast, into the less populated forest area along the Oka and Volga rivers. The Russian infiltration led to amalgamation with the scattered Finnic tribes to form the Great Russian branch of the Eastern Slavs. The princes followed the colonists; the strong Volga principalities came into existence and eventually began offensive operations against neighbouring peoples.

A third current of expansion started from the wealthy trading city of Novgorod and went northeastward to the Arctic Ocean, the Ural Mountains, and even into the northwestern corner of Siberia. Novgorod first sent out trading expeditions, but gradually began to establish permanent colonies. During the twelfth century and the early part of the thirteenth, Novgorod suffered from the predatory inclinations of the Volga princes. These aggressive rulers interfered with Novgorodian river traffic, cut the city's food supply, and tried to establish a hold on Novgorod's 'fur empire' in northeastern Russia. Under this pressure the Novgorodians had to accept princes nominated by the Grand Princes of Vladimir as rulers of their city.

By the second quarter of the thirteenth century, Suzdal had become dominant over Novgorod and was exerting strong pressure to the east against the Bulgars on the Kama and to the southeast against the Mordva in the Oka–Volga area. Although the land was torn by dissension, these developments seem to have presaged an early Russian drive to the Urals. This trend, however, was halted abruptly by the Mongol invasion of 1237–40.

Chapter 2

Russian Expansion Under Mongol Rule

The intrusion of the Mongol Empire into Europe in the first half of the thirteenth century halted the efforts of the Suzdal princes to control Novgorod and its colonies and frustrated their imperialistic plans for the domination of the Volga and its Asiatic trade. The Suzdal princes were crushed, their domains devastated. Yet, although the Mongol or Tatar inundation (the term 'Tatar' refers to the predominantly Turkic peoples in the Mongol forces) swamped the eastern neighbours of Russia (the Bulgars and Mordva), the nomads of the southern steppes, and most of Russia itself, the invaders left Novgorod untouched. The Mongols had little interest in the thickly forested area of northeastern Russia, and Novgorod was able to continue the expansion of her 'fur empire' both in northeastern Europe and northwestern Asia. At the same time, even under Mongol domination, a gradual recovery began in other parts of Russia that would give rise to a new centre of power, which would eventually challenge both Novgorod and the Mongol overlords.

Novgorod was increasingly threatened by its western and northern neighbours and needed strong princes who could not only organize her defensive forces but also contribute troops of their own for the protection of the city.[1] In 1236 the Novgorodians accepted Alexander, the nephew of Grand Prince Iurii II of Vladimir, as their ruler. He proved a happy choice. In 1239 he built fortifications against the Swedes on the Shelon River; in 1240, while the Mongols were overrunning the Russian principalities to the south, he led the Novgorodians to victory over the Swedes in a battle at the mouth of the Neva River (thereby becoming known as Alexander Nevskii—'of the Neva'); in 1241 he captured the fortress of Kopor'e, which was held by the Swedes; in 1242 he recaptured the city of Pskov from the Livonian Knights and inflicted a crushing defeat on them in the 'Ice Massacre' on Lake Chud.[2] Alexander not only defended Novgorod against the Swedes and Germans but also helped the city in dealing with the Tatars. Novgorod was spared the horrors of the Mongol invasion because mud and melting snow stopped the

Mongol armies some sixty miles short of Novgorod. Alexander, who proved to be as good a diplomat as he was a general, was convinced that resistance to the Mongols at this time would be useless and succeeded in establishing good relations with the invaders. The Novgorodians, however, were reluctant to pay tribute to the Golden Horde. As late as 1257 the Tatar tribute collectors received only 'gifts' for the Khan instead of tribute. In 1259, when the Novgorodians were ready to rise in arms against the tax collectors, Alexander saved the city from Tatar reprisals by forcefully persuading the Novgorodians to allow the Tatars to take a census and to submit to the Tatar tax system.[3] Alexander (who became Grand Prince of Vladimir in 1252)[4] ruled Novgorod almost continuously until his death in 1263.

In spite of Alexander's great services to their city, the Novgorodians resented his arbitrary methods and his insistence on participating in the exploitation of their colonial resources. His successors attempted the same policy.[5] After Alexander's death his place was taken by his brother Iaroslav of Tver, who, with Novgorodian financial aid, had been able to outbid his rivals before the Golden Horde and had received the patent for the title of Grand Prince of Vladimir, the position previously held by Alexander.[6] In return for the Novgorodian subsidy, Iaroslav signed several agreements with the Novgorodians in which he recognized the city's territorial claims, including its colonies.[7] Some time between 1294 and 1304, Alexander's son Andrei, a later prince of Novgorod, demanded an exclusive right to exploit Ter, on the Kola Peninsula, for himself, referring to the precedent established by his father. He further demanded free passage and food supplies for his three crews of fishermen and hunters, who were to sail down the Dvina to the sea. Andrei apparently also demanded a share of the Pechora revenues, as can be seen in a later document issued about 1328–40 by Ivan Kalita of Moscow.[8]

On the other hand, during the whole period from the first appearance of Alexander Nevskii in Novgorod until the death of his son Andrei in 1304, the chronicles show little evidence of attempts by the Volga princes to seize any of the Novgorodian colonies. Only twice did the colonies seem to be in danger. In 1274 Vasilii of Kostroma devastated Vologda,[9] and in 1281 Grand Prince Dmitrii invaded and 'did much harm to the Novgorodian possessions.'[10]

THE RISE OF TVER AND MOSCOW

Early in the fourteenth century, the Volga region began to pose a greater threat. This stemmed from the rise and rivalry of the two principalities of Tver and Moscow. It was as if there were elements of strength in that region, which, as soon as recovery from the Mongol invasion began, would again find expression in the northeast, as they had before 1240.

Tver, originally possibly a Novgorodian outpost protecting the river route along the Tvertsa against the Rostov-Suzdal princes, is first mentioned in the chronicles under the dates of 1209 and 1215.[11] In the first half of the thirteenth century, it was tranferred to the right bank of the Volga, and 'after the Batu invasion Grand Prince Iaroslav . . . built a fortress, called it Tver and placed his younger son Iaroslav here and called him Grand Prince of Tver.'[12] Moscow is first mentioned in the chronicles in 1147 and received its first prince in 1213.[13] During the thirteenth century both towns profited from their advantageous positions on the trade routes of Novgorod and from the movement of the population from devastated territories after the Mongol invasion. Around 1295 the relations between the two principalities were still friendly. Prince Michael of Tver concluded a mutual assistance pact with Novgorod in which he promised to come to its aid together with his cousin Daniel of Moscow.[14] The death of Grand Prince Andrei in 1304 marked the beginning of a long period of rivalry between Tver and Moscow.[15] In accordance with the established order of seniority, Prince Michael of Tver should have become Grand Prince. But Prince Iurii of Moscow (the son of Daniel, who had died in 1303) felt himself sufficiently strong to demand the honour for himself. Both princes came to the Horde, and Michael, who promised a greater tribute than Iurii, received the patent.[16]

When Grand Prince Andrei died, before the outcome of the negotiations in the Horde had become known, the officials of Prince Michael of Tver tried to establish control over Novgorod by force. The Novgorodians, however, expelled them, hoping that Iurii of Moscow might become Grand Prince. Moscow was farther away from Novgorod than was Tver and seemed weaker than Tver, while Iurii had not caused any grievances to the Novgorodians in the past. Michael, on the other hand, seemed likely to continue the policy of his father, Iaroslav, and had already periodically cut off the grain supply from Novgorod, as had his father when desiring concessions from the city.

After Michael was chosen Grand Prince by the Khan in 1304, the Novgorodians agreed to accept him as Prince of Novgorod conditionally upon a series of agreements which specified the terms of their relationship. In spite of these agreements, Michael made exorbitant demands on the city and twice, in 1314 and in 1316, the Novgorodians expelled the administrators *(namestniki)* appointed to act as his representatives. In 1314 the Novgorodians invited Iurii to serve as their prince; but he was summoned by the Horde and went there accompanied by a number of Novgorodians, leaving his brother in Novgorod. During Iurii's absence, Michael in turn expelled Iurii's brother from the city, exacted a heavy contribution from it, and restored his own man. In 1316 they were forced to leave again. In 1317 the Novgorodians sent their bishop to Michael to bring about a reconciliation. The plea of the ecclesiastic had no effect, but the military preparations of Iurii restrained Michael and saved Novgorod from reprisals.[17]

Both Michael and Iurii were summoned in 1318 by the Horde. Again some Novgorodians escorted Iurii and presumably, as on the previous occasion, tried to help him gain the favour of the Khan by the judicious distribution of gifts among the influental people at the Khan's court. Even more in Iurii's favour, however, was the fact that he had been married to the Khan's sister. She had been captured by Michael, and had died while in captivity. The Khan blamed Michael for her death and ordered his execution, and in 1319 he gave Iurii the patent of Grand Prince.[18] In 1322 Iurii arrived in Novgorod, led the Novgorodian army in a victorious campaign in Finland, built a fortress at the mouth of the Neva, and organized a punitive expedition against the town of Ustiug, whose inhabitants had plundered the fur convoys coming to Novgorod from Iugra, the territory of both slopes of the northern Urals.[19]

THE NOVGORODIAN COLONIES

In this connection, it may be remembered that probably no other single factor contributed so much to the prosperity of Novgorod in the thirteenth and fourteenth centuries as the export of furs collected beyond the Dvina as tribute or obtained through trade with the natives. The furs were brought to Novgorod along the Sukhona–Vychegda river system, as shown in R. J. Kerner's *Urge to the Sea.* However, this route was too vulnerable. A look at Kerner's maps shows two strategic places where the river traffic could be blocked by the enemies of the Novgorodians.[20] These places were the towns of Beloozero, situated at the lake of the same name, and Ustiug, otherwise called Ustiug Velikii, situated at the junction of the Sukhona and Iug. Beginning with the first quarter of the fourteenth century, these towns played an important role in the struggle of Novgorod to preserve its fur empire.

Both these towns were probably founded by men of Novgorod. During the pre-Mongol period, Beloozero became detached from Novgorod and fell under the control of the Volga princes. In 1169

The people of the Dvina did not want to deliver the tribute to Novgorod, but recognized the authority of Prince Andrei Bogoliubskii; the Novgorodians sent a tribute collector with five hundred men into the Dvina [territory]. . . . Prince Andrei sent his troops fifteen hundred strong against them. Andrei's troops intercepted the Novgorodians at Beloozero, and a battle followed. [Andrei's troops were completely defeated.] [21]

For some time afterwards, men of Beloozero participated in the armies of the Volga princes. Evidently Beloozero at some later time passed to Novgorod; under the date of 1327, the Pskov chronicle lists it among the Novgorodian dependencies. [22]

Ustiug, which was farther east toward the Urals on the Sukhona–Dvina–Vychegda road to the Pechora River region, was even more difficult to by-pass than Beloozero, and at this spot the fur traffic of Novgorod could be more easily intercepted than at Beloozero. In addition to the early Novgorodian settlers, Ustiug's population had been augmented by numerous newcomers who had migrated from the Volga region. The result was a large frontier community resentful of any authority and with predatory tendencies. There was always temptation for its people to prey on passing Novgorodians because of the ease with which the spoils could be disposed of in the Volga region—a circumstance which led to perpetual frictions with Novgorod. In 1220 there were people of Ustiug in the army of the Prince of Rostov, which might indicate that at that time Ustiug was a dependency of Rostov. [23] When Iurii forced the princes of Ustiug to sign an agreement whereby Novgorodian trade would be safeguarded in the future, he rendered his last service to Novgorod. In 1326 he went to the Horde from Ustiug, by way of the Kama, and was killed on the way by his rival, Prince Dmitrii of Tver. [24]

NOVGOROD AND THE EARLY MOSCOW PRINCES

Following Iurii's death there was another contest between Moscow and Tver for the patent of Grand Prince. The Novgorodians maintained their Muscovite 'orientation' and, with their support, Ivan Kalita, a brother of Iurii, received the patent (1328). However, Novgorodian hopes that Ivan would continue the policies of his older brother proved unfounded. Instead, Ivan, the first of a long line of 'gatherers of the Russian land under Muscovite authority', began to quarrel with the Novgorodians soon after establishing himself as Grand Prince. A clever politician, he gained the favour of Khan Uzbek and became his chief financial agent and tax-collector in Russia. In 1332 he demanded the Novgorodian 'silver from beyond the Kama'. He obtained the silver, but as the Novgorodians did not have ready bullion, they had to pay the tribute in silverware. The evidence of this tribute is still preserved in the museums of Moscow, which contain the silverware of Ivan inscribed with the names of Novgorodian bishops and city officials. Often Kalita claimed the right to participate in Novgorodian colonial exploitation, based on privileges supposedly obtained by his uncles and brothers. In 1337 he went so far as to send troops 'beyond the Portage' into the Dvina region. This enterprise ended in failure; his men 'were put to shame, after having suffered serious losses'.[25] Ivan, however, acquired control of Beloozero,[26] and the Novgorodians, having lost hope of its recovery, raided and devastated the town in 1340.[27] In addition to Beloozero, a key point on the Novgorodian colonial riverway, Ivan appears to have acquired control over Kostroma and Galich on the northern tributaries of the Volga, thus establishing a common Muscovite–Novgorodian frontier.[28]

His successors, Semeon, (1341–53), Ivan II, (1353–59) and Dmitrii Donskoi (1359–89), continued his policies of territorial aggrandizement and his demands for participation in the exploitation of the Novgorodian colonies.[29] This is the reason why, in 1353, after the death of Semeon, the Novgorodians tried,though unsuccessfully, to help Konstantin of Suzdal obtain the patent of Russian Grand Prince in the Horde. From 1360, after the death of Ivan II, they had better luck, and, with their aid, Dmitrii of Suzdal became Grand Prince, to the exclusion of Dmitrii of Moscow. According to the chronicle there was great rejoicing in Novgorod when they heard the news.[30] The Muscovite envoys, however, taking advantage of disturbances in the Golden Horde, were able in 1362 to reverse the Khan's decision, in favour of their own candidate. The attempt on the part of Dmitrii of Suzdal to resist the change was easily overcome, and after 1362 the rank of Grand Prince of Russia was associated with Moscow.

THE NOVGORODIAN USHKUINIKI

In spite of such incidents, the Novgorodians enjoyed relatively peaceful relations with Moscow during the second half of the fourteenth century, until the accession of Vasilii I in 1389. During this period there were several important social developments within Novgorod that resulted in the formation of a class of Novgorodian freebooters, the so-called *ushkuiniki*, named after the *ushkui*, a type of river boat. The term 'young man', which was applied to them in the chronicles, apparently referred to their lower-class status and not to their age. These people, apparently without the permission of the Novgorodian authorities, but perhaps with the connivance and help of some Novgorodian capitalists, organized a number of raiding expeditions that plundered the territory along the Volga. Thus, in 1360 the ushkuiniki plundered the Bulgar town of Zhukotin on the Kama.[31] In 1366 a very large party under the command of three voevodas plundered the merchants and population along the Volga

River. They went as far as Nizhnii Novgorod, where they killed a great many 'infidels' (the Mordva). Again, in 1369 the ushkuiniki plundered the land of the Bulgars as well as the Russian population along the Volga, 'doing much evil'. They were sufficiently strong in 1371 to capture and plunder the towns of Iaroslavl' and Kostroma. They looted the town of Viatka in 1374. In 1375, fifteen hundred strong in seventy large boats, they defeated two thousand Muscovite troops near Kostroma, again plundered the town of Kostroma, then went farther down the river and looted the burned Nizhnii Novgorod. They sold many of the women captured in their raids to the Bulgars. This bandit army sailed almost to the mouth of the Volga, where they were intercepted and annihilated by the Tatars.[32]

Following an unsuccessful protest to Novgorod over the activities of the ushkuiniki, Dmitrii of Moscow (later known as Dmitrii Donskoi) arrested the Novgorodian merchants in Moscow-contolled territory. Dmitrii led expeditions against Novgorod in 1366 and in 1386, even though he was preoccupied with the dangers of Lithuanian and Golden Horde aggression, and collected eight thousand rubles in fines from the Novgorodians.[33]

MOSCOW AND THE PERM LANDS

During the reign of Dmitrii Donskoi, Moscow also acquired a strong influence in the region of Perm, northeast of Ustiug (the 'Biarmia' of the Norse sagas), largely as a result of the activities of Stephen, Bishop of Perm (1345–96), who, after his death, became one of the most popular saints in Russia. Stephen, the son of a minor cleric in Ustiug, was educated by the local clergy. Growing up in the frontier community, he also learned the languages of the local Finnic tribes, the Permians and Zyrians (today called Komi). He became the deacon of the church, but soon was sent to Rostov for more education. The monastery at Rostov had a large library for that time, one of the few which preserved books of the old pre-Mongol times, and the monks were famous for their learning. There Stephen learned Greek and prepared for the priesthood. Then he went back to Ustiug to be a missionary and spread Christianity among the heathen. He prepared an alphabet for the Zyrians based on Cyrillic and translated parts of the Bible into their language. From Ustiug he went to the northeast, down the Sukhona and up the Vychegda to the Vym, where he founded a monastery, Ust'-Vymsk, and started preaching the gospel. He built a church, composed hymns in the Zyrian language, and made many conversions. His biography tells how he bested the Zyrian sorcerers in a competition, thereby enhancing his prestige all the more.

The Metropolitan of Moscow appreciated the value of his labours, and in 1383 appointed him Bishop of Perm.

As bishop, Stephen built more churches and established monasteries, ever farther into the wilderness. Around the churches settled Russian peasants and merchants. He became very powerful, a prince of the Church, ruling by virtue of his ecclesiastical authority, holder of a virtual 'frontier mark', or marchland, guarding the eastern approaches of the realm, acting as intermediary between his Zyrian converts and the Muscovite authorities, sometimes pleading their case in person. This conversion of heathen tribes was important in taming the wilderness in preparation for later conquest by Moscow.[34]

NOVGOROD AND THE DVINA REGION

Throughout the fourteenth century, there seemed to be an increase in large landholding by the Novgorodian boyars in the Dvina region. Some of these holdings were acquired through a semblance of legal procedure, others by outright seizure. An example of the former was the purchase in 1315 of the huge area of the Vaga River valley from the local Finns for twenty thousand squirrel pelts and ten rubles by an enterprising Novgorodian, Svoezemtsev.[35] An example of the second type was the action of a certain Luka Varfolomeev, who, in 1342, built a 'hard and thick' fort, Orlets, on the lower course of the Dvina and from there 'captured land on the Dvina and seized all the villages [*pogosty*]' in this area. It should be noted, however, that he did it 'in disobedience to Novgorod and without the blessing of the metropolitan [in Moscow] or the Bishop [of Novgorod]'. For his exploits Luka gathered armed slaves (*sboev*) and Dvina Finns (*Emchane*). Meanwhile, his son, Onitsifor, invaded the Vaga River area. Luka started out on an expedition at the head of two hundred men but was killed by 'men from beyond the Portage (*Zavolochane*).' In Novgorod the news of his death caused rioting among the lower classes of the city, who accused certain boyars of arranging for the assassination of Luka. The rioters were led by a brother of Luka, Matfei, and by his son, the above-mentioned Onitsifor. Apparently they were members of a prominent Novgorodian family. In 1350–54, Onitsifor held the post of *posadnik* (Mayor) in Novgorod.[36]

While along the Dvina there was a noticeable development of agriculture, east of the Dvina the Novgorodians actively continued the exploitation of their fur empire, and in 1363–64 they sent a huge expedition beyond the Urals into northern Siberia. Probably it was the largest expedition that they ever sent there. The expedition reached the River Ob, whereupon one part of it went down the river to the sea while the other part went up the river. On their return, the Novgorodians were attacked without success by the colonists of the Dvina, possibly because the expedition interfered with trade between the Dvinans and the Iugrians.[37]

MOSCOW CONTESTS THE DVINA REGION

During the time of Vasilii I Dmitrievich (1389–1425), the successor of Dmitrii Donskoi, a serious struggle between Novgorod and Moscow took place, which, according to the historian Pokrovskii, was a typical struggle for markets. Moscow attempted for the first time to take away from Novgorod the region of the Northern Dvina and the land 'beyond the Portage', which was the source of the furs which meant so much to Novgorod's economy. Novgorod had practically held a monopoly in the fur trade, and Moscow now attempted to break this monopoly. The warfare was not continuous, but neither did it have the character of a series of predatory raids. It was, rather, more of an intermittent 'colonial war', in which Moscow expected to hold the seized territory.[38] By this time the territory of the Dvina had a large permanent population, not merely visiting government agents who collected tribute, or enterprising businessmen who returned to Novgorod after obtaining the local furs, but permanent settlers, including peasants, merchants, and boyars.

The merchants of the Dvina area had also developed trade with the Volga principalities, and Novgorod did not share in the profits of this trade. In exchange for furs, salt, and other items, the Dvina merchants purchased grain. These merchants visited Kostroma and other Volga towns and established business connections there. Their trade was naturally frowned upon by Novgorod, which wanted to maintain its monopoly of fur exports. The Dvina people resented the interference of Novgorod, and among them a movement began to develop that favoured the establishment of closer ties with the growing principality of Moscow and the severance of their ties with Novgorod. This movement was welcomed by the Muscovite princes, especially since the Muscovite frontier came close to the Novgorodian colonial possessions. Moscow now possessed Beloozero, strategically near the Novgorodian line of communications with its colonies, and also the principalities of Kostroma and Galich, situated on the northern tributaries of the Volga, close to the Novgorodian colonies.[39]

Hostilities started soon after the accession of Vasilii to the throne. In 1392 ushkuiniki from Novgorod, joining with similar elements in Ustiug and other restless border settlements, sailed along the Viatka River, captured Zhukotin and Kazan in the land of the Bulgars, then sailed along the Volga and plundered all the merchants (*gosti*).[40] The exploits of the ushkuiniki did not improve relations between Moscow and Novgorod, for the Muscovites blamed the other city for its lack of effort in restraining the river pirates. A quarrel developed over the question of the jurisdiction of the Muscovite Metropolitan over the Novgorodian bishopric and over certain forms of tribute (*kniazhenina* and *chernyi bor*) which Novgorod was supposed to deliver to Moscow. The Novgorodians rejected the demands of the Prince, and hostilities soon followed.[41]

In 1393 the troops of the Grand Prince marched into Novgorodian territory. Committing all manner of atrocities on the subjects of Novgorod, the Muscovites established control over the rivers which were used to carry grain supplies from the Volga. Simultaneously they invaded the territory of Vologda at the sources of the Sukhona River, which was part of the Novgorodian colonial water route. The Novgorodians hurriedly raised an army of volunteers (*okhochaia rat'*) and retaliated by invading the Muscovite possessions south of Beloozero, capturing Klichen Gorodok and Ustiuzhna.[42]

The area 'beyond the Portage' became another theatre of war. Here the Novgorodians and their Dvina colonists captured and plundered Ustiug, not even sparing the icons in the cathedral. The victors spent four weeks in the town. The Muscovite chronicle describes their atrocities with gusto (although the Muscovities did not behave any better in Novgorodian territory).

They hunted men in the woods, tortured prisoners to make them reveal hidden goods, devastated surrounding villages, and finally went by land down the Dvina, capturing people and cattle. Then, in their boats, they carried away the seized property. A great many prisoners—men, women, and children—were sent to Novgorod.

Next the Novgorodians went to Beloozero, captured and plundered it, and devastated the villages around it, acting as they had in Ustiug.[43]

During this war of 1393, 'much blood was spilled on both sides.' 'Not wishing any further slaughtering of peasants', the Novgorodians were the first to seek peace. They sent an envoy to the Grand Prince to ask for peace 'on the old terms', and also sent a letter of submission to the Metropolitan asking forgiveness for their past offences and for their refractoriness toward the Prince. Peace was concluded with the Prince according to the 'old terms', and the Metropolitan forgave and blessed the Novgorodians. Muscovite envoys went to Novgorod, where they confirmed the terms of peace.[44]

In making peace in 1393, the Novgorodians, as we have seen, made the opening move. They apologized for past offences, including their arrogance and disrespect in dealing with the Prince, made concessions in the question of the Metropolitan's jurisdiction, and agreed to make payments to the Prince. As for the formula, 'on the old terms', each side interpreted it in a light favourable to itself. The peace did not last long.

The Novgorodians were apparently bothered by unrest within their own colonies, particularly on the Dvina, and in 1397 Vasilii took advantage of this situation, the Muscovite armies seizing the grain routes to Novgorod, as well as Vologda and Bezhetskii Verkh, the territory within an angle formed by the Mologa River. This area was greatly cherished by the Novgorodians, and they were always very sensitive about it.[45]

Simultaneously the Grand Prince sent his boyar Andrei Alberdov to the Dvinans with a message addressed to the 'Dvina *sloboda* [district]'. The message advised the Dvinans to accept the authority of the Grand Prince and secede from Novgorod. In return the Grand Prince promised his protection and support and granted a 'bill of certain rights' to the Dvinans.

The message of the Grand Prince was addressed to all the people of the Dvina but favoured the local boyars and merchants. It promised:

1. To protect the dignity of the boyars, establishing punishment for anyone who called them names.

2. To protect the boyars from punishment if they killed a slave 'without intention' while beating him.

3. To give the Dvina merchants special privileges while doing business 'in my patrimony, the great principality', to exempt them from payment of the usual taxes on merchants.

4. To protect the Dvinans against delay in court procedure in case of lawsuits, giving assurance that either the Dvina authorities or the Grand Prince himself should try their cases.

5. That the Grand Prince himself would mete out severe punishment to anyone who should disregard the charter and cause the Dvinans any grievances.[46]

This document, which appears on the surface to be a charter, actually was intended as propaganda to win the Dvinans to Moscow.

Many boyars of the Dvina, including two Novgorodian voevodas (generals), Konon and Ivan Mikitin, as well as some less prominent people of the Dvina, responded to this appeal for secession from Novgorod and took an oath of allegiance to the Grand Prince. Together with the Muscovites, these seceders, operating in the Dvina territory, devastated the holdings of the Bishop of Novgorod and began to divide among themselves the local lands belonging to the Novgorodian boyars. Meanwhile, the Grand Prince sent Fedor, one of the Rostov princes, to the Dvina to act as his Governor. The latter established himself in Orlets (founded in 1342 by the Novgorodian boyar, Luka Varfolomeev) and started to collect taxes in the Dvina territory for the Grand Prince.[47]

Faced with the loss of its colonies, Novgorod made a supreme effort to recover its Dvina possessions. In 1398 a large Novgorodian army entered the Dvina territory and started a campaign against the local traitors and Muscovite forces to recover this valuable region. The army first attacked the vulnerable parts of the Novgorodian river route between Novgorod and the Urals. It advanced against Beloozero, devastating the area and burning the towns and villages. The princes of Beloozero were forced to seek mercy, whereupon the Novgorodians took from them sixty rubles ransom, many spoils, and led away 'innumerable captives'. From Beloozero they entered the areas of Vologda and Ustiug, again devastating and burning. They remained in Ustiug four weeks and from there sent an expedition southwards into the Muscovite-controlled area around the northern tributaries of the Volga, stopping only a short distance from the town of Galich. After devastating this land, which was subject to the Prince of Moscow, they returned, again taking 'innumerable captives'. Some of the captives they left behind (alive or dead?) because there was no room for them in the Novgorodian boats. From Ustiug the army went to Orlets, whither the Novgorodian traitors had fled at the approach of the Novgorodian army, and besieged it for four weeks. When the fortifications began to crumble under the rams of the Novgorodians, the garrison surrendered, 'pleading tearfully' for mercy. The Novgorodians executed their former voevodas, Ivan and Konon Mikitin, and put the other traitors—'the people who brought so much evil to the Dvina land'—in chains. After that they imposed a ransom on Prince Fedor of Rostov, taking from him all the taxes which he had collected. They collected three hundred rubles and imposed a fine of two thousand rubles and three thousand horses on the people of the Dvina territory at large. After the successful reconquest of the Dvina, the Novgorodians sent envoys to the Grand Prince, who, in the same year, concluded peace 'on the old terms'.[48]

Apparently, Ustiug quickly recovered from the devastation; in 1399 we find there many refugees who had fled to escape punishment for the act of treason against their metropolis[49] and who were anxious to take revenge for their sufferings at the hands of the Novgorodian troops. In 1401, without warning, Anfal Mikitin (the brother of Ivan Mikitin) and Gerasim (a renegade monk), supported by troops of the Grand Prince, invaded the territory 'beyond the Portage' and conquered all the Dvina land. The invaders killed and hanged people and seized their property and merchandise. Anfal also captured three distinguished boyars, the posadniks (administrators) of the Dvina. Meanwhile, three boyars loyal to Novgorod gathered the people of the Vaga, pursued and fought Anfal and Gerasim, freed the prisoners, and scattered the invaders.[50]

Anfal escaped to Viatka and did not trouble the Novgorodians further. In 1409 he went with the men of Viatka by way of the Kama and Volga into the land of the Bulgars, was captured by the Tatars, and was taken to the Horde. He somehow obtained his freedom and reappeared in Viatka, but in 1418 he was killed there by another Novgorodian refugee, Rassokhin (or Roz'sokhin).[51]

While officially Moscow and Novgorod were not at war after 1398, the skirmishes and raids along their frontiers continued. The most serious of these conflicts took place in 1417 and 1425. In 1417 a group of refugees from the Dvina (part of those who had tried to secede from Novgorod in 1397), accompanied by adventurers from Ustiug and Viatka, sailed [from Ustiug?] 'without warning' into the land 'beyond the Portage'. At the mouth of the Dvina they seized and burned Kholmogory (an important administrative centre of the Dvina colony) and there captured some Novgorodian boyars. The Novgorodian officials collected a force from the Vaga River, gave chase, recovered the captives and spoils, and pursued the invaders as far as Ustiug, taking this opportunity to plunder that phoenix-like town.[52] In 1425 the people of Ustiug raided the Novgorodian colonies again, whereupon the Novgorodians sent an army to Ustiug and exacted fifty thousand squirrel skins and six 'forties' of sable pelts as retribution for damages caused by the Ustiuzhans.[53]

Thereafter Ustiug became a sharper thorn in Novgorodian flesh. Formerly its people had preyed upon the Novgorodian fur caravans which came from Iugra (especially in 1323 and 1329), but now the town became a recognized tool of Muscovite policy. From Ustiug the Dvina emigrants, with aid from Moscow as well as from the people of Ustiug, made raids deep into the Dvina territory, as far north as Kholmogory. During the reign of Vasilii, the Novgorodians tried many times (1392, 1398, 1417, and 1425) to destroy this Muscovite outpost, located on one of the main arteries of the Novgorodian colonial waterway. Ustiug was repeatedly captured and burned, yet it seemed always to recover quickly and cause Novgorod new grief.

In 1425 Grand Prince Vasilii died. His attempt to seize the Dvina territory outright had failed, but Moscow was now firmly entrenched along the Novgorodian colonial frontier, holding Beloozero, Vologda, and the course of the Sukhona River from Vologda to Ustiug. The Novgorodians still preserved their fur empire, but its position was precarious.

At Vasilii I's death, his son and heir, Vasilii II, was only ten years old. During his childhood, Moscow ceased its aggressive policies towards its neighbours, including Novgorod. Moscow, in turn, was not troubled by its enemies because backing up the youthful Grand Prince was his grandfather, the powerful Grand Prince of Lithuania, Vitovt, appointed as guardian by Vasilii I. The death of Vitovt in 1432 encouraged the uncles and cousins of Vasilii II to come forward with claims to the throne. Vasilii II was recognized Grand Prince by the Horde, but the Horde at this time was too weak to enforce its decision. A civil war started between Vasilii and his relatives that lasted for twenty years. The Novgorodians were delighted by this turn of events because, at least temporarily, it relieved them from the Muscovite pressure. Throughout the conflict they remained neutral, even though at times the military operations spread into their territory.[54]

The Novgorodians adopted a general policy of recognizing the victor as their suzerain while giving aid and asylum to the vanquished. During the struggle Vasilii thrice lost and thrice regained Moscow. In 1435 Vasilii, hard-pressed, made a treaty with Novgorod whereby he promised to return to Novgorod all its former possessions seized by Moscow, including the Volga portages, Vologda, and Bezhetskii Verkh. In 1436, however, the Novgorodians complained that the Grand Prince did not fulfil his promises. When the Novgorodian boyars arrived at the appointed place to establish new frontiers, they did not find the Muscovite emissaries there. In 1441, during the respite in the civil war, Vasilii renounced his concessions and invaded the Novgorodian lands. The Novgorodians counterattacked from 'beyond the Portage' but suffered defeat and had to buy peace from the Grand Prince for eight thousand rubles.[55]

What was probably the last grand expedition of Novgorod into the land of Iugra took place in 1446. Three thousand men participated and returned with a great many spoils and captives.[56] Eighty men, however, lost their lives at the hands of the natives. This happened in the same year that Vasilii was captured by his cousins, who blinded and exiled him to Vologda. Vasilii, however, escaped, gathered a new army, and by 1450 was able to inflict a decisive defeat upon his rivals. In 1453 the chief opponent of Vasilii, Dmitrii Shemiaka, died in Novgorod, apparently from poison. Vasilii, indignant because of Novgorodian neutrality during the civil war and particularly because the Novgorodians gave asylum to the defeated Shemiaka, led a large expedition against Novgorod in 1456. The Novgorod army, although superior in numbers, was defeated, and the proud city had to accept the humiliating terms of the treaty of Iazhelbitsy in 1456. The Novgorodians had to deliver ten thousand rubles as war indemnity (*istoma*). Novgorodian documents in the future were to have the seal of the Grand Prince, the Novgorodian town meeting (*veche*) lost the right to issue written decisions (*gramoty*), and Novgorod was not to offer hospitality to any of the Grand Prince's enemies. Territorial adjustments were not formulated in the document, but apparently all disputed territories went to Moscow.[57]

After delivering this severe blow to Novgorodian independence, Vasilii turned his attention to the old Novgorodian colony of Viatka (also called Khlynov). This colony on the Viatka River, one of the large northern tributaries of the Kama, had a long history. According to a number of Russian historians—Karamzin, Ilovaiskii and others—it was founded in the late twelfth century by the Novgorodians amidst the local Finnic tribes of the Votiaks and Cheremis. Separated from the Russian northern rivers by thick forests, Viatka repudiated the authority of Novgorod at an early date and refused to accept governors from Novgorod or pay tribute to Novgorod. Because of its inaccessibility, remoteness, and general insignificance, Viatka was left alone by the mother city. Within this community the colonists organized a sort of rough democracy patterned after Novgorod, with the town meeting having supreme authority. The Viatkans' geographic position, however, brought them in touch with the colonists coming from the Volga area, and during the civil war of 1432–52 they supported the rivals of Vasilii. To Vasilii this was a crime for which they had to be punished. The Muscovite expeditions in 1459 captured Viatka and some small towns which had grown up around it. The people surrendered and recognized the authority of the Grand Prince.[58]

ANNEXATION OF NOVGOROD AND ITS TERRITORIES BY MOSCOW

Vasilii II died in 1462. It was during the reign of his illustrious son, Ivan III, that Novgorod with its colonies fell into the hands of Moscow, thus ending the three hundred-year long contest between Novgorod and the Volga principalities.

At the time of Ivan's accession to the throne, Novgorod, weakened by Vasilii II, was no longer capable of protecting its colonies against Muscovite encroachment. In 1465, by orders of Ivan, an Ustiug resident named Vasilii Skriaba led an expedition into Iugra, an indisputable colony of Novgorod. The expedition was composed of settlers along the Vychegda and Vym Rivers as well as of native Permians (Zyrians) led by their baptized chief, Vasilii.

It should be recalled in this connection that the missionary activity of St. Stephen had led to the establishment of a bishopric in the land of Perm, with Saint Stephen as its first bishop. His successors continued to spread Christianity in this area and attracted Russian colonists, with the result that there appeared on the Vychegda and Vym rivers a sort of ecclesiastic colony comparable to a frontier mark. The local Permians willingly accepted the authority of the bishops, often seeking their advice and protection and appealing to them as arbitrators in tribal controversies.

45

The bishops, successful with the friendly Permians, attempted to carry their proselytizing efforts beyond their territory to that of another native group, the Voguls, who lived on both slopes of the Urals. Here, however, they met a very hostile reception. The Voguls not only objected to the missionaries but in 1455 came to the Vychegda and killed Bishop Pitirim while he was leading a religious procession. Undaunted by this event, his successor, Iona, continued his work, 'baptized Great Perm and its Prince, built churches in Perm and placed there priests and abbots'.

In doing their missionary work, the Perm bishops served the political ends of Moscow. Thus it was possible to enlist the help of the Permians when the expedition of Skriaba was undertaken. The expedition was successful. It returned with spoils and two captured Iugra chiefs, who were brought to Moscow. Skriaba was rewarded by the Grand Prince, while the native chiefs were graciously received and allowed to return home with appropriate gifts. Before their departure, however, they went through a ceremony in which the Grand Prince confirmed their rank, and they took an oath of allegiance, declaring themselves his vassals. Thus Moscow took the first step toward the establishment of its authority in the Novgorodian colonies and inaugurated its own expansion across the Urals.[59]

Following this unceremonious incursion into Iugra, Ivan took decisive action against Novgorod itself. He took advantage of the fact that the Novgorodians, fearing the aggression of Moscow, had concluded a treaty with Kasimir, who was simultaneously King of Poland and Grand Prince of Lithuania. They recognized his suzerainty and agreed to pay tribute in exchange for protection against Moscow and 'preservation of their liberties'. Ivan announced that the Novgorodians were traitors to the faith and fatherland and declared a 'crusade' against Novgorod. Cleverly utilizing the dissatisfaction of the lower classes of Novgorod, he made himself appear as their champion, who would save them from the oppression of the boyars. With clever propaganda, he weakened Novgorodian resistance and in 1471, after a victorious campaign, he imposed on them the Treaty of Shelon.[60] This treaty restated the provisions of the Treaty of Iazhelbitsy, but strongly emphasized that Novgorod was an inalienable part of the Grand Principality of Russia. (*byt' ot velikikh kniazei neotstupnymi ni k chemu*).[61]

The Novgorodians began peace negotiations before they heard about the disaster in their colonies. The armies of the Grand Prince had invaded them from two strategic bases, Ustiug and Vologda. Among the Muscovite troops were men from Ustiug and Viatka. The Novgorodians gathered a large army consisting of Novgorod, Dvina, and Pechora troops, but were decisively defeated because the Dvinans, according to the Novgorodian chronicle, 'did not follow' their commander. During peace negotiations, Ivan returned to Novgorod its colonial possessions but within them kept a number of important enclaves, including Kholmogory at the mouth of the Dvina.[62]

The year after the conclusion of peace, Ivan sent his troops under the voevoda Fedor Pestrii into the area of Perm east of the Perm bishopric, along the upper course of the Kama. The troops defeated the native Permian chiefs, including the baptized chief, Michael. Then, in a convenient place, they built a fort which served as a base for the conquest of all the Permian tribes. The spoils, including sixteen 'forties' of sable pelts, were sent to Moscow. After the conquest, the Russians allowed the native chiefs to administer their tribes until 1505, when Moscow sent a Russian governor to Perm. Thus, Ivan assumed the leading role in further colonial expansion—in the words of Karamzin, 'Moscow leaned its shoulders against the Urals.'[63]

In 1477 the Grand Prince again quarrelled with the Novgorodians and sent another expedition against them. This time the Novgorodians did not dare to resist and immediately capitulated. They accepted all the terms imposed on them by the Grand Prince. The result was complete subjugation of Novgorod and its colonies. The famous Novgorodian veche was abolished, and henceforth Novgorod was to be administered by a governor (*namestnik*) appointed by the Grand Prince.

ANNEXATION OF VIATKA

Following the downfall of Novgorod, its ancient colony of Viatka also lost its independence. As was shown above, in 1459 the people of Viatka recognized the authority of the Grand Prince.[64] But when, in 1469, the Muscovite generals demanded that the Viatkans join their expedition against Kazan, the Viatkans declared: 'The Khan of Kazan forced us against our will to swear that we shall not help either himself when he would fight the Muscovites, nor the Grand Prince when he would fight Kazan.'[65] However, they proved their loyalty to Ivan during the latter's war with Novgorod in 1471. As was mentioned above, they joined Muscovite forces operating from Ustiug. In 1478, when the Khan of Kazan received false news about a defeat of Ivan by the Novgorodians, he invaded and devastated Viatka territories, but could not take the town, despite a four-week siege. When the Tatars heard that their information regarding Ivan was not correct, they hurriedly retreated.[66]

In 1485, during another expedition of Ivan against Kazan, the Viatkans once more refused to fight in the ranks of the Grand Prince. In the following year they invaded the territory of Ustiug. There is a record showing that the Metropolitan of Moscow tried in vain to induce the Viatkans to mend their ways. He accused them of disregard for the church, insolence toward the Grand Prince, alliance with pagans [the Tatars], and of generally bloodthirsty habits. If they should ask the forgiveness of the Grand Prince and return their spoils and captives, the Metropolitan promised to intercede in their favour before the Grand Prince. Apparently the appeal of the Metropolitan had no effect, because in 1489 the Grand Prince sent a large army to Viatka. Seeing the futility of resistance, the Viatkans surrendered. The Muscovite commanders destroyed the fortifications of the town of Viatka and transferred some prosperous local merchants to Moscow. Some of the local leaders were executed by order of the Grand Prince. The native chiefs of this area were taken to Moscow and, after having sworn their allegiance to Moscow, were dismissed with gifts. Thus disappeared the last vestige of the former colonial domain of Novgorod.[67]

MOSCOW PRESSES BEYOND THE URALS

In his new role as leader of colonial expansion across the Urals, an area formerly monopolized by Novgorod, Ivan sent two large expeditions to Siberia. The first, under Prince Fedor Kurbskii, was sent in 1483. The Voguls had invaded the Perm region, penetrating as far as Cherdyn, where they were defeated by the Russians. The expedition, which included Russian frontiersmen from Ustiug and the friendly Permians, started from Ustiug. It accomplished its mission, punishing the Voguls severely, taking many prisoners, and collecting tribute from the Siberian natives.

It is interesting to note the significant part played by Filofei, Bishop of Perm, in border affairs during the 1480s. Although primarily the protector of the baptized Permians along the Vychegda and Vym rivers, his prestige extended beyond the Urals among the hostile Voguls and Ostiaks. A year after the expedition of 1483, he received a request from the Siberian tribes of Iugra and Koda to use his influence with the Grand Prince to liberate their captured chiefs. Simultaneously Iumshan, the arch-enemy of the Russians and the baptized Permians, a man whose father had participated in the murder of Filofei's predecessor, Pitirim, and who had himself led a Vogul raid on Perm in 1481, appealed to Filofei for safe conduct to Moscow. Iumshan had escaped capture during the expedition of 1483 but had decided to submit to Moscow. Through the efforts of the Bishop, the safe conduct was obtained, and Iumshan, together with the captured chiefs, swore allegiance to the Tsar in Moscow. The bishop also took an active part in the subsequent release of the captured chiefs and their families, who were allowed to return to their people. Furthermore, he acted as an intermediary not only between the Muscovite government and the natives but also among the natives themselves. Thus, about 1485, he held a sort of peace conference at his residence in Ust'-Vymsk, where, in the presence of a representative of the Bishop and a local official of the Prince, six Siberian chiefs swore an oath to two baptized Permian chiefs that they would abstain from any evil action against the Permians. To the Russians they promised faithful service to the Grand Prince. The oath was strengthened by 'drinking water from the gold' in accordance with their custom. Symbolizing his new power, Ivan, in 1484, adopted the title 'Prince of Iugra.'[68]

Ivan sent his last expedition across the Urals in 1499. Prince Semeon Fedorovich Kurbskii and two other voevodas led an army of about five thousand men composed of some government troops, Russian frontiersmen from the Dvina, Vaga, Pinega, and Vychegda Rivers, and people from Ustiug and Viatka. This expedition gathered on the Pechora River and from there went across the Urals to the River Ob in what was later to be known as Siberia. It captured over forty native villages, took over a thousand natives as prisoners, and brought back about sixty captured native chiefs.[69] It would seem that a predatory expedition of such size must have inflicted tremendous devastation and loss of life. Moscow, the leading city of a resurgent upper Volga region, was killing the goose that had supplied the golden eggs to Novgorod.

It is also worth noting that by this time, long before the later 'conquest', the Russians were fairly familiar with the lands beyond the Urals. Novgorod had sent large expeditions to that region in 1364 and 1446, and various smaller enterprises may have gone unrecorded. An ethnographic list compiled at the end of the fifteenth century mentions various types of 'Samoyeds'—peoples dwelling along the Ob, including the 'Malgonzei,' inhabiting an area east of the lower Ob later to become well known as Mangazeia.[70]

SUMMARY

The period of Mongol rule gave Novgorod a new lease on life in the northeast and a respite from aggression at the hands of the Volga princes. This lasted until a new Volga principality, Moscow, grew to a point where it was able to take action against the Novgorodian colonies and Novgorod itself. A seesaw struggle ensued, with the Novgorodian territories as the stakes. The result is not surprising. The upper Volga region had already been dangerous to Novgorod before the Mongol invasion, and the rise of Moscow was a resurgence of this danger. Novgorod, on the other hand, lacked the population and resources of the upper

Volga region, largely because of the lack of a food base, which made a greater population impossible and which, more immediately, rendered her dependent on imports and excessively vulnerable to attack. The decline of Novgorod was also to be expected from her socially disunited polity, with no one class able to direct affairs in a consistent fashion. Unable to establish an effective administration in the conquered regions, to enforce the allegiance of her colonies, or to explore the regions of Iugra and beyond by more than random expeditions, Novgorod lacked what was required for mastery of the east and continued independence. It is likely that its decline before one or another of the Volga principalities would only have been a matter of time in any case. In the course of the fourteenth and fifteenth centuries, the Moscow rulers, particularly Vasilii II and Ivan III, whittled away at Novgorodian sovereignty and sources of prosperity until the northern 'crowned republic' and its possessions were absorbed. Two of the currents of expansion noted earlier—those of Novgorod and Moscow—were thus joined, and Moscow itself began to look beyond the Urals.

Chapter 3

Liberation and Advance

While eroding Novgorod's holdings and independence, the Volga princes had also to deal with their Tatar conquerors and suzerains. The duration of Tatar domination of Russia is usually set at two hundred and forty years, but during the last hundred years of this period Russia began to recover under the leadership of Moscow, while at the same time the Golden Horde crumbled. Conversely, the hundred years that followed the accepted date of liberation saw many adjustments before the change was assured and Moscow could itself take the offensive. These adjustments had direct influence on the nature of Russian activities on the eastern frontier. [1]

DECLINE OF THE GOLDEN HORDE

After the firm, but enlightened, rule of the khan Uzbek (1313–41) and his son Dzhani-bek (1342–57), the throne of the Horde was sullied by a succession of patricides and fratricides, and the Tatar aristocracy was in almost continuous factional strife. All of this was helpful to Moscow, as the rapidly changing rulers of the Horde frequently had little opportunity to interfere in Russian affairs. In the west, on the other hand, the Lithuanians, unified at the end of the thirteenth century, were able to profit from Tatar preoccupation and took half of Russia under their domination, confronting the Moscow princes with a new and powerful neighbour.

Within the Horde there were occasional efforts to stem the dissolution. In the 1370s the able and energetic Mamai, a Mongol general, became the ruler of the part of the Golden Horde west of the Volga through a succession of puppet khans. He tried to restore unity in the Horde and to reduce the Moscow princes to subservience once again. When, in 1378, Prince Dmitrii of Moscow defeated a Tatar force sent by Mamai to raid the principality of Riazan, Mamai entered into an agreement with the Prince of Lithuania for an expedition against Moscow.

Urged by the clergy and the population, Dmitrii resisted the Tatars. The Russian victory at Kulikovo (8 September 1380) raised the prestige of the Muscovite princes, who now appeared as champions of liberation.

The triumph was short-lived, for Mamai was soon overthrown by the still more relentless Tokhtamysh, Khan of the White Horde (or eastern Kypchaks), a descendant of Genghis Khan. Tokhtamysh forced Dmitrii to acknowledge himself a Tatar vassal, then in 1382 treacherously invaded and burned Moscow. Moscow's allies fell away, and the Tatars seemed stronger than ever. In 1389, when Dmitrii died, the Khan proclaimed Dmitrii's son, Vasilii I (1389–1425), Grand Prince in his stead. Vasilii, hard pressed by the Lithuanians, needed Tatar support and therefore remained outwardly loyal.

Meanwhile, changes in central Asia brought forth a new Tatar conqueror. The dynasty of Jagatai, second son of Genghis Khan, lasted until 1335, after which the region became divided into petty states. Out of one of these, Samarkand, came the celebrated Timur, or Tamerlane (1333?–1405), who began wholesale conquests. Tokhtamysh, earlier an ally, finally felt strong enough to challenge Timur, crossed the Caucasus, and captured Tabriz; but in 1395 he was decisively defeated. In the pursuit, Timur went as far as the Caucasus and southern Russia. If he had not been diverted by other concerns, all of Russia might have fallen once more under Tatar rule as implacable as that of Batu a century and a half before.

After the departure of Timur, another important figure rose in the Golden Horde, Edigei. Tokhtamysh had fled to Lithuania, to the protection of the ambitious Prince Viten (or Vytenis, known in Russian accounts as Vitovt). Viten had already taken much Russian territory and after the resubjugation of Moscow used the need to stop the Tatars as an excuse to advance still farther. Had he won, he might have taken Moscow, but in 1399 he suffered defeat on the River Vorskla at the hands of Edigei. Again able to assert Tatar authority, Edigei then played on Moscow–Lithuania rivalries, fomenting a quarrel between the two, which weakened both. In 1409 Edigei made another devastating raid on Moscow, but was soon expelled from the Golden Horde by a rival. The Horde never again produced a capable leader and thereafter gradually declined in power and authority.

BREAKUP OF THE HORDE

The decline of the Horde led inevitably to its destruction. Early in the fifteenth century, several large segments ruled by rival descendants of Genghis Khan seceded from the main Horde. Thus, in the 1440s the middle Volga region became the independent khanate of Kazan. The geographical position of the khanate, on the territory of the former Bulgar state, was highly favourable. The khanate was situated at the junction of several main trade routes: the Volga route to the Caspian Sea, the Kama route to the Urals, the Oka and upper Volga route to the northeast, and the old steppe caravan route to central Asia. Moreover, it was where the forest and the steppe met in a region of good farm land, thus serving as an emporium of forest products and livestock.

In the 1450s the khanate of Astrakhan appeared on the lower Volga. It was in a good position on caravan and water routes, and in a region of good pastures and fisheries.

On the eastern borders of the Golden Horde the Nogai Horde fell away, one of several hordes which arose out of the disintegration of the Golden Horde following the ousting of Emir Edigei in 1411. The Mongol clan of the Mangkyts and sections of the Kypchaks and other Turkic tribes joined this horde.[2] Some of these tribes at the end of the thirteenth century had been among the subjects of Khan Nogai of the Golden Horde; hence they were called the Nogais.[3] Based on the Iaik (Ural) River basin, the Nogais ranged over an area extending from the lower Volga as far east as the Irtysh River, and from the Caspian and Aral Seas northward to the frontiers of the khanates of Kazan and Sibir.[4]

Although for a time a separate political entity, the Nogais remained disunited, divided into many *uluses* (groups) headed by the descendants of Edigei, who often engaged in bloody feuds.[5]

The Tatar lords of the Crimean peninsula, a land of ancient trading centres, with a mild climate favouring alike agriculture and stock raising, at the end of the fourteenth century formed an independent state. With the protection of Prince Vitovt of Lithuania, the Khan Khadzhi-Girei started the dynasty of the Gireis in 1427.

East of the Urals as far as the Irtysh, the land of Sibir or Ibir, famed for its abundant fur resources and traversed by the old trade route from central Asia across the Urals to the Kama and Volga region, also broke away from the Golden Horde. In the fifteenth and sixteenth centuries an independent khanate was formed with its centre at the trading town of Tiumen'. Rule passed in the second half of the fifteenth century from one pretender to another. At the end of the century, one Ibak-Ibragim, who is regarded as founder of the Siberian khanate, set himself up in Tiumen' with the aid of the Nogais. Ibak fell in a struggle with local Tatar nobles, and power passed to a native princely dynasty, which transferred its centre eastward to the mouth of the Tobol, that is, to the town of Kashlyk (known also as *Sibir'*; its ruins, twelve miles from Tobol'sk, were known later as Isker, or the 'old place').

The opportunity for liberation offered by this disintegration of Tatar power may have been clear, but the Moscow state faced the equally important tasks of reuniting the Russian territories divided during the period of anarchy prior to the Mongol conquest, of regaining lands annexed by Lithuania, and of repelling the invasions of the Livonian Order and of Poland and Lithuania, the latter two joined since 1386 by dynastic marriage. The necessity of dealing with all of these tasks simultaneously, with frequent close interaction between events in east and west, posed complex problems of statesmanship for the Muscovite rulers.

TATARS IN RUSSIAN SERVICE

Already, during the Kievan period, the Russians had learned the art of 'divide and rule' in relations with their neighbours. In like manner they gradually learned to take advantage of the divisions among the Tatars, building up a pattern of techniques which was to become characteristic of Russian relations with Asian peoples.

In this connection, the use by the Muscovite government of the so-called 'Tatars in [state] service' (*sluzhilye tatary*) should be noted. Since the days of Ivan Kalita, individual fugitives from the Golden Horde from time to time appeared in Moscow seeking service with the Muscovite princes. In the first half of the fifteenth century various Tatar princelings, descendants of Genghis Khan, with their families and often very numerous retainers and followers, began to offer 'to protect the Russian land during their lifetime'. For the most part, these princelings fled from their enemies and rivals in the Horde. The Muscovite rulers welcomed such 'refugees' and settled them in the frontier towns. The newcomers frequently embraced Christianity, intermarried with the Russian nobility, themselves became progenitors of many Russian noble families, and, on the whole, faithfully served their Muscovite masters.

In 1446 two Tatar princes, the brothers Iakub and Kasim, took service under Grand Prince Vasilii II (the Blind), who gave Zvenigorod to Prince Kasim. The latter, in 1449, fought Tatar raiders set on plundering the Muscovite land, and in 1451, under the command of the Russian voevoda Bezzubtsov, took part in an expedition sent against another marauding band in the steppe. In late 1452 or early 1453, the Tatar khanate of Kasimov was established on the Oka and became a true Russian frontier mark ruled by Tatars in the Russian service. In 1474 Ivan III gave a newly built fort on the Oka to the Tatar Prince Murtaza; in 1486 he gave the town of Kasimov (originally Gorodets, later called Meshcherskii Gorodok, and finally renamed Kasimov in 1471 in honour of Prince Kasim)[6] to Nur Daulet, brother of the Crimean Khan, Mengli Girei; in 1497 he gave Kashira, Serpukhov, and Khotun to the exiled Khan of Kazan, Muhammed Emin; and later granted Kashira to another ex-Khan, Abdul-Letif.[7]

While the Tatars were used wherever possible to help bolster Moscow's defences or, on occasion, to destroy other Tatars, specific measures had to be evolved in each case against the Crimeans, the Nogais, and the Kazan Tatars, all with the aim of preventing any reunion of, or concerted action by, the several parts of the once united and invincible Golden Horde.

The populous Crimea, although dependent on predatory raids for its economic survival, was, at least during the fifteenth century, still no menace to Russia, as it was separated from Russian territory by a broad belt of Polish-Lithuanian territory in the Ukraine. Relations between Moscow and the Crimea were therefore confined to diplomatic machinations of both sides against the Poles and rivalry for influence in Kazan.

Because of their numbers, the Nogais played an important role in the political events in eastern Europe and central Asia. They interfered in the internal affairs of the Kazan and Siberian khanates, sometimes put their candidates on the throne or overthrew the local khans, and, farther south and east, fought the Kazakhs and participated in the wars of the Uzbeks.

At the end of the fifteenth century the Nogais became involved in Muscovite–Crimean relations. Some of the Nogai *murzas* (chiefs) sided with Moscow, while others sided with the Crimea and took part in the Crimean raids into Russia.[8]

After the middle of the fifteenth century, however, it was the khanate of Kazan which posed the most constant danger to neighbouring Russian territory. In spite of the diplomatic efforts of the Muscovite rulers, in spite of annual gifts in gold which were nothing less than tribute, the khans of Kazan would not or could not restrain their subjects from raids. Occasionally they themselves ordered such operations and even led them. Deep in Russian territory as far as Ustiug and Kostroma, no villager could feel safe from the Kazan Tatars, who burned and looted Russian settlements and ravaged the suburbs of walled towns, carrying off thousands of prisoners to be sold into slavery. The problem of how to render Kazan harmless therefore assumed prime importance in the eyes of Muscovite statesmen.

Already, at the time of his accession to power in 1462, Ivan III had sent a large detachment to reconnoitre Kazan territory. In 1467 an opportunity for decisive action seemed to present itself when a faction in Kazan invited Kasim, ruler of the satellite khanate of Kasimov, to take over the throne. Ivan sent troops to support Kasim's claims, but, after a hard march through the cold rains of an early autumn, they found a Tatar force waiting on the opposite side of the Volga below Kazan. They turned back, and Kazan retaliated by raiding the territories around Galich. The Muscovites shielded their territory by fortifying Murom, Nizhii Novgorod, Kostroma, and Galich, and early in 1468 raided the country of the Cheremis, a northern dependency of Kazan.[9]

In the spring of 1468 Ivan organized another force, including boyars and cossacks (the first mention of cossacks being employed in the Muscovite forces as a unit) under Ivan Runo. This army picked up reinforcements successively at Galich, Vologda, Ustiug, and Viatka, all of which had suffered from raids by Kazan. At Kotel'nich, however, most of the Viatkans turned back when word came that a Kazan force had attacked Viatka. Viatka had to submit to the Khan, but Runo's force went on to plunder the country of the Cheremis, went down the Kama toward Kazan as far as the river's confluence with the Volga, then turned and went back up the Kama to return by way of Perm and Ustiug. Simultaneously another Muscovite detachment under Prince Fedor Khripun, setting out along the Volga toward Kazan from Nizhnii Novgorod, slew many Kazan Tatars.

These successful raids, a demonstration of the growing power of the Muscovite state, prepared the way for a major effort against Kazan in the spring of 1469. Viatka, which had had to submit to Kazan the year before, refused to join the effort, citing its promise to maintain neutrality.[10] Ivan, however, raised troops from several other quarters and placed them under the experienced Ivan Runo. By forced marches from Nizhnii Novgorod, Runo took Kazan by surprise. His contingents laid siege to the city and ravaged the suburbs, but shortage of supplies and failure to receive reinforcements seem to have forced Runo to lift the siege and return to Moscow. There Ivan quickly organized another expedition, which, on 1 September, was before the walls of Kazan. Unable to resist, the Khan accepted Russian terms, including return of all Russian slaves, though without surrender of the city.[11]

RELATIONS WITH POLAND-LITHUANIA

The peace on the Kazan frontier—to last for over a decade—enabled Ivan to act more decisively in other quarters. In the west, the Polish-

Lithuanian state, swollen by former Russian lands wrested from Tatar domination, was at the height of its power, although fundamentally unstable. The king of Poland was a figurehead, dependent on the good will of an oligarchy of magnates. In Lithuania, a grand duke, subject to the Polish king, ruled over Russian vassals who maintained their own right of succession. In these Russian territories of Poland-Lithuania, relations between Catholics and Orthodox were deteriorating. A movement toward secession began to develop. Pursuing his policy of unification of the Russian lands, Ivan III therefore took all possible steps to profit from this movement, relying on the Russian sense of unity based on a common language and religion. Beginning in the 1470s, a succession of border raids began, with the evident aim of harassing Poland-Lithuania and persuading princes of Russian extraction on the other side of the frontier to transfer their allegiance to Moscow. Poland-Lithuania, hoping to maintain the *status quo,* refrained from overt action against this harassment, but negotiated with the Golden Horde against Moscow. In the autumn of 1471 the two states apparently concluded a treaty of alliance.[12]

MOSCOW ACHIEVES LIBERATION

Toward the Golden Horde, Ivan was cautious. By nature a statesman and diplomat, he avoided an open break, although he strained relations as far as he could. He acknowledged Tatar domination, but resisted Tatar expeditions.

Akhmat, the Khan of the Golden Horde, was displeased with Ivan's conduct, his negligence in paying tribute, and his acceptance of fugitive Tatars into his service. Although the Horde was increasingly impotent because of internal strife and hostile relations with the Crimean khanate, at Polish instigation the Khan finally decided to punish Ivan for his offences and in July 1472 sent an army into Muscovite territory. Akhmat led his men as far north as Aleksin, which they burned, but turned back when confronted by a Russian army.[13]

Matters then rested until early 1480. Moscow's policy of uniting the Russian lands had by now intensified the opposition of her chief opponents, the Golden Horde, the Kazan khanate, Poland-Lithuania, and the Livonian Order. Ivan III undertook complex diplomatic manoeuvres to keep these opponents from combining.

The best ally available appeared to be Crimea, which might hold back Akhmat and at the same time threaten the southern holdings of Poland-Lithuania. The chronic instability of the Crimea, however, made that state hard to depend on. The Khan Haji-Girei, founder of the

Girei dynasty, had ruled over a prosperous khanate, influenced by Italian culture from the Genoese colony of Kaffa, but upon his death in 1466 his sons began to fight among themselves. The older son, Nur-Daulet, who ruled until 1469, was friendly to Poland-Lithuania, at that time negotiating with the Golden Horde against Russia. Ivan III, on the other hand, had his agents in the Crimea approach Nur-Daulet's brother and successor, Mengli-Girei, with the idea of an alliance. On 23 March 1475 Mengli-Girei concluded a pact of non-aggression with Moscow, with assurances of mutal friendship and mutual aid against Poland and the Golden Horde.[14] Soon afterward an unexpected event occurred: a Turkish fleet appeared, captured Kaffa, and demanded that Crimea recognize the supremacy of the Sultan. The Turks imprisoned Mengli-Girei[15] and set up, first, his deposed brother, Nur-Daulet, and then a candidate from the Golden Horde as khan. Apparently neither of these served the purpose; consequently, at the end of 1478 or early in 1479, the Turks freed Mengli-Girei and re-established him as khan. Mengli-Girei acknowledged himself a Turkish vassal, but, as Turkey was by now involved in war with Venice and Hungary, he revived in 1480 his mutual assistance pact with Russia. As insurance against renewed misfortune, he also concluded an agreement whereby he could take refuge in Russia if the need should arise.[16]

Temporarily at peace with its other neighbours, the Muscovite state was in a more favourable position than ever before regarding the Golden Horde. When, in July 1476, an embassy came to Moscow from the Horde, a break seems to have occurred. There is a story that Ivan III stepped on an image of Khan Akhmat brought by the ambassadors. Some historians doubt this, pointing out that such incautious behaviour was not characteristic of Ivan. In any case, no tribute appears to have been paid after that year.[17]

It would be using hindsight, however, to assume that Ivan III had liberation in mind. In 1477 and 1478 he was occupied with the final subjugation of Novgorod. In January 1480 the Livonian Order, perhaps at the instigation of Poland, struck at the western border and menaced Pskov and Novgorod until finally forced to withdraw in September. At the same time, two of Ivan's brothers rebelled and were brought under control only in October.

At this time, Khan Akhmat, encouraged by Poland-Lithuania, marched against Moscow with a large army. The Khan's intentions had been known for some weeks previously, so that such counter-measures as were possible in the face of the troubles in the west could be taken. When, on 8 October 1480, Akhmat and his army arrived on the River Iugra, he found a large Russian force massed on the opposite bank. The surviving information is scanty and conflicting, but the two armies faced each other until 11 November, when both retreated. Both leaders appear to have been irresolute. Akhmat apparently waited in hope of Polish aid, which never arrived,[18] and finally retired because of the onset of cold weather and news that a small force of Crimeans in Russian service had burned his capital of Sarai.[19] It is likely that Ivan, on the other hand, had never wanted to do battle in the first place and turned back after making sure that the Tatars were in retreat. Although the results of this bloodless 'battle' were inconclusive, it was considered a Russian victory. In history, the event symbolizes Russia's emergence from nearly two and a half centuries of Tatar subjugation.

Akhmat's later fate still further weakened the Tatar cause. Angry at the Polish default, he raided Polish-Lithuanian territory. Returning with the spoils, he was attacked on 6 January 1481 by rebellious subjects led by Ibak (or Ivak), the Khan of the Siberian khanate,[20] operating far west of his usual territory. Akhmat was killed, and his entire camp, his wives, his daughters, and all his wealth, together with a large number of Lithuanian captives and livestock, fell into Ibak's hands. On his return to his capital of Tiumen, Ibak wrote to Ivan to announce to him, 'Your enemy is no more.'[21]

After this blow, the affairs of the Golden Horde went from bad to worse. The realm of Akhmat split into two portions. One of them, subject to his sons, and known as the Great Horde, comprised the nomadic portion of the Tatars between the Don and the Iaik, commanding also the allegiance of the Nogais. The other section, subject to Akhmat's nephews, had its seat at Astrakhan. These heirs of Akhmat lived in constant feud, and their lands became subject to encroachments by Mengli-Girei, Khan of Crimea.

NEW TROUBLE WITH KAZAN

Soon after Ivan's bloodless victory over the Golden Horde, Kazan demanded his attention. In 1482 the Khan Ibrahim died and was succeeded by his son, Ilham (or Ali-Khan), hostile to Moscow. Ivan willingly supported the rival candidacy of another son, Muhammed-Amin, and after some difficulty managed in 1487 to seize Khan Ilham and deport him to Vologda and to seat Muhammed-Amin on the throne of Kazan in his stead. With this, Kazan was ruled by a man who owed much to the Russians, and for a while the Tatar state was in the Moscow orbit. In 1489 Kazan troops helped Moscow to take Kotel'nich and Viatka. Kazan took part with Moscow and Crimea in an operation in 1491 against the remnants of the Golden Horde. Muhammed-Amin even consulted

Ivan III regarding his marriage plans.[22]

Then, in 1496, Muhammed-Amin was overthrown. He was given refuge in Moscow and granted lands. Ivan III tried two other candidates, but the first, Manuk, a Nogai prince, died, and the second, Abdul-Letif (a brother of Muhammed-Amin), who ruled from 1497 to 1501, proved too independent, whereupon Moscow aided the restoration of Muhammed-Amin in December 1501. Abdul-Letif was imprisoned in Moscow for a time, then released and given the fief of Iur'ev.[23]

In the west, meanwhile, Moscow showed the results of its emancipation in a burst of new energy. Ivan, using the pull of common faith and striving to restore Russia to its limits of pre-Mongol times, began to annex more of the Russian-speaking lands of Lithuania, whose dynastic union with Poland was temporarily broken (1492–1501). In May 1500, having achieved a balance of power favourable to his interests, Ivan declared war on Lithuania. Again, Crimea supported the Russians by raids on Lithuania and on the Golden Horde, which suffered new defeats while trying to help its ally, Lithuania. In 1502 the Golden Horde was defeated by the Crimean Tatars and disappeared as a state. Only a small khanate of Astrakhan and the Nogai hordes were left of the nomad empire which had once dominated all of Russia. Ivan, at the same time, made deep inroads into his adversary's territory, though he failed to capture the key town of Smolensk. The war ended with the six-year truce concluded in March 1503, to the satisfaction of neither.

DIPLOMATIC REVOLUTION IN THE STEPPE

The elimination of the Golden Horde by Crimea removed the basis for friendship between Moscow and Crimea. As its spoils in the war, Moscow acquired territories of Poland-Lithuania, in what is now the Ukraine, as far south as Chernigov. Thus, lands long subject to the periodic raids of the Crimean Tatars were now Russian instead of Polish-Lithuanian territory, and Moscow had to protect her new vassals.

Although they had long been bitter rivals, Crimea and Poland-Lithuania nevertheless had now a basis for alliance and friendship, in that Russia was the chief enemy of both. Crimea was interested in wresting Kazan from Russian influence, while Poland-Lithuania sought to weaken Moscow's westward drive. Having thereafter to abstain from raiding Ukrainian lands controlled by their new ally, the Crimeans shifted their attacks to the new border provinces of Moscow. Conversely, a *rapprochement* began between Moscow and Astrakhan. Thus originated a prolonged struggle between Moscow and Crimea, which was not to be resolved until the reign of Catherine the Great in the eighteenth century.

In 1505, just before Ivan III's death, trouble again flared up in Kazan. Russian merchants were slaughtered, and the Khan, Muhammed-Amin, in alliance with some Nogai khans, invaded Russian lands and laid siege to Nizhnii Novgorod. In April 1506, Ivan III's son and successor, Vasilii III, energetic but less able than his father, undertook an expedition against Kazan. One army made its way toward Kazan along the Volga by boat, and another, consisting mainly of cavalry, went by land. After early successes, each force in turn met with a disastrous defeat near Kazan in May and June. For a while, Muhammed-Amin negotiated with Lithuania for an alliance, but then thought better of it and, in 1508, again made peace with Moscow, Kazan remaining at least theoretically a vassal.[24]

The war with Poland-Lithuania was resumed in 1507. Moscow, warding off Crimean attacks on the Ukraine, now had to fight on two fronts. In the west, neither side was able to gain a decisive victory, and in September 1508 the two concluded an 'eternal peace,' on the basis of Polish-Lithuanian recognition of previous Russian annexations.[25] The 'eternal peace' lasted for less than four years. War broke out again in 1512, to last for ten years. This time, Moscow gained its long-sought objective, Smolensk, but, partly because of diversions in the east, was unable to achieve a decisive victory. Again, Mengli-Girei supported Poland-Lithuania, and again trouble arose in Kazan.

STRUGGLE WITH CRIMEA

Crimea at this time wanted to do in Kazan as Moscow had done, that is, to control the election of new khans. In 1515 the Crimeans, probably backed by Poland, negotiated an arrangment with Moscow whereby the latter would allow a Crimean candidate to take the throne of Kazan upon the death of Khan Muhammed-Amin. Russian fortunes, however, soon improved. When Khan Muhammed-Amin of Kazan died in 1518, Vasilii saw the possiblility of at last achieving the aim of Ivan III and placed in Kazan the Khan of Kasimov, Shah-Ali, who was related to the ruling family of Astrakhan, traditionally hostile to the Girei dynasty of Crimea. He did so on the democratic grounds that it was the will of the people of Kazan. This act was to little purpose, however. Shah-Ali antagonized the population of Kazan and a revolution occurred in 1521, sparked by Crimean intrigue. Shah-Ali was expelled and replaced by Sahib-Girei, a brother of the Crimean Khan, Muhammed-Girei.

Rather than await Muscovite retaliation, Muhammed-Girei later in 1521 launched an invasion of Russia. The resultant peril was the greatest since the overthrow of the Tatar yoke. Vasilii III was able to send only a meagre force against the invaders and was badly defeated on the Oka. The Tatars drove directly to Moscow and besieged the Kremlin. Only after Vasilii appeased their leaders with gifts did they finally depart, laden with booty, taking thousands of prisoners, and leaving devastation in their wake.

In the following year, 1522, Vasilii began negotiations aimed at ending the long and inconclusive war with Poland-Lithuania. As a result, his hands were freed in the west, so that he could prepare to meet the Crimeans. This time, however, they did not invade, but went instead against the Circassians,[26] and in the following year, 1523, turned on Astrakhan. The latter, which had remained loyal to Moscow and had even attacked Crimea when Moscow was hard pressed, now asked for aid, but Vasilii III, patently less scrupulous then his father, gave none. Muhammed-Girei captured Astrakhan and forced it to accept a Crimean candidate as khan. This threatened a new concentration of power dangerous to Moscow. But, fortunately, some of Vasilii's Nogai allies attacked the Crimeans; Muhammed-Girei was killed, and the remnants of his force fled back to Crimea.

The quarrel betwen the Crimean Khan and the Nogais ended Crimean aggression for a time. Feeling insecure against rival factions, the new Crimean Khan, Saidat-Girei, adopted a peaceful policy toward Moscow.

VASILII III AND KAZAN

With pressure from the south removed, Moscow was again able to deal with Kazan. Emboldened by his brother's successes against Astrakhan, the Khan Sahib-Girei of Kazan had put Russian merchants and an envoy to death.[27] A Russian punitive expedition sent against Kazan went as far as the confluence of the Volga and Sura, where a fort, Vasil'sursk, was built. In the spring of the following year, 1524, the Muscovite army went on to Kazan itself. Sahib-Girei fled to Crimea, and was succeeded by a thirteen-year old nephew, Safa-Girei. Just when the situation seemed most in Moscow's favour, however, poor generalship cost the Russians considerable losses in men and supplies, and in the end they had to retreat with little accomplished except the devastation of the lands around Kazan.[28]

New troubles now arose with Crimea. For the population of the peninsula, too numerous for the local economy to support, raiding was now a livelihood. In 1527, while envoys of Saidat-Girei were in Moscow, his nephew, Islam-Girei, led a raid into Muscovite territory as far as the Oka, where a Russian army forced him to retreat with heavy losses. When Vasilii III heard of this attack, he ordered Saidat-Girei's ambassadors to be drowned. In Crimea, Saidat-Girei himself was shortly expelled and replaced by Sahib-Girei, formerly (1521–24) Khan of Kazan.[29]

In 1529 Khan Safa-Girei of Kazan sent emissaries to Moscow, proposing that he take an oath of allegiance to Vasilii. A Russian envoy sent to Kazan found that Safa-Girei had changed his mind and was again hostile. This led Vasilii in 1530 to send a large force of cavalry by land and infantry by boat to Kazan. On 10 July the Russians won a victory before the city, but returned to Moscow after receiving assurances that Kazan would accept no khan not approved by Moscow.[30] In 1531 Moscow encouraged the replacement of Safa-Girei with a khan of Astrakhan origin, Dzhan-Ali (or Enali), brother of the Moscow puppet, Shah-Ali.

The new Khan of Kazan was peacefully inclined toward Moscow, but the ousted Safa-Girei appealed to his uncle, the Khan of Crimea, Sahib-Girei for aid. In August 1533 a Crimean army went north toward Kazan and ravaged the Riazan area. The invaders were finally turned back by Russian forces near Zaraisk and retreated southward, boasting that they had taken a hundred thousand prisoners.[31] The Khan of Crimea disclaimed responsibility for the invasion, placing the blame on his princelings, but warned Vasilii to be more generous with presents in the future, lest the raid be repeated. The Grand Prince, however, was already on his deathbed when the Khan's message arrived.

CRIMEA PROFITS FROM A CHANGE OF TSARS

On 3 December 1533 Vasilii III died, leaving a young wife, Helen, and the infant Ivan IV. Officially, the government became the regency of Helen, although power was exercised by a series of courtiers. The uncertain tenure of those in power was reflected in the cautious handling of foreign affairs. The country was at peace with Sweden and the Livonian Order, and satisfactory relations existed with Astrakhan and the Nogai princes. Rivalries in the Crimea worked temporarily to the Russian advantage. Poland-Lithuania, however, hoping to profit from internal dissensions in Moscow, in the summer of 1534 struck at Moscow's Ukrainian provinces and in the west, but concluded peace (1536) after a stubborn defence by Muscovite armies.

Before the Lithuanian war was over, Kazan was again in turmoil. In September 1535 the Khan Dzhan-Ali was murdered and succeeded by the former Khan, Safa-Girei, who returned from his exile in Crimea. Moscow had little choice in the matter. The regency of Vasilii III's widow, Helen, aided by her lover, was short-lived. In 1538 a cabal of Muscovite boyars poisoned Helen and threw her paramour into prison, where he starved to death. The nine-year period of boyar oligarchy that followed was accompanied by a sharp decline in Muscovite prestige in foreign affairs. Profiting from the weakness of authority in Moscow, the Kazan Tatars in 1539 and 1540 raided deep into Russian territory as far as Murom and Kostroma, while the Crimeans raided in the south. As in previous times of weakness, Moscow had again to resort to defensive tactics to protect the borders, establishing towns and forts and foreposts to block the Tatar trails, particularly at fords, and establishing military colonies.

Not until 1545 was Moscow able to take action. In April, determined to deal with the hostile Khan Safa-Girei, the Russians sent another army against Kazan. This force inflicted heavy losses on the enemy, but then retired. Nevertheless, it created internal friction in Kazan, which in January 1546 resulted in the ousting of Safa-Girei. Delegates from Kazan asked Moscow for a new khan, but again received the detested Shah-Ali. Again Shah-Ali's reign was brief, and he had to flee back to the protection of the Russians. Kazan recalled Safa-Girei.

IVAN IV AND KAZAN

Thus far, the problem of Moscow's encirclement by hostile neighbours, particularly Kazan and the Crimea, must have seemed insoluble. For more than a century, Moscow had been beset by either war or threat of war on several fronts. The detachment of Kazan from the Golden Horde in the 1430s had only given that state the privilege of independent action against Moscow. The breakup of the Golden Horde at the beginning of the sixteenth century and Moscow's acquisition of Polish-Lithuanian lands had merely changed Crimea from an ally to a foe. The situation was not to change for the better until after January 1547, when Ivan IV came of age and was crowned. Brilliant, though emotionally unstable, Ivan abandoned the defensive policies of the previous fifteen years and began groping toward a new course in Russian policy.

The change was not solely the effect of Ivan's leadership. In spite of internal and external troubles, Moscow had experienced an increase of trade and prosperity. Merchants were becoming interested in the lands down the Volga and in the furs across the Urals, but Kazan barred the way to both. In addition, there may have been thought of the lucrative trade which Kazan carried on with lands far to the east—Bukhara, Khiva, and Samarkand.

More immediately, Ivan IV himself needed land for his army. He wanted to abolish the old type of military force subservient to his vassals and to create an army whose members would be loyal to him. The state had no money with which to buy the loyalty of such troops; he therefore gave them land, tenable as long as they served the Tsar. Suitable lands were lacking in the older territories of Moscow, but the region around Kazan was fertile and thinly populated. Under Ivan, the fruitless policy of trying to seat a Muscovite candidate on the throne of Kazan gradually gave way to one of outright conquest.

In February 1547 Prince A. B. Gorbaty-Shuiskii raided Kazan territory between the Sura and the Sviiaga rivers. In December Ivan himself led an expedition, but because of a warm winter, this force was unable to follow the Volga to Kazan and had to retreat early in 1548. Matters might there have rested a while, but in March the Khan of Kazan, Safa-Girei, died, opening a new succession problem. Envoys were sent from Kazan to Crimea for a new Khan. Unwilling to permit this, Ivan sent another expedition in November 1549. This one was more successful than its predecessor and arrived before Kazan on 14 February 1550. But again the weather was unseasonably mild. The ice on the river broke up, and the roads became almost impassable. Fearing famine, the Tsar ordered a retreat, which was effected only with difficulty.[32]

These failures emphasized the need for an advance base, and in May 1550 construction began on fortifications at the confluence of the Sviiaga and Volga rivers, only thirty-five miles from Kazan. By using prefabricated materials, the Russians quickly achieved their aim, so that in the record time of two months the Russian fortified town of Sviiazhsk faced Kazan on its very doorstep.

Thus threatened, the people of Kazan were constrained once again to accept the durable Shah-Ali as khan. Placed on the throne for the third time, in August 1551, he was protected by a Muscovite force of three hundred Kasimov Tatars and two hundred *streltsy* (Muscovite regular troops, organized in Ivan IV's reign). The liberation at this time of some sixty thousand Russian slaves, taken by Kazan in former campaigns, indicates the debilitating effect which the Tatar state had exercised upon the Russian border provinces.

Difficulties soon arose. The majority of the nobles of Kazan resented the appropriation by the Russians of the area around Sviiazhsk, the Russian bodyguard around Shah-Ali, and the Russian demands for the return of additional prisoners who allegedly had been hidden. They demanded a fight for independence. A minority proposed that the city might be better off without a khan at all and under a Russian voevoda, as was Sviiazhsk, and offered to take the oath of allegiance to Moscow.[33] To preserve his power, Shah-Ali executed many nobles and forced others to flee to the Nogais. Moscow, turning the screw, proposed that Shah-Ali allow a Russian force to garrison Kazan to prevent disorders. Seeing in this a threat of annexation, the intransigent majority on 6 March

1552 forced Shah-Ali to flee to Sviiazhsk and called on a Nogai prince, Ediger (or Iadiar Muhammed), to become khan.

THE CONQUEST OF KAZAN

Unwilling to see his policies threatened by the accession of a new and hostile prince, Ivan IV overcame the reluctance of his counsellors and organized a new expedition, this time intending to dispose of the problem of Kazan once and for all.

While this army was on the march, the Crimean Khan, Devlet-Girei, attempted to create a diversion by sending a raiding party into southern Russia. Equipped with Turkish artillery, his force laid siege to Tula but was repelled by a force sent by Ivan. Once beaten back, the Crimeans could not quickly form another expedition, and the Muscovites were thus freed from interference from that quarter. Another force was assigned the duty of warding off any attack by the Nogais.

The main Muscovite force reached Sviiazhsk by 13 August 1552, and a week later, 150,000 strong, was before the walls of Kazan. The siege proved spectacular and difficult. The defenders numbered only about 30,000, but they were behind good fortifications and fought bravely. The Tatars made frequent sorties, while groups outside the walls harried the Russians at every favourable moment and wrought havoc with Russian supply lines.

Once, Ivan, in hopes of inducing the Tatars to surrender without further bloodshed, ordered all Tatar prisoners to be attached to stakes near the Tatar fortifications, in order that the prisoners, by their pleas, might induce their fellow-citizens to save them by opening their gates and submitting to the Russians. The Tatars instead directed a volley of arrows against their fellows, saying, 'It is better that they should receive death from the hands of true believers than from those of the accursed *giaours!*[34]

For a time the Russians lived well on supplies captured from surrounding Tatar villages, but soon they were plagued by such bad weather that they were convinced it was the work of Tatar sorcerers. To counter this formidable weapon, messengers were sent to Moscow to fetch the miraculous cross of the Tsars. On its arrival at Kazan, a great ceremony was held: the whole camp was sprinkled with holy water, after which the Russians were cheered by the return of fine weather.[35]

The Russians also made their first large-scale use of artillery. On the advice of a Scottish engineer, Ivan ordered a huge wooden tower erected opposite the main gate of the fortress and on its summit placed sixty cannon, ten of which were of large size. This battery, raised high above the fortifications, kept up a continual fire. The defenders, however, stood firm and replied from the ramparts with an unceasing discharge of small arms, which caused great loss among the Russians. The tower was moved even closer to the fortress until at last it was separated from the wall only by a deep moat. One particularly bloody clash occurred when the Tatars sallied forth and captured the tower, only to have the Russians win it back.

After five weeks, the defenders still held out stubbornly, dismissing all suggestion of surrender. The approach of winter was now causing more concern than the Tatar defence. Ivan accordingly ordered preparations for a general assault.

At dawn on 2 October 1552, mines under the walls were exploded, and the assault began. A furious struggle ensued. The defenders were routed from the walls and towers but then battled desperately in the streets, in houses, and on the roof-tops. The Khan Ediger and his followers were forced from the royal palace. The Russians, considering the contest almost over, began to plunder the town. In the midst of this, the Tatars counterattacked, but the Russians rallied. Finally, some of Ediger's followers stopped to parley long enough to hand over their khan, unharmed, to the Russians, then fought their way out of the town through the Russian forces, across the Kazanka river and into the forest. There, fighting to the last, they were hunted down by Russian light cavalry.

The battle over, at Ivan's order the conquerors killed everyone they met who had borne arms, taking only women and children prisoners.[36] Ivan orderd a *Te Deum* to be sung and marked out a site for the erection of the first Christian church in the city. On the following day, the dead were buried and the town cleaned up. On 4 October Ivan and his retinue made a solemn entry into the town. Ivan chose a site for a cathedral and laid the first stone for its erection. The clergy then sprinkled the streets, walls, and houses with holy water and invoked the benediction of the Almighty on this new rampart of Christianity.

A Russian namestnik was installed in place of the deposed khan, and a Russian bishop was assigned to the city for the conversion of the inhabitants.

THE KAZAN TERRITORIES

As yet, however, only the city of Kazan had been taken. The conquest of its far-ranging possessions was far from being accomplished.[37] The country was large, although with ill-defined frontiers, and very populous, comprising at least six different peoples: Tatars, Mordva, Chuvashes, Votiaks (Udmurts), Cheremis (Mari), and Bashkirs.[38] Many of these had not acknowledged the Russians and had been joined by refugee Tatars from Kazan.

Some of Ivan's entourage advised him to keep the army in the region until the spring and finish the conquest of all the erstwhile subjects of Kazan.[39] This, however, was scarcely possible because some of the nobles were already complaining of the length of the expedition and asking Ivan to return home.[40] Ivan was pleased because some of the 'Arskie' people (the Votiaks) and Cheremis had taken an oath of allegiance to Moscow and had asked to be allowed to pay *iasak*, the same tribute, usually in furs, that they had furnished to the Khan of Kazan. Ivan consented, and thus Moscow took over the institution that was to provide the fiscal and administrative basis for all subsequent Russian eastward expansion and that would even be applied in Russian America.[41] Leaving garrisons in Sviiazhsk and Kazan, Ivan departed for Moscow on 11 October with the bulk of his army.[42]

While Ivan was celebrating his triumph in Moscow, the tribes in the Kazan region on both sides of the Volga rebelled. The Votiaks and Cheremis refused to pay tribute and, when Russian troops were sent against them, resorted to a guerrilla warfare difficult to counter because of the thickly forested terrain. Twice in 1553 the Russians suffered serious reverses. On one occasion a detachment of 350 streltsy and 450 cossacks were massacred; on another, a Russian voevoda and 200 men were taken prisoner.[43] The Russians retaliated in kind. In the winter of 1554, for example, they laid waste the lands along the Kama, taking six thousand native men and fifteen thousand women and children prisoners. Not until 1558 was the resistance of the natives broken.

FORTIFICATION OF CONQUERED TERRITORIES

In their struggle against the Russians, the former subjects of the Khan were often aided by the Nogais of the eastern group. In order to stop the Nogais, forts were built. In 1552 Alatyr was built in the Chuvash land at the junction of the Alatyr and Sura rivers,[44] and in 1554 an advance post, Birsk, was built in Bashkiria on the River Belaia, a southern tributary of the Kama.[45] The Chuvash village of Cheboksary was transformed in 1555 into a Russian fort to keep watch over the Chuvash and Cheremis across the Volga. At the main Kama ford, favoured by the Nogais, the Russians built another fort, Laishev.[46] At about the same time, the Tatar village of Arsk, on the upper Kazanka River, was fortified.[47] In 1557 a fort, Osa, was built on the middle Kama, in the land of the Cheremis.[48]

These forts were placed so that their garrisons could watch over the movements of the tribesmen, especially any large gathering among them. Those manning the garrisons had to be always on guard. They were safe behind the walls, but once beyond them they could often expect arrows from native sharpshooters hiding behind trees and bushes. Several years passed before the Russians obtained firm control over the Nogais.

THE ANNEXATION OF ASTRAKHAN

The downfall of Kazan opened the way to the lower Volga and to Astrakhan. The city at the mouth of the Volga was devastated by the Crimean Tatars in 1549, and many of its inhabitants were carried off. These were later returned at the order of the Turkish Sultan, Suleiman I, and the town was restored under the Khan Iamgurchi. In 1551 Iamgurchi submitted to Russian suzerainty, but in 1554, at the urging of the Sultan Suleiman, he allied himself with the Khan Devlet-Girei of Crimea and with Iusuf, one of the main Nogai chieftains.[49]

Ivan, now determined to unseat Iamgurchi from his throne, sent a force of thirty thousand streltsy, boyars, and cossacks down the Volga. They reached the site of the future Tsaritsyn (later Stalingrad and now Volgograd) on 21 May and after several light skirmishes arrived at Astrakhan. The Khan had retired to a fortified camp nearby, and most of the inhabitants had fled, so that the Muscovites occupied the city without resistance. Many Russian slaves were freed. Dervish Khan, an earlier ruler of Astrakhan, who, after being expelled, had lived first among the Nogais and later on land given him by Russia, was set up as khan. Iamgurchi's forces were pursued and defeated. Dervish Khan soon proved as unacceptable as his predecessor, however. He began to negotiate with the Khan of Crimea, whereupon, in March 1556, Ivan ordered him removed and the khanate put under a Russian governor.[50]

THE FRUITS OF CONQUEST

The conquest of Kazan, besides signalling the destruction of a predatory neighbour and the first Russian conquest of a Tatar state, gave Russia control of the middle Volga and the Kama; the conquest of Astrakhan made the Volga a Russian river all the way to the Caspian Sea. This opened vast possibilities for colonization, exploitation of natural wealth, commercial relations with the Caucasus region, Persia, and central Asia, and new expansion. No longer confined to poor northern lands, the Russian people were now able to resume movements long halted by Tatar attacks.

Thus, the North Caucasus region, then a battleground in the life and death struggle of Turkey and Crimea against Persia, soon became open to Russian influence. In the 1550s many Cherkess and Kabardinian princes turned to Moscow for aid. No direct aid could then be given, but Muscovite operations against Crimea were doubtless aided thereafter by intelligence of Turkish and Crimean operations in the Caucasus region and by the diversion of forces which might otherwise have been brought to bear against Moscow. Ivan IV's marriage to the daughter of a Kabardinian prince and the construction of the town of Tersk (1567) promised a further increase of Russian influence. Although Turkish pressure and Muscovite involvement in the Livonian War later forced abandonment of Tersk, Russian cossacks continued to settle on the Terek river,[51] their colonies constituting informal outposts.

During this period many of the Nogais also came under Russian influence. Never stable, in the middle of the sixteenth century this tribe finally split up. The groups making up the so-called Great Nogai horde submitted to Moscow, while others, the so-called Small Nogais, crossed the Volga into the northern part of the Kuban region and submitted to the khanate of Crimea.[52]

The conquest also brought closer contact with the land beyond the Urals, which had been economically and politically connected with the Kazan khanate. In 1555 the Siberian Khan Ediger acknowledged himself a vassal of Moscow and commenced to pay an annual tribute of a thousand sables.[53]

The submission of Kazan and Astrakhan also gave rise to the possibility of disposing of the last remnant of the Golden Horde, the Crimean khanate. Between 1556 and 1559, the routes of the Crimea were reconnoitred and several expeditions against the khanate were undertaken. The most successful was that led in 1559 by Daniil Adashev, which descended the Dnepr to the Black Sea and entered the Crimean peninsula itself.

However, the Livonian war, which Ivan IV undertook in 1558, halted offensive operations against the Crimea and slowed consolidation of the new possessions. During the ensuing twenty-four years of struggle in the west, the armed forces elsewhere had to be reduced, and as a result almost every year (with the exception of 1566, 1575, and 1579) the Crimean Tatars raided Russia (chiefly west of the Volga),[54] while in the land of the Cheremis there was continuous unrest, with particularly serious rebellions taking place in 1567, 1570, and 1571.[55]

DEFENCE LINES AGAINST CRIMEA

Owing to the persistent hostility of the Crimeans, whose ranks were swelled with the Nogais, such attention as the Muscovite government could spare from the Livonian war was given to the Russian frontier along and south of the Oka. The river formed a natural barrier against the invaders. Accordingly, during the reign of Vasilii III, the Russians had begun to fortify the towns along this river. Strongpoints were placed at Nizhnii Novgorod (1508), Tula (1530), Zaraisk (1531), and later Serpukhov (1556), and Tatar colonists on the Oka were employed successfully as frontier guards.[56]

During the time of Ivan IV, the Oka line became obsolete. The line of defence then shifted southward to the old Russian towns of Putivl, Ryl'sk, Mtsensk, Novosil, and Pronsk (rebuilt 1536),[57] and the new strongpoints of Mikhailov (1551), Shatsk (1552),[58] and Orel (1564).

In spite of these measures, in 1571 the Crimean Khan Devlet-Girei succeeded in reaching Moscow and in plundering and burning the suburbs. To prevent future raids, the Muscovite government thereupon undertook further improvements of the frontier protective system. Forts were built at key points on the favourite routes of the Crimean and Nogai Tatars. In 1571 the towns of Dedilov, Epifan, Donkovo, and Riazhsk were built.[59] These and older towns formed the defensive 'line of 1571', comprising Novgorod-Severskii, Putivl, Ryl'sk, Orel, Mtsensk, Novosil, Dedilov, Epifan, Donkovo, Riazhsk, Radom, Temnikov, and Alatyr. The fort Tetiushi, built on the western bank of the Volga near a convenient crossing point[60] about 1570, can be considered as the Volga terminal of this line. These frontier strongpoints, connected by minor fortifications, formed a continuous line along the border. Ahead of the line were outposts and observation points. Each fort kept in touch with its neighbours by means of mounted frontier guards, who patrolled the line and were ready to give the alarm in case of attack.[61] Special trails were cut through wooded areas for the convenience of the Russian patrols. Where a Tatar trail went through a forest area, it was blocked by barricades of felled trees. Fords were blocked by sharp pointed stakes fixed in the river bed. Outposts that communicated with the rear by means of smoke signals and fast riders served to give warning of approaching danger. A decree of October 1571 even ordered that the grass on the steppe be burnt in order to deprive the nomads of pasture for their livestock. Thus, Prince M. I. Vorotynskii was ordered to burn the steppe from the sources of the Vorona to the Dnepr and Desna, taking care, however, to preserve the grass near the Ukrainian towns, the forested areas, and the forts.[62]

The defence line could stop only small raiding parties, but it enabled the frontier guards to warn the people of the countryside, giving them time to hide or seek protection within the walled towns, which the Tatars rarely attacked. The system was also effective for assembling forces to intercept returning raiders, and often these forces were able to retake captives and spoils. As time went on, the settlement of the territory protected by one line permitted the building of another line farther south.[63]

SUMMARY

The offensive by Moscow against Novgorod was greatly complicated by hostile neighbours. Activity on the northeastern frontier was inextricably bound up with the complex situation of Moscow's striving for reunification while coping with the declining, but still strong, Tatar power and with the rising power of Lithuania in the west.

The rise of Moscow in the fourteenth century coincided with a decline of Tatar power, at first gradual, then accelerating, until the Golden Horde ceased to exist in 1505. The principal feature was the breakup of the Golden Horde into the khanates of Crimea, and Kazan, Astrakhan, Sibir', and the loosely organized Nogai state in the 1440s, and the defection of several groups to Russian service. Moscow, confronted with powerful foes on all sides, strove first of all to prevent them from uniting. This was possible because of the rivalries within the khanates themselves. But the process was complicated by Moscow's own internal divisions, by the disinclination of her boyars to put themselves under unified command—especially during the minority of Ivan IV—by backward technology and inability to use her human resources, and, finally, by lack of a standing army and consequent dependence of the Tsar upon the boyars for military support.

The conquest of Kazan by Ivan IV removed the principal barrier in the east, although there was long trouble with the peoples who had been in the Kazan realm. Crimea, to the south, remained a major foe, against which Moscow could not cope for two centuries. However, in spite of the continuing need for defensive arrangements, the expansionist tendencies of Russia, restrained by alien rule and hostile neighbours for almost three centuries, were now released as of yore. Although harassed by the Crimean Tatars until the eighteenth century, peasant colonists flocked into the lands at least partially protected by the border defence systems, and many, attracted by the free life and by love of adventure, went far beyond the outposts.

Chapter 4

The Rise of the Cossack Hosts

By the middle of the sixteenth century, about the time Moscow was moving toward a solution of the problem of Kazan, a particular social element, the cossacks (from the Russian *kazak*), was becoming prominent on the frontier. This element is of uncertain origin, and in fact seems to have existed in several forms from early times.[1] S. M. Solov'ev saw it as a militant border population, containing Slavic and Turco-Tatar elements, a natural consequence of the geographic position of early Rus'.[2] Karamzin and Pogodin linked the cossacks with the 'Black Caps' (*chernye klobuki*), bands of Turkish warriors hired by the Russian princes in the late eleventh century as auxiliary troops against the Polovtsy (Cumans) in southern Russia.[3] Kliuchevskii saw the cossacks as originally a social class to be found throughout Russia, hired labourers without definite occupation or fixed residence, workers on the land.[4] Ukrainian nationalist historians have placed their origin in Kievan times, the 'golden age' of Ukrainian history, when brave border settlers guarded the Russian land against invading nomads.[5]

Such early elements were indeed analogous to the cossacks of later times, but there is no evidence of any genetic connection, nor do these theories allow for the intermixture of Tatar elements.

The word itself is of little help. Vernadsky derives *kazak* from *kozak*, which in turn came from 'Kasog' or 'Kosog', the term for the Cherkess or Circassians in the early Russian chronicles.[6] However, *kazak* is more usually believed to be of Turco-Tatar origin, with the meaning 'free man', 'free frontiersman', 'freebooter', and so on. Solov'ev states that in the Tatar armies this name was applied to common warriors, a class below the *murzas* (lesser nobles) and *ulans* (members of the Khan's family not in line for the throne).[7]

Following the Mongol invasion the term begins to acquire more definite usage. A reference in the *Codex Cumanicus* of the end of the thirteenth century, indicates a *kosak* as a person manning a watch post. The Greek Synaxarion, or chronicle, of the Crimean town of Sugdaia (now Sudak, west of Feodosiia) mentions in an entry for 1308 the slaying of a young prince 'by the sword of the kosaks'. Subsequent entries indicate these 'kosaks' to have been hostile Tatars, evidently irregular cavalry.[8]

The Russians, unless one follows Vernadsky's reasoning, borrowed the appellation *kazak* from the Tatars, but at first it is difficult to tell the nature of the warriors mentioned. The first reference to cossacks in the Russian chronicles occurs under the year 1444, when it is mentioned that *kosaks*—either Russians or Tatars in Russian service—helped the frontier principality of Riazan fight off a Tatar attack.[9] Under the year 1468, as noted in Chapter Three, the Arkhangel'sk Chronicle mentions participation of cossacks under Ivan Runo in an expedition to the Kama River.[10] Whether Runo's cossacks were Tatars or Russians is not clear; probably the former, for in 1471 Ivan III, leaving Moscow, left his son in charge, protected by various followers including the Tatar princeling Murtaza 'and his cossacks', almost certainly Tatars.[11]

From the 1490s there is frequent mention of cossacks. Some of these are in service with the Tatars. Thus, in 1491 Satylgan the son of the Crimean Khan Mengli Girei 'and his kosaks' is mentioned, and in 1499 'kosaks of the Horde and the Azov kosaks'. Later the term came to be applied in a general sense to men of the Crimean khanate. Similarly, under 1499, the Chronicle tells of the Tatar cossacks of Azov who raided Russian territory near the town of Kozel'sk.[12] These Azov Tatar cossacks are further mentioned in the correspondence of Vasilii III addressed to the Sultan of Turkey. In 1516 and again in 1523 the Sultan is asked to restrain their predatory activities.[13]

Other cossacks were in the service of Moscow. Thus, in 1508 the princeling Abdul-Letif, a vassal of Moscow, refers to 'my ulans, princes, and kosaks'.[14] Beginning with 1534, envoys from Gorodets-Meshcherskii (Kasimov, the small Tatar state whose rulers were vassals of Moscow) are referred to as cossacks.[15] In other cases the envoys themselves were Russians accompanied by Kasimov Tatar cossacks acting as guides and interpreters.[16] It seems obvious that the Gorodets cossacks, sometimes also referred to as Meshchera or Riazan cossacks, were Tatars in the Russian service. Until that time, then, cossacks were mainly a special class of Tatars in Tatar or Russian service.

The presence of cossacks of Russian or Slavic origin is not certain until the early sixteenth century, when in 1502 there are references to the Riazan cossacks, and again in 1515, when a number are mentioned by name, either Russian or Russified.[17] In 1503 Mengli Girei complained regarding 'Russian cossacks'. He referred to those of Kiev and Cherkassy, and one can therefore assume these to have been 'Russian' or at least Slavic since the first reference to them was made in 1493.[18] As used by the Russians, the term acquired broader significance. During the time of Vasilii III, King Sigismund I of Poland complained about the raids of the Smolensk cossacks in Lithuania.[19] In this case, apparently, the cossacks were Russian frontiersmen. Some documents of northwestern Russia also refer to the cossacks as free, homeless men, tramps, or itinerant workers.[20]

In the frontier towns a special class of military servicemen was established, known as the town cossacks (*gorodovye kazaki*). These men had to ride into the steppe to keep watch over the trails used by the Tatars, to follow the movements of the Tatars, to capture prisoners who could tell about the Tatar plans, and to report the news to the voevodas and the Tsar. In case of a surprise attack, it was their duty to defend the frontier towns. The men in this service were enrolled from various classes of society but had to be free men. They received for their service grants of land and, with their families, were exempt from payment of taxes. Sometimes they received their salaries in money; but they had to obtain arms at their own expense. These town cossacks should not be confused with the 'free' Don or Volga cossacks. The town cossacks were established by the government and were wholly subordinated to it. In the time of Ivan IV they were under the *Streletskii prikaz* (the government department or bureau concerned with the streltsy) and, like the streltsy, formed a special branch of the army distinct from that of the nobles and boyar sons (lesser nobility), who were under the *Razriad*,[21] a military affairs department of the Muscovite government.

The Azov cossacks, who later, as the Don cossacks, became one of the largest and best known groups, were, as previously mentioned, at first Tatars. It appears that the first cossacks of Russian origin among the Azov, or Don, cossacks are found during the second third of the sixteenth century. To account for their presence there, it is customary to trace them as fugitives from the north, fleeing serfdom or the severity of Muscovite justice, or as adventurers from the Russian borderlands. A document of 1538 seemingly supports such an explanation. In a message to one of the Nogai chiefs, the government of Ivan IV states that 'there are many cossacks in the steppe—men from Kazan, Azov, Crimea, and other cossack adventurers [*balovni*]—and people from our frontiers go with them and mingle with them. All of them are bandits and robbers, although no one incites them to work their evil doings. After their evildoing is over, they return to their land.'[22]

However, one simple and seemingly logical explanation of the origin of the Azov, or Don, cossacks has been neglected. In the fourteenth century, as a result of raids made on Russian lands by the Crimean Tatars and Nogais, thousands of Russian captives were sold in the slave markets of Crimea almost every year. Some of them were shipped to Turkey or to the Mediterranean, and a great many were sold to be used as galley slaves in Turkish vessels. It is more than likely that some of the Russian slaves escaped from their masters in Crimea and from the galleys and, having no place to go, joined the Tatar desperadoes. Among the cossack leaders on the Don in the early seventeenth century was a certain Katorzhnyi, a nickname derived from *katorga,* which means a galley in Turkish. Katorzhnyi, no doubt was a former galley slave like many of his companions. The commonly advanced explanations of the rise of the cossacks hold true for the later growth of the cossack movement, but it would seem that cossack origins may be sought, at least in part, among runaway Russian slaves from Crimea and the Turkish galleys.

By 1549 the Russian element among the Azov (Don) cossacks had grown enough to build three or four forts on the Don which served as bases for raiding the Nogais. It is curious, however, that their leader had the Turkic name Sary Azman (Osman), indicating the presence of Tatars among them.[23] Further evidence of the increase of the Russian cossacks on the Don can be illustrated by a message dated 1551 from the Sultan Suleiman I of Turkey to Izmail Murza: 'The hand of the Russian Tsar Ivan is high [too far reaching]. . . . He took the land and rivers away from me, he took away the Don and left Azov devastated. . . . His cossacks from the Don collect tribute from Azov.'[24]

In describing the Russian expedition against Kazan, the chronicles constantly refer to the cossacks as an important part of the Russian army. These cossacks were probably common warriors, freemen of Russian but of non-noble origin. Thus, before the middle of the sixteenth century, when the sources mention Russian cossacks they might refer to various categories: itinerant, homeless labourers; the Tatars in Russian service; the warriors in the Russian army as distinct from the nobles' militia and regular troops of the streltsy; and, finally, predatory frontiersmen of the self-governing communities established far out on the boundary of the Russian state. Since the middle, and particularly since the end, of the sixteenth century, the term cossack is used, as a rule, with reference to two groups. One group formed a sort of frontier guard which was composed of free men of non-noble origin employed for the protection of the frontier, who, in return for their service, were granted parcels of land and freedom from taxes. They garrisoned forts and outposts and were employed as scouts in the patrols along and across the frontier. Another group consisted of independent settlers along the Don, Iaik, and Terek rivers who were ruled by their own elected leaders, the atamans.

Similar cossacks appeared for similar reasons about this same time in the Polish Ukraine, some as 'registered cossacks' in the government

ervice, others forming the free host of the Zaporog cossacks on the
Dnepr River.[25]

THE COSSACK HOSTS

Both the Russian 'service cossacks' and the free cossacks owed their
origin to a large extent to internal conditions within Russia, which took
the form of a social revolution. Ivan IV continued and intensified the
policy of his grandfather, Ivan III, of creating a numerous class of
petty nobility, the so-called *pomeshchiks*. They owed allegiance directly
to the ruler of Moscow instead of to their former suzerains, the appanage
princes or boyars. In return for military service they received parcels
of land which belonged to the state, and the free peasants on this land
became tenants dependent upon the pomeshchik who had received the
grant. This was the beginning of the institution of serfdom. Many peasants,
dissatisfied with the change, deserted their villages and fled to the frontier,
joining either the frontier guards or the free cossacks.

The continuous wars of Ivan IV created an economic crisis in Russia.
Many people contracted debts which they could never hope to repay
because of the exorbitant interest rates of the time. Rather than face
the consequences, they also fled to the frontier. Finally, there were many
fugitives from justice and plain adventurers among the cossacks. The
mass movement to the frontiers swamped the cossack elements of the
early sixteenth century and gave the cossack communities the form since
regarded as characteristic.

It is very likely that the depopulation and weakening of the Nogais
was an important factor in the development of these communities of
free cossacks beyond the borders of the Russian state. As was explained
above, the intertribal wars among the Nogais resulted in great losses
of population. Before the Russian annexation of Astrakhan, the Nogai
Prince Izmail informed the Tsar that his people were suffering from
famine and that their cattle and horses were perishing, and he asked
the Tsar to send some grain for his people.[26] The official of the British
Muscovy Company, Jenkinson, testifies that in 1558, when he was at
Astrakhan, about a hundred thousand of the Nogais perished through
civil war, famine, and pestilence. In his words, 'The like plague was
never seen in those parts, so that the said country of Nogay, being
a country of great pasture, remaineth now unreplenished, to the great
contention of the Russes, who have had creul warres a long time together.'[27]

In the vacuum caused by the depletion of the Nogais through wars,
famine, and disease, a number of self-governing cossack communities
appeared along the rivers flowing into the Black and Caspian seas.

Establishing their settlements in the midst of the hostile nomads, these bold outlaws lived a dangerous life, always expecting sudden attack. Their settlements, curiously enough, were known as *stanitsas,* a word meaning a flock of migrating birds ever ready to take flight. Although they gave lip-service to the Muscovite tsar, usully referring to themselves as his subjects, they defied the Russian frontier authorities more often than they cooperated with them. On the other hand, Moscow, in its diplomatic relations with the Nogais, Crimeans, Turks, or Caucasians, refused to accept the responsibility for the cossacks' actions and called them thieves and bandits. Moscow was always none the less ready to use the cossacks for conquests and colonization.

Toward the late 1570s the cossacks of the Don became more numerous, and their enterprises increased in both scope and boldness. They not only attacked Tatars but ranged along the Volga plundering passing merchants and even the tsar's envoys and foreign ambassadors.[28] In 1577 Ivan IV sent an army to disperse them and 'they scattered like wolves.'[29] One group of the now fugitive cossacks sailed down the Volga to the Caspian, by-passed Astrakhan, and went farther east to the Iaik (now the Ural) River, where they raided the Nogai town of Saraichik. In their search for spoils, apparently, they even dragged corpses out of their tombs, for the Nogai Prince Tin Akhmet complained to the Russian envoy that 'the Sovereign's men' had violated the body of his father.[30]

The cossacks attacked Saraichik again in 1581, captured it, killed many inhabitants, burned the town, and once more violated the cemeteries. Incidentally, this event caused an internal disturbance among the Iaik Nogais, who blamed their prince for it. 'He plundered the Russian envoys . . . and now the Tsar might order his cossacks to drive us away from the Volga, Samara, and Iaik rivers, and we shall all perish from the cossacks.'[31] Some of the Nogais moved their camps to the north. In 1583, incited by the Khan Muhammed-Girei II of Crimea and by Kuchum, Khan of Siberia, they ravaged the banks of the Kama.[32] About 1584 the cossacks themselves built a town on the Iaik. A document of 1586 quoted by Karamzin states, 'And at this time about six or seven hundred of the cossacks came to the Iaik River and built a strong fort there.' Karamzin adds that there were no streltsy (regular troops) in the garrison.[33] The founding of this fort, which was called Ural'sk, marked the beginning of the Iaik (later Ural) cossack Host.

In about 1582 another section of the Don cossacks crossed the Manych, Kuma, and Terek rivers to the Caucasus Range. This group formed the nucleus of the Greben or Terek cossack host. But the most famous for its exploits was a third group of dispersed Volga pirates who, fleeing rom the Tsar's voevodas under their leader, Ermak, sailed up the Kama River and entered the domain of the Perm merchants, the Stroganovs.

UMMARY

The cossacks became prominent on the Russian frontier about the middle of the fifteenth century. Their early history is uncertain, but the term appears to have been of Tatar origin, first used to denote a class of common warriors. The name is attached to Tatars in the Russian service in the middle of the fifteenth century, and at the beginning of the sixteenth century begins to be applied to Russians as well—frontiersmen, itinerants, or frontier guards. Simultaneously, a heterogeneous element came together on the southern borders, composed of fugitive serfs from Muscovite territory, fugitive slaves from the Crimea, outlaws, and river pirates. These formed, first, the Azov, or Don, cossack host, and, later, other hosts on the Dnepr, the Volga, and the Iaik (Ural) rivers. Though turbulent and unruly, the cossacks were of great use to the Moscow government as a buffer against the steppe peoples and as an advance force.

Chapter 5

The Stroganovs and Their Frontier Mark

The reign of Ivan IV, surnamed the Terrible, saw many remarkable changes in the internal structure of the Muscovite state. The legends surrounding this ruler obscured for a long time the true significance of his undertakings, so often marked by grotesque and gruesome details. An objective analysis, however, reveals a certain method in his apparent madness. In his reforms and persecutions, Ivan pursued a definite aim: the destruction of all agencies, social groups, and institutions which could contest his autocratic power. Thus, he mercilessly mistreated the descendants of former appanage princes and crushed the last remnants of liberty in the once proud free city of Novgorod. Curiously enough, however, in apparent contradiction of his general policies, he allowed a strange phenomenon to occur on the outskirts of his empire, namely, the appearance of a semi-independent, essentially feudal principality ruled by a family of merchants, the Stroganovs. A history of the Stroganovs and an explanation of their unusual position in the Muscovite state has direct bearing on the subject of Russian expansion beyond the Urals.

ORIGINS OF THE STROGANOV FAMILY

The Stroganovs were already an old-established business family at the time of the so-called conquest of Siberia by Ermak. Omitting the legends surrounding their origin which were recorded from a Russian source by a Dutchman, Isaak Massa, and later incorporated into Nicolaes Witsen's remarkable work, *Noord en Oost Tartarye*,[1] it seems safe to accept the fact that the Stroganovs originally came from Novgorod.[2] The first member of this family about whom we have definite information was Spiridon Stroganov, who, according to one genealogy, died in 1395 (another states 1361).[3] By the fifteenth century his descendants already possessed considerable wealth and social prestige. In 1445–46 the Stroganovs were among the chief contributors to the fund raised by the Muscovite government to pay the prince's ransom after the Grand Prince of Moscow, Vasilii II, was captured by the Tatars.[4]

The name of the Stroganovs reappears during the reign of Ivan III In 1471 Ivan, after a successful war, forced the Novgorodians to turn over to Moscow certain lands along the Northern Dvina that according to Muscovite claims, had been previously seized by the Novgorodian republic from the princes of Rostov and Moscow. Among the surveyors commissioned to define the Muscovite claims was Luka Stroganov, the grandson of Spiridon,[5] an enterprising businessman who had some interest in the Dvina area and was therefore well acquainted with the economic importance of the disputed territories. After the death of Luka, his business fell to his son Fedor, about whom information is lacking, and was in turn inherited by Fedor's sons.[6]

Three of Fedor's sons, Stephan, Osip, and Vladimir, together with a certain Roman Frolov, in 1517 obtained a concession from the Muscovite government to open a salt-making enterprise in the district (*volost*) of the town of Ustiug. They received a large forest tract because the primitive technique at that time required an enormous amount of fuel in making salt. They also obtained the right to invite and settle colonists on their concession. The grant exempted the proprietors of the colony from paying the Ustiug administrators any state dues or taxes for fifteen years. The proprietors were also exempt from the jurisdiction of the Ustiug officials and any legal action against them had to be taken directly to Moscow Within their colony the Stroganovs exercised seignorial rights and themselves attended all court cases arising among the colonists, with the exception of cases of murder or robbery. The disputes between the colonists and outsiders were to be handled by a mixed court composed of the Stroganov and the Ustiug officials.[7]

Fedor's fourth son, Afanasii, apparently was also a successful business man, for it is known that his son Grigorii, in the middle of the fifteenth century, operated a large saltworks in Tot'ma, where he also held an administrative post as the local *volostel* (holder of a volost).[8]

ANIKA STROGANOV

However, it was the fifth son of Fedor, Anika Fedorovich Stroganov (1497–1570), who is responsible for the foundation of the distinguished business dynasty of the Stroganovs. Anika deserves special mention, as he was a curious representative of the Russian middle class of his time Very modest in his personal habits, wearing the 'kaftans' and overcoat which he inherited from his father and grandfather, he spent money lavishly for pious purposes. A devout Christian (he took monastic vows before his death), he built a number of churches, 'which he constructed with the same zeal as he showed in the construction of his saltworks' and reports of his religious activities reached the ears of the Metropolitan. With the increase of his wealth, he also became known to Tsar Ivan IV. At their request, Anika ably executed various commissions for both the Metropolitan and the Tsar, and he put to good use the favours from both the Metropolitan's see and the Tsar's court in combating his business rivals, among whom were the monastery of Solovetskii (Solovki) and Prince Iurii Tokmakov, a courtier of Ivan IV. In 1555 and 1556 Anika received letters from the Tsar commending him on the purchases he made for the court in Arkhangel'sk and other places,[9] and in 1566, because of the special favour of the Tsar, he and his sons were accepted into Ivan IV's special military-political structure, the *oprichnina*.[10]

Anika was a patron of learning and art. Sparing of money for personal needs, he spent it lavishly on ancient icons, manuscripts, and books, leaving after his death a considerable library. A celebrated singer of the time of Ivan IV, Stepan Gladysh, who travelled all over Russia, often stayed in the Stroganovs' house as the guest of Anika. Gladysh was known as the originator of the so-called *Usol'skii raspev*, a choral arrangement in church singing, and as a teacher of another well-known church singer, Ivan Lukoshko.[11]

Anika started his business career at the age of seventeen, when he appeared as a pioneer in founding the saltworks in Sol'vychegodsk, at that time an insignificant hamlet on the River Vychegda, situated near a salt lake. That was in 1515. Others followed Anika's example, and Sol'vychegodsk became a small town; but by the middle of the sixteenth century, Anika managed to eliminate most of his competitors and acquire half of the town.[12]

While making salt, Anika became interested in mining iron ore. The making of salt required a large rectangular iron boiler made of iron plates, pipes, and supports, and iron was very expensive. The documents show that when, in 1562, Anika bought a certain saltworks, he paid six rubles for the boiler, while the land, buildings, and the rest of the equipment cost him only one ruble. To save expenses in operating his saltworks, Anika decided to engage in the production of iron and in 1556 obtained permission from Ivan IV to search for iron and copper ores in the vicinity of Ustiug, Perm, and other places.[13] In addition to salt and iron, Anika Stroganov was also interested in grain. As a grain dealer, he was commissioned in 1556 to sell to the government surplus supplies of rye, oats, and barley.[14]

A particularly important line of Anika's business activity was the trade in furs. There is information that Anika was not satisfied merely with the purchase of furs which were brought by the natives and Russian traders to the Vychedgda, but himself tried to tap the main sources

83

of furs, namely, the area around the River Taz, east of the lower Ob, known as Mangazeia. He sent agents there to trade with the Samoyeds, and, according to Isaak Massa, Anika's wealth originated chiefly from trade with the Samoyeds along the lower Ob.[15]

Anika was one of the first merchants to introduce new methods in his business relations with the natives. He was able, at least, to create an illusion of giving profit and advantage to the formerly cheated and robbed clients, whom he supplied with 'German' trinkets and Russian articles.[16] The ignorant natives were still exploited, but, with the different approach, they saw in Anika a friend and were anxious to deal with him. Anika's trade is described in the above-mentioned book, *Noord en Oost Tartarye.*

Much of Anika's success was due to the able help which he received from his sons, whom he put to work at an early age and who, by the time they reached the age of twenty or twenty-five, became his invaluable assistants. Even when married, they did not break away from their father but constituted a large and friendly family with their father's authority as the mainstay of family solidarity. Anika was a stern father. According to a legend, he once threw his daughter into the River Vychegda. Of course, the unity of the family did not depend on such methods but on the strong ties of a patriarchal family and a common interest in the father's enterprises.

After his death in 1570, the sons divided the property, but for the most part carried on business together, remaining as one business firm, wherein the members often regulated their relations by written agreements.

THE CHARTERS OF 1558 AND 1564: A FIEFDOM ON THE KAMA

In 1558 the Stroganovs, by the Tsar's charter given to Anika's son Grigorii, had received permission to occupy 'empty lands, the lakes, rivers and forests' on both sides of the Kama as far as the Chusovaia River, at a distance of eighty-eight versts from the town of Perm.[17]

Within this enormous grant, the Stroganovs were allowed to build a fort (*gorodok*), equip it with cannon, and to maintain there a garrison armed with muskets and other arms. They were expected to cultivate land, to found villages, and to invite and settle colonists from the free population not assigned elsewhere (*nepismennye*) and not under any obligation to the state (*netiaglye*). But the Stroganovs were warned not to attract colonists already settled in Perm and were also forbidden to accept as their colonists any lawless elements. The colonists were to be exempt from any state taxes or duties for twenty years.

The colony as a whole was specifically exempt from obligation to provide guides, wagons, boats, food, and so forth, to the Muscovite ambassadors passing to or from Siberia. The Stroganovs were to enjoy free trade in the colony with the Russian or foreign merchants who might visit the colony to buy fish, salt, or other goods or who might be passing through the colony for other destinations. There were no customs or sales duties. The Stroganovs were allowed to establish saltworks and to fish, but in case of discovery of any ore, silver, copper, or tin, they first had to notify the state treasury and were not to smelt the ore without the state's knowledge. Within the colony, the Stroganovs obtained special rights: 'Grigorii administers and holds court over his settlers himself.' The state administration of Perm could not interfere, visit, or make any demands for the colonists to appear in the State court.[18]

Having received this charter, the Stroganovs built a fort, Kankor, on the Pyskorskii Mys (cape), a promontory formed by a bend in the Kama River, where later they also founded the monastery of Pyskor.[19] In order to make gunpowder, the Stroganovs needed saltpetre, and the Tsar, after receiving a petition from the Stroganovs, permitted them to make saltpetre in the Vychegodskii Posad (Ust' Vychegodsk) and in the Usol'skii Uezd (near Kamskoe Usol'e-Solikamsk), but no more than thirty puds.[20] Several years later the Stroganovs also petitioned for permission to build another fort twenty versts below Kankor. Here the Stroganovs had found brine and wanted to establish saltworks, but did not dare to do so because they had heard from 'the captives and the Voguls that the Siberian Khan and the Sheibanids wanted to invade Perm, and that in the past they had captured Solikamsk twice'.[21] This was a reference to the seizure of power in the Siberian khanate by the aggressive member of the Sheibanid family, Kuchum, in 1563.

In response to their requests, the Stroganovs received a new charter dated 22 January 1564:

I, Tsar and Grand Prince Ivan Vasil'evich of all the Russias, grant permission . . . to build another fort on the Kama, on the Orel on the Navoloka where there is brine . . . below this new fort Kankor, which he [Grigorii Stroganov] had established. The walls are to be about [30 sazhens] 210 feet and the sides to be fortified by stone . . . There should be in both towns [Kankor and the new fort, later named Kergedan] artillery, cannon, muskets and pistols, which should be made by an armourer, hired by Grigorii, from among men not under contract to the Government.[22]

In the charter of 1564, the privileges of the charter of 1558 are repeated. Some privileges were made a little more specific: 'The Tsar's officials cannot handle cases of the Stroganovs and their men, unless the latter commit murder or are caught while plundering.'[23]

During the early days of the existence of their Kama colony, Grigorii Stroganov received permission from the Metropolitan Makarii to invite priests and to build churches in the colony. In 1565 Metropolitan Afanasii allowed the ecclesiastics in the Stroganovs' colony to baptize those Tatars and Voguls who expressed the desire to become Christians.[24]

GRANT OF THE CHUSOVAIA VALLEY (1568)

In an extension of the former charters, Iakov Stroganov in 1568 received permission to build another fort, this time on the Chusovaia, and to maintain artillery and a garrison in order to protect the newly established saltworks there. He received a new grant of land which included some territory along the Kama (twenty versts downstream from the mouth of the Chusovaia) and all of the Chusovaia valley.[25] In 1570,

. . . by order of the Tsar Ivan Vasil'evich . . . Iakov Stroganov built ostrozheks [small forts] with artillery and proper garrisons on the Rivers Sylva and Iaiva, for the protection of the towns of Perm against the raids of the Siberian and Nogai men and for the control of the Tatars and Ostiaks of the Sylva and Iren, of the Voguls of the Chusovaia, Iaiva, Inva, and Kosva.[26]

Thus the Stroganovs' settlements, which were started for purely business reasons, because of their strategic position on the frontier became not only advanced posts of Russian colonization by also a substantial agency for the protection of the Russian lands and the river route from Siberia to the Kama.[27]

CLASHES WITH THE NATIVES

The infiltration of the Russian colonists bothered the local tribes. The Russians would come to hunt and fish and clear the forests for agriculture, thus seizing the hunting grounds used by the local natives. There were conflicts, and whenever they could do so the natives complained that the Russians 'drove them away from the lands which had always been theirs, that the Russians destroyed their sacred places of worship and treated the natives with great violence'. The resentment against the Stroganovs was especially strong because they 'founded villages and settled colonists on the natives' possessions and seized the places where the natives hunted beavers and gathered honey and fished, and deprived them of the means to pay iasak.'[28] It was small wonder that the local natives were not reliable Russian subjects and instead were always ready to conspire with their free brethren beyond the Urals.

On the other hand, the Stroganovs always had reasons for complaints: 'These places are covered with forests [affording opportunity for a sudden ambush] and the men and peasants cannot leave the forts and plough the land or cut firewood. They [the natives] come furtively and drive away horses and cattle and kill men, and prevent salt making.'[29] The Voguls of the Chusovaia constantly harassed the Stroganovs' villages, burned them, destroyed crops, kidnapped peasants with their wives and children, and ruined the saltworks and flour mills.[30]

The native unrest also interfered with trade. Russian merchants had visited these regions even before the fall of Kazan. As early as the first half of the sixteenth century, the merchants of Perm used to send their agents to the 'portage of Tiumen' (Tagil portage) and to the Sylva River with goods. With the fall of Kazan, the trade grew rapidly, and the merchants of Cherdyn started doing business along the Kama and Chusovaia, trading largely with the Ostiaks.[31]

In 1572, according to a message of Ivan IV to the Stroganovs,

This year [1572] our voevoda in Perm, Prince Ivan . . . Bulgakov reported . . . about the Cheremisian attacks on the merchant boats of the Kama; Prince Ivan wrote that he received a letter . . . dated 15 July from your man Tret'iachko that forty Cheremisian traitors [rebels] came to the Kama with the Ostiaks, Bashkirs, and Buintsy and killed eighty-seven merchants and workmen [*vatashchiki*] from Perm on the Kama.[32]

The Siberian Chronicle adds that the massacre took place near the Stroganovs' forts, Kankor and Kergedan.[33] It is interesting to note that some of the merchants were saved by the native chiefs with whom they traded[34] and that others participated on the side of the natives, notably 'Andrei Danilov, son of Moshevskii, and his companions.'

Iakov and Grigorii Stroganov were advised in the above-mentioned message of 1572:

Exercise great caution. Choose a good commander [*golova*], put under him as many volunteer [*okhochie*] cossacks as you will be able to hire equipped with arms, get such Ostiaks and Voguls as are loyal to us [and add them to this army] while their wives and children should find safety in the ostrogs. . . . Send the golova with the musketeers [streltsy], cossacks, Ostiaks and Voguls againt our traitors—Cheremis, Ostiaks, Votiaks, and Nogais.

However, if among the Cheremis and Ostiaks there are some good men who might persuade their fellows to desert the insurgents and to become our loyal subjects, then spare them, do not kill them, and we shall show them favour.

If some took part in rioting but now are willing to obey us and give proof of such intentions, announce to them our forgiveness and we shall favour them. . . . They are to fight with you against traitors, and after victory they can take the property of the traitors and their wives and children as slaves. . . . If these [repentant natives] fight and acquire spoils, traitors' wives, horses, cows, and clothing, do not let anyone take it away from them.[35]

These disturbances were followed by a general uprising of the Cheremis in 1573. To suppress this uprising, the Muscovite government sent a punitive expedition into the territory of Kazan, under the command of Princes Kurakin, Serebrianyi, Khovanskii, and Paletskii, which is indicative of the seriousness of the situation.[36]

The uprisings and massacres along the Kama and the Chusovaia probably happened not without some incitement by Kuchum, the Khan of the trans-Ural Siberian khanate, who was disturbed by the activities of the Stroganovs.[37]

About 1573, Mamet-Kul, nephew of Kuchum,[38] was apparently sent by Kuchum to destroy the settlements of the Stroganovs. In his first raid Mamet-Kul came into territory where Iakov and Grigorii Stroganov had their saltworks and massacred the Ostiak chief, Chagir, and his men there. In another raid, also directed against the Ostiaks of Perm who recognized Russian authority, he again killed a great number of the Ostiaks and took women and children into captivity. On this occasion Mamet-Kul approached within five versts of the Stroganovs' settlement but found the Russian positions too strong and contented himself with further massacres of the natives who paid tribute to the Russians.[39]

Apparently by a system of terror, Mamet-Kul tried to intimidate the tribes on the European side of the Urals who had accepted Russian rule. He expected that the fear of retribution by the Siberian Tatars would prevent the tribesmen from paying tribute to the Russians and from taking orders from the Russians. However, he did not limit himself to attacking and plundering the unfortunate Ostiaks, but also dared to attack the envoys of the Muscovite government.

Seeking, as a part of its frontier policy, to establish relations with the Kazakh Horde in Asia, the Muscovite Government sent the boyar-son (lesser nobleman) Tret'iak Chebukov, accompanied by Tatars in the Russian service, to the ruler of the Kazakhs. Apparently taking the route along the Chusovaia, the mission was intercepted by Mamet-Kul and all of its members killed. This act naturally provoked the wrath of Moscow, but the Tsar was then engaged in the Livonian wars and in no position to send a punitive expedition against Mamet-Kul.

By this time the Stroganovs had firmly established themselves in their frontier colony. They brought many Russian settlers into their possessions along the Kama and Chusovaia Rivers and not only searched for mineral resources there but sent scouts and prospectors beyond the Urals, where, along the Tura River, deposits of silver and iron ores were discovered.[40] The exploitation of this region could be undertaken successfully only if the Stroganovs had military control of this territory. So they petitioned for new land grants, beyond the Urals, practically within the limits of the Siberian khanate, and at the same time complained strongly about the depredations of Mamet-Kul and asked for permission to fight the Siberians.

AUTHORIZATION TO INVADE SIBERIA (1574)

The Muscovite government saw the economic advantage of expansion in an area rich in the mineral resources which it badly needed. It was also an opportunity to retaliate against the Siberians without any expenditure of money or men on its own part. As a result, the Stroganovs received a new charter.

The charter of 30 May 1574[41] confirmed and expanded the former privileges of the Stroganovs and urged them to look for iron, tin, lead, and sulphur, but the most significant provisions contained recommendations that an aggressive policy be adopted in regard to the Siberian Tatars. The Stroganovs were authorized to drive a wedge between the Siberian Tatars and the Nogais by occupying land in Takhcheia[42] and along the Tobol and its upper tributaries. There the Stroganovs were to build forts (*kreposti*) manned by garrisons equipped with firearms, to mine ore, and to cultivate land. As an afterthought, at the end of the charter, the Stroganovs were given permission to build forts on the Irtysh and Ob Rivers and along other rivers where it would seem expedient. In other words, the Stroganovs received a *carte blanche* for penetration into the territory of the Siberian khanate.

The Stroganovs were instructed in this charter to give asylum in their forts to various natives, the Ostiaks, Voguls, and Iugra, from the Siberian Tatars who tried to impose tribute on them. Some of these natives had formerly paid tribute to the Kazan khanate, others (the Takhcheia natives) had formerly paid to the Nogais. The Stroganovs were now to 'persuade' them to pay their tribute to the Russians. If any subjects of the Siberian Khan were to desert their master and go over to the Russians, they were to be allowed to deliver the tribute themselves. If they were to remain loyal to Kuchum, then the Stroganovs were to send their agents to collect the tribute from them.

The following passage of the charter is particularly significant: 'Iakov and Grigorii are to gather volunteers, and Ostiaks and Voguls, and Iugra, and Samoyeds, and send them together with their hired cossacks and artillery (*nariad*) against the Siberian Khan, and take the Siberians into captivity and make them pay the tribute.'[43] The above passage actually granted the Stroganovs permission to start a private war with the Khan of Siberia. In 1574 the Stroganovs seem not to have had any desire for such a hazardous undertaking, particularly in view of the rumoured strength of the Khan. They may have known that in 1555 Ediger, the predecessor of Kuchum, offered to deliver tribute to Ivan IV from a population of 30,700 male subjects, not counting the privileged Tatars, who might have numbered several thousands.[44] However, sometime after 1577, when over five hundred cossack river pirates appeared in the Stroganovs' colony, it is possible that their attitude changed toward expansion into Siberia.

It is worth noting that when the Stroganovs were planning a land expedition into the regions of the Irtysh and the Ob, they were also planning to establish communication with the Ob by sea. During the middle of the sixteenth century, foreign ships, first the English and afterwards the Dutch, began to visit the Russian north. The Stroganovs did not lose any time in entering into commercial relations with them. To their operations stretching from Ustiug and Vologda to Kaluga and Riazan within the Muscovite state, they now added 'foreign trade' in Kola on the Murman coast and in Kholmogory at the mouth of the Northern Dvina River. Starting with the exchange of their goods for English and Dutch imports at the Russian fairs and market places, the Stroganovs began to think of reaching foreign markets abroad. For accomplishing such a purpose they needed competent agents, whom they found in an unusual way.

The long wars of Ivan IV with Lithuania, Livonia, and Sweden brought to Russia numerous prisoners of war, who were for sale like any other spoils of war. The sons of Anika purchased some of these foreign captives. Among them the Stroganovs discovered a remarkable man, Oliver Brunnel from Brussels, whom they obtained from Iaroslavl' prison in 1570. Brunnel was not actually a war prisoner. He had arrived in Kola on a Dutch ship at the very beginning of the Russian-Dutch trade relations, probably in the 1560s. From Kola he went to Kholmogory for the purpose of learning the Russian language. Suspected of being a spy, he was arrested, sent to Moscow, and then to Iaroslavl'.

Brunnel's ability was soon appreciated by the Stroganovs, who did not treat him as a slave, but paid him the salary of a regular employee. Soon he became indispensable in the Stroganovs' relations with foreigners. Together with the Russian business clerks of the Stroganovs, he made a few trips from Kola to the Netherlands, selling furs and once visiting Paris. Then in 1577 he was sent to Mangazeia in Siberia—which apparently he visited twice—to trade with the Siberian natives. The first time he went there by land, and the second time by water, along the River Pechora and then by sea. These journeys to Siberia gave him the idea of reaching China by way of the Ob River and the Arctic Ocean, and apparently he passed this idea on to his employers.

While abroad in 1581 he visited the famous cosmographer, Gerhard Mercator, in Cleve, as well as his friend Johann Balak (or Balach), and explained to them his plan for a trip via the Ob to China and told them what preparations had been made for this enterprise. According to his account, a Swedish master had already built at the Stroganovs' wharf on the Northern Dvina two ships capable of sailing through Arctic waters to China, and Brunnel himself was now on his way to Antwerp to find skilled mariners. This expedition was organized about 1584. It sailed, but because of ice was not able to proceed eastward beyond the islands of Vaigach and Novaia Zemlia. Apparently the failure of the expedition led to quarrels between Brunnel and the Stroganovs. Brunnel left Russia and went to the Netherlands.[45]

SUMMARY

The Stroganov family rose to prominence in the fourteenth century. After 1471 it gained a foothold in the former Novgorodian lands on the Northern Dvina. In 1517 it began a salt-making enterprise in the Ustiug area. Anika Stroganov (1497–1570), who established the family as one of the great commercial dynasties of Europe, made his fortune in salt making, iron smelting, grain dealing, and furs. The latter caused him to send agents across the Urals to the area around the lower Ob, known as Mangazeia.

After Anika's death in 1570, his sons carried on business together. Their possessions were located throughout the Russian north, but chiefly on the Vychegda, the Kama, and the Chusovaia rivers. All the natural resources from the Kola peninsula to the Ob seem to have been explored by the Stroganovs and to have provided them with valuable articles for trade within the Moscow state and abroad.

Like their father, the sons of Anika continued to have a strong interest in furs, and Ivan IV commissioned them to acquire furs for him. That explains the significance of distant Mangazeia for the Stroganovs and also why Ivan IV dealt with them when he wanted to obtain furs of the best quality. Their interest in the fur resources of the Ob region led them to seek to reach this area by land and by sea. They were therefore ready to employ the fugitive Don cossacks under Ermak who appeared in their domain sometime after 1577.

Chapter 6

The Expedition of Ermak, the Russian Cortez

While the expedition of Ermak, which heralded the establishment of the Russian colonial empire in northern Asia, is of momentous interest to the historians of Siberia, a great many details of this expedition are still under dispute, and some will probably never be cleared up. It is not possible to establish with certainty whether the initiative for the expedition belonged to the cossacks themselves or to the frontier merchants, the Stroganovs, from whose domain the cossacks started on their odyssey across the Urals. It is difficult to decide whether the Stroganovs invited the Volga pirates in order to enroll them in their service or whether the cossacks appeared in the Stroganovs' colony as unwelcome fugitives from the Tsar's troops. If the Stroganovs were the initiators of the expedition, it is not clear whether their chief motive was a desire to acquire the land 'in Takhchei and on the Tobol River' situated within the realm of the Siberian khanate which was granted to them in 1574 by Ivan IV or whether the Stroganovs persuaded the cossacks to go to Siberia merely in order to get rid of them. The Siberian chronicles conflict on the question of whether the Stroganovs provided assistance to the expedition voluntarily or yielded to threats and force.

Although the chronicles tend to represent the exploits of Ermak and his cut-throat cossack companions as a sort of planned holy crusade against the 'godless Sultan Kuchum', it would be difficult to say with certainty whether the cossacks went across the Urals with the definite aim of destroying the Siberian state or, what is more likely, went simply to get the spoils. Once in Siberia they learned how weak the Tatars were, and their attack on the Tatar capital of Isker (also called Kashlyk or Sibir') might have been merely an accident in their predatory career, even though it had serious political repercussions.

In the abundant historical literature on the subject, there is no agreement as to exactly when Ermak left the domain of the Stroganovs or the length of time he spent on the way to the capital of the Siberian khanate. For that reason, the date of the capture of Isker, as well as the general chronological sequence of the events, is uncertain. The difficulties of a study of the so-called conquest of Siberia by Ermak are due to the conflicting information found in the Siberian chronicles, which allows only an approximate reconstruction of the historical events. Below, an attempt at such a reconstruction is offered, based on the study of the chronicles themselves and of their commentators, notably of the late Professor S. V. Bakhrushin, one of the foremost authorities on Siberian history and an editor of the incomplete modern reprint (1937–41) of the history of Siberia (first published in 1750) by G. F. Müller, the father of Siberian history.[1]

In the narrative which follows, the exact data are given only when they are indicated in the contemporary official documents of the Muscovite Government. In other cases it is possible only to determine limits of time within which an event took place. Thus, it might be said with certainty that the cossacks did not arrive at the chartered colony of the Stroganovs in Perm before 1577, the year when the Muscovite troops dispersed the cossack pirates on the Volga, Ermak being one of those cossacks. All the chronicles agree that the cossacks did not merely pass through Perm on the way to Siberia but spent some time there. It is evident that the cossacks departed for Siberia not later than the fall of 1582 (probably in 1581) because a document dated 16 November 1582 shows that the Government had already heard about it.[2] After careful analysis of the available information, Bakhrushin suggests that the cossacks departed for Siberia in 1581, captured Isker in 1582, and sent envoys with a report of their feat to Moscow also in 1582. The Tsar ordered reinforcements in 1583; these troops spent the winter of 1583–84 in Perm and arrived at Isker in November 1584. Ermak perished in August of 1585.[3]

ORGANIZING THE EXPEDITION

According to the generally accepted version of the chronicle, at its outset the expedition consisted of 840 men, 540 of whom were cossacks while the remaining 300 came from the Stroganovs' domain either as volunteers or by orders of their masters. Among the men provided by the Stroganovs there were Russians, Lithuanian, and German war prisoners redeemed from captivity and employed by the Stroganovs, and possibly a number of Tatars. According to some chronicles this army was equipped with three small cannon (probably abandoned on the way as they were never mentioned afterwards),[4] muskets or bows and arrows, battle-axes, swords and pikes.

The military supplies and food were provided by the Stroganovs. The cossacks apparently demanded more than the Stroganovs were willing to contribute, and there is an account of how the cossacks threatened to kill Maksim Stroganov, plunder his house, and divide his possessions if their demands were not satisfied. When an agreement was reached it was decided that if they returned, the cossacks were to pay for the supplies from their spoils or, if they perished during the expedition, they were to redeem the expenses incurred by the Stroganovs by prayer in the next world.

According to the chronicles, an attempt was made to introduce a semblance of military discipline among this motley crowd. Ermak was to be in supreme command and assisted by two atamans (senior officers) and four *esauls* (captains). The men were to be organized into *sotnias* ('hundreds'), or companies, each under the command of a *sotnik*, or 'commander of a hundred'. The companies were subdivided into 'fifties', each under the command of a *piatidesiatnik*, or 'commander of fifty'. Each company had colours with an image of the Saviour, the Virgin Mary, or one of the saints. The spiritual needs of the men were to be taken care of by three priests and a runaway monk who, the chronicle comments, was also a good cook. Discipline was to be maintained by the adoption of the Don cossacks' custom of weighting the offender with sand and submerging him in water.[5]

CROSSING THE URALS

The expedition went by water up the Chusovaia River, a tributary of the Kama. The boats carrying the men and supplies were driven by oars and sails. The flotilla was cumbersome, and, as it approached the source of the river, the cossacks had to drag their boats through the shallow water, which became increasingly difficult. As they came closer to the mountains, some time was lost in choosing that tributary of the Chusovaia which would lead to an easy pass across the mountain range, because the guides did not know the way. By the time the cossacks reached the foothills, where they could no longer use their boats, the season was well advanced. Ermak deided to spend the winter in the mountains and ordered a fortified winter camp to be built. Müller, who wrote in the middle of the eigthteenth century, states that the remains of this camp, surrounded by a palisade, still existed in his time.[6]

The cossacks had been supplied with flour by the Stroganovs and were expected to supplement their diet by fishing and hunting. They preferred, however, to obtain their supplies by plundering the natives (in this area they were mostly the Voguls) not only of dried fish and meat but of anything which attracted their eye, particularly furs. The rumours of their cruelty spread, and, when one exploring party of the cossacks reached a village belonging to a certain Tatar chief (*murza*), the latter attacked them, and only a few cossacks escaped.[7]

Early in the spring the cossacks crossed the mountains to the River Barancha, which would lead to the Tura, a tributary of the Tobol. At first Ermak thought of dragging his boats across the portage, but he found the task practically impossible. The cossacks had to abandon their boats and carry their arms and supplies toward the river. Because the water was shallow, they built rafts and used them until they reached a place whence they could continue their journey in boats. The construction of the boats took several weeks, but eventually the cossacks sailed down and reached the River Tura. On the Tura the Tatar princeling Epancha gathered the Tatars and Voguls over whom he had authority and tried to stop the cossacks. However, a few salvos from the cossack muskets were sufficient to put the natives to flight. The resistance of Epancha gave the cossacks an excuse to plunder and burn his village (later the site of the town of Turinsk).[8]

THE ADVANCE FROM TIUMEN

Going farther along the Tura, the cossacks reached the town of Tiumen, a former residence of the Siberian rulers. The 'Tiumen Gates' in Kazan probably indicate the early commercial relations between these two cities. According to the Remezov Chronicle, Tiumen was captured and thoroughly plundered. Here the cossacks found plenty of provisions, including dry fish, barley, and spelt flour (*polba*), and Ermak spent the second winter in Tiumen. The other chronicles do not mention the occupation of Tiumen, and Bakhrushin doubts the Tiumen episode. He thinks that Tiumen was in ruins during the time of Ermak and was rebuilt later by the Russians.[9]

The Remezov Chronicle states that while Ermak stayed in Tiumen, parties of cossacks explored the vicinity and collected provisions and furs from the natives. In one of the villages they seized an official of Siberian Khan Kuchum, one Kutugai, who had been sent there to collect tribute. This official was brought to Ermak, who treated him with courtesy, inquired about the health of the Khan and his family, and assured him of his peaceful intentions. This man, who had never seen the use of firearms before, was given a demonstration of musketry fire. He was then released and presented with gifts for Khan Kuchum, his family, and his courtiers. For himself, the official received a brightly coloured Russian dress. When he returned to Isker and made a report to Kuchum, the Khan did not put any trust in the peaceful declarations of Ermak and sent messengers to all his subjects to collect an army

96

to be sent against the Russian invaders. The other chronicles do not mention this tribute collector but contain a similar story of one of Kuchum's officials who was captured near the confluence of the Tavda and Tobol Rivers.[10]

Going down the Tura, Ermak moved slowly and cautiously. His tactics proved to be wise because six Tatar princelings were waiting for the cossacks at the mouth of the Tura, thus blocking the entrance to the Tobol River. The names of three of these princelings were still preserved in Müller's time in the names of three Tatar villages in the region of the Tura and Tobol. One of the princelings later entered the Muscovite service under the first Russian voevoda in Tiumen and participated in numerous expeditions and battles as well as in the construction of the Russian forts in Tiumen, Tobolsk, and Tara. In 1617 he was the golova of the Tiumen Tatars in the Russian service. His four sons continued in the Muscovite service after his death.

The battle with these six princes lasted several days, with victory seeming to be first with one side and then the other. Eventually the Russians won, seized many spoils, and were able to enter the Tobol. No sooner had they sailed along the Tobol than they were attacked once more by the Tatars at a place called Berezovyi Iar. The attacks lasted several days again, but the Russians broke through without many casualties. Farther down the Tobol the cossacks met a large crowd of Tatars waiting for them at the place where the Tobol becomes rather narrow. To deceive the Tatars about the number of the cossacks, Ermak let his boats proceed along the river loaded with manikins made of dry twigs inside cossack costumes. While the Tatars watched the strange flotilla, a landing party attacked them from behind. Fearing that they were surrounded, the Tatars fled.[11]

Proceeding along the Tobol, the cossacks came to the mouth of the Tavda. The native guides explained that people travelled to Russia by going up this river. Hearing this, many cossacks began to clamour in favour of going back. Their mood changed, however, when they caught a certain Taussan nearby who was a personal servant to the Khan Kuchum. Taussan gave detailed information about the conditions in the Tatar capital, the number and quality of the men Kuchum could muster under his command, and the arms of Kuchum's army. The story sounded as if the cossacks would not have much trouble in defeating the Tatars and in capturing Isker. Hesitation disappeared; the cossacks were cheered up, and they decided to proceed.[12]

Kuchum was disturbed upon hearing that the cossacks were continuing their advance. He made a supreme effort to gather a large army, probably several thousand men of Tatar, Vogul, and Ostiak origin. Remaining with the bulk of his army near the capital, he sent his nephew, Mamet-Kul, with a strong vanguard to try to stop the Russians. Meanwhile, Kuchum himself started to fortify his capital.

The forces of Ermak and Mamet-Kul met about twenty miles below the mouth of the Tavda River near the village of Murza Babassan. The scouting boat of Ermak, ahead of the rest of the flotilla, was showered with arrows and would have been captured if the rest of the flotilla had not arrived in time for its rescue. The ensuing battle lasted five days before the Tatars retreated. A pious chronicler explains the cossack victory by the personal intervention of St. Nicholas, who roused the spirits of the cossacks.[13]

Instead of proceeding farther along the Tobol, Ermak turned next toward Karacha-Kul, an oxbow lake about twelve miles from the confluence of the Tobol and Irtysh. This lake has both narrow ends close to the Tobol, to which it is connected by a channel. At this lake there was the residence of one of Kuchum's notables, 'Karacha, beloved by Kuchum, his councillor and maker of his coats of mail and breastplates'. Here, in accordance with expectations, the cossacks seized 'great wealth and Tsar's [Kuchum's] honey . . . gold, silver, and precious stones besides grain and cattle'.[14] It should be noted here that 'Karacha' was not a proper name, as the chroniclers seemed to think, but a designation for the chief councillor or vizier of Kuchum.[15]

Apparently hostilities then ceased for a while. At Karacha-Kul the cossacks rested and, evidently expecting heavenly aid in reward of their piety, fasted. At Isker the main Siberian army waited for them, assembled in response to Kuchum's call to all his subjects to rally for the defence of the capital. 'A multitude of his princes, murzas, ulans [horsemen] as well as Tatars, Ostiaks, Voguls, and other tribes assembled under his command.'

After forty days Ermak decided that the cossacks had fasted long enough to gain the grace of the Lord and ordered the advance. The Tatar scouts maintained a close watch over the cossacks who, after some difficulty and constant guard against a sudden attack, reached the mouth of the Tobol, where it flowed into the Irtysh. Then the cossacks proceeded for a short distance along the southern bank of the Irtysh, upstream, until they reached the Tatar village of Atik-Murza, below Isker. The village was captured without much effort and became the base for further operations.[16]

CAPTURE OF ISKER (SIBIR)

Farther up the Irtysh, before Isker, 'the natives looked like a dark cloud'; the cossacks thought that they were outnumbered by at least ten, and possibly twenty, to one. Many began to question the wisdom of giving battle. Some favoured retreat, especially in view of the previous losses from fighting, desertion, and illness (in all likelihood, mostly scurvy). Only after some hesitation did the cossacks muster their courage, take to their boats, and advance to the palisade at the base of the hill held by the Siberians. The victory would bring them a relatively secure place to spend the winter because 'it was well fortified by earthworks, walls and moats'. However, the first Russian attack failed, and they had to return to Atik-Murza.

Following this unsuccessful assault on the stronghold of Kuchum, the cossacks spent several days in Atik, occasionally engaging in minor skirmishes. Short of food, they organized several foraging expeditions into the neighbourhood which brought back small quantities of barley, wheat, and oats. Finally an all-out attack was decided upon. The cossacks stormed the palisade defended by Mamet-Kul in hand-to-hand fighting, while Kuchum watched the battle from the top of the hill. Mamet-Kul was carried away wounded. The loss of the leader and the casualties from musket fire among the massed defenders, together with their lack of fighting spirit, decided the outcome of the battle. According to the chronicle, some of Kuchum's warriors were forced to fight the cossacks against their will (probably they were the Ostiaks and Voguls pushed from behind by the Tatars). At any rate, it was the Ostiaks who turned first in flight and disappeared into the forest. Soon afterwards the Voguls followed their example and deserted Kuchum.[17] Only the Tatars kept on fighting.

At night, despairing of victory and worn out by fatigue and grief, Kuchum decided to leave his capital. Under the cover of darkness he fled hastily with his people into the steppe, hoping to find asylum and assistance with the Kazakh Horde. The chronicler here portrays a dramatic vision which prompted Kuchum to make his decision:

Suddenly the skies burst open and terrifying warriors with shining wings appeared from the four cardinal points. Descending to the earth they encircled Kuchum's army and cried to him: 'Depart from this land, you infidel son of the dark demon, Mahomet, because now it belongs to the Almighty.'[18]

The next morning the cossacks entered Kuchum's deserted capital, which the natives called Isker and the Russians called Sibir', a name long in use by the eastern writers in reference to the territory between the Irtysh River and the Urals.[19] The capture of Isker cost the cossacks 107 lives; it was the bloodiest engagement they fought in Siberia. The list of the killed was preserved in the Cathedral of Tobolsk and used in memorial services on the anniversary of the capture of Isker.[20]

DISINTEGRATION OF THE SIBERIAN KHANATE

Almost immediately after the capture of Isker, the motley khanate of Kuchum began to fall apart. Earlier during his reign (in 1574), Kuchum had tried to bring about greater cohesion in his state by the conversion of the Ostiaks and Voguls to Islam. Moslem mullahs were brought from Bukhara, but their missionary efforts had little effect except to create antagonism toward the Tatars among the intended converts. This fact might possibly explain the readiness with which the Ostiaks and the Voguls deserted Kuchum during the crisis. But even among the Tatar chieftains there seemed to be a notable lack of loyalty, especially following the appearance of Seid Akhmat from Bukhara as a political rival of Kuchum soon after the fall of Isker. For a century there had been rivalry in the Siberian khanate between two ruling families, the Toibuga family and the Sheibanid family. The uncle of Seid Akhmat of the Toibuga family had been Khan of the Siberian khanate until he was killed by Kuchum of the Sheibanid family. At that time Seid Akhmat fled, but now, hearing about the plight of Kuchum, he returned to dispute the throne. Kuchum almost immediately lost many of his Tatar subjects, who recognized the authority of Seid Akhmat. Particularly serious for Kuchum was the defection of the already mentioned Karacha, whose treason was probably largely responsible for the eventual fate of Kuchum.[21]

On the fourth day after the occupation of Isker, an Ostiak chief from the River Dem'ianka (a right tributary of the lower Irtysh), by the name of Boiar, came to pay his respects to Ermak and offer his allegiance. He brought gifts, numerous furs, and food supplies, mostly fish. Ermak received him graciously. After that many Tatar families who had fled at the approach of the cossacks began to return and were assured by Ermak of safety and protection against violence, especially against reprisals by Kuchum.[22] After the cossacks had been in possession of Isker for about a month, two Tatar chiefs, Ishberdei and Suklem, came to greet Ermak, bringing gifts and ample food supplies. The chronicle has high praise for Ishberdei, who later served the Russians loyally and helped them to impose tribute on the other chiefs.

Ermak found himself, perhaps unexpectedly, in the position of ruler over the former Siberian khanate, accepting allegiance and tribute from the former subjects of Kuchum. The moment seemed to be propitious for making an appeal to the Tsar. Ermak felt that he could offer the Tsar the conquered khanate and even ask for his assistance if he desired to accept the new land and its subjects. One of Ermak's atamans, Ivan Kol'tso, was chosen to go to Moscow with fifty men and a large quantity of furs (according to Witsen, sixty 'forties' of sables, twenty black foxes, fifty beavers, and three noble captives). The envoys did not proceed by the rivers, but by land using skis and sleighs drawn by dogs and reindeer. Chief Ishberdei offered his services as guide across the Urals and promised to show the Russians the shortest route, the so-called 'wolf path'.[23]

While Ermak was engaged in his various exploits in Siberia, the Perm land suffered from successive invasions by the Voguls. In 1581 the Pelym Ostiaks and the Voguls crossed the Urals and invaded the Stroganov settlements, burned many villages, and carried many people into captivity. Two of the Stroganovs (Semeon Anikievich and Maksim Iakovlevich) appealed to the Moscow Government, asking aid from Cherdyn. They also complained about the lack of cooperation from Nikita (Grigor'evich) Stroganov. In answer, the Tsar sent a message, dated 6 November 1581, to the namestnik of Perm requesting him to gather about two hundred men from among the settlers in his province and send them to the assistance of Semeon and Maksim Stroganov. In turn, if the Voguls invaded the region of Perm, the Stroganovs were to send their men to help the Perm colonists. Another message was sent to Nikita Stroganov at the same time ordering him to cooperate with his cousins.[24]

A year later the Voguls attacked the Russian town of Cherdyn. Many inhabitants were killed and their property plundered. The military governor (voevoda) of Perm, in his report to Moscow, attributed the Vogul hostility to the actions of the Stroganovs, who had sent their armies to Siberia, leaving the frontier without protection. Their men had attacked the Voguls, provoking retaliation, and it was likely that the Khan of Siberia himself would undertake to avenge the cossack outrages. Now the ire of Ivan IV was thoroughly roused, and he sent a thundering message to the Stroganovs, dated 16 November 1582:

Without our permission you invited the Volga atamans . . . who killed the Nogai envoys at the Volga crossings, plundered the Persians, and caused much damage and loss to our men. They should have expiated their crimes by guarding the Perm frontier, but they continued to act here as they acted on the Volga. Instead of helping the Permians when the Voguls came to Cherdyn, Ermak and his companions went to fight the Voguls [across the Urals]. You are guilty of disobedience and treason. If you served us well, you would have sent them and your men to protect our Perm *ostrogs* [forts]. . . . If you do not send the Volga cossacks, ataman Ermak, and his companions to Perm immediately . . . you shall be punished severely, and we will order the atamans and cossacks who took orders from you and served you to be hanged.[25]

At the height of the Tsar's indignation, the envoys of Ermak appeared in Moscow announcing the conquest of a kingdom and offering gifts of precious furs as the evidence of their exploits. Coming on top of the disappointment caused by the Livonian Wars, the arrival of the cossacks produced a sensation. According to Witsen, as quoted by Müller, special services of thanksgiving were held, accompanied by the distribution of generous alms to the beggars. The chronicles tell us that the Tsar gave an audience to the cossacks during which the message of Ermak was read.

Their crimes forgotten, the envoys received many tokens of the Tsar's favour; each received money and a piece of wool cloth (foreign?). They were also fed at the State's expense. The envoys were given a special laudatory message for Ermak, which praised his achievements and contained a full pardon for him and his followers. In addition, they received gifts for Ermak: two excellent suits of armour, a silver cup, a fur coat 'from the Tsar's own shoulder', and a piece of wool cloth. [26]

The Tsar promised to send a voevoda with troops to Siberia, but ordered Ermak to remain in charge meanwhile. It was later claimed by the Siberian cossacks that they had received a charter at this time permitting them to transport women to Siberia, presumably as wives. Later, when accused of kidnapping, the Siberian cossacks tried to justify themselves by reference to this charter. [27] On the return journey the envoys of Ermak brought along more adventurers, who were attracted by the stories of Siberian wealth and the prospects of a free life. [28]

Upon hearing the news, the Stroganovs rejoiced at the success of the expedition but apparently did not profit by it, although the Stroganov Chronicle mentions grants of some trading privileges on the Volga as a reward for their service to the State. [29] In the spring of 1584 they received a message from the Tsar requesting them to prepare boats for the troops which were assigned to Siberia. [30] The message is dated 7 January 1584, and the date on this official document enables one to determine the chronology of events from then on more accurately than was possible before from the data given in the chronicles, which are both contradictory and confusing. All chronicles agree that the capture of Isker took place late in October, but there is disagreement as to the year. The message to the Stroganovs indicates that Isker was captured not later than the year 1583. According to the document, the troops were already on the way to Siberia, and their commander, Prince Semeon Bolkhovskoi, was already in Perm on the date when it was issued. Therefore, in all probability, the reinforcements reached Isker in the winter of 1584.

NATIVE RESISTANCE

While waiting for the outcome of his mission to Moscow, Ermak was busy in Siberia collecting fur tribute in the neighborhood of Isker. Kuchum and his followers seemed to have disappeared. Cossacks in small parties visited the native villages without noticing any hostile feelings and consequently grew careless. A group of about twenty cossacks went to Lake Abalak to fish. Apparently they did not bother to keep guard, for at night, while asleep in their camp, they were attacked by Mamet-Kul, who had been watching them from a distance. All the cossacks were killed except the one who brought the news to Ermak.[31]

Ermak immediately set after Mamet-Kul, who disappeared once more. The reprisal party soon encountered 'a number of the infidels', some of whom were killed and the rest of whom fled. It is not likely that the cossacks in boats or on foot could move faster than Mamet-Kul's party, presumably on horse. Therefore, it is quite possible that Ermak did not attack the killers of the cossacks, as stated by the chronicle, but an entirely different group. If such was the case, this action was intended to serve as a sort of object lesson. The dead cossacks were buried in the cemetery of the Siberian khans, a few miles below the site of Isker.[32]

Soon afterwards the Russians were informed by one of the friendly Tatar murzas about the position of Mamet-Kul's camp. Immediately sixty picked men were sent there, and in the night they surprised and killed many Tatars and captured the prince. Mamet-Kul was the first distinguished prisoner of Ermak, who treated him with respect and courtesy and assured him of the favour of the Tsar. For a while Ermak thought that Kuchum might start negotiations to liberate his nephew, but Kuchum did nothing, and later Mamet-Kul was sent to Moscow.[33] He arrived there after the death of Ivan IV,[34] and the Government of Tsar Fedor Ivanovich gave him a princely reception. He remained in Russia, and in 1590, as a Russian voevoda, he took part in the war against the Swedes. In 1598 he served in the army which was sent against the Crimeans.

As has been mentioned, Isker was captured in late October. Early in March, Ermak sent a party of fifty cossacks under the command of one of his lieutenants, Bogdan Briazga, to visit the native villages along the Irtysh below the mouth of the Tobol. Apparently they started out on sleighs but when the ice broke up continued their journey by boat. Most of the natives whom they met were Ostiaks, although the chronicle also mentions the Voguls and Tatars. On the way the cossacks heard about strange native rites, such as pouring water over a golden image of some deity and drinking it for good luck. During the prayer, in place of incense the natives burned sulphur and lard in front of this image. Interested in gold, the cossacks tried to locate the deity but without success. The chronicle also describes numerous sorcerers and witch doctors.[35]

While going down the Irtysh, the cossacks encountered resistance in several places. On such occasions the captured natives were shot or were hanged by one foot. If the natives submitted, their treatment was then lenient in order to keep them from flight and to encourage them to pay tribute in the future. In token of their obedience, the natives took an oath of allegiance to the Russians by kissing, according to their custom, a bloody sword. Judging by the success of such a small party of cossacks, the resistance was never too serious. Only once, when they reached the Ob River, of which the Irtysh is a tributary, did they face real danger—when they came into the territory of the Ostiak princeling Samar, who met them together with eight other Ostiak chiefs at the head of a large number of warriors. The cossacks, however, defeated this gathering by a sudden attack. Luck favoured them, and Samar was killed by one of the first musket shots. Confused by the death of their leader, the Ostiaks fled. After reaching the Ob, Briazga and his men turned back and arrived in Isker at the end of May, bringing a quantity of furs which they had collected. Going back from the Ob to Isker, the cossacks did not have any more trouble with the natives. Terrorized by the cossack methods, they resigned themselves to their fate and met their masters with obsequiousness, bringing the imposed fur tribute. It is interesting to note that, according to the chronicle, while accepting the tribute the cossacks dressed themselves up ('wore coloured dress'), apparently to impress the natives. Incidentally, later the Siberian officials always made a 'gala' occasion of the reception of the fur tribute.[36]

It was at about this time that the chronicle mentions the return to Siberia of Seid Akhmat of the Toibuga house, the desertion of Kuchum by his 'Karacha', and the migration of Kuchum to 'places of safety'. Possibly Ermak heard of the feud between the Sheibanid and Toibuga families and thought that while the Tatars were fighting among themselves he could safely undertake some expeditions himself, leaving only a small garrison in Isker. First, he repeated the journey of his lieutenant along the Irtysh and returned with more spoils. Then he ascended from the Irtysh up the Tavda River. One of the historians thinks he went there to meet the coming Muscovite troops, as the Tavda–Loz'va route was one well known to travellers from Russia to Siberia. Indeed, when the Muscovite reinforcements eventually came they used this route, but the approaching winter forced Ermak to return to Isker before their arrival. The cossacks pillaged the Voguls while on the upper course of the Tavda and the Tatars along the lower part. The attempts at resistance on the part of the petty princelings there were met with wholesale massacre. 'Lake Poganoe was filled with dead.'[37]

Although the cossacks were victorious in their encounters with the natives, their casualties mounted and their numbers were becoming dangerously depleted. On one occasion they suffered severe losses. They received a request from the Karacha to render assistance against either the Kazakhs or the Nogais.[38] Ermak, hoping to bring this influential Tatar to his side, sent him forty cossacks under Ivan Kol'tso. They were all treacherously murdered. The cossacks then sent a punitive expedition against the Karacha, and it was repulsed. These events seemed to serve as a signal for a general uprising against the Russians. Russian tribute collectors were killed in many villages, and it became unsafe to leave Isker. Being dependent on foraging expeditions to bring food supplies, the cossacks were seriously threatened with food shortage. The Karacha meanwhile turned against his former master, Kuchum, and inflicted on him a serious defeat. He must have then joined his forces with Seid Akhmat, with whom he was captured in 1588 in Tobolsk.[39]

In November 1584 the long expected reinforcements, five hundred men strong, arrived from Russia. They included troops (streltsy) from Kazan, Sviiazhsk, Perm, and Viatka. While, from the point of view of general safety, their appearance was welcome, it brought about a food crisis. Expecting to find plenty in Isker, they came without any food supplies. Confined to Isker during the severe Siberian winter, the garrison starved. 'Many people died, the Muscovite soldiers, the cossacks, and the natives; the voevoda, Semeon Bolkhovskoi, also died and was buried in Siberia. . . . Men were forced to eat the bodies of their own companions' who had died from hunger. Only in the spring did the situation improve, when some neighbouring natives started bringing fish, vegetables, and other food.[40]

In March the Karacha, probably having heard of the desperate plight of the Russians in Isker, came with a large number of warriors and besieged the town. This siege, which lasted two months, brought further suffering to the garrison. In May a large party of cossacks managed to slip unnoticed through the lines of the besiegers. On this sortie the cossacks went to the tents of the Karacha, who had established his headquarters at some distance from Isker. A sudden attack, during which two sons of the Karacha were killed, caused panic in the camp. The Karacha fled, and the besieging army dispersed.[41] It was a story which was repeated many times in the subsequent conquest of Siberia. The natives would have the Russians in desperate straits in a besieged fort on many occasions but could never maintain the siege for more than one or two months.

THE DEATH OF ERMAK

In August of the same year 'some men from the steppe' appeared in Isker with the exciting news of a rich Bukharan caravan on the way to Isker and about Kuchum, who was waiting for it in the vicinity of the Vagai River (a tributary of the Irtysh) with intentions of intercepting it. Ermak, with a party of fifty men, set forth either to plunder the caravan or to rescue it from Kuchum and bring it safely to Isker. On the way he subdued a number of the Tatar villages along the Irtysh and Vagai but found that the news about the caravan was false. Returning, he camped near the mouth of the Vagai. During the stormy night the tired cossacks did not keep a good watch. Suddenly the men of Kuchum, who had been following the movements of Ermak, attacked the camp, and most of the cossacks were killed in their sleep. Ermak supposedly tried to jump into a boat but fell into the water, and his heavy coat of mail (the gift of the Tsar) pulled him to the river bottom.[42]

EVACUATION OF SIBERIA

With the death of Ermak, the whole undertaking directed by him and held together by his ability and energy started to crumble. After his catastrophic last venture, only 150 men were left in Isker out of the 840 men who had come with him and of the 500 reinforcements.[43] According to another chronicle, all the men sent by the Government perished from starvation, and only ninety of the original companions of Ermak survived.[44] Among the survivors was a Muscovite officer by the name of Ivan Glukhov. A few days after the news of Ermak's death reached Isker in August 1585, Glukhov, convinced that he could hold the conquests of Ermak no longer, boarded boats with the remnants of the Russians and sailed down the Irtysh and Ob Rivers to return to Russia by the northern route which the Russian merchants had long used in their trade with the Ostiaks and Samoyeds.[45]

The deserted town of Isker was immediately occupied by Ali, the son of Kuchum. He remained there only for a short time before he was expelled by Seid Akhmat. Late in 1585 a new Russian voevoda, Mansurov, came within sight of the town. He had been sent with an additional hundred men to Isker before the news of its evacuation reached Moscow. Finding Isker in the hands of the Tatars, Mansurov sailed down the Irtysh until he reached the Ob, which was frozen. He then erected a wooden fort on the high east bank of the Ob, opposite the mouth of the Irtysh, wintered there, collected tribute from the neighbouring Ostiak tribes, and in the spring recrossed the Urals, leaving Siberia once again to its native inhabitants.[46]

SUMMARY

Although the exact date is uncertain, Ermak and his men appear to have left the domain of the Stroganovs in 1581. They ascended the Chusovaia, spent the winter in the Urals, and in the spring crossed the mountains to the River Barancha, which led to the Tura. They occupied the site of the old Siberian capital of Tiumen and then continued down the Tobol. There they captured Isker, the capital of the Siberian Khan, Kuchum. The khanate thereupon disintegrated, and the cossacks and the Stroganovs were able to gain the favour of the Tsar Ivan IV with a substantial addition to his realm and a rich source of furs. Reinforcements were sent, but in August 1585 Ermak died in battle. A relief force under Mansurov, finding the region again in the hands of the Tatars, returned to Moscow.

With Mansurov's departure, the prelude to the Russian occupation of Siberia ended. Though a fiasco, the expedition of Ermak had taught the Russians an important lesson: it had shown the weakness of the Tatar state beyond the Urals and had demonstrated the easy access to the fabulous wealth of Siberian furs. It had indicated certain methods that would have to be followed. Siberia was to be conquered not by the raiding, cut-throat cossacks, nor through the private enterprise of men like the Stroganovs, but by the deliberate and systematic efforts of the Muscovite state.

Chapter 7

The Frontier Policies of Boris Godunov

The advance into Siberia which followed Ermak's expedition was only one of a number of important developments on the Russian frontier at that time. Though often in areas far removed from one another and from Moscow, these developments usually indicated government policy of great wisdom. In view of the centralized structure of the Muscovite government, the control exercised over frontier affairs, and the nature of the man himself, most of these developments would appear to have originated in the policies of a single prominent figure, Boris Godunov.

FORTIFYING THE FRONTIER

During the last years of Ivan IV, especially following the end of the Livonian War (1582), the Tsar's adviser, Godunov, exerted a considerable influence on government affairs. Source material is inadequate, so the extent of this influence is hard to weigh; but the period of his assumption of power, first as regent for the incompetent Tsar Fedor (1584–98), and later as Tsar (1598–1605), coincides with a new era in the history of the Russian frontier. It therefore appears likely that he had a major share in the direction of operations in this sphere.[1]

Thus, during Godunov's time, Moscow recaptured most of the territory lost by Ivan IV to the Swedes, thereby obtaining limited access to the Baltic Sea. In 1584 the port of Arkhangel'sk was built at the mouth of the Northern Dvina. Iarensk, on the Vychedga, built at about the same time, aided the development of local trade. Even more important, a whole network of fortified towns was built along all of the Russian frontiers, some for defensive purposes, others as outposts of the Russian advance. Against the menace of invasion from the west, Smolensk, the key to Russian defence on the Polish-Lithuanian frontier, was transformed (1595–99) into a powerful stone-walled fortress, later able to resist the Poles for two years during the Time of Troubles. In the south new fortified towns were built to lessen the danger of the Crimean invasions. Livny was built in 1586 on the Bystraia Sosna, the western tributary of the Don, and Voronezh was built near the confluence of the Voronezh and Don Rivers. Livny was situated directly on one of the main routes used by the Crimeans (the *Iziumskii shliakh*). Voronezh was on the main route which ran from Russia into the territory of the Don cossacks, whom Moscow tried to utilize for its own purposes, and with whom a lively trade soon developed. In 1587 the old Russian town of Kursk was refortified. Kursk, situated near the confluence of the Tuskor and Seim rivers, was located between two branches of another famous route of the Crimean invasions (the *Muravskii shliakh*).

The strengthening of Kursk was followed in 1592 by the building of Elets, also on the Bystraia Sosna.[2] Under the date 1593, the chronicler narrates that 'in this year Tsar Fedor Ivanovich took notice of the many wars with the Crimean people and decided to establish forts on the Tatar trails. He sent his voevodas with many warriors and they built the towns of Belgorod, Oskol, Valuiki, and others on the steppe in the Ukraine.'[3] This bold stroke established Russian forts at the junction of practically all the favourite Crimean trails (*Svinaia doroga, Pafnutsova doroga, Muravskii shliakh*). Here the Crimeans and their allies, the Nogais, gathered from various directions and chose the trail or trails for invasion. Somewhat to the east of this area, Tsarevo-Borisov was built in 1600 near the confluence of the Severskii Donets and the Oskol. This fort blocked the *Iziumskii shliakh*. Thus, under Boris Godunov the Russians abandoned a purely defensive strategy and advanced into the no man's land which separated them from the Crimeans. To consolidate the defence, Kromy was built in 1595 in the rear, at the sources of the Oka.[4]

In the area of the Cheremis and Chuvash, following a serious rebellion in 1584, according to the chronicle, 'when these infidel Kazan people heard that Tsar Fedor Ivanovich had ascended the throne . . . they asked for clemency. He, the generous and pious ruler . . . forgave them. . . . Seeing, however, that he might expect treason from them in the future, he sent his generals [*voevodas*] to build forts [*gorods*] in all the land of the Cheremis. They [the generals] built Kokshaisk, Tsivil'sk, Urzhum, and many other towns.'[5] Kokshaisk was situated on the Volga near the mouths of the Bol'shaia Kokshaga and Malaia Kokshaga. Tsivil'sk was built on the Tsivil, a southern tributary of the Viatka River. The 'other towns' mentioned by the chronicle included Koz'modem'iansk, built in 1583 on the southern bank of the Volga near the mouth of the Vetluga, and Sanchursk, built in 1585 on the upper course of the Bol'shaia Kokshaga. These towns were built to maintain peace in the land of the Cheremis and Chuvash, between whom the chronicle makes no ethnic distinction.

As early as 1555 the Nogai Prince Izmail, an ally of Ivan IV and leader of the western group of the Nogais, had asked Ivan to build forts on the Volga, 'at the mouth of the Samara River', at the portage [*perevoloka*]', and 'on the Irgiz River'. The Samara and Irgiz rivers are eastern tributaries of the Volga and, because of their rich meadows, were favourite camping grounds of the Nogais. The portage was the place where the River Don flows at a relatively short distance from the Volga. Izmail wanted Russian garrisons there to restrain the movements of his hostile kinsmen, the eastern Nogais. Ivan appreciated the significance of establishing Russian forts at these three strategic points. He consented but was distracted by the Livonian War. The project was realized by Boris Godunov, who built Samara at the mouth of the Samara River in 1586, Tsaritsyn at the Volga–Don portage in 1589, and Saratov, between the first two, not far from the mouth of the Irgiz, in 1590.[6] These fortifications enabled the Russians to police the Volga and protect the river traffic against both the Nogais and the cossack pirates.

About the same time (in 1586), Godunov founded Ufa at the juncture of the Rivers Ufa and Belaia in the heart of Bashkiria. The Siberian princelings, Ablai and Tenkei, tried to interfere with the construction of Ufa but were defeated by the Russians, who captured them and took them to Moscow. The building of both Ufa and Samara threatened the Nogais, toward whom the policy of Godunov can be illustrated by a quotation from the chronicle under the year 1599:

[Tsar Boris] heard that the Nogai population had increased and that they lived among themselves in accord. Fearing that they might threaten Astrakhan or even invade the Muscovite state and start war, he ordered the voevodas of Astrakhan to provoke quarrels among them. [When the voevodas followed these instructions] there was a great war among them, they [the Nogais] killed each other and many of their encampments [*ulusy*] were depopulated. . . . They became so impoverished in this war that many fathers sold their children in Astrakhan.[7]

The building of Samara and Ufa provoked immediate protests from the eastern Nogais,[8] who asked for the demolition of the fortifications and the removal of the Russian garrisons.[9] The government of Boris Godunov tried to mollify the Nogais, and in September 1586 envoys were sent to all Nogai chiefs of any importance reassuring them:

The Nogais . . . complain that the Volga cossacks plunder their encampments. . . . These thieving cossacks also attack, plunder, and murder the Sovereign's merchants. Seeing that, the Sovereign ordered the construction of a fort on the Samara so that the Nogais and their camps would no longer suffer from the cossacks on the Volga or on the Samara. The Sovereign ordered the capture and the punishment of the bandits to make life secure for the Nogais on the Volga, Samara, and Iaik. If the bandits establish themselves on the Iaik, then, by the Sovereign's order, the streltsy will be sent from Samara together with your men [the Nogais] against them. . . . The Sovereign ordered also the building of a fort, Ufa, on the Ufa and the Belaia Volozhka, because Tsar Kuchum [Khan of the Siberian khanate] fled to Bashkiria from Siberia and began to wander here and collect iasak from the Bashkirs. The Sovereign ordered the building of the fort on the Ufa where his men would be stationed to protect the Bashkirs in the Kazan area. The Sovereign's men have already built many forts in Siberia. From this fort . . . [on the Belaia Volozhka] many Kazan people travel to Siberia. This fort is built to prevent the flight of the cossacks from the Volga to the Belaia Volozhka and also to prevent them from doing any harm to your [Nogai] camps.[10]

The document is interesting for several reasons. Although it tactfully passes over in silence the fact that one of the chief reasons for building Samara and Ufa was the intention of the government to restrain the activities of the Nogais, it stresses the importance of Samara for the protection of the Volga traffic against the cossacks. Samara, built at the mouth of the river of the same name, was one of the best of the Volga River ports and a logical place for passing flotillas to dock. On the other hand, right across the river Nature had provided a most suitable answer to a river pirate's prayer. At this place the Volga makes a sharp horse-shoe bend (the Zhiguli Bend) around a large rocky promontory which is thickly forested and honeycombed with caves. Also, a small river, the Usa, flows almost across the base of the bend, forming a short cut which can be used by small boats. From the summit of the Zhiguli Hills the cossacks kept watch over the river. On sighting laden ships approaching from one direction, they could sail their small craft by the shorter route along the Usa and thus have sufficient time to prepare an ambush for the boats approaching on the other side of the bend. There are still villages on this promontory bearing the names of famous Volga cossack pirates.[11]

The document is also of great interest for the insight it gives on the government's Siberian policies. In stating that 'the Sovereign's men have already built many forts in Siberia', the document was, of course, premature, but indicated intent.

RE-ESTABLISHMENT IN WESTERN SIBERIA: TIUMEN (1586), TOBOLSK (1587)

As with events on other frontiers, the evidence concerning Boris Godunov's role in Siberia is indirect. For example, according to Witsen, as quoted by A. A. Vvedenskii, while still a young man Boris made the acquaintance of the Stroganov family. Karamzin mentions one of the Stroganovs who cured Godunov of wounds. It would seem likely that through the Stroganovs Godunov became well informed about, and interested in, the Siberian frontier. It might be significant that in 1586 Tsar Fedor granted Godunov the title of Namestnik of Kazan, possibly in view of the latter's interest in this area.[12]

Be that as it may, in Godunov's time the government realized the desirability of recovering and consolidating the conquests of Ermak, and the Russians re-entered the khanate of Sibir. However, instead of rash thrusts into the country, the government adopted a method of slow, cautious advance based on seizure of control over the river routes. The instructions to the officers sent to establish Russian authority there contained detailed directions as to how to choose a site for a new town, how to build fortifications, how to maintain military preparedness, how to treat the natives, how to provide the garrisons with military supplies and food, how to settle Russian colonists, and how to collect tribute. These directions show that there was a carefully worked out program behind the Russian expansion in western Siberia.

It was deemed necessary first to establish on the River Tura a fortified base for further expansion. In 1586 a small detachment of three hundred men—cossack irregulars and streltsy—under the voevodas Vasilii Sukin and Ivan Miasnoi, was sent to build a fort on the site of the old trading town of Tiumen. This was accomplished in the same year that the fort of Ufa was built in Bashkiria. The fact that Ufa, among other purposes, was supposed to protect the Bashkir tributaries of the Russians against the Siberian Khan Kuchum and to protect merchants traversing the ancient caravan route through the Ufa steppe which connected Kazan with Tiumen[13] indicates the establishment of Ufa and the fortification of Tiumen to have been part of the same general plan. The Kazan–Ufa–Tiumen route was thereafter much used for trade and troop movements.[14] Significantly, in the eighteenth century there were still a Tiumen Gate in Kazan and a Siberian Gate and a Siberian Street in Ufa. It is also interesting to note that the Trans-Siberian railway, built in the 1890s through the gap between the southern and middle ranges of the Ural mountains, followed approximately the same route. The building of a chapel in Tiumen was an indication tht the Russians had come to stay. They started collecting iasak from the native villages along the Tura, Tobol, and some of their tributaries. The natives in this area were sedentary, cultivating land and raising cattle. Apparently they delivered the tribute without protest.[15]

The garrison of Tiumen, however, was too small to undertake any further advance. The commanders petitioned Moscow to send some reinforcements, pointing out that they would not be able to hold the fort in case of a war with Seid Akhmat, who had established himself as khan in Isker. In response to this request, another detachment of five hundred men arrived at Tiumen in the spring of 1587 and brought instructions for the *pismennyi golova* (an official capable of preparing reports), Danilo Chulkov, to construct another fort at the mouth of the Tobol. Chulkov sailed down the Tura and Tobol and erected a small fort within a short distance of Isker. This became known as Tobolsk. From there he kept a close watch over the movements of the Tatars, who so far did not show any open hostility. In 1588 he invited Seid Akhmat to visit the Russian fort and by a rather ignominious trick captured him as well as his main supporter, already

113

known to us, the Karacha. Both were sent to Moscow.[16] The population of Isker, disheartened by the loss of their ruler, either left Isker or submitted to the Russians. The former capital of the Siberian khans quickly declined, and the new Russian fort, Tobolsk, soon became the chief base of Russian expansion in Siberia as well as the main administrative centre there.[17]

Following the establishment of Tobolsk, the Muscovite government began to send new troops to Siberia regularly. Beginning at Tobolsk and branching out over most of the Ob–Irtysh river system, within a decade and a half the Russians had established a network of forts in western Siberia, which brought that area securely within the fold of Moscow.

TARA (1594) AND THE END OF KUCHUM

But Kuchum was not finished. In 1590 he approached Tobolsk, raided the Tatars who delivered iasak to the Russians, and fled with the spoils before the voevoda of Tobolsk could do anything. Later he attacked his former subjects in the Tatar settlements along the upper Irtysh, presumably because they had accepted Russian domination.

In 1591 the voevoda of Tobolsk sent an expedition under voevoda Kol'tsov-Masal'skii into the steppe to search for the former khan. Kol'tsov found him on the Ishim River near Lake Chilikul. In a sudden attack he killed many of Kuchum's followers and captured two of his wives and his son Abdul-Khair.[18]

In 1593–94 a large expedition under Prince Fedor Eletskii was sent up the Irtysh River and built a fort near the river bank on the very edge of the steppe frontier. This fort was named Tara, after the small river which entered the Irtysh at that point. The importance which the government attached to this southern outpost can be seen in the number of men who participated in the expedition, in spite of the scarcity of Russian forces in Siberia at that time. The expedition included about 1,200 men on horse and 350 on foot, the largest number ever sent to found a new fort in Siberia. Among the men participating were 100 Polish war prisoners from Kazan, about 450 Kazan Tatars and Bashkirs under the command of Russian officers, 150 cossacks and Litvins (Lithuanian war prisoners) from Tobolsk and Tiumen, 100 Tobolsk Tatars enrolled in the Russian service, 450 tribute-paying Tatars, and 20 Russian carpenters from Perm. It is worth noting that the Tatars outnumbered the Russians.

The instructions set forth in detail the type of fort which was to be built. The completed fort was to contain a church, the office of the voevodas, warehouses for military supplies and furs and grain, a jail for native hostages, and living quarters for the officers, priests, cannoneers, and streltsy. Outside the walls, places were to be assigned for vegetable gardens and for cooking in the summer. This was a precaution against fire. No one except the officers were to be allowed to cook inside the citadel (*gorod*). The cossacks and Tatar cavalry were to be located in the ostrog, the part of the fort outside the citadel but fortified with palisades. Special care was taken to provide water. Wells were dug, and palisades protected a passage to the river bank.[19]

The commandant of the new fort was instructed to enter into diplomatic relations with Kuchum before resorting to force and to demand one of the sons of Kuchum and two or three distinguished Tatars as hostages. In exchange, Moscow offered to release Abdul-Khair, the captured son of Kuchum, who was then in Moscow. If the negotiations failed, military action was to follow against Kuchum and his son Ali, who found support among the Nogai chiefs. The commandant of Tara was further advised to use the Tobolsk Tatars in order to enter into negotiations with the chiefs under Kuchum and to induce them to desert Kuchum and go over to the Russians. If any of them could be persuaded, they were to be treated well and given some woollen cloth and bread. Some of the most distinguished were to be sent to Moscow, where they were to be given additional proof of the sovereign's favour. At the same time the Tara commanders were ordered to maintain strict vigilance to prevent sudden attack by Kuchum. Guards were to be kept constantly on the walls, and scouts were to be sent regularly into the steppe.

The commandant was also to collect iasak from the surrounding native settlements. The amount of the tribute was to be the same as they had formerly paid to Kuchum. It was recommended that 'easy' iasak be collected from those natives who would recognize Russian authority. However, if any chiefs showed hostility and refused to pay, they were to be executed and their property seized and sorted. The sables and black foxes were to be taken for the sovereign; and the red foxes, beavers, martens, squirrel furs, as well as horses, cattle, and other spoils were to be divided among the army men. The subjects of hostile chiefs were to promise under oath that they would deliver iasak and give hostages as security for their future conduct.

The territory between Tobolsk and Tara was to be delimited so that the natives would not have to pay iasak twice, to both Tobolsk and Tara. The instructions also mention that some natives were paying iasak both to the Russians and to Kuchum. It was hoped that with the foundation of Tara this practice would cease and that all the iasak would go to the sovereign. Careful records of received furs were to be kept. In addition to the furs obtained as iasak, the commander was directed to get more furs through barter. He was to receive thirty-five copper kettles or pots, of 370 pounds total weight, from the Government to be exchanged for furs. Directions were also given to obtain salt from the salt lakes farther up the Irtysh.

It may be noted that the instructions mention the necessity of making the route from Tara to Ufa safe for travel.[20] This interest was probably due in part to a desire to foster the trade long carried on by the Bukharan merchants who traded extensively with the Siberian khanate over the same route. Thus, the officials at Tara were instructed to establish trade and other relations with the peoples of southern Siberia and central Asia. For this purpose it was decreed that

if Bukharan and Nogai merchants come to the town of Tara with merchandise, horses, and horned cattle, [they should] allow them to carry on free trade with the local people, treat them as friends, attract them in this way, and allow them to sell their goods without hindrance. Whoever of them wants to go to Tobolsk or Tiumen with their goods and cattle, then allow them to do this also.[21]

The officials were also to collect information from the merchants about Asiatic affairs. Finally, they were to open diplomatic relations with the most influential rulers of the central Asiatic countries, 'duly receiving their ambassadors at Tara, listening to their proposals, reporting to Moscow, and allowing them to return to their [own] countries'.[22] Thus, besides its significance in the conquest of Siberia, the founding of the town of Tara in 1594 might also be considered the first step of the Russians toward central Asia.

Although the initial instruction counselled the voevoda of Tara to negotiate with Kuchum, subsequent instructions enjoined him 'to squeeze Tsar Kuchum to the end', that is, to destroy this restless ruler of the Siberian wilderness. Immediately after the fort at Tara was built, steps were taken to remove the danger of raids by Kuchum. In the neighbourhood of the new fort, some of the Tatars, fearing the Russians, fled at their approach up the Irtysh River toward the camp of Kuchum and his family. Kuchum sent his son Ali to take care of them and, together with some of Kuchum's men, they built a village of about two hundred families. In December of 1594 a scouting expedition composed of ninety cossacks and Litvins under the command of Grisha Iasyr was sent by the voevoda of Tara up the Irtysh to discover the whereabouts of Kuchum. Returning, the expedition brought along about two dozen captured Tatars. The Tatars declared after torture that Kuchum was then farther up the Irtysh River not far from the settlement of the prisoners and that he camped between two rivers with his wagons drawn up to protect the camp.

The voevoda of Tara then sent 276 men under the *golova* (senior officer) Domozhiroz, who located the settlement and captured four chiefs and about sixty Tatars along with their families. Kuchum escaped, however, and the Cossacks sent in pursuit scattered his men but failed to capture the Khan.

116

Domozhirov burned the village and returned to Tara.[23]

With the arrival of reinforcements from Tobolsk and Tiumen, Domozhirov led another expedition, composed of 483 men, to conquer the Tatars in the region of the Om River, who still recognized the authority of Kuchum. One of the villages showed some resistance and was burned. The rest took an oath to the Tsar and promised to pay tribute. The followers of Kuchum continued to desert him, including some of his relatives, who came to Tara and threw themselves upon the mercy of the Russians. Among them was the mother of the captured Mamet-Kul, the chieftain Chin Murza and his wife, and thirty-eight other men.[24] Next, the 'Zhigat' Murzas, former allies of Kuchum, sent a request to Moscow asking for friendship and the release by Moscow of two captives.[25]

In 1597 Kuchum himself sent a letter to the voevodas of Tara in which he wrote:

You wanted to enter negotiations with me. Do you have the order of your sovereign, the White Tsar to this effect? If so, I shall be glad to negotiate. . . . I am asking the White Tsar for the banks [the valley] of the Irtysh. My eyes are ailing. . . . The two merchants whom you have captured . . . had for me a medicine and a description of how to use it, and I am asking for them. Since the coming of Ermak, I have tried to resist you. I did not give Sibir to you; you have seized it yourselves. Now let us try for peace, perhaps it would be better. I am allied with the Nogais, and if we would take a stand from two sides, the Prince's [Tsar's] treasury would suffer, but I want a just peace (*pravdoiu pomiritsa*) and for the sake of peace I shall make concessions.[26]

In 1597 Abdul-Khair, who had been captured by the Russians in 1591, wrote a letter to his father, Kuchum:

Previously you had sent to . . . Tsar Fedor . . . your man Makhmet with a letter . . . asking for the return of your villages (*iurty*) and our brother [cousin] Mamet-Kul. . . . The Tsar then granted me a favor and allowed me to write to you . . . and you did not do anything, that I wrote to you about. . . .

At present the Great Tsar . . . has granted estates [*volosti*] to me and my brother Mamet-Kul, and we hear that you are in great need and poverty, and our brothers, princes Kanai and Idelin, with many men deserted you, and you have very few men left. . . .

So I and Mamet-Kul asked for permission to write to you again, and the Tsar has permitted us . . . and we know from . . . *d'iak* [clerk] Vasilii . . . Shelkalov . . . that if you will recognize the Tsar's authority you will have a choice either of residing here [in which case] the Tsar will give you a town, estates, and a subsidy in money, or you might live in your Siberian yurt as Tsar. Here at the Court many tsars and princes serve, receiving abundant subsidies.[27]

At the same time, Tsar Fedor himself wrote a letter to Kuchum:

From olden times the Siberian state has been a patrimony of our ancestors. . . . When your grandfather Ibak lived, tribute was delivered from the Siberian land to our ancestors. After . . . Ibak, the Siberian kingdom was ruled by the princes of the Toibuga family—Mekhmet and Prince Kazyi and Prince Ediger—and all of them gave tribute from the Siberian land to Grand Prince Vasilii and Grand Prince and Tsar Ivan Vasil'evich. And when you, Kuchum, became Tsar of the Siberian land, at first you were also obedient to our father of sacred memory, Ivan Vasil'evich, and you delivered tribute from the Siberian land, and our father . . . held you in favour under his exalted hand. . . .

But you spurned the favour of the Tsar and became disobedient, ceased to deliver tribute, and killed Tret'iak Chebukov, who was sent after the tribute, and your men raided our frontier possessions in Perm, and you know yourself what happened to you for your arrogance and violation of justice. By order of our Royal Majesty, our men came to Siberia and drove you away from kingship and took away from you the Siberian land. You have to wander now like a cossack [that is, as a man without any social ties and standing].

After having been expelled you continued to insult and disobey our Royal Majesty and raided Siberian volosti. . . . [In retaliation] your nephew Mamet-Kul and son Abdul-Khair were captured and many men of yours were killed. Mamet-Kul and Abdul-Khair deserved the death penalty, but in spite of your arrogance and injustice, we granted them favours and established them in our state according to their rank. And now with the Lord's aid, forts are established in the Siberian land, and in these forts [*gorods*] are garrisons with firearms. We did not send a large army against you, in the hope that you will realize your guilt and injustice and will submit and seek the favour of our Royal Majesty. Because if we were to send a large army to Siberia, our men would find you no matter where you would be and would take vengeance for your crimes.

Three years ago [*chetverty god*—1594] you sent your man Makhmet with a letter asking us to return your *iurt* [state] to you and to release your nephew and promising that you would be under our exalted hand and under our favour.

[Upon receipt of this message] we, the Tsar Fedor, intended to render you a favour, to place you as the Tsar of the Siberian land where you would enjoy our favour steadily and permanently. Your nephew Mamet-Kul received favours, towns and volosts, in accordance with his rank and is now established in our state and in the service of our Royal Majesty. Afterwards Chin Murza . . . with his clan [*ulus*] arrived from your state and they all received favours and serve us now. . . . But you wander now in the steppe [*pole*] like a cossack, with just a few men.

The Nogai uluses and Taibuga's iurt deserted you. . . . Some of those on whom you relied so much left with Princes Kanai and Idelin . . . your other men went to Bukhara, to the Nogais or to the Kazakh Horde. . . . You know there were once great Moslem states, Kazan and Astrakhan . . . and they were captured . . . by our father. . . . Likewise we should have sent against you a great army with firearms . . . to destroy you altogether, but because of our clemency we grant life to those who deserve death and mercy to the guilty.

[There follows a repetition of the previous offer, that if Kuchum will become a subject he will either receive favours at the court or be established with a Tsar's rank in Siberia.] [28]

The correspondence with Kuchum did not achieve any results, so in 1598 the Russians delivered him a final blow from which he was unable to recover. In his report to the Tsar of 4 September 1598, the voevoda of Tara, Andrei Voeikov, wrote: 'Last year the ataman of Tara, Elistrat Mikitin, brought your orders . . . to go against Kuchum. . . . I led the army . . . altogether 397 men . . . and learned from a scout that Kuchum was at Ub Lake with 500 men. There were also 50 Bukhara merchants there.' [29] Voeikov went to Ub Lake, found seven clans which followed Kuchum, seized most of the important men, and ordered the rest to return to their old homes (which were in the area controlled by the Russians). They were

118

to pay iasak and 'enjoy the favour of the great Sovereign' there. Going farther, Voeikov found Kuchum himself on the Ob River. A battle started, lasting from dawn till noon. In the battle, two sons of Kuchum, a great many of his notables, and 150 men were killed. Five of Kuchum's sons, eight wives, eight daughters, and a number of princes and murzas were captured. The Russians killed the male prisoners of low rank. Kuchum fled, but a great many of his followers perished in the river during the flight or were later killed by the pursuing Russians.

Voeikov was afraid to go too far because he had heard that a group of five thousand Kalmuks were two days distant from the camp of Kuchum. Voeikov returned to Tara and sent a certain Seit Tul Mamet (a Moslem ecclesiastic) to Kuchum to persuade the Khan to surrender.[30] In his report of 20 September 1598, Voeikov reported the return of a Russian traitor, Iakub Grigor'ev, a Litvin who had been with Kuchum for ten years and had now deserted him.[31] In October 1598 another report was sent from Tara stating that Seit Tul Mamet had returned after visiting Kuchum. He told about advising Kuchum to submit to the Russians and quoted the answer of Kuchum.

I did not go to the Sovereign when I was well and had a sword, so why should I go now when I am deaf and blind and without any subsistence? They took away my son Asmanak; if I lost all my children but still had Asmanak, I could live, but without him I shall go to the Nogais, and I am sending my son to Bukhara.[32]

That was the last contact the Russians had with Kuchum, who later perished at the hands of either the Nogais or the Kalmuks.[33] So passed from the Siberian scene this defiant warrior, a King Lear of the steppe, who remained true to himself to the end. Even by this time, however, Kuchum was already an anachronism. His death probably attracted little notice in view of the widening sphere of Russian activities in the Ob basin, where new lands and tribes were being subjugated each year.

IMPROVEMENT OF COMMUNICATIONS

The Muscovite government fully realized that permanent occupation of Siberia depended largely on convenient and safe routes to the region beyond the Urals.[34] The route first chosen was from the Chusovaia, a tributary of the Kama, to the Tagil, a tributary of the Tura, which in turn flows into the Tobol. At the sources of the Tagil, the small fort (*gorodok*) of Verkhne-Tagilsk was built. This route had to be given up because the mountain rivers were too shallow.[35] A route from the Vishera, another tributary of the Kama, to the Loz'va and Tavda, the latter a tributary of the Tobol, was tried next. Accordingly, in 1590, the small fort of Loz'vinsk was built on the Loz'va, at the place where this river becomes navigable.

Here the boats were to be constructed for going down the river, and during the time when the rivers were frozen, goods were to be stored until the navigation season opened.[36] The fort of Loz'vinsk also served the purpose of protecting the portage and providing assistance to the traffic across the portage.[37] This route, however, was dangerous for a long time. To the northeast of Loz'vinsk were the warlike and restless tribes of the Voguls, who had caused the Russians such trouble by their raids in the past. It may be remembered that on one occasion they had murdered the Bishop of Perm, and during Ermak's expedition they had devastated this region.

THE DESTRUCTION OF THE PELYM PRINCIPALITY

The Voguls were hunters. By the time the Russians came to Siberia they had barely started agriculture and cattle breeding. Politically they were broken into many clans led by elders. There was, however, a princely family. (Their Princes Asyka and Iumshan have been mentioned before in connection with the history of the Perm region.) This family resided in a settlement called Pelym, which was situated on the eastern slope of the Urals, and exercised some control over their people on both sides of the Urals. It was in Pelym that their predatory expeditions usually originated.

In order to remove the threat of the Voguls, the Russians decided to destroy this dangerous nest, the Pelym principality. It was not an easy task. Systematic attempts to subjugate them began in 1592 or 1593, and in 1593 the Russian fort of Pelym was built in the place of the former residence of the Pelym princes.[38] It might be noted that the builders of the fort had instructions to bring to Pelym the first Russian exiles to Siberia, the family of Ignatii Khripunov from Rzhev.[39]

Apparently energetic and warlike, Abdul Kerim (or Ablegirim), who was at that time the Prince of Pelym, was considered a dangerous enemy. That the Government was anxious to destroy him is evidenced by instructions sent to the officials in Pelym: 'Build the ostrog first, then try to lure Ablegirim [Abdul Kerim], the Prince of Pelym, his oldest son Tagai, his nephews and grandsons [into the ostrog] and execute them all.' The instructions go on to say that other important leaders were to be executed and others were to be taken as hostages. The 'iasak men' (tribute-paying natives) were to be encouraged to continue paying tribute but to the Russians instead of native princes and were to be promised the favour of the sovereign. They were also to be told that they did not owe any allegiance to the Prince of Pelym. If Abdul Kerim were to flee, the voevodas were to hunt him and his family down and kill them. Any subterfuge necessary to lure the prince into Russian hands was authorized.[40]

The Russians finally achieved success in the struggle in 1594 with the aid of the bitter enemies of the Pelym Voguls, the Ostiaks from the Koda region. The aid of the Ostiak chief, Igichei Alachev, was very useful in the impassable forest and swamp area. In return, Igichei and his descendants enjoyed particular favours from the Government.[41]

VERKHOTUR'E (1598) AND TURINSK (1600) SECURE THE ROAD TO THE IRTYSH

With the destruction of the Pelym principality, the route along the Tavda became safe. However, in 1597 a certain Artemii Babinov found a better route which shortened travel by about seven hundred miles. This road led from Solikamsk directly to the Tura River.[42] It remained the principal land route to Siberia until 1763, when the Siberia–Moscow road by way of Kungur and Ekaterinburg was established.[43]

After the establishment of the Babinov road, the Tavda route was deserted, and the fort of Loz'vinsk was dismantled. Instead, in 1598, a new town, Verkhotur'e, was founded on the Tura. In about 1600, midway between Verkhotur'e and Tiumen, another ostrog, Turinsk, was built. The site of Turinsk was formerly the possession of the Tatar chief Epancha, whose vigorous resistance twenty years earlier had caused considerable difficulties for Ermak. The role of these two towns is illustrated by the dispatch of a great number of carpenters to Verkhotur'e (in 1603 and 1609),[44] chiefly to build and repair boats for river navigation, and by the establishment of a postal *iam* (station) in Turinsk. Fifty *iamshchiks* (drivers) were settled there and organized into units consisting of two to four men. Each unit was to be provided with at least three good horses, sleighs for winter use, saddles and carts for the summer, and rowboats, oars, ropes, and other equipment for boat travel.[45] Besides the river route, a land route was laid out between Verkhotur'e and Turinsk, along which bridges were built across the swampy places and across the small rivers.[46] By the establishment of Verkhotur'e and Turinsk, the Russians consolidated the route which connected the Kama with the Irtysh. With the development of this system of transportation and communication, the newly acquired Siberian khanate was firmly attached to the Muscovite state.[47]

OPERATIONS ON THE LOWER OB: BEREZOV (1593)

The regions of the lower Ob had been visited by the Russians at an early date. As mentioned previously, the Novgorodians had sent a large expedition there as early as 1364. Subsequently, the Ostiak tribes on the lower Ob had paid fur tribute more or less regularly, first to the Novgorodians,

121

then to the Muscovites. When Russian troops appeared in their territory
in the early 1590s, therefore, many Ostiak princelings did not resist the
imposition of tribute.[48]

Nevertheless, in 1593 the fort of Berezov was founded on the River
Sos'va, about thirteen miles (twenty versts) from its confluence with the
Ob, for the final subjugation of the Ostiaks and the strengthening of the
Russian position on the lower Ob. The River Sos'va served as a route
toward portages leading to the tributaries of the Pechora. Formerly the
tribute of the Ostiaks and Voguls had been transported by this route on
the Pechora and thence to the Vym (a tributary of the Vychegda) for
delivery to the Russians.[49] There are reasons to believe that during the
reign of Ivan IV a Russian trading post already existed on the site of
Berezov.[50]

The new fort occupied a strategic position relatively to the Ostiaks of
the Kazym and Koda regions and the Voguls along the Sos'va. The two
tribes constantly fought and plundered each other and carried off women
and children into captivity. At the outset, the Russians took the side of
the Ostiaks, who cooperated in the subjugation of the Voguls of Pelym
principality. Expeditions against the Voguls along the Konda River were
carried out by Russian troops under the command of the golova Zmeev
and by the Ostiak tribesmen under the aforementioned Prince Igichei
Alachev.[51]

That did not prevent the Russians from quarrelling with their allies,
and in 1595 a considerable uprising against the Russians took place among
the Ostiaks, who besieged Berezov, unsuccessfully in the event. They were
led by a man whose father, Prince Lugui, had received a special charter
from the Russian Government in 1586. But on the whole, the Koda Ostiaks
remained Russian allies, and in return the Alachev princes were permitted
to retain some independence, ruling over certain territories where they
were complete masters and collecting iasak for themselves.[52]

It appears, however, that the Ostiaks took advantage of the Russian
favours to oppress their enemies, the Voguls, who sent a petition to Moscow
in 1600 enumerating the plundering and murders committed by the Ostiaks.
By this time native warfare was no longer in the Russian interest, as it
interfered with the collection of iasak. The Government ordered an investigation, took measures to stop the feuds, and reprimanded the Koda Ostiaks.[53]
Nevertheless, in 1604 they received another charter, which granted them
special privileges.[54]

FOUNDING OF MANGAZEIA (1601)

Berezov served as a base for further operations in the north. About 1595
an expedition was sent toward the mouth of the Ob, inhabited by the

so-called Ostiaks of Obdora and the Samoyeds. The Ostiaks were already delivering iasak, but the Samoyeds proved less docile. However, they were in turn subdued with the aid of the local Ostiaks and the Ostiaks of Kazym (from the Berezov region).[55]

The coast of the Bay of Ob had been known to the Russians for a long time and had been visited by them for trade with the Samoyeds. The Siberian authorities had received information about this region from the enterprising people of Pomor'e, the White Sea coastal region, who had sailed there from the Dvina and Pechora and had gone as far as the mouth of the Taz River. On the Taz River the Russian traders had founded their own fort and had gathered abundant furs either by imposition of iasak for their own benefit or by barter.[56]

About 1600, two officers (Prince Miron Shakhovskoi and D. Khripunov) with a hundred cossacks of Tobolsk, who were to be reinforced by some cossacks from Berezov, were sent to the coast, and there they built four ships. The party descended the Ob, entered Ob Bay, and set out toward the entrance to Taz Bay, north and east of the mouth of the Ob. However, the ships were wrecked and a large part of the food supplies lost. Undaunted, the voyagers obtained reindeer from the Samoyeds and continued toward the mouth of the River Taz. Near the River Pur, another group of Samoyeds attacked the party, killed thirty Russians, seized the supplies, and forced the rest to flee. There was a strong suspicion that the attack was instigated by traders who did not want Government competition. However, the remnants of the expedition reached the Taz and about 150 miles from the mouth of the river began construction of the ostrog of Mangazeia. The next year (1601) large reinforcements arrived.[57] This settlement, in a desolate spot almost on the Arctic Circle, became an important fur trading and administrative centre and a base for an advance to the Enisei.

OPERATIONS ON THE UPPER OB: SURGUT (1594), NARYM (1598), KETSK (1602)

Simultaneously with the conquest of the lower Ob, the Russians started up the same river from the point of its confluence with the Irtysh. At the mouth of the Irtysh they re-established the fortified camp founded in 1585–86 by Mansurov. It served as an outpost until 1594, when another fort, Surgut, was founded further up the Ob River. Surgut was situated at the site of the residence of the Ostiak Prince Bardak, who, unlike the other Ostiak princelings, submitted only after the Russians used cannon against his forces.[58] The main significance of Surgut was military: it was intended to keep watch over the Ostiak tribe of the middle Ob, known as the Grey Horde, whose chief, Prince Vonia, was in the habit of raiding the Russian-controlled territory along the Ob.[59] Four years later, in 1598,

Vonia had to submit to the Russians, who proceeded to build a fort, Narym, in the very centre of the Horde's territory. The subjugation of the Ostiak tribes was completed in 1602 with the building of another fort, Ketsk, on the River Ket, a tributary of the Ob which would lead toward portages to another great river system, the Enisei.[60]

THE TATARS AND KIRGIZ OF THE TOM RIVER COUNTRY: TOMSK (1604), KUZNETSK (1618)

The foundation of the Narym and Ketsk forts brought the Russians to a region inhabited by various Tatar and Kirgiz tribes. In 1604 one of the Tatar princes, Toian, voluntarily recognized Russian authority and was persuaded to ask the Muscovite Government to build a fort in his territory to protect him from his enemies. The Russians were glad to comply and on the river Tom, a tributary of the Ob, built Tomsk, another advanced southern outpost like Tara. Penetration of this region was temporarily halted because of possible conflict with the Kalmuk and Kirgiz peoples, already paying tribute to the powerful Mongol Altyn khans residing on the Kemchik River (the upper Enisei).[61] Only in 1618 was another step taken with the establishment of Kuznetsk (three centuries later a major source of coal) farther up the river Tom.[62]

SUMMARY

A study of Russian frontier policies during the two decades while Boris Godunov was at the helm of the State would seem to reveal new aspects of his generally recognized statesmanship. That he had a clear vision of the development of trade, particularly with the outside world, was borne out by the later significance of the territory recaptured from the Swedes, by the building of the port of Arkhangel'sk, and by the security afforded commercial traffic along the Volga by the founding of Samara, Tsaritsyn, and Saratov. The building of Ufa and Tara established terminals for the overland trade routes from cental Asia.

That Godunov was a guardian of the Russian frontier is attested by his fort-building program in the south, which prevented the Crimean Tatars from taking advantage of the Time of Troubles to invade Russian territory. Finally, Godunov appears to have played a most significant part in preparing for the future expansion of Russia. A series of forts in the former khanate of Kazan established order in the territory of the Cheremis and served also as a bridge to Siberia, making safe the route from Kazan to Tiumen. The building of Ufa created a Russian outpost in Bashkiria; the building of Tara was a first step toward expansion into central Asia.

Although Godunov's interference in Georgian affairs and his attempt to gain a foothold in the Caucasus failed, he more than made up for this failure by the conquest and organization of western Siberia. During his period of power (1585–1604) plans for the systematic occupation of this region seem gradually to have been worked out. The plans involved acquiring control of the rivers and formulation of a policy toward the natives. As they advanced, the Russians penetrated the forests by following the rivers and crossing from one to another on portages. The rivers were the best means of transportation and communication. Also, the fur-bearing animals and the natives who hunted them lived near the rivers and streams. Accordingly, the troops sent to Siberia built forts at strategic places on the River Ob and its tributaries. These forts served as military bases for the subjugation of the surrounding natives and as centres for the collection of fur tribute. Moscow insisted that the commandants of the forts pursue a benevolent policy toward the natives, particularly the chieftains. The reason behind this paternal policy was not philanthropic: dissatisfied natives could rebel or migrate into the innaccessible wilderness, thereby depriving the Government of the tribute they were expected to pay.

During Godunov's time, the Russian hold on the valleys of the Ob and Irtysh as far as Tara and Tomsk was made sure, and the basis was laid for further expansion, at a pace which would have been impossible without the groundwork which he laid. Indeed, it seems that if the one man most responsible for the early establishment of the Russian Asiatic empire were to be chosen, he should be Godunov.

Chapter 8

From the Ob to the Pacific

Until the death of Boris Godunov, Russian expansion in Siberia proceeded along plans carefully worked out by the Government in Moscow. By 1604 the cornerstone of the Russian Asiatic empire had been laid. The valley of the Ob–Irtysh Rivers, with the exception of its southern part, was under Russian control.

But then, in the so-called Time of Troubles, the movement slowed. During the period 1605–18, unsettled conditions west of the Urals diverted the attention of the Muscovite Government from the new lands in Asia. The Siberian garrisons were neglected, and transports of grain, used in payment of salaries, which had arrived regularly since the beginning of the period of systematic occupation, ceased. Attempts to induce the natives to expand their limited agriculture failed, and when produce was demanded of them they petitioned Moscow asking to be freed from the obligation. Hardly more successful were efforts by the Russians themselves to develop agriculture. Hungry, without supplies and reinforcements, the garrisons dwindled from death and desertion.[1]

THE ADVANCE TO THE ENISEI: TURUKHANSK (1607)

But even without much aid from Moscow, the inhabitants of the eastern frontier towns continued to explore and conquer, extending the area under Russian control. Primarily through the initiative of local officials, they developed Mangazeia in the north and Ketsk on the middle Irtysh and continued eastward toward the great River Enisei. Russian *promyshlenniks* (private traders and hunters) from Pomor'e, the maritime region of northern Russia, had been operating in the territory of Mangazeia throughout the sixteenth century and were apparently familiar with the portage route to the Enisei.[2] They had discovered a sea route from Arkhangel'sk to Mangazeia, which, under favourable circumstances, could be covered in four and a half weeks. Goods acquired from foreigners in Arkhangel'sk were taken to the native Ostiaks and Samoyeds in the Mangazeia area and there exchanged for furs.

British and Dutch merchants, interested in acquiring furs directly, and in finding a northern route to the Orient, tried from 1553 to find a way into the Kara Sea but were blocked by ice and the massive barrier of Novaia Zemlia. The Moscow Government feared the intrusion of foreigners into the exploitation of Siberian furs, as well as the loss of customs dues from the development of illicit trade. Accordingly, in 1616 the Government warned the promyshlenniks not to show the sea route to foreigners and in 1619 forbade the promyshlenniks themselves to use the sea routes from European Russia to Mangazeia and the mouth of the Enisei.[3] Thereafter the commerce in furs had to depend exclusively on land transport and inland waterways.

With the establishment of the office of voevoda in Mangazeia, *sluzhily liudi*, or 'service men'—men in government service—went after iasak over routes discovered previously by the private traders. Going overland from the river Taz, they reached the River Turukhan, a western tributary of the Enisei. About 1607 the *zimov'e* ('winter quarters', usually a blockhouse) of Turukhansk was founded at the mouth of the Turukhan. On a slight eminence, the site is surrounded in the springtime by a vast swamp, covered with myriad ponds and small lakes. Later the blockhouse was transformed into a fort, to which in 1643, after the decline of the parent centre, the voevodas of Mangazeia moved their administrative apparatus, so that it became known as 'New Mangazeia'.

From Turukhansk parties went in several directions. Thus, in 1610 Kondratii Kurochkin (or Kurkin) and other Dvina merchants in Mangazeia organized an expedition to the lower Enisei. The participants built *koch* (decked boats) in Turukhansk and sailed down the river to its mouth a four-weeks journey, with the intention of exploring the seacoast. Although it was already June, the explorers were stopped by ice floes that blocked the bay. They had to wait five weeks until a south wind drove the ice away.[4] Proceeding eastward, the party reached the Piasina, the first large river between the Enisei and the Lena. In 1614 a fort was built on this river to collect iasak from the Samoyeds. Other Mangazeian parties went up the Enisei as far as its western tributaries, the Rivers Sym and Kas But there they found that iasak collectors from the rival centre of Ketsk far to the south, had preceded them and were already collecting iasak from the local tribes.[5]

The men from Ketsk had entered this area for the first time in 1605 A party reached the Enisei in 1608 by way of the Ket–Enisei portage and went up the Enisei as far as the River Kan, where they encountered a Turkic-speaking tribe called the Arins. This tribe refused to pay tribute and sought aid against the Russians from the neighbouring Kirgiz, a related but more powerful group.[6]

In the same year, the Tungus (part of a large East Siberian ethnic group centred in Manchuria) from the Upper Tunguska region invaded the Ketsk area and attacked the Ostiaks there. Two local Ostiak chiefs, Urnuk and Namak, who had formerly provided guides and interpreters for the Russians, told officials at Ketsk that the Tungus intended to kill Russian iasak collectors if they appeared in Tungus territory and to punish Ostiaks who paid iasak to the Russians.[7] Joint Russian-Ostiak forces defeated the Tungus in a bloody battle. The Tungus continued, nevertheless, to raid the iasak-paying Ostiaks, especially those near the Enisei.[8]

In 1612 Chief Namak came to Ketsk with the news that the Tungus and the Arins were ready to submit and pay iasak. But when Namak, accompanied by some Russians, arrived in the territory of the Tungus, the latter denied any intention of giving up their freedom. They plundered Namak and took away all his possessions. When Namak and the Russians visited the Arins, they discovered that the latter had been plundered recently by numerous and warlike Mongol tribesmen from farther east, the Buriats, and had nothing left to offer. Namak and his companions took solace for their own losses by seizing a few of the Arins' remaining sables.[9]

Mangazeia and Ketsk became rivals for control of the Sym and Kas. Each side accused the other of mistreating the natives and each inspired petitions to Moscow purporting to come from the natives to prove its point. One complained about the officials of Ketsk and asked for control by the Mangazeians. Another complained of the hardships suffered by the natives in carrying tribute all the way to Ketsk, although in actuality it was still farther to Mangazeia; yet another took the side of Ketsk.[10]

NATIVE REBELLIONS

A critical development during this period was the organization of several widespread conspiracies among the native tribes of western Siberia, aimed at the expulsion of the Russians. Aware of the difficulties of their conquerors, toward the end of 1604, the Ostiaks, Tatars, Kirgiz, and other groups that had been paying tribute to Ketsk and Tomsk, began to lay plans for revolt. At the head of the conspiracy were three chiefs, Basandai of the Tomsk Tatars, Nemcha of the Kirgiz, and Baibakhta of the Ob Ostiaks. In the winter of 1604–5 these leaders sent messengers to Mogula, a prince of the Ostiaks in the vicinity of Ketsk, demanding that he attack Ketsk and threatening that if he refused they would destroy his tribe after they had captured Tomsk. The Ostiaks of Ketsk were ready to rise against the Russians without any threats, however. In 1602 they had joined the Ostiaks of Narym in a mutiny against the Russians that was suppressed by the garrison of Surgut. Now they responded readily to the invitation and began to hold secret meetings under the leadership of chief Mogula.[11]

The Russians learned of the conspiracy through information obtained by Posnik Belskii, the *prikashchik* (factor or commandant) of Ketsk, from an Ostiak woman. Belskii immediately sent a party of service men who captured the leaders just as they were departing for their meeting place. Questioned under torture, they revealed their plan. [12] The capture of the leaders averted the threat, and the Russians punished the conspirators.

To the north, in 1607, the Ostiaks of Berezov and Obdora rebelled. They were led by the princess of Koda, Anna Ignat'evna, and by the prince of Obdora, Vasilii, both Christian converts. The natives laid siege to Berezov for two months but, lacking any skill in breaching fortifications, finally abandoned the siege. In spite of their relative weakness—the garrison consisted of only 314 men—the Russians caught the leaders and punished them. They hanged Vasilii and some of the other chiefs and whipped others. Only Princess Anna, presumably, escaped punishment, [13] for in the next year, 1608, she reappeared at the head of an even larger and more dangerous conspiracy against Russian authority.

In the fall of 1608 Princess Anna and her brother-in-law, Chumei, collected iasak from her own Ostiaks in the Surgut area. From there, accompanied by the Surgut Prince Neuna and other local chiefs and princes, she went to the native village of Samar, at the mouth of the Irtysh. There she met Prince Tair Samarov and the Belogorsk Ostiaks, and together they laid plans for another attempt to overthrow the Russians. Evidently the schemers also entered into an agreement with the Tungus and Kirgiz of the Enisei, the Tatars of the Tobol and the Ostiaks of the Konda, the Sos'va, and the Obdora regions. One Ostiak chief, Mamruk, brought in the Samoyeds. From the Ostiaks of the Sos'va the threads of the conspiracy extended to the Voguls and to the Tiumen and Tura Tatars. The Russian agent of the Sos'va, Vlas'ev, reported unusual inquisitiveness on the part of the Voguls concerning the news from Moscow, the number of Russians on the Sos'va, and their supply of firearms. When they got no information from Vlas'ev, the Voguls told him that they knew themselves that the Russians were killing each other in Moscow. The conduct of the natives also aroused the suspicion of the voevoda of Verkhotur'e, who reported apparent preparation for an uprising in his district.

The nature and extent of the conspiracy, which involved almost all of the native tribes in western Siberia, was discovered by accident. The cossacks seized an Ostiak who had in his possession an arrow with eleven symbols of various deities (*shaitans*). He turned out to be a messenger from the Surgut chief, Neun, and Chief Tair Samarov to the Ostiaks of Koda. Put to torture, the messenger disclosed the details of the conspiracy to exterminate the Russians and seize Berezov 'in the fall when the nights are dark' and later to attack Tobolsk. [14] Revealed in time, the conspiracy disintegrated.

Four years later, in 1612, a rumour that the natives were to be drafted into the army to fight in Russia brought another crisis. Whether there was any foundation for this rumour is not known. The idea of revolt originated among the Voguls of Verkhotur'e and the Ostiaks of Berezov, who then contacted the Tatars. The conspirators planned to take Pelym when the members of the garrison were out attending to the fields. After the capture of Pelym they planned to cross the Urals and attack Perm, hoping thereby to prevent the Russians from coming to Siberia. Their final aim was no less than the organization of an independent state, as in the time of Kuchum. The voevoda of Pelym, Peter Islenev, hearing of the danger, prepared for a siege and notified the voevoda of Tobolsk. The ringleaders were rounded up, ten were hanged, more than thirty were flogged, and others kept as hostages. [15] Thus the network of strategically located forts erected during the period 1585 to 1604 stood the test of the native uprisings. The sporadic attempts of the natives to free themselves from Russian domination were suppressed.

The restoration of order in European Russia permitted the Moscow Government to resume an active role in affairs beyond the Urals. In 1618 the garrison of Ketsk was augmented, and an expedition composed of men from Ketsk and Tobolsk was sent to explore the routes to the Rivers Enisei and Upper Tunguska and to build an ostrog for the systematic exploitation of the area. [16] Peter Albychev, a boyar-son of Pelym, and Cherkas Rukin, a cossack, led the expedition. The party took their boats up the River Ket to a place where the river ceased to be navigable, then searched for a route to the tributaries of the Enisei. In order to protect the boats and supplies while the men were scouting, the leaders built a small fort, Makovsk, at the head of the Ket, named after a local chief, Namak, already mentioned. [17]

The founding of Makovsk provoked the resentment of the voevoda of Ketsk. He had already been ordered to hand over some of his territory to the jurisdiction of the fort which was to be erected on the Enisei, and the building of Makovsk meant that he might lose even more territory. As a result, when a large group of Tungus besieged Makovsk in 1619, the voevoda of Ketsk not only withheld assistance from the besieged fort but actually detailed a messenger sent from Makovsk to Tobolsk with a request for aid. [18] Fortunately a strong palisade and a few shots from guns and muskets were sufficient to keep the attackers away and eventually to scatter them. In the following year a special commission appointed by the voevoda of Tobolsk, Kurakin, investigated the conduct of the voevoda of Ketsk. [19]

Sometime after the siege, the founders of the fort, Albychev and Rukin, explored the territory east of Makovsk. They ascended the Ket River, then

131

portaged to the small River Kem, and followed it to the Enisei. There, on the low left bank of the river, they built an ostrog, Eniseisk. The situation, in a swampy area, was unattractive, but within a short time this settlement completely overshadowed Ketsk as a frontier outpost and itself became a base for expansion. Eniseisk was at first administered by boyar-sons sent from Tobolsk, but in 1623 was placed under a voevoda.

Before the end of 1619, Albychev and Rukin sent cossacks to the Upper Tunguska to collect iasak.[20] Two chiefs on the first tribe of Tungus whom they met came to the Russian flotilla and declared their willingness to submit, but explained that their 'common people' were hostile and were even planning to raid the Russian and Ostiak settlements at the portage. The next tribe was willing to submit, but other tribes proved hostile.[21] Thus drawn by the abundance of furs, the Russians extended their control and collected iasak along the tributaries of the Enisei: the Lower Tunguska, Stony Tunguska, and Upper Tunguska rivers.

MANGAZEIANS EXPLORE THE LOWER LENA

Meanwhile, men from Mangazeia had continued to explore the lower Enisei and its eastern tributaries. As sable and beaver became scarce along the Taz and lower Enisei, the Mangazeians had increased their efforts on the Lower and Stony Tunguska rivers.[22] During the years 1621–25 they collected large amounts of iasak. Some natives had sable coats and even used sables as foot pads on their skiis. The Russians decided that the Tungus could use cheaper furs for themselves, so they confiscated even worn sable coats and the sable pelts on the skiis, recommending the use of reindeer skins instead.[23]

On the Stony Tunguska, about 1620, the men from Mangazeia were told by the Tungus of another large river to the east, which was abundantly stocked with sables of unusually high quality. Upon it were people who lived in houses, wore clothes like the Russians, and kept horses.[24] The river was the mighty Lena, three thousand miles long, with a thousand tributaries, draining an area of nearly one million square miles. The people were the Iakuts, a tribe of Turkic origin. Originally pastoral nomads in more favoured regions farther south, they fled northward during the upheavals accompanying the rise of Genghis Khan and settled along the middle Lena. There they continued to practise cattle and horse breeding in spite of the severe climate, keeping the animals in their houses during the winter.

As usual, the rumours caused a rush to the new region. Men from Mangazeia ascended the Lower Tunguska, portaged to the sources of the Viliui River, descended it to the Lena, and soon reported to Tobolsk and

Moscow the first contacts with the Iakuts.[25] Later the voevodas of Mangazeia claimed the discovery of the Lena on the basis of this report.

Apparently the first Russians actually to sail on the Lena were promyshlenniks led by a certain Penda. Starting about 1620 from Turukhansk with forty companions, he spent three years on the Lower Tunguska, reached its upper course, portaged to the Lena at a point opposite its right bank tributary, the Kirenga, and then descended the Lena. Still a clear mountain torrent, the river bore them past forest-clad cliffs of red sandstone until joined from the right by the Vitim, then flowed through thickly wooded plains until joined by another right bank tributary, the Olekma. Some distance farther down, where the Botama joins it, they would have passed the Lena *stolby*, or columns, perpendicular limestone cliffs with remarkable green and red strata, rising in places to two thousand feet. Penda went as far as the site of the future Iakutsk, then turned and went all the way back up the river and still farther to the mouth of the Kulenga, opposite which on the high right bank of the Lena, was the future (1641) site of Verkholensk. From there he crossed the Buriat steppe by land until he reached the Upper Tunguska, or Angara. This swift-flowing stream brought Penda and his men back to the Enisei, by which they reached Eniseisk at the end of 1623, whence they returned to Turukhansk, after a journey of more than five thousand miles.[26]

Upon hearing of the wealth of sables on the Lena, the voevodas of Tobolsk dispatched an expedition in 1629 under the command of the boyar-son Samson Navatskii 'to protect the Russian promyshlenniks against attack by the Tungus and Iakuts'. Like Penda, Navatskii also ascended the Lower Tunguska, but portaged to the Chona, a tributary of the Viliui, and descended both to the Lena. There he collected iasak and built a small fort, Ust'-Viliuiskoe. Natives attacked the fort on 9 November 1630 and, although beaten off, killed half the Russians, leaving only fifteen to get back to Turukhansk.[27] In spite of this experience, other promyshlenniks followed, and the Viliui soon became a well-known route.

ENISEISK MEN EXPLORE THE UPPER LENA

While the Mangazeians were operating on the Lena in the north, the service men and promyshlenniks of Eniseisk reached the river from the south.[28] In 1628 the *desiatnik* (petty officer) Vasilii Bugor led ten men from Eniseisk, ascended first the Upper Tunguska and its small tributary the Idirma, then portaged to the River Kuta and followed it to the upper Lena. He ascended the Lena as far as the mouth of the Kirenga, collecting iasak from Iakuts along the way, then turned and retraced his route, arriving in Eniseisk in 1630.[29]

The excellent quality of the furs brought back by Bugor led to the organization of another expedition to Eniseisk, this time under the command of the cossack ataman Ivan Galkin. He was given thirty men and instructions to collect iasak along the Ilim, a tributary of the Upper Tunguska. He was then to portage to the Lena and sail down it in peace, inducing the natives 'by clemency and persuasion' to deliver tribute. He was also to study the most effective means of extending the authority of the Sovereign over the Iakuts. Galkin discovered a route from the Ilim to the Lena much better than the Idirma–Kuta portage used by Bugor and secured the two ends of the portage by building a zimov'e, Lenskii Volok (Lena Portage), later known as Ilimsk, on the Ilim, and another zimov'e, Ust'-Kut at the mouth of the Kuta.[30]

The systematic conquest of the Lena began with the arrival from Eniseisk of sotnik Peter Beketov, who had already won a reputation by his exploits against the Buriats and Tungus along the Upper Tunguska and its western tributary, the Oka. In 1631 Beketov portaged from Ilimsk to the Lena with about thirty men. Leaving ten men at Ust'-Kut, he led the rest up the Lena as far as the mouth of the Kulenga.[31] He then turned west into the Buriat steppe, where, on the fifth day, he found a large number of Buriats. He demanded iasak and built a fortified camp of fallen trees. About sixty Buriats approached, supposedly with iasak, and were admitted into the camp after they had left their bows and arrows behind. The quality of the furs they brought caused an altercation, during which the Buriats pulled out knives and daggers, which they had hidden under their clothes, and attacked the Russians. However, Beketov had expected something like this and he and his men shot and killed most of the Buriat party. Masses of Buriats eager to avenge the death of their kinsmen milled outside the camp, but the Russians made a sortie, seized some horses, and escaped. Riding without rest for twenty-four hours, they finally found safety on the Lena at the mouth of the Tutura River, where they were among friendly Tungus who had been oppressed by the Buriats. At this place, not far from Lake Baikal, Beketov built an ostrog, Tutursk. Leaving ten cossacks there, he took the rest back to Ust'-Kut, where they spent the winter.[32] Tutursk served as a base for collecting furs from the local Tungus, protected them from their Buriat enemies, and served as a base for conquering the people along the Kirenga.[33]

In the spring of 1632, Beketov took his small force down the Lena, where he accomplished the outstanding achievement of his adventurous career, the conquest of most of the Iakut people. The Iakuts were scattered over an enormous territory, yet in spite of this they were conquered within a few months by only twenty men. The first tribe with which Beketov came into contact met him with arrows and tried to cut off the landing party from their boats. The cossacks, however, succeeded in capturing some important hostages and as a result were able to open negotiations that not only won them a free passage but also the promise of the natives to swear allegiance to the Tsar and to deliver iasak. On the right bank of the Lena opposite the *ulus* (settlement) of one of the most powerful tribes,[34] Beketov built an ostrog, the forerunner of the town of Iakutsk. With this fort as a base, he continued his conquest. He was also able to detach some of his men and send them down the lower Lena into the territory of the Lena Tungus, who agreed to deliver iasak. There he built a zimov'e, Zhigansk. In 1633 Beketov extended his activity with the same success along the Aldan, a large eastern tributary of the Lena.

The ease of Beketov's conquest was due to several factors. Most important was the use of firearms, and next the existence of bitter intertribal feuds, which prevented united action by the natives. Instead, each tribe and each clan fought the Russians separately. The natives also easily lost courage and surrendered at the first setback. Besides, many natives accepted Russian authority without protest because they were attracted by trade, through which they obtained highly valued copper pots, tin plates, and brightly coloured beads. Presents judiciously distributed among friendly chiefs won many of them to the Russian side.[35]

RIVALRY BETWEEN MANGAZEIAN AND ENISEISK MEN ON THE LENA

The force dispatched by Beketov to collect iasak on the lower Lena had a harder time. In 1633, at the mouth of the Viliui, Beketov's men met a Mangazeian party under Stepan Korytov. The meeting was not friendly. Korytov seized the sailboat used by Beketov's men, so that without a means of transportation 'to escape death in a desolate place'[36] they had to go along with Korytov. Korytov then sailed up the Lena and the Aldan, collecting iasak from Iakuts who had already delivered tribute to Beketov. From the Aldan, Korytov proceeded up the Amga, a western tributary of the Aldan. Here, also he collected iasak for the second time, so that by September 1633 the natives had become exasperated. They killed five cossacks, caused the rest to move on, and declared that from then on they would pay no tribute to anyone.[37]

Upon his return to Eniseisk in 1633, Beketov was replaced by Ivan Galkin, who took reinforcements to Iakutsk, among them the future conqueror of the Amur, Erofei Khabarov.[38] This brought the garrison to about two hundred men. Upon arrival, Galkin sent notices to the Iakuts demanding the payment of iasak. They refused, and Galkin therefore sent out four expeditions in as many directions to reconquer them.

Late in 1633 Galkin learned that a Iakut chief, Umymak, had assembled six hundred men and intended to take Iakutsk either by assault or by starving out the garrison. On 5 January 1634, Galkin gathered as many men as he could—about forty-seven—and marched against Umymak. In the battle that followed, only two Russians were killed, but most of the remainder were wounded. The Russians also lost all of their horses, which were struck by arrows, and were forced to retreat to the ostrog on foot. Forty Iakuts were killed, but the others pursued the Russians and laid siege to the fort. Under protection of shields, they carried straw and birch bark up to the walls and attempted to set the fort on fire, but were beaten back by musket fire. The siege lasted almost two months, and the Russians suffered greatly from lack of food. With a little more patience, the Iakuts might have forced the Russians to surrender, but they finally gave up and withdrew.[39]

As soon as the siege was raised, Galkin notified the Iakuts that the rebels would be forgiven if they stopped fighting and resumed payment of iasak. Some of the natives were placated by promises of better treatment. Against the recalcitrants, Galkin sent an expedition of 150 men. The effort accomplished little, however, for many of the Iakuts had by now migrated to inaccessible mountain regions, northern tributaries of the Viliui, the Iana river, and the Arctic coast.[40]

In the spring of 1634, the Mangazeian commander, Korytov, returning from the Amga, was surprised at the mouth of the Aldan by Galkin's men. A battle followed in which one cossack was killed and several wounded. Korytov broke through and went down the Lena to rejoin the rest of his party at Zhigansk, but the Eniseisk men managed to recover the sailboat and the men of Beketov's detachment whom Korytov had seized. Galkin pursued Korytov and overtook him at the mouth of the Viliui. Another skirmish ensued, with forty Eniseisk m   ~~inst thirteen of Korytov's. Korytov was captured, sent to Iakutsk, and there forced to surrender his native hostages and the iasak taken from the Iakuts. However, he was allowed to keep what he had collected from the Tungus along the Viliui and to take it to Mangazeia.[41]

TOBOLSK AND TOMSK MEN ON THE LENA

When the news spread of the abundance of sable furs on the Lena, other Siberian towns, including Tobolsk and Tomsk, tried to obtain a share in the exploitation of the Lena region. In 1633 a boyar-son, Voin Shakhov, was sent there from Tobolsk with forty cossacks. He went by way of Mangazeia, Turukhansk, and the Lower Tunguska. On the latter he met a party of Mangazeians under command of Ostafii Kolov, a Litvin (properly, a Lithuanian, but used collectively to designate a group comprising prisoners of war, immigrants, and foreign mercenaries exiled to Siberia for punishment). Because the Litvins rated below the boyar-sons on the Siberian social ladder, Shakhov demanded that the Mangazeians join his party and accept his command. The Mangazeians refused, and the two parties, quarrelling among themselves, came to the Viliui River, where the Mangazeians had previously established a zimov'e. Still unable to agree, both parties started to collect iasak. The local Tungus resented the double iasak and rose in arms, attacking both groups without discrimination. Most of the Russians were killed, but Shakhov escaped: a few years later we find him in an administrative capacity on the Viliui River.[42]

From Tomsk, in 1636, a detachment of fifty-four men under the command of ataman Dmitrii Kopylov was dispatched to the Lena by way of Eniseisk. In vain the voevoda of Eniseisk protested against the encroachment on what he considered territory under his jurisdiction. Kopylov's boats went on the Lena and up the Aldan. Above the mouth of the Maia River, a right bank tributary of the Aldan, Kopylov established the zimov'e of Butal'sk, and proceeded to collect iasak from the Tungus and the Lamuts (the latter a Tungus sub-group) of the region.

MOSKVITIN REACHES THE PACIFIC (1639)

In 1639 Kopylov sent a detachment of twenty men under the command of Ivan Moskvitin to reconnoitre the Maia River. The detachment spent six weeks going up the Maia, seeking the best way to reach what the natives had told them lay beyond, 'the great sea-ocean'. Moskvitin led his men up the Iudoma, a tributary of the Maia, then through a pass in the Dzhugdzhur Mountains to the River Ul'ia. Following the Ul'ia downstream for five days, they reached the Sea of Okhotsk, part of the North Pacific.[43] One may note that the Portuguese discovered the Pacific when Antonio de Abreu entered it from the south in 1511. Balboa discovered it from the east by crossing the land bridge between the American continents in 1513. The Russian petty officer, Moskvitin, discovered it from the west in 1639.

How Moskvitin and his men may have felt about their achievement is not recorded in the laconic reports of that time. At the mouth of the Ul'ia, the party built a zimov'e and began to collect iasak from the natives. Moskvitin sent out two groups to reconnoitre the coast to the north and south. The first group went as far north as the mouth of the Taui River and the bay of the same name. The other group went as far south as the mouth of the River Uda. There the local Lamuts, a Tungus sub-group, told them about the Rivers Zeia and Amur still farther south. This region was said to be inhabited by two tribes, the Giliaks and Daurs, who kept

137

several kinds of domestic animals and raised grain. The Lamuts, however, refused to act as guides, and the Russian discovery of the Amur was delayed until a few years later.[44]

As was mentioned, the group which reached the Pacific was part of the expedition sent from Tomsk to the Lena under Kopylov. While Moskvitin and his men were exploring the seacoast, Kopylov, who had remained on the Aldan River, became involved in the intertribal wars of the Iakuts. With his aid one tribe was victorious and obtained three hundred head of cattle and three hundred horses as war spoils.

At this moment another expedition appeared on the scene, this one from Eniseisk, under the command of the boyar-son Parfen Khodyrev. The vanquished tribe of the Iakuts appealed to Khodyrev for assistance. As we have seen, the Eniseisk men had a grudge against the 'encroaching' expedition from Tomsk and did not need much persuasion. Together with their native allies they attacked the cossacks of Tomsk and their allies. In the battle the Tomsk cossacks sought protection against the musket fire behind their animals, 'and many of their horses and cattle were shot down by the Eniseisk cossacks'. Thirty Iakuts were killed, and the Tomsk cossacks were captured. Khodyrev wanted to incite the Iakuts to massacre the men of Tomsk, but was prevented by his own men saying, 'It is not proper to send the natives to kill Russians. You had better kill them yourself.' Khodyrev then changed his mind and merely flogged the Tomsk men with canes and whips, and seized all their spoils and arms. Although these spoils had been taken by the Tomsk cossacks from Khodyrev's allies, Khodyrev did not return the seized property to the former owners, but characteristically kept it for himself.[45]

Thus, detachments from Mangazeia, Eniseisk, Tobolsk, and Tomsk came into the Lena region in the name of the Muscovite sovereign and often conducted themselves as bandits and outlaws. Not only did they perpetrate crimes on the natives (murder, rape, plunder, and general violence) but often fought among themselves. Such disorder antagonized the natives, especially the newly conquered Iakuts and Tungus.

The disturbances and a decline of revenue for the Treasury impelled Moscow to establish a separate Lena administrative unit with voevodas of its own who had a degree of independence from the other towns and were responsible for the state of affairs on the Lena. The service men from

Mangazeia, Eniseisk, and other towns henceforth had to stay away from the Lena.[46] An order of 1638 appointed Petr Golovin and Matvei Glebov voevodas of Iakutsk with instructions to assemble 395 cossacks and strel'tsy from various towns of Siberia and proceed with them to Iakutsk.[47]

Describing conditions on the Lena, the Tsar's instruction stated:

> The service men from Mangazeia visit the frontier of these lands, along the great River Lena, from its mouth up the river a small distance, while the service men from Eniseisk ostrog go down the river as far as the mouth of the Viliui. . . . They [either group] land and lure the natives with goods as if for trade. Then they fall on the natives, take away their wives, children, and possessions, steal their cattle, and commit many acts of violence. They themselves amass great wealth, but obtain little for the Sovereign. And because of their wretched greed, these service men of Tobolsk, Eniseisk, and Mangazeia fight each other, and beat to death promyshlenniks who gather sables on the Lena. They grieve and oppress the natives, make them resentful, and thus drive them away from the sovereign.[48]

Golovin and Glebov started out with a large caravan carrying supplies and ammunition, but because of the difficulties of transportation reached Iakutsk only in 1640.[49] The new voevodas made a census of the population and made each individual deliver his quota instead of exacting collective delivery by the whole clan.[50] But they did not improve the treatment of the natives, who during the period 1638–41 grew increasingly restive. A petition from the promyshlenniks to the Government stated:

> Last year [1639–40] forty-four promyshlenniks were killed by Shamagirs [Tungus] on the upper Lena, and twenty-six men were killed on the lower Lena. This year [1640–41] fifteen men were killed on the Aldan and their zimov'e destroyed. In the last three years sixty-four men have been killed along the Viliui, and this year seven more were killed. Many promyshlenniks have been plundered or besieged by the natives.[51]

By 1642 the demands of Golovin and his brutality in collecting tribute resulted in a general native uprising. Forty-five cossacks in outlying areas were annihilated. The uprising threatened Iakutsk for a while but finally collapsed because of quarrels among the natives. As soon as the danger was over the Iakutsk administrators carried out punitive measures. 'For over a month Golovin tortured, burned, and flogged the Iakuts involved [in the murder of the Russians] without mercy.'[52] This uprising was the last great outbreak among the natives on the Lena. Thereafter, sporadic explosions of protest did occur, but on the whole, Russian authority was firmly established.[53]

SUMMARY

During the first two decades of the seventeenth century, known as the 'Time of Troubles', internal disturbances in European Russia retarded the advance into Siberia. With the restoration of order, the government's interest in Siberia revived, although much of the initiative in expansion thereafter passed from the central Government to the local officials and private frontier traders.

Primarily this expansion was a huge business enterprise on the part of the Russian government, albeit the government was not able to carry it out alone. As they moved eastward, the frontier officials had to rely more and more on private traders because of the insufficiency of regular army men.

On their march the Russians encountered numerous aboriginal groups, among them the Finnic tribesmen on the Ob River; the Tungus, related to the Manchus, on the Enisei River; the Iakuts, who are related to the Turks, on the Lena River; and the Buriats of the Baikal area, who are Mongols. The natives of Siberia greatly outnumbered the Russians, but they were scattered, lacked political organization, and were unable to check Russian penetration. The government troops and private traders explored distant areas searching for furs. When the government learned of a new region where it expected to collect large fur tribute from the natives, commandants of the established forts sent expeditions to build forts or blockhouses in the midst of still unconquered tribes. The advance then slowed temporarily until the supply of animals in the area was exhausted or a new Eldorado of furs was discovered farther on. Each discovery led to a fur rush, both of government men and private traders, comparable to a gold rush in America. 'Boom towns', like Mangazeia, grew up during the rush, only to be left later as 'ghost towns', in its wake.

The expansion in Siberia proceeded by leaps. By 1619 the Russians had gained all the important river routes and portages from the basin of the Ob to the basin of the Enisei. They had reached the Enisei in the north via Mangazeia, and later by 'New Mangazeia'—Turukhansk—between the Taz and the Turukhan Rivers; they reached the middle Enisei by way of the portage of Makovsk, between the Ket and the Kem; and they reached the upper Enisei by way of Tomsk. Once on the Enisei, they continued eastward by ascending the two large Enisei tributaries, the Lower and Upper Tunguska, and portaging to the Lena. Within a decade of Penda's journey (1620–23), they had discovered most of the course of the Lena and its chief tributaries.

Thus it was that in a little over two generations—within a single lifetime—the Russians advanced from the scene of Ermak's crossing of the Urals to gain control of three great river basins of northern Asia—the Ob, the Enisei, and the Lena. Command of the Lena opened the way south to the Baikal region and the Amur, north to the Arctic Ocean, and east to the Pacific.

Chapter 9

The Conquest of Buriatia and Transbaikalia

In acquiring the Enisei region, the Russians had come into conflict with the strong and warlike Buriats, or 'Braty', a Mongol tribe. Their existence became known in 1609, when the officials at Tomsk were informed that the eastern Kirgiz clans paid tribute to the *Bratskie liudi* (Brat or Buriat people). The first actual meeting occurred in 1612, when the Buriats raided the iasak-paying Arins who lived on the upper Enisei. The Buriats themselves occupied a vast territory stretching from the Biriusa and Uda tributaries of the Upper Tunguska (known as the Angara in its upper reaches) to the Iablonovyi range in Transbaikalia. Their southern border was the Saian Range and their northern border was at approximately 55–57 degrees north latitude. Hunters and farmers, they traded with other Mongol groups and with the Chinese.[1] The Russians of that time clearly distinguished between the Buriats and the Mongols, although the difference was only cultural. Cut off from the civilizing influence of Chinese culture, the Buriats were less advanced than the other Mongol tribes, though they were more advanced than the Siberian tribes around them.

EXPEDITIONS FROM ENISEISK UNDER KOZLOV, SAVVIN, ALEKSEEV (TIUMENETS), AND PERFIL'EV

In 1622 the Buriats raided the iasak-paying natives of the Kan River (a tributary of the Enisei) region, and demanded that these tribes deliver iasak to them instead of to the Russians. They reappeared, in 1623,[2] and there were rumours that a Buriat army of three thousand was advancing on Tomsk.[3] Probably in connection with these rumours, Iakov Khripunov, the voevoda of Eniseisk, on 11 December 1623 sent Zhdan Kozlov with instructions to collect information about the Buriats and, on promise of favours and gifts, to invite them to become subjects of the Tsar. In his instructions Khripunov asked:

What kind of people are they? Sedentary or nomadic? What are the names of the local chiefs? What fortifications have they and what is their manner of fighting . . .? How many men can they put to horse? If they are not warlike people, what are their occupations? In what wares do they trade? Do they have good sables or other furs? Do they have anything else to offer? Should the Great Sovereign expect any profit from them?[4]

The outcome of Kozlov's mission is not known; he probably did not even reach the Buriats. Matters rested for a time, while the Eniseisk authorities subdued a revolt of the Tungus on the Rivers Chona and Lower Tunguska and a revolt of cossack service men.[5]

A detachment of Eniseisk cossacks under the command of Vikhor Savvin was sent in 1624 to the Upper Tunguska (Angara) to collect iasak from Tungus who had previously been conquered. Near the mouth of its left tributary the Uda (also called the Taseeva and Chuna in its lower course) the Tungus attacked, killed some of the cossacks, and besieged the others for six days until they managed to escape. As a result, on 30 May 1625 another expedition of twenty-five men,[6] under the cossack ataman Vasilii Alekseev, or as generally known, Tiumenets,[7] was sent from Eniseisk to this place. Tiumenets was told to restore Russian authority and to collect iasak from the Tungus, then to take along some friendly Tungus and proceed to Buriat territory. There he and his party were to collect additional information on the Buriats. Tiumenets first ascended the Upper Tunguska and then its tributary, the Uda, until he reached rapids. There he was attacked by the Tungus and, after losing five men, turned back.[8] Although he did not reach the land of the Buriats, Tiumenets did bring back some information on them: he wrote that the Buriat land had a common frontier with China, that there were about twenty thousand horsemen in this country, and that they fought with the Chinese practically every year. Their chief occupation was tilling the soil.[9]

Next we find Tiumenets collecting iasak among the Tungus along the River Pit, an eastern tributary of the Enisei below the Upper Tunguska. Here, apparently without any justification, he killed several Tungus and captured others as slaves. The cossacks were forbidden to take slaves, and when Tiumenets returned to Eniseisk the voevoda, Andrei Oshanin, ordered their release.[10] The cossacks, who valued the women slaves as workers and concubines, rebelled at this. They held a meeting, "swore on the cross to stand by each other', came noisily to the voevoda's office, 'called the voevoda names, pulled out his beard, and threatened him with arms'. The rioters shot from bows and muskets, killed a Litvin, and beat to death some merchants and promyshlenniks who sided with the voevoda. Fortunately, a detachment from Tobolsk arrived and restored order. Some of the rebels were beaten with the knout, and Tiumenets and ten other ringleaders of the revolt were taken to Tobolsk.[11] The *pod'iachei* (clerk), Maksim Perfil'ev, who had received a severe beating at the hands of the mutineers, replaced Tiumenets as cossack ataman.

The raids, rumours, and reports of scouts had by now convinced the voevodas of Eniseisk that the Buriats were dangerous and should be subjugated, if only to secure the Russian possessions on the Enisei and the Upper Tunguska. Rumours of fur and silver mines in the land of the Buriats provided another reason for conquest.[12]

In the summer of 1626, Perfil'ev was sent from Eniseisk with forty men to the Tungus of the Upper Tunguska with instructions to collect iasak there and also to obtain information 'about the unknown Buriat land'. He visited first the Tungus princelings who had murdered the iasak collectors two years before, pacified them, and persuaded them to pay iasak. He continued up the river until he was stopped by the great Shaman Rapids. However, he gathered new information from a tribe which paid tribute to the Buriats:

The Buriat land is large and abundant. The Buriats are a sedentary people; they have countless horses, cows, and camels. They plant barley and buckwheat. There are many valuable articles in the Buriat land: sables, foxes, beavers, Bukharan cloth . . . and much silver. The Buriats trade with their neighbours and collect tribute from many small tribes.

The most important part of this intelligence was that, supposedly, the Buriats were expecting the Sovereign's service men, that they were willing to become subjects of the Great Sovereign, to pay iasak and to trade with the service men.[13] Hearing this, the voevoda of Eniseisk, Oshanin, sent an enthusiastic report to Moscow, anticipating real profits from the opening of the Buriat territory.

In 1627–28 Perfil'ev led a new expedition of forty cossacks up the Upper Tunguska, again as far as the Shaman Rapids, where he built an ostrozhek. He collected a large amount of iasak from the Tungus on the way, but on the return journey, three days away from Eniseisk, the Tungus attacked. A *strelets* (musketeer) was killed, and Perfil'ev and many of his cossacks were wounded, but the attackers were beaten off and the iasak brought back to Eniseisk.[14]

DUBENSKII FOUNDS KRASNOIARSK (1627)

Among the men attached to the staff of the voevoda at Eniseisk was an interesting adventurer of the lesser nobility by the name of Andrei Dubenskii. He became interested in the exploration of 'distant regions' and on a number of occasions participated in iasak collecting expeditions. Because of the Kirgiz and Buriat threat to the Arins, former vassals of the Kirgiz,[15] along the west bank of the Enisei, Dubenskii was sent in 1624 to investigate the region with a view to building a fort there. As a result of his observations, he prepared a project for a fort on the Enisei south of Eniseisk and was sent to Moscow to present his proposals personally. The government accepted the plan, and the voevoda of Tobolsk was instructed to inspect the proposed site to see if it was situated in a place convenient for agriculture and further expansion. It was expected that the fort would prevent future raids on this territory by the Buriats and Kirgiz, and would serve as a base for their subjugation.[16]

In 1627 Dubenskii was assigned three hundred men, given sufficient food and military supplies, and sent to build the proposed fort. He selected as a site a tongue of land on the left bank of the Enisei where the River Kacha flows into it. The soil in this place is of a reddish colour, hence the fort was called Krasnoiarsk (red bank).[17] Before the ostrog was completed, the prospective subjects, the Kacha Tatars and the Arins, at the instigation of the Kirgiz, came in large numbers to destroy it. They killed several cossacks, but they were repelled and soon submitted.[18] In a few months the fort was completed, and the Russians, following the example of the local Tatars, began to till the soil.[19]

With the building of Krasnoiarsk, the Russians reached the extreme southern point of expansion on the Enisei during the seventeenth century. A further advance eastward was made in 1628 when Ostaf'ev built the zimov'e of Kansk on the Kan River. This was in turn abandoned in 1640 in favour of the ostrog of Kansk, farther up the river.[20] Krasnoiarsk and Ketsk functioned as Russian strongholds against the Buriats, and from these two forts the Russians started the conquest of the neighbouring Tatars as well as the Kirgiz of the upper Enisei. However, here, as in the upper Ob, they were stopped by the advance of the Mongols from the south.[21]

BEKETOV'S EXPEDITION (1628)

Thus far the main significance of the expeditions of Perfil'ev and others lay in the collection of information about the Buriats. The actual conquest of the Buriats started in 1628 with the expedition of the strelets sotnik Peter Beketov, the same Beketov who, in 1632, was to sail down the Lena, build Iakutsk, and accomplish the preliminary conquest of the main course of the Lena and Aldan. In 1628 Beketov led thirty cossacks into the land of the Buriats. He built the ostrozhek Rybnoi (later Rybnoe) at the mouth of the Uda, pacified some rebellious Tungus in the area, and then continued up the Upper Tunguska. Overcoming tremendous difficulties, he and his men passed not only the Shaman Rapids, which had stopped previous expeditions, but even the more formidable Padun Rapids. Here one of the two boats (*strugi*) used by the expedition was wrecked, and the supplies it carried were lost, the crew barely escaping death. Beketov reached the mouth of the Oka, where the local Buriat

144

princelings gave him iasak, the first collected from the Buriats, then proceeded some distance farther along the Upper Tunguska (Angara). His return trip was complicated by the loss of some of his men in fights with the Tungus and of others from the food shortage and from scurvy. Finally, in July 1629, the expedition arrived in Eniseisk. The voevoda was presented with a beautiful fur coat obtained as a 'gift' from the Buriat princelings.[22] A great celebration was held because the Buriats had delivered iasak 'without war'.[23]

KHRIPUNOV'S EXPEDITION (1629)

The powerful Buriats appeared to have submitted to Russian authority, but disappointment soon followed. Among the factors which upset the peaceful relations established by Beketov between Eniseisk and the Buriats, probably the most important was the expedition of Iakov Khripunov, the former voevoda of Eniseisk, organized by the voevodas of Tobolsk with the knowledge of the Tsar and the Siberian Prikaz. Since the first decade of the seventeenth century, rumours of gold and silver had circulated among the Russian population of Siberia. Prompted by these rumours, Khripunov had sent a dozen cossacks from Eniseisk up the Upper Tunguska River in 1625–26 to search for silver ore. The cossacks brought back some rocks which, when smelted, yielded pure silver.[24] Khripunov's prospectors also brought back a rumour of a whole mountain of silver ore in the territory of a certain Buriat princeling, Okun. The Buriats actually did wear silver trinkets on their dress and decorate their weapons with silver, but obtained this silver from Mongolia and China in exchange for grain.[25]

Khripunov drew up a plan for a large expedition to look for the silver mountain. Moscow, chronically short of precious metals, approved the plan and subsidized the enterprise, granting two years' salary for 150 men. Due to the shortage of troops in Siberia, 'Khripunov's regiment', as his detachment was called, was made up chiefly of adventurers and *guliashchie liudi* (vagabonds) from a number of towns. Departing from Tobolsk in the spring of 1629, his men took to plundering the Russian promyshlenniks and iasak-paying natives along the Irtysh and Ob. On the way, they ignored the orders of Khripunov and proceeded leisurely, 'half a day travel, half a day camp'. Coming to Narym they broke into the ostrog with noise and yells and looted the shops of about a hundred merchants. Twice they attempted to kill Khripunov, who tried to maintain discipline. Such was the band which went up the Angara prospecting for the silver mountain. They did not find any traces of silver ore, but terrorized the Buriats on the Oka and Angara.[26]

145

Concurrently with the plundering by Khripunov's men, the Buriats were pillaged by men from Krasnoiarsk. Since the founding of Krasnoiarsk (1628) the relations between this fort and Eniseisk were far from cordial. Eniseisk men resented the fact that they had to bring supplies to Krasnoiarsk. Krasnoiarsk men, who could not explore the south because of the Kirgiz there, envied the opportunities which the Eniseisk men had to explore the Buriat country. There was a direct road from Eniseisk to Buriatia along the Angara, whereas the Krasnoiarsk men could reach the Oka region only by going overland through dense forests *(taiga)* and by crossing mountain streams. As soon as the voevoda of Krasnoiarsk, Dubenskii, heard about Beketov's expedition of 1628 he protested, contending that the exploitation of the Buriats should be the business of Krasnoiarsk. In 1629 there was a food shortage in Krasnoiarsk. When Ataman Kol'tsov (who had led the punitive expedition against the Arins and Kacha Tatars after they attacked the men building Krasnoiarsk in 1628) arrived without any grain, a mob of local service men killed him. They then decided to seize Eniseisk itself. Early in July about 130 of them suddenly appeared at the walls of Eniseisk, but the local voevoda had been warned and met them with cannon and musket shot. Then the rioters went up the Angara, without food and supplies, 'naked, barefoot and hungry'.[27] Plundering as they went, they reached the Oka and there joined Khripunov's men, the two groups apparently dividing the territory between themselves. Khripunov planned to go on to Lake Baikal, but he died.[28] Without food, some of his men and the men from Krasnoiarsk turned back, passing Eniseisk on the way. Seeing that they had a number of captive Buriats intended for sale as slaves, the voevoda of Eniseisk took seventy of the Buriats from their captors. To punish the rebels, and to placate the Buriats, he ordered the latter fed from grain that had been intended for the garrison of Krasnoiarsk.

However, it was too late to undo the harm that had been done. The formerly friendly Buriats were now hostile. The promyshlenniks were afraid to visit the Angara. Nevertheless, envoys were sent to the Buriats from Eniseisk to ask for iasak. Hoping to pacify the Buriats, they took along some of the prisoners who had been recovered from the brigands and were instructed to reassure them against future depredations. The Buriats, however, met them in a hostile fashion, killing one envoy, Vikhor Savvin, and seizing another, though he was later returned.[29]

PACIFICATION BY PERFIL'EV: BRATSK (1631)

The delicate task of pacifying the now enraged Buriats was imposed on that 'efficient and skilful man', Maksim Perfil'ev, who had already led two exploratory expeditions to collect information about the Buriats in 1626 and in 1627–28.[30] He started in 1630, and in 1631 built a fort called Bratsk (from 'Brat' or 'Buriat'), on the Angara River above the Padun rapids, near the mouth of the Oka. Bratsk guarded the Lena–Enisei line of communication from the south. It became an important base for iasak collection and further exploration.[31] From Bratsk, Perfil'ev sent out Buriat-speaking Tungus with promises of the Tsar's favour and protection against a repetition of the plundering and violence they had suffered at the hands of the Russians.[32]

Perfil'ev succeeded in establishing contact with the Buriat chiefs in the vicinity of the new ostrog. He returned some of the prisoners who had been carried away by Khripunov and the Krasnoiarsk marauders and obtained at least nominal iasak. He had to be satisfied with a small quantity of furs because the Buriats claimed that they had lost everything the previous year. But with the departure of Perfil'ev, the situation at Bratsk once more deteriorated. Warned by the Buriats that they would not deliver iasak and that if the cossacks appeared outside the walls to collect iasak, catch fish, or hunt animals, they would be killed,[33] the garrison of the fort led a precarious existence.

In 1634 the garrison was replaced by new men, all armed with muskets. Soon afterwards news reached Eniseisk that the new party had been massacred, the fort burned to the ground, and all of the arms, bullets, and gunpowder captured by the natives.[34] The Buriat victory had a curious aftermath. The natives did not know how to use firearms, so they decided to burn them with the bodies of the dead men. The fire caused the muskets to discharge, and stray bullets killed a few Buriats, creating panic among the superstitious natives, impressed with the fact that even after the Russians were dead their weapons continued to do battle.[35]

The authorities of Eniseisk could not remain indifferent to the military defeat, which was likely to undermine the legend of Russian invincibility and the futility of resistance. In 1635 a punitive expedition of a hundred cossacks, led by the boyar-son, Radukovskii, was sent to the site of the destroyed fort. The Buriats scattered at the approach of the detachment. Radukovskii achieved a degree of submission, obtained some hostages from the princelings' families, and restored Bratsk.[36] In 1638 the Buriats once more besieged the fort, this time without success. Afterwards some of the Buriats began to deliver iasak, while many others migrated up the Oka.[37]

Thus, during the first decade of the conquest of Buriatia the Russians obtained control of the Angara to the mouth of the Oka and part way up the course of the latter.[38] The 1640s were marked by the energetic advance of the men of Eniseisk along the Angara and the Oka, of the men of Krasnoiarsk along the Uda, and of men of Iakutsk along the upper

Lena. This period is also marked by the penetration of the Russians into the region to be known as Transbaikalia (*Zabaikal'e*), beyond the still undiscovered Lake Baikal.

RECONNOITERING TRANSBAIKALIA: PERFIL'EV'S EXPEDITION (1638–1640)

The first Russian to penetrate the Transbaikal region is already familiar to us, Ataman Maksim Perfil'ev of Eniseisk. In 1638 he left the ostrog of Eniseisk, went along the Upper Tunguska, crossed the Ilim portage, and then sailed down the Lena. He spent the winter in Olekminsk ostrog at the mouth of the Olekma River and in the spring of 1639, with a party of 36 men, partly service men and partly volunteers, went back to the mouth of the Vitim and then up that river. He proceeded through the great Vitim Rapids before stopping to spend yet another winter. In 1640 he continued up the Vitim, thus entering the Transbaikal region, until he reached the mouth of an eastern tributary of the Vitim, the Tsipa. Hearing that numerous Tungus lived along the Tsipa, he ascended the river until rapids, scarcity of food, and the reluctance of his men to go farther forced him to turn back.

From the Vitim Tungus, Perfil'ev obtained information about the tribes inhabiting the sources of the Vitim and the area farther east. These natives were the Daurs or Dahurs, related to the Manchus, who occupied the valleys of the upper Vitim, Shilka, and Amur. According to the Tungus, the princeling of the Daurs of the upper Vitim, Botoga, had many sables, much silver and silk cloth. These articles he obtained from Lavkai, another Daur princeling who lived on the Shilka, in exchange for sable furs. Four days' travel from the habitation of Botoga there was a dense population of Daurs, who cultivated land, gathered large crops, and mined silver, copper, and lead ore. By following the Shilka one could reach the sea. Perfil'ev returned to Eniseisk with this news.[39]

IVANOV DISCOVERS LAKE BAIKAL (1643)

The fact that Iakutsk had become a separate voevodship and had its own voevodas after 1640 barred the people of Eniseisk from further operations on the Lena, and their attention therefore turned to the still unexplored parts of the Buriat country. But the voevodas of Iakutsk also developed an interest in this area, especially in the sources of the Lena and its tributaries, and in 1643 one of their men, Kurbat Ivanov, a cossack piatidesiatnik, made his way from Verkholensk to discover Lake Baikal.[40]

What Ivanov and his seventy-five men, mostly promyshlenniks, may have thought about the lake, may only be conjectured. One of the natural wonders of the world, it is over four hundred miles long, twenty-five to forty-five miles wide, over a mile deep, rimmed by mountains a mile high, and it has waters of incredible clarity. Several hundred species of animals, including a type of seal, are native only to the lake. Yet, Ivanov and those who came after him, intent on other matters, left only the usual terse accounts of their activities. He and his men crossed the lake to Olkhon Island, where they attacked and defeated more than a thousand Buriats, from whom they then collected iasak. After that, Ivanov returned to Verkholensk with half of his party, sending the remainder, under one Skorokhodov, northward along the lakeshore to the Verkhniaia (upper) Angara (not to be confused with the Angara proper), which flows into the northern tip of Baikal. Skorokhodov circled the northern end of the lake and came to an eastern tributary, the river Barguzin, where he built a zimov'e. Here he was attacked by the Tungus. Some of his men were killed, two escaped to the lake by boat, and the rest endured a long siege.[41]

KOLESNIKOV FOUNDS VERKHNE-ANGARSK (1646)

Several other expeditions were soon sent from Eniseisk to the Transbaikal region. The most significant were those led by Vasilii Kolesnikov, Ivan Pokhabov, Ivan Galkin, and Peter Beketov.

In 1644 the ataman, Vasilii Kolesnikov, was sent with a hundred men to get information about silver or silver ore 'wherever it might be found'.[42] He had already by-passed the River Ilim and had gone as far as the Shaman Rapids when news came that a number of boats of merchants and promyshlenniks had arrived at the mouth of the Ilim, and that they carried ample supplies of provisions and trade goods. Kolesnikov's party turned back and robbed the merchants, an indication of conditions then prevailing in Siberia. After that, his group continued as far as the Osa River, an eastern tributary of the Angara. There, near the future site of Balagansk (1653), they built an ostrog and spent the winter. They collected furs in this vicinity, causing the commander of Verkholensk ostrog to complain that Kolesnikov was encroaching on his territory. However, in 1645 Kolesnikov resumed his journey to Lake Baikal. After his departure, the local Buriats destroyed his ostrog.

Kolesnikov had intended to go to the southern end of the lake, but upon meeting superior forces of Buriats he and his men turned and went along the west shore toward the northeastern end instead. Before he reached the Verkhniaia Angara, he had had to fight the Tungus and had captured a princeling, Kotuga. He treated Kotuga well, and the latter became of great help to the Russians. At the mouth of the Verkhniaia Angara, Kolesnikov founded the ostrog of Verkhne-Angarsk, where he spent the winter of

1646–47. While there, he heard that at 'Lake Eravna' (Lakes Bolshoe and Maloe Eravnoe, at the head of the Uda River) there was a camp of Mongols who had much silver. Afraid to advance farther, however, he sent envoys, the captured Tungus chief (whose wife and son remained as hostages), and four cossacks. The Mongol chief, one Turukai Tabun, received them well and gave them some gold and two silver cups. He said that there was no silver in his land and that he bought these things from the Chinese. But Kolesnikov sent four cossacks to explore further for silver mines, while he himself turned back to Eniseisk with the news.[43]

POKHABOV VISITS THE EASTERN KHALKA MONGOLS

Another, and more important, pioneer in this region was the notorious boyar-son, Ivan Pokhabov. In 1644, the same year in which Kolesnikov set out, the officials in Eniseisk sent Pokhabov to Bratsk ostrog to collect iasak and to look for 'new iasak lands'. He succeeded in collecting more iasak around Bratsk than his predecessors and built a new fort, this time with parapets (*nadolby*) and moats, around the 'small and unsatisfactory' former fortifications. He then led a party of thirty service men and promyshlenniks up the swift-flowing Angara. In the last five miles, the river gradually widens, until it is more than a mile across; and this great body of water roars down a steep incline, over huge rocks, forming a rapid nearly four miles in length. At the head of this cataract lay the broad expanse of Lake Baikal. The party crossed the lake to the mouth of its chief source, the Selenga River. Ascending the Selenga for two days, Pokhabov, the first Russian to traverse this river, found everywhere natives who until then had not delivered iasak. In his words, 'They fought with us; we killed many of them, and captured more than forty women and children.'

In 1645 Perfil'ev was sent to replace Pokhabov. During his administration the Buriats again withdrew their allegiance and refused to pay iasak, so that he had to ask for reinforcements.[44] Pokhabov was sent out again in 1646 to pacify the rebellious Buriats, to search for new lands, and particularly to look for silver ore. In spite of Khripunov's failure, the government persisted in believing that silver would be found. Pokhabov was also directed to find Kolesnikov, who had not been heard of for some time,[45] and to obtain information about the Chinese state. He departed with a party of about a hundred men.[46] It is worth noting that Pokhabov financed part of this expedition from his own resources: he evidently expected an enormous return.

Repeating Kolesnikov's work, Pokhabov built an ostrog on an island in the Angara, just opposite the mouth of the Osa River, thereby separating the Osa Buriats from those of the Angara. In the spring of 1647, after collecting iasak from the local Buriats, Pokhabov again proceeded up the Angara to Baikal, crossed the lake 'as soon as the ice melted', and landed near the mouth of the Selenga River. Finding Mongols there, he attacked and captured a few of them. Then he learned that these Mongols were subjects of Turukai Tabun, who had been so friendly to Kolesnikov. Four cossacks left by Kolesnikov were still with Turukai, who sent word that he would treat them precisely as Pokhabov treated his prisoners. Pokhabov thereupon went directly to Turukai, and restored peace and friendship.[47]

While still on the Angara, Pokhabov heard that the local Buriats bought their silver from a relative of Turukai, the powerful Tsetsen Khan, of the Eastern Khalka Mongols, who had his headquarters at Urga, near the sources of the Selenga River. Pokhabov asked Turukai for guides and himself went to Urga. Tsetsen Khan received Pokhabov in a friendly fashion but assured him there were no gold or silver deposits in Mongolia, that these metals came to the Mongols from China. Pokhabov, anxious to get to the sources of the gold and silver, wanted to go to China, but the Khan would not give him guides. Nevertheless, Tsetsen Khan agreed to send an embassy to Moscow.[48]

In 1648 Pokhabov returned to Eniseisk. He had not succeeded in conquering the Transbaikal area, he reported, because the Buriats were numerous, mounted, and lived some distance from the rivers. However, he did bring back rich spoils and prisoners, among them the important local chief, Narei of the Irkut Buriats. As a result of his exploration, Pokhabov prepared a plan for the conquest of all Buriatia by means of a network of forts established in strategic places, and the plan was reported to Moscow.[49]

GALKIN FOUNDS BARGUZIN (1648)

Even before Pokhabov returned, however, measures were already being taken in Eniseisk to organize the Buriat land by establishing forts and collecting iasak regularly. In the summer of 1648 a new expedition to Transbaikalia was sent out under the boyar-son Ivan Galkin, with the usual instructions to impose iasak on new peoples, to describe accurately the places seen, and, most important, to seek veins of gold and silver ore. Going around Lake Baikal from the north, Galkin reached the Barguzin River and there, amidst Buriat settlements, founded the ostrog of Barguzin. This fort became the point of departure for further Russian conquests in Transbaikalia. From its beginning it had a permanent garrison of seventy men, replaced every two years along with its commandant. With the new ostrog as a base, Galkin undertook several expeditions against the Vitim Tungus and the Transbaikal Buriats who lived along the Barguzin and along the lower Selenga and its tributary, the Khilok.[50]

A subordinate of Galkin, who had been sent up the Vitim, discovered that promyshlenniks from the Lena, posing as government agents, had taken hostages from the local Tungus and had collected iasak. He seized this iasak from the promyshlenniks and brought it to Galkin.[51]

In 1650 Vasilii Kolesnikov reappeared in the region, coming from Eniseisk with seventy men to replace Galkin in Barguzin. He spent two years there, maintaining order and continuing explorations. During that time his scouts crossed the Stanovoi Range to the Shilka and brought back important news. They informed Kolesnikov that the route from Barguzin to the Shilka, where the Daurs lived, was not a difficult one. It would be necessary only to establish two ostrogs for the safety of communications, one on Lake Irgen at the head of the Khilok River, and the other on the Shilka at the mouth of its tributary, the Nercha. In order to better link the ostrogs together, the best route lay across Lake Baikal, along the Selenga, and thence to Lake Irgen. In 1652 Kolesnikov left for Eniseisk to report this information.[52]

Kolesnikov was replaced in Barguzin by Ivan Pokhabov. Enroute from Eniseisk, Pokhabov built a zimov'e on an island in the Angara River at the mouth of the Irkut, thereby assuring control over the river route from Eniseisk to Lake Baikal.[53] The ostrog of Irkutsk, founded nearby in 1661 on the right bank of the Angara, later became the capital of Eastern Siberia. On arrival at Barguzin, Pokhabov treated the local Tungus so cruelly that they fled the region. To reimburse the Tsar's treasury for the resultant loss of tribute, he explored the region north of the Vitim, where he imposed iasak on the inhabitants and built the ostrog of Bauntovskii.[54]

In his later years, Pokhabov became ever more notorious. Taking command of Balagansk, on the Angara, in 1657, he treated the local Buriats with particular severity. Among other things, he practiced enforced baptism in order to make slaves of the natives. Only baptized natives could be enslaved, the unbaptized being tributaries of the Tsar. Two or three men or women would be tied to a long post, and, at a signal, cossacks submerged them in water through a hole in the ice.[55] On 5 June 1658 the Buriats submitted a desperate petition to the Tsar complaining of Pokhabov's reign of terror and begging that he be replaced.[56] Later in the month, many of the Buriats, driving their flocks before them, fled into Mongolia.[57] Trying in vain to head off the fugitives,[58] Pokhabov instead provoked a general uprising. Appealing to Eniseisk for reinforcements, he took refuge at Bratsk and was for a time under siege. Finally, at Moscow's order, Iakov Turgenev came to arrest and replace Pokhabov and to bring him to Eniseisk. Enroute to Eniseisk, however, Pokhabov escaped and fled to Ilimsk, which was under the jurisdiction of the voevoda of Iakutsk and where he was able to evade punishment.[59] Subsequently, in 1660 and 1661, expeditions were sent from Balagansk to seek the fugitive Buriats. Although the expeditions had little success, privation in Mongolia eventually forced many of the Buriats to return.[60]

Meanwhile, in 1652 the voevoda of Eniseisk sent an old and experienced officer, Peter Beketov, to Transbaikalia in charge of a hundred men to carry out the program outlined by Kolesnikov. Since 1648 Beketov had been the commandant of Bratsk, where he had made notable efforts to introduce agriculture. He sent a detachment of men along the northern route by way of Verkhne-Angarsk and Barguzin to build a small craft. With the rest of his men he took a southern route around the lake, arriving on the eastern shore in December. Throughout the winter and spring of 1653 he explored the lower course of the Selenga and at its mouth built an ostrog which received the name Ust'-Prorva. In the summer he went by boat up the Selenga and Khilok to Lake Irgen, which he reached in September. There he founded the ostrog of Irgensk.

The second part of Beketov's mission was to build an ostrog at the mouth of the Nercha River, south of the Iablonovyi Range. To accomplish this, he travelled to the Ingoda River and started making rafts for navigating the Shilka. When the rafts were ready, the party went down the Ingoda but were halted by the freezing of the river. Not wishing to lose time, Beketov sent a small band of service men, under the desiatnik Urasov, to the mouth of the Nercha with orders to choose a convenient place and there to build an ostrog. In the winter of 1653–54, Urasov reached the Shilka and on its bank, across from the mouth of the Nercha, began building an ostrog, the future Nerchinsk.

With the coming of spring, Beketov himself arrived at the new ostrog. He and his men were short of supplies, which were hard to replenish because the Tungus-Daur population in the neighbourhood had fled. Hoping to secure food for the winter, Beketov ordered the planting of grain near the ostrog, but some of the men wanted to go down the Shilka and join other Russians on the Amur. Fearing famine, Beketov refused, but when some then left anyway, he felt constrained to follow with the remnants of his force. After the departure of the Russians from Nerchinsk, the Tungus destroyed the deserted ostrog. Beketov remained on the Amur until 1660, when he returned to Eniseisk via Iakutsk and Ilimsk. He brought with him a large quantity of furs, perhaps intended as a redemption payment for his abandonment of Nerchinsk.[61]

After Beketov left Transbaikalia, the voevodas of Eniseisk continued to strengthen the Russian hold over this territory by building new ostrogs. In 1658 the ostrog of Telembinsk was built above the Khilok, and in the same year the ostrog of Nerchinsk was restored. The zimov'e of Udinsk (later the ostrog of Verkhneudinsk, and now Ulan-Ude) was founded in 1665 at the confluence of the Uda and the Selenga, and the ostrog of Selenginsk was founded farther up the Selenga.(The Uda mentioned here, it should be noted, is not to be confused with two other rivers of the same name already mentioned in this account). With the erection of these new fortifications, the Russian domination encompassed more and more of the Tungus, Buriat, and Mongol clans, and many Buriats who had migrated to Mongolia began to return to Transbaikalia and accept Russian overlordship.

SUMMARY

Several parties sent out from Eniseisk in the 1620s brought back information on the Buriats, a Mongol group to the south. The expedition of Peter Beketov (1628) was the first to penetrate the Buriat country, and although good relations were established, the plundering expedition of Khripunov in 1629 and depredations by men of Krasnoiarsk (founded in 1628) aroused the Buriats' hostility. Maksim Perfil'ev pacified them and in 1631 built a fort called Bratsk on the Angara River to guard the Lena–Enisei communications line from the south. Bratsk became a key to control of the region, and a base for further exploration.

During the 1640s, men of Eniseisk advanced along the Angara and the Oka Rivers, men of Krasnoiarsk along the Uda, and men of Iakutsk along the upper Lena. Simultaneously others penetrated into the region to be known as Transbaikalia. Perfil'ev in 1638–40 ascended the Vitim and heard of the Daurs, related to the Manchus, who inhabited the valleys of the upper Vitim, Shilka, and Amur.

In 1643, Kurbat Ivanov, of Iakutsk, ascended the Lena and discovered Lake Baikal. Other expeditions from Eniseisk explored the Transbaikal region. Kolesnikov founded Verkhne-Angarsk in 1646 and made contact with the Mongols, as did Ivan Pokhabov who ascended the Selenga River in the same year. Ivan Galkin founded Barguzin in 1648 on the Barguzin River. Other forts secured the Russian hold on the region.

Peter Beketov, sent out from Eniseisk in 1652, explored the lower course of the Selenga and built an ostrog at the mouth of the Nercha River, the future Nerchinsk, gateway to the Amur River.

Chapter 10

The Seizure and Loss of the Amur

In the late 1630s rumours began to spread among the Russians on the Enisei and the Lena of a great river in eastern Siberia. In 1639 Ivan Moskvitin and his men from Tomsk, the first Russians to reach the Pacific, heard of the Amur and Zeia rivers from the Lamuts. The people who lived along the Amur, they were told, practised agriculture and possessed rich silver deposits.[1] Moskvitin wanted to go there, but the Lamuts refused to act as guides.[2]

The Perfil'ev expedition of 1638–40, from Eniseisk, while on the Vitim and its tributary, the Tsipa, heard of the Daurs on the Shilka and the Amur. To verify these rumours, the voevodas of Eniseisk sent expeditions to the land of the Daurs. These expeditions, as we have seen, resulted in the conquest of Transbaikalia and the discovery of a direct route into the Amur region from the west (the Barguzin–Nercha route discovered by Kolesnikov in 1650). However, it was not to be the service men and promyshlenniks of Eniseisk, but those from Iakutsk, who were to conquer this new territory.

The Lena and its tributaries the Vitim, the Olekma, and the Aldan offered three obvious routes to the Amur. As soon as the voevodas of Iakutsk heard of Perfil'ev's expedition,[3] they sent seventy service men under the command of a pismennyi golova, Enalei Bakhteiarov, along the Vitim. Bakhteiarov had orders to investigate the sources of the Vitim and to secure accurate information about the Daurs and Daurian silver, but failed in this mission.

POIARKOV'S EXPEDITION DOWN THE AMUR TO THE SEA OF OKHOTSK

In June 1643 the voevodas of Iakutsk sent another pismennyi golova, Vasilii Poiarkov, to the Amur, this time by way of the Aldan. Poiarkov was instructed to reach the Zeia and the Shilka, collect iasak, and check the reports of Perfil'ev about the copper and lead ores of the region and about the agriculture of the natives. He was to find out whether the Shilka offered a route to China, and whether ships could travel on it. He was ordered to subdue

the inhabitants of Dauria and the rest of the Amur region and to secure
the new territory for Russia by building a series of forts.[4] Poiarkov left
Iakutsk with 133 men, supplied with a half-pounder cannon, 280 pounds
of gunpowder, 280 pounds of lead, and ample numbers of hand arms.
Counting on the grain of the Amur natives, he took provisions for a one-way
trip only.

The expedition spent a month ascending the Aldan, then its right tributary
the Uchur, and then the Gonam. Progress was particularly difficult along
the narrow, boisterous Gonam; in all, they overcame sixty-four rapids,
losing almost all their lead at one of them. In five weeks they traversed
only about half of the river. At the approach of winter, Poiarkov stopped
to build a zimov'e at the mouth of the Niuiamka River and left forty-nine
men there with instructions to follow him in the spring. With the rest
of the party, he crossed the Stanovoi Range with sledges, found the River
Brianta, and descended that river to the Zeia, a tributary of the Amur.[5]

Along the Zeia, the Russians saw no native settlements until they reached
the Umlekan River, a tributary, where they came upon a Daur village.
They built a zimov'e nearby and stopped there. The Daurs met Poiarkov
in a friendly fashion, gave him iasak and hostages, and provided the first
more or less reliable information he had had about the population along
the lower course of the Zeia and along the Amur. In spite of his insistent
demands, however, they denied knowledge of any deposits of silver, copper,
or lead ore, declaring that such ores were not to be found anywhere along
the Zeia, Shilka, Amur, or Sungari. They admitted having articles made
of metal, from the Mongols and Chinese in exchange for furs. They told
of a Daur town called Moldikichid at the mouth of the River Selemdzha,
where abundant foodstuffs could be obtained, and of a Prince Lavkai on
the Amur, who ruled over three hundred men, and of three Mongol chiefs
on the Shilka, who ruled over five hundred men.

As his food supplies were running low, Poiarkov sent a piatidesiatnik,
Iurii Petrov, with a detachment of seventy service men to Moldikichid.
He told Petrov to lure and seize the local chiefs as hostages, then escape
toward the forest, where he and his men were to fortify themselves and
await developments. Petrov, however, did not have to follow the recommended
precautions: upon his approach to Moldikchid, the chiefs met him with
honours and gifts a half mile from the town. They voluntarily offered
themselves as hostages and gave the Russians ample foodstuffs (forty large
baskets of oats or groats and ten head of cattle), but would not allow
them to enter the town. Instead they installed their visitors in three large
yurts outside the town.

Still not satisfied, however, Petrov and his men, after a parade with
colours to impress the chiefs, demanded admission to the town. The Daurs

answered that they were afraid it might lead to trouble, because their people did not know the Russians. Petrov then threatened the hostages with torture if they did not order their people to submit. Hearing of this, the men of the town came out, some on horseback, and advanced against the Russians. In the battle which followed, the Daurs captured ten Russians and drove the remainder to the shelter of their yurts, to which the Daurs laid siege. After a three-day siege, Petrov and such men as remained alive fled secretly from the yurts and returned to Poiarkov at the Umlekan zimov'e.[6]

Relations between the Russians and the Daurs now changed sharply for the worse. The Daurs realized what a dangerous adversary they had and took up arms. Poiarkov's position became critical. His supplies were at an end, and after the return of Petrov and his men there were even more mouths to feed. The hostages escaped, the natives on the Umlekan ceased to supply food, and the Russians spent the winter of 1643–44 eating pine bark and roots. Forty men died of starvation, some committed suicide, and others even resorted to cannibalism to survive. The situation improved only with the coming of spring, when the detachment left on the Gonam arrived with supplies.

Having gathered all his men, Poiarkov went down the Zeia, through mountain gorges and grassy plains. At its mouth the Zeia is over a half mile in width, and on this broad course the party entered the even greater Amur.

The mighty river of the east, the Amur, is comparable in length and volume to the north-flowing Ob, Enisei and Lena. Formed by the confluence of the Shilka and the Argun, the Amur is from that point 1,767 miles long, but followed to its most distant source it is over 2,700 miles long, one of the greatest rivers in the world. It carries an immense quantity of water, and varies greatly in depth and breadth. In the mountains it rushes through deep canyons. In the plain it is slower and often branches out, forming islands which are covered with forest. Five hundred miles from its mouth the river is one and a half miles wide, but at its mouth it is ten miles wide. The great amount of silt it carries in suspension gives the river a brownish tinge, which has led the Chinese to call it the Hei-lun-kiang (Black Dragon River) or Hei-Ho (Black Water).

Starting down the Amur Poiarkov and his men entered the land of the Duchers, and for three weeks saw Ducher villages all along the banks. The tribesmen at first met the Russians peacefully and paid iasak, but then became hostile. Near the mouth of the Sungari, the Duchers attacked a Russian scouting party of twenty-five, killed all but two. Poiarkov continued his journey and in six days reached the mouth of another of the Amur's great affluents, the Ussuri. There he and his men entered the land of the Ol'chi and Gol'dy, or, as Poiarkov called them, the 'Natki'. For two weeks they travelled among these tribes and then entered the territory of the Giliaks, whose settlements extended to the seacoast. Like the 'Natki', the Giliaks were at that time independent and did not pay tribute to anyone. After a month of river navigation, the Russians reached the mouth of the Amur, ten miles in width, a constantly shifting mass of sandbars. There they spent the winter of 1644–45, managing 'by the grace of God and the good fortune of the Sovereign' to seize hostages from the Giliaks and to collect foodstuffs and iasak.

Poiarkov had only sixty men left and dared not try a return journey back up the river through the territory of the now thoroughly hostile natives of the Amur. Instead, in the spring of 1645 he and his detachment sailed their small craft into the stormy Sea of Okhotsk. After a dangerous trip of three months they finally reached the mouth of the Ul'ia and the zimov'e built a few years before by Moskvitin's party. There, with some of Moskvitin's men, they spent the winter of 1645–46. During the winter, Poiarkov collected iasak from the local Lamuts. In the spring of 1646, Poiarkov left twenty service men at the zimov'e (Ust'-Ul'insk) and led the rest, with sledges, across the Dzhugdzhur Range. Reaching the sources of the Maia after two weeks, the party built boats and travelled downstream six days to the Aldan, then four days to the Lena, and finally six more days up the Lena to Iakutsk, where they arrived on 12 June 1646.[7]

Although he had lost more than half of the 133 men who had started with him, Poiarkov thus completed one of the most remarkable expeditions of his time. The party had covered an enormous distance, in the form of a wide arc, through previously unexplored country. Poiarkov was the first European to travel on the Amur and the first to investigate the region seriously. He placed on the maps all the rivers he and his men had sailed upon and wrote down everything they had seen or heard on their way. As a result of his trip, the Russians also learned about the Okhotsk coast from the Amur to the Ul'ia, information supplemented in the following year, 1647, when Stadukhin investigated this coast from the Okhota River to Penzhinsk Bay.[8]

Upon his return, Poiarkov submitted an elaborate plan to the local voevodas for the conquest of the Amur region. In this plan, he suggested that a force of three hundred men or more be sent 'to collect iasak and bring new lands under the hand of the Tsar'. These men would build three ostrogs, each garrisoned by fifty men, to dominate the Daurs and Duchers, leaving the 150 men to be sent along the Amur and its tributaries to conquer the other tribes. 'That will bring great profit for the Sovereign,' wrote Poiarkov, 'because these lands have a large population, are fertile, bring in large crops, and are abundant in sables and other animals; there are plenty of fish in the rivers, and the warriors of the Sovereign will not go hungry in this land.'[9]

ALTERNATIVE ROUTES TO THE AMUR: THE VITIM, THE ALDAN, AND THE OLEKMA

Looking into the project, the voevodas had first of all to decide what route to choose for any new expedition from the Lena to the Amur. Two routes had already been tried. Perfil'ev had nearly reached the Amur by way of the Vitim River, while Poiarkov had used the Aldan. The Vitim route was inconvenient because the upper course of the river had a great many rapids and from there the route led into the mountainous and hardly passable Transbaikal region to the sources of the Shilka. The Aldan route was longer, had an even greater number of rapids, and in addition, there was the dangerous crossing of the Stanovoi Range. However, a third route, by way of the Olekma, was straighter and more convenient, and led almost to the confluence of the Shilka and the Argun—the beginning of the Amur.

The Iakutsk voevodas learned about the Olekma route from the promyshlennik Grigorii Vizhevtsov, who ascended the Olekma as far as its tributary, the Tungir (or Tugir). Vizhevtsov, who reported simultaneously with Poiarkov, told how it was possible to cross the Iablonovyi Range with loaded reindeer from the Niukzha, a tributary of the Tungir, to the Shilka or the Amur in nine or ten days. He reported hearing from the Tungus that beyond the mountains there was a large Daur tribe, headed by a princeling named Levkai (that is, Lavkai, of whom Perfil'ev and Poiarkov had heard already) and his two brothers. According to the Tungus, Levkai was very prosperous, with plenty of grain, wine, and cattle. The women of Levkai's tribe wore silver bracelets, and both sexes wore dress embroidered with strips of silk. Other promyshlenniks brought similar tales.[10]

Thus, toward the end of the 1640s, the voevodas of Iakutsk had learned of three routes to the Amur region and were in a position to judge the merits and drawbacks of each. The Olekma route seemed to have many advantages over the others and was therefore chosen for an expedition led by a famous promyshlennik and entrepreneur, Erofei Pavlovich Khabarov.

KHABAROV'S FIRST EXPEDITION TO THE AMUR (1649–1650)

Khabarov was born at Ustiug, and in his youth operated a saltworks at Sol'vychegodsk. About 1636 he moved to Siberia and was one of the first to start farming on the Enisei. Successful, he became a *slobodchik,* a local administrator who found places well-fitted for agriculture, sent to Russia

159

for peasants, and supplied equipment in exchange for future rent. He was soon attracted by the profits to be had in the sable trade and started an extensive trade in furs in the new area, employing his own hunters. As the Lena region opened up, this energetic and enterprising man began farming on the Ilim and on the upper Lena and engaged in the transport business, hiring out horses and boats and importing necessities for sale in the region. He also started a saltworks at Ust'-Kut, but the government took this from him. Living and working near the portage to the Ilim, the main line of communications from the Lena to the west, Khabarov became well informed about the wealth of the Amur, which attracted his interest as a new place in which to invest his capital, and learned of the attempts of both privately operating promyshlenniks and the voevodas of Eniseisk and Iakutsk to penetrate the region.[11]

In March 1649 Khabarov submitted a petition to the voevoda of Iakutsk, Dmitrii Frantsbekov, asking permission to organize a private expedition into the new Amur land without any government support in either money or grain. He emphasized the advantages to the state of having the natives of the Amur subjugated to Russia. The voevoda, attracted by the idea of extending his administrative area, gave Khabarov his permission and personal backing. He instructed Khabarov to gather up to 150 volunteers—promyshlenniks and service men—and to proceed to the Shilka, 'against the men who disobey the Sovereign and do not submit to him . . . against Lavkai and Batoga and also against their villagers (*ulus* men) and other independent (*zakhrebetnye*, literally, transmontane) men who do not pay iasak—all this for the collection of the Sovereign's iasak and for the subjugation of new lands'.[12]

After gathering about half of the volunteers and all the necessary military supplies and provisions, Khabarov set out by boat up the Olekma in the spring of 1649, collecting more men along the way. The party advanced very slowly and reached the Tungir only by the beginning of autumn. They went up the Tungir as far as the mouth of the Niukzha and remained there part of the winter. Toward the end of January 1650, they put their supplies on sledges and crossed the Iablonovyi Range. Then, by way of either the Urka or the Amazar, they reached the Amur.

Soon, Khabarov and his party came to the Daur village which belonged to the princeling Lavkai, of whom both Poiarkov and Vizhevtsov had heard. The village was empty. Puzzled, the Russians continued down the river and found first one and then another deserted village. Near the latter, however, they encountered five horsemen, one of them Prince Lavkai himself. From the conversation that followed Khabarov found out that shortly before his appearance on the Amur a promyshlennik, Ivan Kvashnin, had been there to trade in sables and to collect unauthorized iasak. Knowing about the proposed expedition of Khabarov, and not wishing to cede him all the profits of the sable trade on the Amur, Kvashnin told Lavkai and the other Daur princelings that a detachment of five hundred men under Khabarov was coming and that it would be followed by an even larger force. Kvashnin predicted that these Russians would rob and murder the Daurs and capture their wives and children. The story so frightened Lavkai and his fellows that they deserted their villages and fled down the river. Khabarov tried to reassure Lavkai and his companions by stating that he and his men had come to trade and had brought presents for the local rulers. Lavkai, however, remained dubious. 'Why do you try to deceive us?' he asked, 'We know all about you cossacks.' When Khabarov proposed that he recognize the authority of the Tsar, Lavkai turned without giving a positive answer and galloped away.

Proceeding down the Amur, Khabarov found two more deserted villages. Feeling it useless now to journey farther, he then returned to the first village, which belonged to Lavkai, and prepared to stop for a while. Luck was with him, for, buried in the ground, his men found supplies of barley, oats, wheat, buckwheat, hemp seeds and peas. Khabarov calculated that there was enough to last the party for two years, perhaps three.

While at Lavkai's village, Khabarov learned more about the situation on the Amur. He was told, evidently by captives, that the Daur princelings paid tribute to the Emperor of China, and that war with the Daurs would therefore lead to a struggle with China. It was clear that with the insignificant forces at his disposal, Khabarov could not think of risking such a conflict. Leaving a garrison of fifty men in the village, he returned to Iakutsk to make a personal report, arriving on 26 May 1650.

Reporting on the expedition, Khabarov declared that if the Muscovite government wanted to take possession of the new region, and thereby risk involvement with China, it would be necessary to send at least six thousand service men to the Amur. He insisted that the conquest of the Amur was a matter of vital interest to the state. The region was more abundant and beautiful than any place in Siberia, and it looked as if it would be even more profitable than the Lena region. It would be possible to start farming there and supply Iakutsk with grain, making it unnecessary to import grain all the way from Russia. The transport of grain from the Amur to the Lena region would be very easy, because Lavkai's village was only sixty-six miles from the portage of the Tungir, and the trip between the portage and Iakutsk could be made in only two weeks. The picture seemed very attractive to the voevoda of Iakutsk, who sent a report to Moscow.[13]

161

With the permission of the voevoda, Khabarov began to gather volunteers for another expedition to the Amur. Within a short time he had recruited 117 promyshlenniks; the voevoda contributed twenty-one service men, three cannon, arms, and supplies. As before, Khabarov was ordered to conquer the Amur natives, and this time was also directed to search for silver ore. He was given wide powers to judge and punish his men, and was required to refer only the most serious cases to the voevoda of Iakutsk.

In the fall of 1650 Khabarov and his detachment started for the Amur, joined along the way by other volunteers. But this time, when they reached the Amur they found the Daur villages occupied. The Daurs had decided to resist and not allow the Russians to come into their land. The garrison left by Khabarov in Lavkai's village had already repulsed several attacks. Khabarov went on down the river. Not far from the large town of the princeling Albaza, the Daurs gave battle, but soon fled.

With winter approaching and the Daurs hostile, it was dangerous to continue, so Khabarov fortified Albaza's town, thereafter called Albazin, and prepared to winter there. However, as a precautionary measure against possible attack, on 24 November he sent out two scouting parties, one down and one up the river. The latter group went as far as the confluence (*strelka*) of the Shilka and Argun where they built the ostrozhek of Ust'-Strelochnyi, thus securing the upper part of the Amur. The party brought a number of hostages back to Albazin. The men were drowned and the women, children, and goods were divided among Khabarov and his followers. Now confident, Khabarov wrote the voevoda of Iakutsk that 'the Daur men can never drive [*me*] out of this place . . .' and boasted of having enough grain for five years.

Khabarov further reported that it would only be necessary to send men, equipment, and supplies for him to attack the Chinese Emperor, in whose possession there was a mountain of silver, and many pearls and precious stones. He indicated that the struggle might not be easy, because the Emperor had wooden and stone fortresses and artillery, but that it was necessary to acquire this wealthy region. An army would be needed, and it would be necessary to colonize the Amur. 'If it be the Sovereign's will, he should send here exiles or any other men to start agriculture. There are many arable lands on the Amur, grassy meadows, places abundant in fish, and many other attractions.'[14] Thus, Khabarov understood that the Amur region could not be held by military force alone, but must be colonized as well.

The voevoda of Iakutsk sent Khabarov's proposals to Moscow, where they were read with interest. Russia was then in a period of growing strength and prosperity. The reports of the Amur were attractive, and the prize evidently seemed worth the risk of involvement with a major power. On the basis of the information at hand, the Moscow officials decided to send to the Amur an army of three thousand under the command of the voevoda Prince Lobanov-Rostovskii. The voevodas of Verkhotur'e and Tobolsk were told to prepare boats for the transportation of the army. During 1652 and 1653, with the aid of carpenters to be sent from the coastal towns of northern Russia, they were to build up to eighty boats and to prepare timber for sixty more.[15]

Meanwhile, with the coming of spring, in 1651, Khabarov and his men built boats at Albazin and on 2 June started down the Amur. The going was difficult. As Khabarov later reported, the population resisted obstinately everywhere. After some fighting he took several villages and devastated many unfortified settlements. Some of the natives submitted and agreed to pay iasak, but others fled into the interior of the country. In this manner, Khabarov conquered both banks of the river as far as the mouth of the Sungari. Below this tributary were many villages of the Duchers, but even this region was completely devastated within a week's time. The Russians seized and destroyed large settlements and cut down the natives 'like trees'.

Eight days' travel below the mouth of the Sungari, Khabarov passed the mouth of the Ussuri and entered the region inhabited by the Ol'chi and the Gol'dy, both of whom he called the 'Achany' in his reports. For two days he and his men passed through their possessions. Large villages with a hundred or more houses were situated along the banks. Whenever the Russians tried to land, they met such strong resistance that they had to sail farther. Under such circumstances Khabarov feared to proceed. Toward the end of September, his men stormed an Ol'chi village and built an ostrog, Achansk, where they spent the winter of 1651–52. The Duchers and the Ol'chi joined forces and attacked the ostrog, but they were repelled with great losses. The Ol'chi then began to pay iasak and to supply the Russians with provisions, but harsh and violent treatment soon forced them to turn to the Manchus with complaints and requests for assistance.[16]

During Poiarkov's expedition, the Manchus had been engaged in conquering China; they could give no attention to frontier disturbances. But as soon as the Empire began to be consolidated, the Court hastened to cope with the situation. Under the Shun Chih Emperor (1644–61) the Chinese Court in 1652 ordered Hai Se, the special commissioner stationed at Ninguta, to attack the Russians.[17] At dawn on 24 March, Hai Se suddenly appeared before Achansk with an army of two thousand men and some artillery and started a bombardment. The cossacks were taken unawares and rushed to the walls wearing only shirts. At first they were panic-stricken, but they soon recovered. In an all-day battle, the Chinese destroyed part

163

of the walls, but were handicapped by orders to take the Russians alive. The cossacks learned of this and fought all the harder. Expecting the attack where the wall was breached, they placed their large brass cannon there. When the Chinese approached the opening the Russians made a successful shot, followed by rapid gunfire, killing many of the enemy and throwing the rest back in confusion. They then made a sortie and after hand-to-hand fighting finally routed the Chinese, capturing two iron cannon, seventeen 'rapid firing' matchlocks with three or four barrels, 830 horses, large supplies of provisions, and one prisoner. Khabarov lost only ten killed and eighty wounded.

The fact that this first encounter between the Manchus and the Russians had ended in victory for the latter had a tremendous moral effect on both the Russians and the natives of the Amur region. The natives saw that in spite of small numbers the newcomers represented a dangerous force which the Manchus, in spite of superior numbers and arms, could not overcome.[18]

Khabarov nevertheless realized that once China had intervened in Amur affairs she wold not be satisfied with sending a comparatively small army but would defend the natives with more decisive measures. To resist the Manchus with a small force of tired men was impossible, and in April 1652 he abandoned Achansk and went up the Amur to await aid from Iakutsk. Already, as he sailed past the mouth of the Sungari River, he saw a large gathering of Manchus which he estimated at about six thousand men.

Passing the mouth of the Little Khingan River, Khabarov met a detachment of more than a hundred men under one Tret'iak Ermolaev Chechigin, sent to his aid by the voevoda of Iakutsk with a cannon, gunpowder, lead, and money. This party, coming by way of the now familiar Olekma–Tungir route, had arrived on the Amur in the autumn of 1651 and had gone down the river looking for Khabarov. Not finding him, the party had wintered, and in early May 1652 Chechigin had sent a subordinate, Ivan Antonov Nagiba, with twenty-six men on ahead to continue the search. Nothing had been heard from these men, and Khabarov and his party had not seen them.[19]

Refusing the request of Chechigin's men to go down the Amur to hunt for their comrades, Khabarov instead added their party to his own and continued to move up the river, collecting iasak from the Duchers as he went along. From Chechigin, Khabarov heard that the Emperor of China was gathering an army of forty thousand to expel the Russians from the Amur. Some signs of threatening Manchu activity began to be seen. On 1 August the combined detachment of Khabarov and Chechigin reached the mouth of the Zeia, where Khabarov decided that they should stop and build a strong ostrog (the present day Blagoveshchensk). The decision caused a rebellion. Dissatisfied with Khabarov, about a hundred men deserted, dragged along thirty more by force, seized three boats 'with the treasury', two cannon, and other supplies, and sailed down the Amur. En route, they treated the natives so badly that even former friends accused the Russians of treachery, referring to 'your men who went down the river and plundered our land'.

After this affair, which cost him a third of his force, Khabarov had only 212 men left. He could not count on successful resistance in case of a Manchu attack, and therefore, after staying at the mouth of the Zeia for approximately a month and a half, collecting iasak from the local Daurs and Duchers, he led his men up the Amur to the mouth of the Kumara, where he founded the ostrog of Kumarsk (or Kamarsk) on what is now the Chinese side of the river. From there Khabarov wrote the voevodas of Irkutsk about the mutiny, stating that with such insignificant forces he could not conquer the region ('this land is populous and the people fight with firearms'), but that he would not leave without orders from the Sovereign.[20]

A RUSH TO THE AMUR

Thus far the results of Russian operations on the Amur had been indecisive, but along the Lena and its tributaries wild rumours spread of the wealth of the newly discovered territory. These rumours were further inflated when some of the returning cossacks paraded around in silk, spent money lavishly, and assured everyone that this was quite the ordinary thing on the Amur. Excited by this, the farmers, promyshlenniks, and service men left their homes, plundered the stores of the Tsar and of merchants of money, food, gunpowder, lead, guns and everything else which might be needed, and rushed to the Amur.[21] Everyone wanted a share in the wealth. In the words of the eighteenth-century historian of the conquest of Siberia, Fischer, 'Neither home, wife, children, nor the laws of God or man could turn the people from their intention to change their habitation for the far-famed Dauria.'[22] As early as August 1653, the voevodas of Iakutsk wrote to Moscow that the region was becoming depopulated: 'Free immigrants, who settled voluntarily on the Lena to till the land, have gone without permission to the Amur,' and 'All the remaining service men, promyshlenniks and peasants . . . will run away.'

The colonists arrived on the Amur in large parties, sometimes several hundred men at a time, and began to live off the new region, oppressing and plundering the natives. This confused situation continued until 1655, when the particularly severe ravages of a group of three hundred men

165

under the brothers Sorokin caused the Government to order the establishment of a barrier station on the Olekma to prevent further flight to the Amur.[23]

KHABAROV OUSTED BY ZINOV'EV

The importance of acquiring the Amur was nevertheless well understood both by the voevodas of Iakutsk and by the Muscovite Government. In March 1652 Moscow dispatched the nobleman, Dmitrii Ivanovich Zinov'ev, to aid Khabarov. He was supposed to investigate the state of affairs along the river, and make preparations for the forthcoming grand expedition under Prince Lobanov-Rostovskii. Zinov'ev took along a detachment of 150 service men, a large quantity of gunpowder and lead, and back pay and 320 gold medals for Khabarov's men.

Zinov'ev reached the Amur in the spring of 1653, but Khabarov was at that time on the march, and the two did not meet until the fall, at the mouth of the Zeia. By that time, the Muscovite emissary had apparently learned enough of Khabarov's activities, for he announced to Khabarov that he had an order from the Tsar authorizing him to supersede Khabarov and to inspect the whole Daurian land. When Khabarov demanded to see the order, Zinov'ev seized him by the beard and beat him. He questioned the men, and made their accusations the basis for a formal complaint. Khabarov was accused of sending false reports to Iakutsk, of persecuting and enslaving his subordinates and the natives, of being devoted to his own affairs instead of to the business of the Sovereign, of appropriating the best furs for himself instead of for the Tsar's treasury, and of laying waste the entire region.

Zinov'ev from the very first began to carry out measures aimed at the establishment of order and at making the Russian occupation of the region permanent. Thus, he demanded that Khabarov's men build three new ostrogs, one at the site of the small one already erected at Albazin, and two others at the mouths of the Zeia and the Urka, and to start the cultivation of land to provide food for the army of Lobanov-Rostovskii.

The demands were reasonable, but Zinov'ev erred in the manner with which he tried to carry out his policies. While Khabarov was informal in his relations with his men and consulted them in all important affairs, Zinov'ev was pompous and arrogant and decided everything himself, demanding at the same time absolute obedience. This behaviour caused such discontent among the men that Zinov'ev soon felt it prudent to leave for Russia, taking Khabarov along.[24]

Arriving in Moscow early in 1654, Zinov'ev and Khabarov were able to give the government a first-hand view of affairs on the Amur, especially of the efforts of the Chinese. Khabarov was tried in the Siberian Prikaz. Accounts of the trial are confused, but it seems to have featured a cross-fire of accusations between Khabarov and Zinov'ev. In the end, Khabarov was exonerated, given the rank of boyar-son in reward for his services, and appointed prikaschik in the ostrog of Ilimsk, where he remained to the end of his days.

Even before Zinov'ev and Khabarov had left the Amur, however, attitudes in Moscow toward the region had changed. Earlier in 1653, pressures elsewhere had caused cancellation of the ambitious expedition of Lobanov-Rostovskii. The men and resources allocated for the expedition were diverted to areas adjoining Poland, and Lobanov-Rostovskii himself was sent on a mission to Persia.[25] Instead of an army, Moscow in 1653 sent a minor official, Fedor Isakovich Baikov, to China to seek trade and learn whatever he could about the country. Sending a Bukharan of Tobolsk, Seitkul Ablin, ahead to announce his coming Baikov himself reached Peking in 1656. He obtained valuable information about China, but failed in his mission because of his refusal to kow-tow before the Emperor. He returned to Russia in 1658.[26]

STEPANOV CLASHES WITH THE CHINESE (1655–1658)

Meanwhile, Zinov'ev had left affairs on the Amur in charge of the prikashchik Onufrii Stepanov, enjoining him to build the three ostrogs already planned, and to prepare the ground for growing 5,000 to 6,000 puds (180,000 to 216,000 pounds) of grain for the supposedly forthcoming expedition of the grand Muscovite army. But there was not even enough grain at the mouth of the Zeia to feed the 320 men left under Stepanov's command. He and his men moved down the Amur to the mouth of the Sungari, where they extorted grain from the Duchers, took hostages and collected iasak, and spent the winter still farther down the river. In the spring of 1654, they started the return trip. At the mouth of the Sungari, Stepanov encountered a newly-arrived party of fifty service men, who joined his group, giving him a total of 370 men.

After consulting his men, Stepanov sailed up the Sungari, subjugating the Duchers along the way. On 6 June, according to his later report, his party met

a large force of the Bogdoi's [*Manchu Emperor's*] soldiers armed with firearms, cannon, and muskets. We had a battle with them in which the Bogdoi's men fought on land on horses and on the river in boats. They bombarded our boats with cannon [*but*] we also used cannon.

167

. . . We succeeded in forcing the Bogdoi's men to leave their boats and retreat to land, [*but*] there they fought from fortified positions and many service men were wounded in the battle. . . . From the captured Duchers we learned that the Bogdoi's army had been sent hurriedly from three territories and included men of the Bogdoi, the Daurs, and the Duchers. . . . They fought as trained men, in companies, under white, black, red, and yellow colours, and wore uniforms corresponding to the particular colour of the standard under which they fought. . . . We could not overcome the Bogdoi's men because of our shortage of gunpowder and lead [*so we retreated*]. They prevented us from gathering grain on the Sungari river, so after consulting the whole detachment we sailed back up the Amur.

During the same year, 1654, three parties of service men, some sixty-five in all, under the well-known boyar-son Peter Beketov, arrived on rafts from the Baikal region. Beketov had been sent to Dauria from Eniseisk two years before, and had had his share of misadventures. To continue Stepanov's account:

They came here because of a lack of food, and privations, and I, Onufrii, at their request, accepted them. . . . On one expedition we captured a Ducher woman . . . who told us that five envoys [*including the above mentioned Chechigin*] whom Dmitrii Zinov'ev had sent to the Bogdoi Tsar . . . had been killed by the Duchers, who divided their property among themselves and did not notify the Bogdoi Tsar about it. . . . [*Stepanov later went to the tribe which had killed the envoys and discovered kettles, axes, and other remnants of their possessions.*] We cannot built the ostrogs [*which Zinov'ev had ordered built*] because of intense hostilities with the men of the Bogdoi. As for grain, there is very little of it on the Amur because the Bogdoi Tsar has forbidden the natives to sow grain and has ordered them to move into his territory. . . . From the captured natives we heard that the men of the Bogdoi have built a fortress at the mouth of the Sungari to prevent our entering the river where grain is abundant. . . . A captive . . . said that the Bogdoi's army has been sent to the mouth of the Sungari to remain there for three years . . . and they have been ordered to fight us. At the present there are about 3,000 men there and the Bogdoi intends to send 2,000 more, not counting Ducher and Daur men . . .[27]

Stepanov and Beketov spent the winter of 1654–55 in the ostrog of Kumarsk, which was strongly fortified in anticipation of a Manchu attack. As described by Stepanov in a report to the voevoda of Iakutsk, the ostrog consisted of a timber stockade on top of an earthern wall with towers or bulwarks at the corners of the stockade. The fort was surrounded by a moat seven feet deep and fourteen feet wide, which the cossacks had to dig in frozen ground. Beyond the moat there was a palisade of wood, and beyond this palisade the men dug pits in the ground at the bottom of which they placed iron stakes. The pits were then covered lightly so that during an attack the besiegers would fall into them and be transfixed by the stakes. The walls of the fort had upper and lower embrasures, and inside they were strengthened with earth. Water from a well was piped to the four corners of the fort to be used in case the fort was set on fire from outside. On top of the walls were iron baskets filled with resin, to be lit in case of a night attack. Against the ladders and shields of the besiegers the Russians had long poles similar to those used in propelling boats, which were hung on the walls of the fort for use in pushing the ladders of the enemy away from the walls. A high platform was built within the fort mounted with guns which could be turned in any direction.

In March 1655 a Manchu army appeared under the walls of the ostrog, putting these elaborate preparations to the test. About this attack, Stepanov reported:

The Bogdoi's army came on 13 March and besieged us in the ostrog. . . . They intercepted 20 service men and Amur volunteer cossacks and killed them in their camp. . . . This army of the Bogdoi arrived with firearms of all sorts, cannon and muskets. They had standards of various colours and the army was organized into companies. . . . At a distance of between 1,700 and 1,800 feet from the ostrog, there was a hill 300 feet high. The Bogdoi's men put their large cannon on this hill and bombarded the ostrog . . . other Bogdoi men approached the ostrog to within a distance of about 500 feet and opened fire from cannon and they also shot incendiary arrows. . . . On 24 March the Bogdoi's men stormed the ostrog from all four sides. . . . They had large wooden shields covered with leather on wheels, and also ladders equipped with wheels on one end and grappling hooks on the other end. They brought fire-wood, resin, and straw on two-wheeled carts to set the ostrog on fire, and they had all kinds of machinery for the siege. . . . By the grace of the Lord and the luck of the Sovereign we, his service men, answered the fire by shooting cannon and muskets from the upper and lower embrasures and from the towers . . . and killed many of the Bogdoi's men. . . . Then the service men made a sortie and captured two iron cannon, gunpowder, cannon balls, other assault equipment and some wounded men.

I questioned the captives and they said that this army was sent by the Bogdoi Tsar . . . and among them were people from various territories: the Bogdoi's men, Munguts, Nikans, Duchers, Daurs, and others subject to the Bogdoi; they had 15 cannon and an abundance of small firearms. This army came at the request of the Daur princes . . . to defend them, so they would not have to pay tribute to the Sovereign nor obey him. . . . Altogether this army numbered up to 10,000 men.

The struggle continued for more than two weeks, but in the end, in spite of their numerical superiority (perhaps exaggerated in Russian accounts) and elaborate preparations, the Manchus lost heart, perhaps because of a lack of food, and on 4 April retired.[28]

But not even this victory improved Stepanov's position. After the siege, Stepanov wrote, he had neither provisions nor military supplies left, and with his men on the verge of starvation he therefore prepared to abandon Kumarsk and sail down the Amur to seek some point where they could continue their service to the Sovereign and at the same time feed themselves. The prikashchik pointed out that the position of the Russians on the Amur was becoming exceedingly difficult and precarious. The Daurs and Duchers, exasperated by the perpetual plundering and violence of the Russians, refused to submit. Large, well-armed Manchu detachments gave Stepanov and his men no chance to settle anywhere. The party lived on the move, seizing grain and fish from the natives, and gathering crops from the fields. Thus, the military operations of the Russians on the Amur were reduced to piratical raids on the ruined local population.[29]

Revisiting the Duchers of the Sungari in the summer of the same year, Stepanov seized enough grain to last for twelve months, but when he appeared there the next year, 1656, he found the lower course of the Sungari deserted. By order of the Chinese Government, the local Duchers had moved toward the sources of the river, where it would be impossible to reach them. Stepanov knew now that the Manchus wanted to starve the Russians out. There was no more grain in the Amur valley, where recently native agriculture had flourished. He and his men tried to raise grain themselves, but they were poor farmers, and the military situation on the Amur was in any case unfavourable for this peaceful occupation. A number of setbacks occurred, including the loss of thirty-one men, killed by the Giliaks, and there was more and more insubordination within Stepanov's detachment. In vain Stepanov tried to get assistance—men, equipment, and food—from the voevodas of Iakutsk. He wanted to leave the Amur altogether, but not having permission to do so, was forced to remain in the now desolate region.[30]

Meanwhile, the Muscovite Government had learned of the precarious condition of the Russians on the Amur and sought to improve matters by more immediate direction. Because the voevodas of Iakutsk and Eniseisk were too far away, it was decided to organize an independent voevodship in the Amur. To this end, at about the beginning of 1655, the voevoda of Eniseisk, Afanasii Pashkov, was ordered there with three hundred service men. Arriving on the Amur in 1658, the new voevoda first of all restored the ostrog of Nerchinsk and set up his residence there. From Nerchinsk he sent a messenger to Stepanov informing him of the administrative changes and demanding his subordination.[31]

But Stepanov never received the message. In the spring of 1658, still short of supplies and provisions, he led five hundred men down the Amur to get food. Below the mouth of the Sungari, he met a Manchu fleet of forty-five barges armed with cannon. At the sight of this fleet, 180 of his men deserted. The Manchus surrounded the remainder of the party and killed or captured 270. One of the slain was Stepanov himself. Only forty-seven escaped; some of them bore the news to Pashkov at Nerchinsk.[32]

THE AMUR A NO MAN'S LAND (1658–1672)

When the voevoda reported this crushing defeat to Moscow, the government put aside any remaining plans it might have had for an early conquest of the Amur and narrowed its aims. For the time being it was decided to establish a strong hold on Transbaikalia and to confine interference in affairs on the Amur to Nerchinsk. The Amur valley became a no man's land.

Nevertheless, for the next fifteen years after the destruction of Stepanov and his detachment, individual Russians continued to struggle with the Manchus for possession of the region. From time to time there appeared small groups of service men and promyshlenniks who restored the old ostrogs or built new ones. In 1665, for example, Nikifor Chernigovskii, a Pole in the Russian service who had killed the voevoda of Ilimsk, came to the Amur with a band of eighty-four mutineers, deserters, and outlaws. He restored Albazin, which became known as the 'outlaw ostrog', and built other ostrogs along the Zeia and its tributaries, founding a sort of cossack republic. His men established control over the middle Amur but, fearing the Chinese, pretended to recognize the control of the voevodas of Nerchinsk. In 1669 they began to send iasak to Nerchinsk.[33] For the Government, this unofficial extension of Russian power served a purpose. Instead of continuing in jeopardy for murder, mutiny, and desertion, Chernigovskii and his followers found themselves forgiven, and Chernigovskii received a reward of two thousand rubles.[34]

RUSSIA RETURNS TO THE AMUR

The Muscovite Government now began a cautious attempt to restore the conquests of Khabarov. In 1672 it formally established its protectorate over Albazin and established a number of peasant families there. From 1674, the voevodas of Nerchinsk began sending their officers to Albazin as commandants.[35]

Besides the Russian presence on the Amur, another issue in Russo-Chinese relations arose in the defection of Gantimur, a Tungus chief who had originally lived on the Nonni River in Manchuria and had paid an annual tribute to the Chinese in sables, receiving in return gifts of gold and silver.[36] Brought by Khabarov 'under the hand of the Great Sovereign' in 1651,[37] Gantimur nevertheless managed for some years to hold double allegiance. In 1655 he took part in the Chinese attack on Kumarsk and, in 1658, after Pashkov founded Nerchinsk, migrated to the right bank of the Argun River in order to escape submission to the Russians. In 1667, however, when the Chinese asked him to take part in another attack on Kumarsk (probably then held by outlaws), he left the Chinese and set out for his old grounds on the Nercha.[38]

As an important person, whose defection would influence other Tungus-Manchu tribes and weaken the Chinese claim to the entire region, Gantimur was pursued by the Chinese but escaped and asked permission of the Russian authorities to become a Russian subject. He brought with him three hundred armed men, nine wives, and thirty children, 'not counting daughters'. The Chinese offered Gantimur forgiveness and gifts if he would return, and when this failed they demanded of the Russians his extradition as a Chinese subject. Since this was a question of prestige, and moreover involved the whole Muscovite colonization policy as expressed in the system of taking oaths of allegiance and exacting iasak, in return for which Moscow undertook the obligation of protecting the vassal, the Russians refused. The question of Gantimur was to remain an irritant in relations between the two powers for the next twenty years.[39]

The Chinese tried to get explanations from Baikov, Ablin, and other envoys to Peking about Russian activity on the Amur, but the envoys gave evasive answers or claimed that the Russians on the river were brigands. In order to get information, the Chinese in 1669 sent spies to Nerchinsk disguised as merchants. The spies tried to find out who really held the place, cossack outlaws or Government troops. The voevoda of Nerchinsk, Danila Arshinskii, treated them well, allowed them to trade, and gave them provisions for the return journey. (The appearance of these 'merchants' would seem to indicate that sporadic frontier trade already existed between the Russians and the Chinese). On a second visit, the merchant-spies delivered a letter from the Chinese defence commissioner at Ninguta and sent by order of the K'ang Hsi Emperor. In it the Chinese complained about the depredations of the cossacks at Albazin, informed the Russians that they had given refuge to Chinese brigands, and demanded the return of the fugitives. Arshinskii assured the emissaries that Nerchinsk and Albazin were held by Government troops at the order of the Tsar who, however, was anxious to have peace and friendship with China.

The merchant-spies were also scouts for a six thousand-man Chinese army sent to recover Gantimur, but upon learning that Nerchinsk was garrisoned by Government troops, and not outlaws, the Chinese commander turned back.[40] Further Chinese military action was postponed because of a long-drawn-out rebellion in the southern provinces of China (1673–80).

THE SPAFARII EMBASSY TO CHINA (1675–1677)

For Moscow, meanwhile, troubles in Europe and the corresponding need to avoid a conflict on the remote eastern frontier was making it increasingly essential to reach some agreement with China. Discussion could no longer be limited to questions of commerce and protocol; discussions of political questions were becoming an urgent necessity. Moscow thereupon, early in 1673, ordered the Moldavian emigré Nikolai Milescu-Spathari to China as ambassador, with instructions to establish diplomatic and commercial relations and to arrange other matters affecting the two countries.

Spafarii, as he is known in Russian accounts, left Moscow on 3 March 1675, accompanied by a suite of 160 persons. He took all the information he could gather on China and at Tobolsk talked at length on the subject with the Croatian priest and early pan-Slavist, Iurii Krizhanich, then in exile. He doubtless absorbed Krizhanich's convictions of the danger to Moscow of a war with China to the prejudice of her affairs in Europe, the need to colonize Siberia, and the need for peace and trade with China.

Gathering copious notes along the way about everything he saw and heard, Spafarii arrived in Peking in May 1676. Conferring in Latin, he and Father Verbiest, one of several Jesuit missionaries in Peking, got on well. Verbiest served as a valuable intermediary in talks with the Chinese. The Chinese treated Spafarii well at first, then became arrogant and demanding. He finally left Peking in September 1676, with little to show for his visit except a copy of a decree—not a letter—issued by the Emperor reiterating his demand for the return of Gantimur and the cessation of disturbances on the frontiers as preconditions for amicable relations between the two countries.[41]

Having gauged the mood of the Chinese, on his way back Spafarii warned the local authorities in Nerchinsk that it would be dangerous to provoke China by operating on the Amur River beyond Albazin, and urged maintenance of the status quo at least until he had returned to Moscow. But the warning was not heeded. Instead, the new voevoda of Nerchinsk, Voeikov, pursued a more active policy than ever, founding several new ostrogs, forts, and villages.[42]

CHINA OUSTS THE RUSSIANS FROM ALBAZIN (1685)

The Chinese reaction to the new Russian encroachments bore out Spafarii's predictions. The K'ang Hsi Emperor, his hands finally freed by the end of the rebellion in South China in 1680, set about a campaign to restore Chinese sovereignty in the Amur region. The second ruler of the new Manchu dynasty was energetic and astute and directed the campaign against the Russians with characteristic thoroughness. On account of the failure in 1655 to defeat the Russians at Kumarsk—primarily because of lack of provisions—the Emperor and his advisers paid special attention to the problem of supply. In 1680, 250 transports were sent to the Liao, the Itung, and the Sungari, and 130 transports to the Amur with provisions for garrisons which were to be established along the way.[43] In 1681 Generals Lang Tan and P'eng Ch'un were dispatched to investigate the water route from Ninguta through the Ussuri to the Amur and to study the situation in the vicinity of Albazin. General Lang Tan received the following instructions from the Emperor:

The Lo Ch'a [*Russians*] forcibly entered the district of Heilungkiang [*Amur*] and robbed and killed our hunters. I sent my troops against them, but they effected nothing. Many years have since passed, and the number of the Lo Ch'a on the Amur increases. I order you and those who shall accompany you, that you shall conscript, in addition to the soldiers which you shall take along with you from the capital, 100 men from Korchin [*Eastern Mongolia*] and 80 men from Ninguta. When you reach the Daurs and Solons, you must immediately dispatch a courier to Nipchu [*Nerchinsk*], to spread the news that you have come on a hunting trip. While still on the way, you should make preparations for hunting, betake yourself to the Amur and advance towards Yaksa [*Albazin*] and with all foresight study the Lo Ch'a, their customs and means of defense. I am convinced that they will not venture to attack you. If they offer you provisions, accept them and give some presents in return, but if they attack you, you must in no case take up arms to kill them, but must withdraw. This is my war plan. On your return you must sail down the Amur, until you reach the village Ussuri. Having arrived there, send some people to Ninguta, in order to make out which is the shortest way thither.[44]

An edict of the emperor, issued in the same year, 1681, describes further preparations for the campaign:

I share completely in the view of Lang Tan that 3,000 soldiers is enough to besiege the Lo Ch'a. Still I would prefer not to commence hostilities, for war is a great misfortune. On this account, for the present I order 1,500 troops to be collected in Kirin-ula [*Kirin*] and Ninguta; ships, cannons and guns to be prepared, and the toops trained. Everything should be finally concentrated in two places, namely, Saghalien-ula [*Aigun*] and Kumarsk. Here, redoubts are to be built. The supply of provisions must come through the Imperial farms in the province of Kirin. It is easy here to produce 13,000 sacks of millet. That will suffice for three years. The town Saghalien-ula [*Aigun*] is five days' journey from Hulunboir, the capital of the Solons. I order a station to be established between these two points. Cattle and sheep can be forwarded from Hulun-boir.[45]

In 1682, in execution of these and other orders, a party was sent to measure the volume of water in the Liao, and on the basis of this knowledge a canal was dug later in the year connecting the Liao with the Sungari. Four granaries were established on the upper Liao, and a number of stations were established between Kirin and Aigun.[46]

In the same year, the Chinese presented an ultimatum to the Russian officials demanding the demolition of the ostrogs on the Zeia. The voevoda of Nerchinsk, Voeikov, ordered the evacuation of the ostrozhek of Dolonskii, on the Zeia, but this concession did not satisfy the Chinese. In 1683 a Chinese flotilla appeared on the Amur, and under its protection the Chinese established the fort of Aigun at the mouth of the Zeia (it was moved to its present location on the south side of the Amur two years later). They then destroyed everything the Russians had established beyond Albazin, killing or capturing the cossacks and peasants.

Albazin itself was a more difficult problem. Thus, on 17 July a detachment of sixty-seven Russians from there, under Grigorii Myl'nikov, was captured near Aigun.[47] Trying first to achieve his objective by peaceful means, the

Emperor sent a message in the nature of an ultimatum to the commandant of Albazin:

I am benevolent and merciful to every man as a father to his children. I govern peacefully and attack no one. But you have broken into my country and driven out my subjects and destroyed their sable trade. You have received Gantimur and his comrades and have inspired revolutions along my frontiers. Therefore, I sent a large army against you to compel you to give up your evil intentions, to forsake my territory and to give up Gantimur, who has gone over to you and concerning whom I have several times written and especially besought Nicholas [*Spafarii*]. . . . You have not esteemed my requests but persist in your bad conduct. Last year by treachery you enticed Ordighi and his companions belonging to my tribute-paying Tungus and Daur tribes, who carried on sable hunting, into a house and there burned them. . . . I have sent my general with a numerous army against you and I have ordered him to build forts on the Amur, the Zeia, and their tributaries and to prevent your navigation on these rivers. Formerly I ordered him to attack and capture you whenever you will be found, but at present I have ordered him to appeal to you with kindnesses and to treat you well. Last year thirty of your men descended the Amur . . . and met my troops. They surrendered, and I was kind to them and executed none. . . . And you, the Russian people of Nerchinsk and Albazin, abandon your evil deeds, return Gantimur, and go away . . . to hunt sables and other animals elsewhere . . .'[48]

The Russians did not reply to this message. By the spring of 1685 the Chinese had established two lines of communication, one by land and another by water, and were ready to start military operations. A force variously estimated from two thousand to ten thousand, with cavalry and artillery, led by Lang Tan, came partly by land and partly by water and on 23 May appeared before Albazin.[49]

The garrison of Albazin consisted of the serving men, promyshlenniks, and peasants, not more than 350 men in all, according to Bantysh, with not enough muskets to go around. There were three cannon and some swivel guns (*zatinnye pishchali*). The voevoda Aleksei Tolbuzin was in command. When the Russians refused to surrender, the Chinese built earthworks around the fort and started shooting incendiary arrows and bombarding the fort with cannon. During the first days, the Chinese lost 150 killed and the Russians 100. When the Russians ran short of lead and gunpowder they offered to surrender the fort if allowed to depart with arms and baggage. The Chinese consented and kept their word. The Russian artillery fell to the Chinese. The Chinese claimed that Nerchinsk and Selenginsk had already been captured and directed the Russians to retreat to Iakutsk. Some did so, but Tolbuzin went to Nerchinsk with about three hundred men, women, and children. The Russians were allowed to take their Russian wives, but had to leave behind their native women and hostages. The Chinese convoyed Tolbuzin's party as far as the mouth of the Argun. According to Chinese accounts, a number of Russians elected to become captives, perhaps fearing punishment by the authorities for past offenses. They became the nucleus of the 'Albazinians', a special force of troops at Peking.[50]

After the arrival of Tolbuzin at Nerchinsk, the local voevoda, I. Vlasov, sent scouts to Albazin. They reported that the Chinese had withdrawn, leaving the crops intact. Vlasov then sent back Tolbuzin with his men and the cossack golova, Afanasii Beiton, to gather the crops and to rebuild the fort. Although this was contrary to the terms of the surrender, Tolbuzin carried out his mission, and the fort was reoccupied by a garrison of 826 men.[51]

THE GOLOVIN EMBASSY

Meanwhile, in 1685, two Russian cossacks previously captured by the Chinese were released and sent to Nerchinsk with letters from the K'ang Hsi Emperor to the Tsar and to the voevodas of Albazin and Nerchinsk. The letter to the Tsar was forwarded to Moscow. In his message the Emperor of China regretted the Russian failure to settle frontier affairs and notified the Tsar that a large Chinese army was being sent to Albazin. He suggested that the Russians leave Chinese territory and promised to withdraw his troops if the Russians would come to terms.

Moscow was receptive to the overture. The possiblity of a new war with Poland, the death of Tsar Fedor in 1682, and subsequent uncertainty as to the succession had drawn the attention of the government away from Far Eastern affairs. In reply, the Moscow government appointed the *okol'nichii* (an official rank next to boyar in importance) Fedor Alekseevich Golovin as ambassador plenipotentiary for concluding a treaty with China.[52]

THE MISSION OF VENIUKOV AND FAVOROV TO PEKING (1686)

Two clerks of the Foreign Office (*Posol'skii prikaz*), Nikifor Veniukov and Ivan Favorov, were sent ahead to Peking in advance of Golovin's main expedition. Leaving Moscow on 20 December 1685, they carried a message giving notice that Moscow was sending Golovin to Albazin to investigate the situation there and to punish those who were guilty of causing trouble. There was also a request to stop hostilities and to recall the Chinese troops. In secret instructions the envoys were ordered to seek information from the Jesuits about the strength of the Chinese army, its equipment, the presence of western instructors, and Chinese relations with neighbouring countries. They were given letters to the Tushetu Khan of the Eastern Khalka Mongols (whom the Russians called Ochiroi Sein Khan) requesting that the envoys be given safe conduct through his territory and that they be assisted with provisions and guides.

Veniukov and Favorov arrived in Selenginsk on 1 August 1686. There they learned that the Chinese had again attacked Albazin. Upon discovering that Tolbuzin had returned to Albazin and refortified it, the Chinese had sent out a second expeditionary force. On 7 July 1686 they appeared before the settlement in 150 boats, each carrying 20 to 50 men, and with 40 cannon. Most of the Chinese were armed with bows and arrows, and only a few with muskets. The Russian garrison at this time consisted of 826 men, with 12 cannon. At the very beginning of the siege, voevoda Tolbuzin was mortally wounded by a Chinese cannonball, and the command was assumed by the Cossack golova, Beiton.

The envoys also learned that the K'ang Hsi Emperor had sent several missions to the Tushetu Khan of the Eastern Khalka Mongols and his brother, the Khutuktu (living Buddha), requesting military assistance against the Russians and recommending attacks on the frontier ostrozheks. Evidently China was trying to gain every advantage possible before engaging in peace talks. The Khutuktu was reluctant, but the Tushetu apparently was willing to attack the Russians, resenting the flight of many of his subjects to Russian territory. In spite of this attitude, however, the Tushetu gave the envoys guides to China, although he refused to give them provisions.[53]

On 31 October Veniukov and Favorov arrived in Peking. Here the usual bickering about kow-tow took place. Like Spafarii, the envoys finally agreed to leave the letter of the Tsar in a certain place instead of delivering it directly to the Emperor. Afterwards, they were received by the Emperor, and they informed him of Moscow's willingness to settle the Amur question by peaceful means. They left Peking in November.

Meanwhile, the siege at Albazin dragged on through the winter, the Chinese army being unable to cope with the firearms of the besieged Russians. Finally, in May 1687, the impending arrival of the Russian ambassador led the Emperor to order his commanders to cease hostilities and to retreat some short distance from the fort. It was none too soon for the defending garrison, so ravaged by scurvy that only seventy men remained able to carry on the defense.

GOLOVIN'S JOURNEY ACROSS SIBERIA

Golovin had left Moscow on 23 January 1686, accompanied by a large retinue and five hundred of the Muscovite streltsy. He was given elaborate instructions which were amplified further while he went through Siberia. He was to settle the border question, making the Amur the frontier if possible. If this could not be obtained, he was to get the Amur as the frontier as far as the mouth of the Zeia, and if this were to fail, he was to agree to the cession of Albazin. He was to arrange for the exchange of war prisoners but to refuse to deliver Gantimur, who had already been baptized. He was to suggest a regular exchange of embassies and to obtain the right for Russian merchants to visit Peking with goods and to obtain permission for Chinese merchants to import silver and gold into Russia.[54]

Making unusually rapid progress, the embassy reached Tobolsk on 24 March but remained there till the end of May. At the end of September, Golovin reached Rybnyi, on the Angara, wintered there, and on 15 May 1687 set out again, arriving in Selenginsk in October. There, he and his party were held up for more than a year by events in Mongolia.[55]

KOROVIN'S MISSION TO MONGOLIA

From Selenginsk, Golovin sent an envoy, Stepan Korovin, to the Mongolian–Chinese frontier to notify the Chinese authorities of the arrival of the embassy and to ask them to report to the Emperor so that the latter could send a similar Chinese embassy to the frontier for negotiations. Golovin suggested that the negotiations be held at Selenginsk. En route through Mongolia, Korovin was to approach the Tushetu Khan and the Khutuktu at Urga to ask for a free passage through the Tushetu's territory and for military aid in case of a Chinese attack. Instead, the Khutuktu detained Korovin at Urga from 7 December 1687 to 2 February 1688.

Chinese diplomats at Urga meanwhile persuaded the Mongol leaders to take action against the Russians. Early in January 1688, four thousand Mongols armed with Chinese cannon and small firearms, under the command of the Tushetu Khan's brother, Batur, invaded Russian territory, laying claim to the Buriats, who wandered on both sides of Lake Baikal, and besieged Selenginsk and Udinsk. Several encounters took place, but Golovin, with his five hundred Moscow streltsy and fourteen hundred men from the Siberian ostrogs, managed to hold the upper hand. Then, as suddenly as he had come, Batur lifted the siege and hurriedly returned with his troops to Mongolia, to stave off an invasion by a rival Mongol chieftain, the famous Galdan, leader of the Oirat (Ölöt) or Dzhungar tribe of the west.

The Tushetu Khan had provoked Galdan by his invasion of the territories of the Jassaktu Khan, a protégé of Galdan, and by his encouragement of the pretentions of his brother, the Khutuktu. Early in 1688 Galdan led thirty thousand men into the territory of the Tushetu Khan. The latter and his brother summoned other Khalka princes to their assistance, but quarrels broke out among the allies, and the Tsetsen Khan and others deserted the Tushetu Khan. The forces of the Tushetu Khan were routed, his camp was seized, the temples built by the Khutuktu were burned, and the country was devastated. The Tushetu Khan and his brother fled to the southern desert country and acknowledged themselves as vassals of the Chinese Emperor.

After the battle, Galdan sent an envoy to Irkutsk with presents and an offer of an alliance. The Russians were friendly but declined the alliance, not wishing to become embroiled in Mongol warfare, fearing that it would spoil their Chinese negotiations, and not wishing to see an increase in the power of Galdan, who might become too dangerous a neighbour.[56]

At this time the Chinese delegation was already on the way to Selenginsk, which was at first chosen as a place of conference, expecting to find the Russians there in serious difficulties with the Mongols. Instead, the rout of the Khalkas and the nearness of Galdan forced recall of the mission to Peking. The Russians profited from the Mongol disturbances because some Mongol chieftains signed agreements making themselves vassals and tributaries of Russia.[57]

NEGOTIATING THE TREATY OF NERCHINSK

The conference was next set to be held at Nerchinsk. The ambassadors of the K'ang Hsi Emperor arrived on 20 July (old style) 1689. They had travelled overland escorted by a large force commanded by the experienced General Lang Tan, with supplies borne by several thousand camels and horses, followed by herds of cattle and horses. Simultaneously a fleet of large war vessels arrived, armed with cannon and bearing about fifteen hundred soldiers. According to Russian estimates, the entire Chinese force comprised about fifteen thousand men. Overnight a Chinese tent city sprang up beside the modest Russian town of Nerchinsk, surrounded by its log palisade. The garrison at Nerchinsk, numbering only six hundred men, was in effect under siege from the time of the Chinese force's arrival.[58] Golovin arrived on 9 August, his force of less than fifteen hundred troops insignificant beside that of the Chinese.

On 12 August the Russian and Chinese ambassadors met. Latin was to be the language of the negotiations, for which both sides had interpreters: for the Chinese, two Jesuit missionaries residing at Peking, Father Gerbillon and Father Pereira, and for the Russians, Andrei Belobotskii, a Pole. Each side wanted peace. In Moscow, the unsuccessful expedition against the Crimea had emptied the Treasury, and the nobles were hostile to Tsarevna Sophia and were struggling for power. The Chinese faced prolonged struggles on their northern and western frontiers with the Mongols. Neither could afford a costly war on the distant Amur.

The negotiations were nonetheless acrimonious. Golovin's instructions were to try to obtain a boundary at the Amur,[59] the Chinese were instructed to get the Russians to renounce the Amur. Each began with excessive

179

demands, the Chinese negotiators at first demanding that the Russians set the boundary at Lake Baikal. When the Russians insisted on the Amur, the Chinese refused and broke off negotiations. From 14 to 27 August the ambassadors did not meet at all, but negotiated through their interpreters, who crossed back and forth from camp to camp several times daily. Several times the negotiations were nearly broken off. At last, thanks largely to the patience and tact of Fathers Gerbillon and Pereira, agreement was reached, and on 27 August (7 September m.s.) 1689, the treaty was signed and copies exchanged. The Russians handed one copy in Latin and one in Russian to the Chinese, who reciprocated with one copy in Latin, and one in Manchu. The Latin copies were regarded as official.[60]

By the treaty, the frontier was to follow the River Argun—the left bank to be Russian, the right bank Chinese—to where the Argun joins the Shilka to form the Amur. The line then doubled back along the Shilka to the River Gorbitsa, a left tributary of the Shilka, then ran up the Gorbitsa to its sources in the Stanovoi Range, thence along that range to the River Uda and along that river to the Sea of Okhotsk. Certain ambiguities in the treaty texts were later to cause dispute, but, by following the watershed separating the Amur and its tributaries from the northward-flowing tributaries of the Lena, the new frontier barred Russia from the entire Amur Valley. The town of Albazin was to be destroyed and its inhabitants transferred to Russian possessions. On the other hand, the Chinese had in the end consented to allow the Russians to retain Nerchinsk. Fugitives who had crossed the frontier before the treaty was signed were to remain where they were, but any future ones were to be delivered to the frontier authorities of the country from which they had fled. The subjects of each of the two countries were to be allowed to visit the territory of the other in order to sell or purchase goods, provided they had proper passports. Subjects of either party who were guilty of thievery, banditry, or murder were to be punished by their respective governments through the frontier authorities, by corporal punishment or the death penalty.

Immediately after conclusion of the agreement, Golovin wrote to voevoda Fedor Ushakov in Selenginsk instructing him to maintain peaceful relations with the Mongols, who were Chinese subjects. Voevoda Beiton in Albazin was ordered to destroy the town and fort and to bring the arms and food supplies as well as the men under his command to Nerchinsk. Milovanov, the commandant of the ostrog of Argunsk, was ordered to transfer the fort to the left bank of the Argun river.[61]

SIGNIFICANCE OF THE AMUR TO RUSSIA

The treaty concluded in 1689 ended the first Russian effort to gain the Amur. The task had proved too difficult, and the Russians had been able to maintain their hold only as long as the Chinese did not take energetic action.

The main cause of the Russian failure was the predatory policy which had been followed from the outset. The natives had met the first Russians without special hostility, but after learning that they could expect nothing good from the newcomers, most of them fled the region. Another circumstance which hurt the Russians was their failure to establish an orderly administration. They entered the Amur in comparatively small parties, which scattered quickly over the vast basin of the river. This had been sufficient to bring the greater part of eastern Siberia under submission but was not effective in a region bordering upon the domains of a great power. The smallness of the Russian bands and their lack of central direction and discipline could not create respect for the might of the Russian State among either the natives or the Manchus. A third factor was the failure to colonize the region. Although the Russians were attracted by the natural wealth of the Amur, they lacked the wisdom to exploit it properly. Khabarov in particular understood the necessity of colonization and even tried to encourage the Russians to cultivate land, but the same Khabarov mercilessly ruined and destroyed the native agriculture, thereby dooming the entire Russian enterprise to failure.[62] Yet, in spite of their small size and the egregious policy errors of the men in charge, the Russian establishments on the border and their determined garrisons had their use, so hindering the Chinese operations there as to make negotiation and compromise seem the wiser policy.

From a diplomatic standpoint, the treaty between the two empires, stabilizing the long frontier, may be considered one of the most successful ever made, inaugurating a period of peace which lasted for 170 years. From a short-term standpoint, Russia gained coveted trading privileges, Chinese acknowledgement of her right to be in the Far East, and a free hand for dealing with matters in the west. Faced with the possibilities of renewed hostility from Poland over the Ukraine, and conflict with Turkey and Crimea, Russia had to avoid a major struggle in the Far East, of uncertain duration and outcome. At the time, the treaty was even regarded in Moscow as a victory, and Golovin was honoured for the part he had taken in the negotiations.[63] China, on the other hand, was relieved of a threat on her northern frontier, which gave her a free hand against the Mongols.

From a long-term standpoint of imperial advantage, however, loss of the Amur was a major defeat for Russia, creating a lasting weakness which would hinder all operations on the Lena and east of Lake Baikal. The Russians remained active north of the Amur valley, but were engaged almost exclusively with furs and trade, which drew only a handful of population to the region in comparison with what agriculture might have brought. Russian historians have frequently pointed out that loss of the Amur cost Russia her best route to the Pacific, to the detriment of all later operations on that coast and to her future enterprise in America.[64] Whether in fact there is basis for this is debatable. The Russia of the seventeenth and eighteenth centuries would not have been in a position, even with the Amur, to have undertaken significantly more than she did. And the Amur itself, even after it was regained in the mid-nineteenth century, proved less useful for agriculture than had been thought, remaining neglected until colonization was fostered in the early years of the twentieth century.[65]

SUMMARY

The Russians on the Enisei and Lena heard rumours of the Amur River in the late 1630s. The Lena and its tributaries the Vitim, the Olekma, and the Aldan offered routes to the Amur, and although an expedition from Iakutsk sent by way of the Vitim in 1640 failed to reach it, another, sent in 1643 under Poiarkov, did so by following the Aldan, crossing the Stanovoi Range, and descending the Zeia. Poiarkov and his men terrorized the Amur natives, descended the river to its mouth, went northward along the coast, ascended the Maia, and returned to Iakutsk in 1646. In 1649 and 1650, Khabarov reached the Amur by way of the Olekma. Remaining there until 1652, he further antagonized the natives and had a battle with a Manchu and Chinese force. Rumours of the wealth on the river caused a rush to the Amur from all over eastern Siberia.

Moscow planned an expedition to consolidate the Russian hold on the Amur region, but although this was cancelled in 1653 because of more pressing needs west of the Urals, the government continued to strive for the territory. The Russians remaining on the Amur under Stepanov held out against the Chinese until 1658, when they were defeated and expelled. The Amur was then a no man's land until 1672, when the Moscow government established a protectorate over the irregular post of Albazin, but at this same time trying through the Spafarii mission (1675–77) to reach some kind of accord with China. The Manchus, once their position in China was secure, began to move against the Russians on the Amur and conquered Albazin in 1685.

Unable to undertake a major struggle in the Far East, the Moscow government drew back. The Russian envoy, Golovin, made peace with the Chinese at Nerchinsk in 1689, and Russia withdrew from the Amur, not to return until 1850.

Chapter 11

To Arctic Shores

Even while exploring and subjugating the Lena and Amur regions, the Russian administrators, service men, and promyshlenniks there began to turn their attention to regions farther north and eastward. The story of their explorations is incomplete. The documents which make up the record are often vague as to dates and itineraries, making it difficult to establish continuity and priority. Modern scholars, re-examining materials already published, or using unpublished archival materials, have shed light upon some questions, but are uncertain regarding others.

The exploration of this region involved seafaring. Many of the techniques used were outgrowths of those used in river transport throughout European Russia and Siberia, but others stemmed from Pomor'e, the maritime region of northern Russia mentioned earlier. This area, which might be called the cradle of Russian seafaring, produced a hardy and enterprising population of fishermen and traders. In small, relatively crude vessels they became familiar with the European Arctic coasts. As early as the fifteenth century they even reached Spitzbergen.

The principal craft of the Pomorians was the *koch,* a wooden, single-masted, decked vessel with one sail. Although unable to use any but a following wind, the koch was otherwise well suited to Arctic coastal waters, sturdy enough to withstand stormy weather or floating ice. With a favourable wind, such vessels could cover as much as two hundred miles in a twenty-four hour period. They ranged up to sixty feet in length, and fourteen feet in width. Besides a crew of from ten to fifteen, the largest of such vessels could carry thirty to forty passengers. [1]

EARLY VOYAGES ALONG THE ARCTIC COAST

After the founding of Mangazeia in 1601, the new centre was often reached by sea. In 1602 a detachment of forty men in four vessels under Lev Ivanov Shubin arrived from Kholmogory, wintered at the mouth of the Pechora River, crossed the Iamal Peninsula by rivers and portages to the Ob estuary, and from there went up the Taz to Mangazeia. Others followed, and soon the voyage became commonplace. In 1610 sixteen vessels, with a total of 150 men, visited Mangazeia. In the same year, as mentioned earlier, the Dvina trader, Kondratii Kurochkin, sailed east from the Ob estuary to the mouth of the Enisei and then still farther eastward to the mouth of the Piasina River, near the Taimyr Peninsula.

No written records remain, but various finds show that Russian vessels may even have rounded the Taimyr Peninsula itself at this time. A camp site on Faddeia Island, on the east side of the peninsula, discovered in 1940 by seamen from a Soviet hydrographic expedition, and another site on the shore of nearby Sims Bay, found in the following year, seem to establish this fact. The two sites yielded copper vessels, tin plates, earrings, rings, crosses, ivory chess men, a solar watch and compass, and nearly thirty-four hundred Russian silver coins ranging in date from the reign of Tsar Vasilii III to that of Tsar Michael. These indicate a voyage, evidently clandestine, for it was made at about the time of the decrees of 1616 and 1619, forbidding sea travel, and doubtless of fatal conclusion.[2] Other finds, of single objects, on Bol'shoi Begichev Island at the mouth of Khatanga Bay, on Preobrazheniia island, and on Kotel'nyi Island in the Novosibirskii group are less certain, but may also belong to this period.[3]

This eastward striving was halted by the stern decrees of 1616 and 1619, already mentioned, forbidding all voyaging in the Kara Sea.[4] The experience, energy, and enterprise of the Pomorians thereafter found an outlet in inland waters and in the exploration of the lower Lena and adjacent coasts.

PERFIR'EV AND REBROV DESCEND THE LENA AND EXPLORE THE IANA AND THE INDIGIRKA

The initiative for the exploration and exploitation of northeastern Siberia was first taken by service men and promyshlenniks from Mangazeia and Eniseisk. In the spring of 1633, when the question of rivalry between the two centres for predominance in the new region was still undecided, and before the Iakut uprising which would break out in the autumn of that year, men of both centres gathered at the newly founded outpost of Zhigansk, eager to follow the Lena northward as soon as the ice went out.

Prominent among the group were the Eniseisk piatidesiatnik, Il'ia Perfir'ev, and the Tobolsk cossack, Ivan Rebrov (or Robrov). On their own initiative, Perfir'ev, Rebrov, and a few companions asked the prikashchik of Zhigansk for permission to descend the Lena and 'to go by sea to the new place, the Iana river', concerning which rumours had evidently reached Zhigansk, to subjugate new tribes and to collect iasak. Permission was granted, but they received no Government aid in either money or supplies. Rebrov instead invested over a hundred rubles of his own money in the enterprise.[5]

The expedition went down the Lena in kochi. Throughout this part of its course the Lena is already a vast, majestic stream, from four to twenty miles in breadth, with many unstable alluvial islands and broad sandy banks on either side. The low, flat islands are covered with moss and grass during the summer. When they reached the great delta at the mouth of the river, the voyagers would have made their way through islands still frozen to a depth of several feet, and covered with great blocks of ice carried down by the spring floods.

From the Lena, Rebrov and part of the group followed the coast westward as far as the Olenek River. There they remained for about four years, collecting the first iasak from the Olenek Tungus. For subsistance they would have fallen into the hunting cycle of the natives, by whom they were doubtless supplied, in the spring living off the reindeer when they made their annual migration, in the summer relying on the myriads of geese which nested in the region. These would be killed with bow and arrow, or snared, especially while flightless during a two-week moulting period. This would have tided the party over until the end of the summer, when swarms of fish ascended the rivers to spawn. After the fishing season, the reindeer could again be hunted while migrating southward.

While Rebrov was on the Olenek, Perfir'ev sailed east along the coast to the Iana River. The interior valleys of this river along with the Indigirka system to the east, enclosed by the curving Verkhoiansk Range along the right bank of the Lena and the Cherskii Range are the coldest inhabited regions on earth. During the winter, as with all of the polar mountains of this region, the summits are warmer than the valleys. As the warm air ascends, the icy air from the mountain-tops drains downward into the enclosed basins, causing them to become increasingly colder. In this forbidding region Perfir'ev collected iasak from the local Iakuts and also from the Iukagirs, a tribe not previously encountered.

In September 1637 Rebrov came to the Iana, and Perfir'ev then took the collected iasak and returned to Eniseisk. In the summer of 1638 Rebrov and a few others went by sea to the next major river eastward, the Sobach'ia (Indigirka). There they collected more iasak and built a zimov'e at the river mouth. Petitioning the Tsar for back pay and a promotion some years later, Rebrov claimed, somewhat inaccurately, to have been the first Russian to visit the Iana and the Indigirka, to have spent, in all, seven years in the region, during which he had suffered greatly from cold and hunger, sometimes having to subsist 'on roots and grass', and to have been wounded five times in fights with natives.[6]

BUZA EXPLORES THE IANA, THE INDIGIRKA AND THE OLENEK

Another early visitor on the Iana was the desiatnik Elisei (or Eleska or Elesa) Iur'ev Buza. In 1635 Buza petitioned the voevoda of Eniseisk for permission to go and seek new lands and collect iasak at the mouth of the Lena and on the rumoured 'Siviriui' and 'Lama', the latter supposedly a great river comparable to the Lena. Permission was granted, but again, as in Rebrov's case, no money, foodstuffs, boats, or other supplies were forthcoming.[7]

The party made the journey in winter, by sledge, to Iakutsk, where Buza had been assured that the authorities would assign him service men and supply him with beads and objects of copper and tin for trade. Again he received nothing. Buza was able to recruit ten service men and about forty promyshlenniks on his own account, however, to buy boats and supplies, and to furnish his men with arquebuses and powder, food, fishnets, and other equipment.[8]

In the spring of 1636[9] the party set out down the Lena, reaching the ocean in two weeks.[10] From the mouth of the Lena, Buza appears next to have turned west, to have sailed for a day until he reached the Olenek, and then to have gone upstream until he found a Tungus village, where he collected iasak.[11]

In the fall of 1636[12] Buza and his men travelled overland from the Olenek to the Lena. Near the mouth of the River Molodo he and his men built two kochi, again descended the Lena in the spring of 1637, and sailed east in an attempt to reach the Iana. He got as far as the River Omoloi, where he found the way blocked by ice.[13]

The party ascended the Omoloi, built sledges, abandoned what supplies they could not carry with them, and headed farther eastward. In September, after travelling for about eight weeks, they reached the Iana,[14] where they built four kochi and sailed up the river. On the middle Iana they found Iakuts and tried to collect iasak. But the Iakuts resisted and laid siege to the party for six weeks; two of the men were killed.[15] In the end, however, the Russians prevailed and wintered among the Iakuts.

In the spring of 1638[16] Buza and his men, after aiding the Iakuts in a war on the Iukagirs,[17] built another vessel, descended the Iana, and proceeded eastward to the next river, the Chondon. At the mouth of the Chondon they encountered a Iukagir shaman. They took his fur coat and made him lead them to his village, where they imposed iasak.[18] Buza then selected four of his men to take the accumulated iasak to Iakutsk and to report his progress,[19] while he himself, with seventeen men, returned to the Iana. He remained there until 1641, when he left for Iakutsk,[20] arriving in July 1642 after a five-year absence.[21]

Buza brought along three Iukagir princelings, who told of new rivers, as yet unvisited by Russians, especially the 'Neroga' or 'Pogycha', situated east of the Iana. They said that on this river lived a settled tribe called the Natty, who herded reindeer and dwelled in 'earth yurts'. They had a prince who wore bright blue beads in his nose; they went to sea in two-man boats; they obtained silver in a very original fashion, shooting arrows into mountain sides so that the silver fell down in fragments, out of which they made rings which they wore on their foreheads; they got pearls from lakes near the river Neroga; and they made arrowheads of walrus bones and arrows of iron.[22]

POSNIK IVANOV GOES OVERLAND TO THE IANA AND THE INDIGIRKA

Simultaneously with the opening of the sea route to the Indigirka, a land route was found across the Verkhoiansk Range. This route is exceedingly difficult: the mountains are only 4,000 feet high, but the north side is very steep, and the summit is apt to be lashed by howling, gusty winds. Another service man from Eniseisk, Posnik Ivanov (Gubar'), appears to have been the first to make this journey, in 1636–37.[23] Nothing more is known of that pioneer venture, which established the way that was to serve as the principal northeast land route until the end of the century,[24] but it was followed by another which earlier writers thought to be the first. On 25 April 1638 Ivanov, with thirty companions, set out from Iakutsk on horseback. They crossed the mountains to the Iana, by-passing the sources of the river, held by the still unsubjugated Lamuts, and descended the Iana to the Iakut settlements on the river near the ostrog of Verkhoiansk, probably built previously by the Eniseisk piatidesiatnik Perfir'ev.[25] There they wintered, and in 1639, guided by native prisoners, Ivanov led the party down the Iana, collecting iasak as he went, and sending it to Iakutsk with six of his men. A like number of men would be sufficient to collect iasak on the Iana in the future, he reported, and no hostages would have to be taken.

While Ivanov and his men were at Verkhoiansk, the Iakuts there complained about their neighbours the Iukagirs. Ivanov accordingly set upon the Iukagirs and subjugated them. The Iukagirs told him of the Indigirka, farther east, and so interested Ivanov in its riches that early in 1640 he set out for it.

Collecting iasak from the previously hostile Lamuts *en route*, Ivanov and his party reached the Indigirka on 28 May 1640.[26] The Iukagirs on the Indigirka tried to resist, but, never having seen horses, they supposed them to be more dangerous than their riders and concentrated their attack on them. The cossacks won and, on 11 October 1640, built an ostrozhek there. Returning to Iakutsk in the summer of 1642,[27] Ivanov told of the Indigirka, 'into which many rivers flow, along all of which live many hunting and reindeer people', and of the wealth in sables to be had.[28]

ZYRIAN TRAVERSES THE INDIGIRKA, UIANDINA AND ALAZEIA

News of the activities on the Iana and Indigirka and of the fabled River Pogicha fired imaginations at Iakutsk. Early in the summer of 1640[29] a detachment of fifteen men[30] under Dmitrii Zyrian was sent—again by the overland route—to the Indigirka.[31] Reaching their destination, Zyrian and his men built two kochi and sailed down the river. During the summer they conquered the Iukagirs of the middle Indigirka as far as the Uiandina River, a western tributary, where they wintered at a place they called Uiandinsk or Indigirsk.[32] In the spring[33] they went on to the mouth of the Indigirka. While on the Indigirka, Zyrian was joined by several men from Ivanov's detachment.[34]

Captive natives told Zyrian and his party of the sea route to a neighbouring river to the east, where Iukagirs lived who had never seen Russians. The news had its usual allure, and the detachment went three days by sea in kochi to the River Alazeia, the first Russians known to have travelled in the East Siberian Sea. A six-day passage up the winding, marshy Alazeia brought them to the edge of the timber region, where they found not only Iukagirs, but also a new and hitherto unknown people, the Chukchi.[35]

The Iukagirs on the Alazeia put up a stout resistance to Russian attempts to make them pay iasak. In one fight the Russians lost two men, and all were wounded. However, they wintered on the river and subdued the Iukagirs in the following spring.[36] Doubtless eager to be rid of their unwelcome overlords, the Iukagirs told the Russians the usual story of a greater river beyond, the Kolyma, three days' journey eastward by sledge, inhabited by people 'as numerous as the hairs on one's head, with many sables, all kinds of animals, and many fish'.[37] Zyrian wintered on the Alazeia, and when the ice went out in the spring of 1643, he took eleven men from the mouth of the Alazeia to the Indigirka by koch, he sent four men to Iakutsk with the iasak collected thus far,[38] and himself returned to the Alazeia.

STADUKHIN REACHES THE KOLYMA (1644)

The voevodas of Iakutsk, as news of the explorations trickled in, were particularly interested in the reports that the Iukagirs had silver,[39] and gathered reinforcements to assist the service men who were operating in the Iukagir country. In the winter of 1641–42, a small detachment was organized under the veteran serviceman, Mikhail Stadukhin, and in the spring was sent overland to the upper Indigirka. The detachment included Semeon Ivanovich Dezhnev, who, because of his later exploits and the somewhat fuller record concerning him, is now best known of all the explorers of Siberia.

Stadukhin imposed iasak on Iakuts and Tungus on the Oimiakon River (one of the headwaters of the Indigirka), but only after a battle in which his party lost almost all their horses. There they spent the winter of 1642–43 amid temperatures which would have been around the modern recorded minimum for the settlement of Oimiakon of minus 90 degrees Fahrenheit. Nevertheless, they built kochi and in the following summer sailed down the Indigirka[40] and eastward to the Alazeia. At the mouth of the Alazeia, Stadukhin found the party of Dmitrii Zyrian. Here Stadukhin's detachment split, Dezhnev and part of the men joining Zyrian and remaining on the Alazeia, while Stadukhin and the remainder bypassed the Alazeia and went eastward toward the Kolyma.[41] While proceeding along the Arctic coast, Stadukhin thought he saw snowy mountains to the north and assumed that there was a great island there, 'a new land', contributing to a legend already in existence by which earlier Russian seafarers had explained various small islands off shore, which under certain lighting conditions had seemed to merge into one another.[42] In the summer of 1644 Stadukhin and his party reached the Kolyma. At its mouth, at the usual large delta characteristic of eastern Siberian rivers, they took Iukagir hostages and founded the zimov'e of Nizhne-Kolymsk. The site is bleak, buffeted by freezing north winds off the Arctic Ocean, so the settlement was later transferred upriver to the mouth of the Malyi Aniui,[43] to become a base for future expeditions.

Returning from the Kolyma to the Lena with a great supply of sables in the fall of 1645, Stadukhin and Zyrian rejoined, then met a party bound for the Kolyma with word that Zyrian was to be prikashchik at Nizhne-Kolymsk. Zyrian turned back to take charge, but died early in 1646. Stadukhin meanwhile continued his homeward journey to Zhigansk and Iakutsk. There he reported hearing that the elusive River Pogycha, with much sable and many inhabitants, was to be found three days' sail eastward from the Kolyma.[44]

In the summer of 1646 a party of nine promyshlenniks, led by the kormshchik, Isai Ignat'ev (nicknamed 'Mezenets', possibly because he was from Mezen, just east of the White Sea), set out from Nizhne-Kolymsk by sea to seek the 'sable river'. Ignat'ev and his party sailed eastward for two days and would appear to have reached Chaun Bay. Obtaining a small cargo of precious 'fish teeth', or walrus ivory, from the coastal Chukchi, they returned to Nizhne-Kolymsk.[45]

The experience of Ignat'ev and his men caused a stir at Nizhne-Kolymsk. On the basis of their report, added to that of Stadukhin, it was thought that the mouth of the 'sable river', Pogycha, which now began to be called the Anadyr, must lie only a day or two farther east. In the following year, 1647, a company was formed among the servicemen and promyshlenniks to search for more walrus ivory and for the Anadyr. The company was headed by Fedot Alekseev Popov, a prikashchik of a wealthy Moscow merchant Aleksei Usov. Popov, from the White Sea port of Kholmogory, had in 1642 sailed from the Lena to trade on the Olenek.[46] After about two years, trade there declined, and in 1647 Popov turned up on the Kolyma. At Popov's request, Semeon Dezhnev was attached to the expedition to lead a group of servicemen who would protect the force from hostile natives. In the summer of 1647 the company left Nizhne-Kolymsk in four kochi, sailed down the Kolyma to the Arctic Sea, but had to return because floating ice rendered the sea too dangerous for navigation.[47]

THE FIRST VOYAGE THROUGH THE STRAITS BETWEEN ASIA AND AMERICA

Undeterred, Popov and Dezhnev during the winter of 1647–48 formed a new company from the merchants, promyshlenniks, and servicemen on the Kolyma. Popov again led the 'civilians'—some twenty-nine in number—while Dezhnev commanded the eighteen servicemen.[48] Another detachment was headed by Afanasii Andreev and Besson Astaf'ev, prikashchiks of the merchant Vasilii Gusel'nikov. Still another detachment, headed by Gerasim Ankudinov, consisted of thirty unattached men, virtual outlaws, who proceeded independently of the others. By the summer of 1648 all preparations were finally complete, and early in June seven kochi, including that of Ankudinov, loaded with over a hundred men and supplies, left Nizhne-Kolymsk and headed for the open sea. The weather was fine and the sea was relatively free of ice.[49]

Along the Arctic coast, four of the kochi became separated from the others, never to be seen again. Rumours among the Chukchi a century later of men similar in appearance, dress, language, and customs to the Russians, living on the coast of Alaska, were taken as indicating possible survival of some of those lost,[50] but the chances of this are remote. The remaining three kochi, with Popov, Dezhnev, and Ankudinov, continued eastwards, and during the month of August rounded what they called the Bol'shoi Kamennyi Nos (Great Rocky Cape), the easternmost point of the Eurasian continent, now called Cape Dezhnev. While rounding the cape, Ankudinov's koch was wrecked, and he and his men were distributed between the two remaining boats. The loss of the boat and the lack of drinking water forced the expedition to land in the vicinity of the Nos. They were attacked by hostile Chukchi, and Popov was wounded. Dezhnev assumed command of the expedition and continued the voyage, unaware that they were sailing between continents and thereby close to solving one of the greatest of geographical mysteries.

Thus Dezhnev and his men came into the Pacific and sailed down the coast. Toward the end of September, stormy weather ended their sea journey.[51] Popov's boat vanished. Years later Dezhnev reported that on a subsequent expedition he took from the Koriaks Popov's Iakut mistress, who said that Popov and another had died of scurvy, that others had been killed, and that the remainder had fled by boat.[52] Some later held the belief, based on native rumour, that this party had even managed to round Kamchatka, or that it may have been they who gave rise to the rumours among the Chukchi, mentioned above, of a group living on the coast of Alaska.

DEZHNEV FOUNDS ANADYRSK (1649)

Whatever the fate of the others, Dezhnev and twenty-five men in the sole remaining boat were driven south, their koch leaking and almost out of control in the stormy sea. Eventually they ran the boat ashore somewhere beyond the Anadyr on what was probably the Oliutora coast of the Bering Sea.[53] They salvaged what they could, especially weapons and tools, but found themselves in a desperate plight. The Arctic winter was at hand; barren mountains made up the landscape; they could find no animals to kill, nor would the winter permit fishing.[54] The men made skis and sledges from the wreck, loaded their salvage, and started 'climbing mountains, not knowing where we were going, suffering from cold and hunger, lacking clothing and footwear. For all of ten weeks we wandered, finally reaching the Anadyr not far from the sea.'[55]

At the mouth of the Anadyr they were not much better off. There was no forest, only a vast tundra as far as one could see; there were no animals to hunt, and no means to catch fish. Twelve of the men left camp in search of food, but at three days' distance they had found nothing and stopped to rest. Only three of this group were able to attempt the trip back, and of these only two arrived. When Dezhnev reached the men who had stopped 'to rest', he found them all dead. Later, four other men died, so that Dezhnev survived the winter with only twelve men.[56]

In the summer of 1649 the remaining men built a boat out of driftwood and ascended the Anadyr. It would have been a case of necessity, for as soon as the ice breaks up it forms dams downstream, the country side is flooded, no fish are to be caught, the wild fowl go elsewhere, and supplies are exhausted or spoil in the warm weather. They would have had to find their way through the innumerable channels which make the whole country a succession of large islands. Along the way they obtained food from the natives, and hunted where they could (probably for water fowl). Yet they managed to subdue the Iukagirs and Anauls (a local sub-group of the Iukagirs) whom they found living near the river, and collected iasak. On the mid-course of the Anadyr, Dezhnev established a zimov'e, which became the important ostrog of Anadyrsk.[57]

Thus far, people on the Kolyma had remained ignorant of the fate of the expedition. Then Iukagir prisoners captured at the source of the right tributary of the Kolyma, the Bol'shoi Aniui, told the officials at Nizhne-Kolymsk that beyond the mountain range there was a large river called the Anadyr, where plenty of walrus ivory was to be had. This greatly interested the people on the Kolyma, and in June 1647 Michael Stadukhin went out of Iakutsk to explore the region, possibly to find at last the River Pogycha, and to subdue the natives there. Simultaneously and without authority, twenty men set out under Vasilii Bugor (known to us earlier for his exploration of the upper Lena in 1628.)[58] Both groups, however, had to turn back because of ice. During the winter of 1647–48, Stadukhin and Bugor, now together, went overland to the Iana and the Indigirka and, the next summer (1648), to Nizhne-Kolymsk. In the summer of 1649 Stadukhin and his party tried to go by sea to the Anadyr, but ran out of provisions before Shelagskii Nos and again had to return to the Kolyma,[59] arriving back on 7 September 1649. In the same year, N. Semenov went to the upper Bol'shoi Aniui, returning with news that the great River Anadyr lay beyond the mountains. In March 1650 Stadukhin and his party and, at almost the same time, another group under Semeon Motora set out overland for the Anadyr. Quarreling as they went, with Stadukhin trying to subordinate Motora and his men to himself,[60] the two parties crossed the steep and barren Aniui Range together. After a perilous journey, both groups arrived on the Anadyr, and there encountered Dezhnev and his surviving comrades.

The reunion of Stadukhin and Dezhnev, however, was neither joyous nor peaceful. Stadukhin had long planned to find the Anadyr and had already made several unsuccessful attempts. And now, after great hardship, he had arrived only to find the local natives already paying iasak to Dezhnev. The two groups began to fight each other, but both found themselves under unfavourable circumstances. In spite of the fact that the natives had already paid iasak to Dezhnev, Stadukhin began to collect it again, using violence and threats. Some of the Anauls and Iukagirs fled to the lower Anadyr and toward Kamchatka, and later had to be subjugated all over again, this time with considerable bloodshed. Some of Stadukhin's men, including Bugor, deserted to Motora and Dezhnev. At last, early in 1651, Stadukhin left the Anadyr and turned south, seeking the Rivers Penzhina and Gizhiga, reputed to be rich in sables. After two months of difficult travel, he arrived on the lower Penzhina, where he imposed iasak on the Iukagir and Koriak people of the region. He later subjugated the Koriaks and Tungus on the north coast of the Sea of Okhotsk.[61]

Dezhnev and Motora meanwhile built a vessel on the Anadyr in which they could seek new regions, but in 1651 the Anauls killed Motora. Dezhnev went down the Anadyr himself and on the north side of the river mouth, on a long bank or shoal, he found a mass of walrus bones and ivory. In 1654 he made a second visit to the beach with Iurii Seliverstov, a new arrival from Iakutsk. Seliverstov's subsequent efforts to claim the honour and profit of the discovery for himself caused Dezhnev to write denials of this to the authorities, thereby providing posterity with the stark details of the exploit for which he is best known, and which provides a climax to the earlier stage of explorations in the far northeastern part of Asia.[62]

SUMMARY

Seafaring played an important role in the exploration of northern Siberia. Although sea travel eastward from the north coast of European Russia was halted by the decrees of 1616 and 1619, ships were much used in the exploration of northeastern Siberia. In 1633 Perfir'ev and Rebrov descended the Lena to the Arctic Ocean, and from there Rebrov and part of the group followed the coast to the Olenek River, while Perfir'ev sailed east along the coast to the Iana River. In 1638 Rebrov went by sea to the Iana and eastward to the Indigirka. In 1635–38 Buza explored the Omoloi, the Iana, and the Chondon, gaining submission from the Iukagirs.

In 1636 and 1638, Posnik Ivanov found a land route from Iakutsk across the Verkhoiansk Range to the Iana, and in 1640 reached the Indigirka, subduing the Iukagirs in that region.

Rumours of activities on the Iana and Indigirka and of a River Pogicha still farther to the east brought other expeditions from Iakutsk. In 1640 Zyrian and a small detachment took the overland route to the Indigirka, descended it, subduing the Iukagirs, and then went by sea to the Alazeia River.

Word of the Kolyma and other rivers still farther eastward led to the despatch of a small expedition under Mikhail Stadukhin, with Semeon Dezhnev. Stadukhin and his party sailed down the Indigirka to the sea, thence eastward to the Alazeia, and from there to the Kolyma, which they reached in 1644. In 1648 a party under Fedot Alekseev Popov, including Semeon Dezhnev, left Nizhne-Kolymsk and sailed down the Kolyma to the Arctic Sea. All the boats were lost except that of Dezhnev, who made it around East Cape to the Anadyr, thus solving, had he but known it, the problem of whether Asia and North America were joined.

After the 1650s, the activity on these coasts declined, evidently reflecting the decreasing number of furs attainable and absence of new lands to be won. Fewer ships were sent out, and the region remained little frequented until the eighteenth century, when government-sponsored expeditions began to make scientific surveys. Although undertaken on a different basis, these nevertheless owed much to the fur-seeking promyshlenniks who had gone before, scouting out so much of the region in such a short time, with limited means and largely on their own initiative.

Chapter 12

The Conquest of Kamchatka and Chukotka

Although Dezhnev's voyage of 1648–49 was a notable achievement, the exploration and conquest of the northeastern extremities of Siberia had still scarcely begun. The ostrog of Anadyrsk, built on the Anadyr River in 1656 following the explorations of Dezhnev and Stadukhin, was for a time the main base for activities in this region. From it the cossacks imposed iasak upon the Koriak reindeer herders to the south, as far as the rivers Aklan and Oliutora. The ostrog of Aklansk, built in 1669, served as an added guarantee of Koriak submission. Little new exploration seems to have been carried on, however, probably because of diminishing returns and inadequate forces, until 1695, when the voevoda of Iakutsk appointed the cossack piatidesiatnik, Vladimir Atlasov, as prikashchik over this difficult region. Atlasov was an apt choice. He was typical of the rough, cruel, but at the same time courageous cossacks, able to stand almost unbelievable privations, who played such an important role in the conquest of Siberia. Born in Ustiug, he was poorly educated but possessed a great deal of native intelligence, as indicated in his reports.

FIRST INFORMATION CONCERNING KAMCHATKA

When Atlasov arrived in Anadyrsk, the local cossacks already had heard about a land farther south, called Kamchatka. This knowledge probably came from the reports of natives or from unrecorded journeys of the cossacks themselves. They may have heard of the legend, still current as late as 1737, when it was noted by Müller and Krasheninnikov, of Fedot Alekseev Popov and others of Dezhnev's companions who were stranded there and later killed by Koriaks.[1] The Kamchatka River appears on the earliest Russian map of Siberia which has come down to us, that made at the order of the voevoda of Tobol'sk, P.I. Godunov, in 1667, and the name or variants of it, appears thereafter on various Russian and western European maps. On Nicolaas Witsen's map made in Amsterdam in 1687, it is called 'Kamtzetna'. Isbrandt Ides, who went to China as an ambassador of Moscow, 1693–95, writes in his account of his trip, first published in the Netherlands in 1704, that 'Kamsatka and the country farther along by the sea-side is inhabited by a people called *Xuxi* [Chukchi] and *Koeliki* [Koriaks] . . .', that 'there is a gulf which comes up to Kamsatka, that affords prodigious quantities of sea-horses and other sea fish . . .', [the Penzhina gulf, well-known today as a fishing ground] and that 'not far above Kamsatka is a passage which the seal-fishers and others make very good use of.'[2]

In 1696 Atlasov sent the cossack, Luka Morozko, to the River Opuka in the land of the Koriaks. Morozko went much father, down the west coast of Kamchatka as far as the River Tigil. There he seized a native fortified settlement and brought back some mysterious writings, probably from a wrecked Japanese ship.[3]

ATLASOV'S EXPEDITIONS TO KAMCHATKA

With the information obtained by Morozko, Atlasov organized an expedition to Kamchatka in 1697. It consisted of sixty servicemen and sixty Iuka-girs.Travelling on reindeer, Atlasov and his party crossed the mountains and after two and a half weeks reached the River Penzhina, the same route taken by Stadukhin a half century earlier. There Atlasov found three settlements with a total of about three hundred Koriaks. This tribe inhabited the region as far as the River Tigil.[4] The Koriaks were frightened of the newcomers and surrendered their villages without fighting. Atlasov collected iasak in red foxes because there were no sables there. In describing this people he wrote that they were of average height, had no beards, were sedentary, and had no domestic reindeer. They were armed with spears and bows, were dressed in reindeer skins, used seal skin for the soles of shoes, and covered their tents with reindeer hides; they ate fish and the flesh of seals and other animals; they hunted seals and whales in large seal skin boats about forty-two feet long and ten feet wide, which carried thirty to forty hunters. They had no religion, wrote Atlasov, only sorcerers who shrieked and beat drums. In barter, they were anxious to get iron knives and axes.[5]

From the mouth of the Penzhina, Atlasov continued for two weeks along the west coast, the route taken by Morozov. He then turned east, crossed the Seredennyi Range, and in February 1697 found himself on the Oliutora Gulf. The Koriaks of the Oliutora were a backward people who did not even know of iron. Atlasov found them to be very similar to the Koriaks of the Penzhina. He imposed iasak in foxes because the local sables were of a pale, inferior variety. He then divided his group into two parties. One, under the command of Morozko, was to explore the eastern coast of the peninsula; the other, under Atlasov, recrossed the range to investigate the western coast.

On the Palana River, Atlasov ran into trouble. The Iukagirs of the Anadyr rebelled and besieged the ostrog of Anadyrsk. Somehow the news reached Atlasov's men, and some of the Iukagirs in his party attacked the Russians, killing three and wounding fifteen, including Atlasov himself. Forced to ask aid from Morozko, Atlasov sent word of his situation by a loyal Iukagir, and Morozko came to the rescue. Meanwhile, the mutineers heard that the revolt of their tribesmen on the Anadyr had failed; so they came back to Atlasov asking forgiveness. He flogged them and accepted them back.

After this incident the expedition went farther south along the western coast to the Tigil. Here the servicemen and promyshlenniks in the party heard of the rich and populated Kamchatka River country and persuaded Atlasov to go there. He recrossed the range and in June came to the Kamchatka River. He found there four large fortified settlements containing about four hundred huts. The inhabitants were Kamchadals, a people related to the Koriaks and Chukchi.[6] Surprisingly, they were glad to see the Russians and gave iasak readily. They were at the time hard pressed by other Kamchadals who lived along the lower course of the river and asked Atlasov for help against their enemies. Atlasov consented, built some boats, and sailed down the river.[7]

On the way, the Russians noticed numerous Kamchadal settlements along the banks, containing between three hundred and five hundred huts. In three days they reached one such village of about four hundred that was inhabited by the enemies of their friends. Atlasov demanded submission and iasak. On being refused, he attacked the village, captured it, and burned it, killing a number of the natives. This friendly service done, Atlasov returned to the upper course of the Kamchatka. From there he sent out scouts to investigate the lands and people along the Kamchatka and its tributaries. As a result of this survey, it was determined that about 25,000 Kamchadals lived on the river and its tributaries.[8]

In his description of the Kamchadals, Atlasov said that they were of short stature, bearded, and looked like the Zyrians of the Ural region. They wore clothes made of sable, fox, and the skins of reindeer and seal. They sewed the skins together like a quilt and used dog fur to decorate the collars, sleeves, and hems of their coats. In the summer they lived in huts called *balagans,* built on stilts about twenty feet high, which they reached by ladders. The buildings were constructed of wood and pine bark. During the winter they lived in dwellings dug in the earth, lined with timber on the inside, and with an opening in the ceiling which served as a door, window, and chimney. Their diet consisted mainly of raw fish and meat. For winter use they split fish and hung them up to dry or buried them in the ground. Afterwards they dug up the decayed fish, put it in large wooden basins, added water and heated it with hot stones. They then drank the soup-like mixture. They also used fish fat obtained by filling their boats with water, bringing it to a boil with hot stones, boiling the fish and rendering the fat. They used wooden utensils and clay pots. In addition they had wooden lacquered articles, apparently of Japanese origin, which they had acquired by barter. From the Russians they preferred blue beads and knives.[9]

When the Russians came, the Kamchadals were still living in the Stone Age; metal was unknown to them. Krasheninnikov notes that their bows were made of whalebone, arrowheads of sharpened rocks and bones. Their axes were made of reindeer and whalebone and attached to the handles by leather thongs. With them they chipped out of wood their boats, bowls, and troughs; but the labour required was so great that it took them three years to finish a boat and a year to make a wooden bowl. They made needles of sable bone, and they could sew with them very skillfully.[10]

The Kamchadals were terrified at the first sight of Russian firearms and called the Russians 'men of fire', believing that they breathed fire. According to Atlasov, they were sometimes very courageous in war and sometimes cowards. In winter they fought on skis; in summer they sometimes fought naked. He also said that they seldom fought among themselves. After the Russians came they fortified their settlements by earthworks and palisades. From these they threw rocks and stones, either by hand or by a sort of sling; but these caused little harm. The Russians approached the fortifications under the cover of large shields and then tried to throw burning objects into the Kamchadal huts. Then, when the Kamchadals tried to escape through the gates, the Russians fired on them. Sometimes the Russians dug through the earthen walls under the cover of musket fire. The Kamchadals built boats which carried from ten to twenty people. They had no livestock, but kept dogs with exceedingly long fur and sometimes used their skins for clothing. They used traps to catch animals and nets to catch fish. The Kamchadal social system was simple, like that of most of the Siberian peoples, being based on the clan, and their religion was based on shamanism. They derived hallucinations of a semi-religious nature from a drink prepared from a variety of toadstool,[11] which had an effect similar to lysurgic acid (L.S.D.). The men had from one to four wives, depending on their means.[12]

When Atlasov returned to the upper course of the Kamchatka, he discovered that the 'reindeer Koriaks' (so-called in distinction from others of a more sedentary way of life) had driven away his reindeer (which he had presumably left with the friendly Kamchadals while going down the river to fight their enemies). Setting out in pursuit, he caught up with the Koriaks on the coast. After a fierce battle which lasted almost twenty-four hours, and in which 150 Koriaks were killed, Atlasov recovered his reindeer, so important for transportation and food.[13]

The party then proceeded south for six weeks, as far as the River Icha, whence Atlasov sent out scouts to investigate the tribes in the surrounding area. He heard there that farther south there was yet another people, the Kuriles. This was the first heard of the Ainu, the strange sub-group of the Caucasian race aboriginal to the Japanese islands and the Kuriles. Some, with an admixture of Kamchadal blood, inhabited the southern tip of the Kamchatka peninsula.

On the Icha River Atlasov also heard of a strange prisoner kept by the Kamchadals of the River Nana. Atlasov ordered them to bring the captive to him. He described him as a man who somewhat resembled a Greek, slender, dark haired, with a small mustache. He said he was from the state of 'Uzaka' (Osaka), subject to the government of 'India' (probably Hondo [Nippon] or Endo [Tokyo]), as the Russians understood it, which made them think him to be a Hindu. Atlasov spoke very highly of the prisoner's courtesy, intelligence, and cleanliness, and contrasted these qualities with those of the Siberian natives. This prisoner was, of course, a Japanese. He had been captured along with two compatriots by the Kuriles, but the other two, unaccustomed to a diet of roots and decayed fish, had died in captivity. The survivor wept when he met the Russians, and seeing Russian icons said that there were similar images in his own land. He was literate and had a book with 'Hindu' writings. Atlasov took him away from the natives and later brought him to Anadyrsk, whence in 1701 he was sent to Moscow and presented to Peter I, who commanded that he be taught Russian, so that he might then teach three or four boys Japanese.[14]

From the Icha, Atlasov continued south as far as the mouth of the Golygina River. Although he went no farther, from that point he was able to perceive an island, Alaid (now Atlasov Island) which later explorers found to be the northernmost of the Kurile islands.

At the Golygina, Atlasov came in contact with the Kurile tribesmen, darker and more heavily bearded than the other peoples of Kamchatka, living in six settlements. As the Kuriles refused to pay iasak, the Russians seized one of their settlements and killed fifty of them. Afterwards finding the Kuriles to be poor and unable to give iasak, they left the other settlements alone. Sables and foxes were abundant in their land, but the country was warmer than in the north, and thus the fur was of poorer quality.[15]

Atlasov then returned to the Icha, where he founded a zimov'e, and dispatched Potap Seriukov with twenty-seven men (fourteen Russians and thirteen Iukagirs) to the River Kamchatka, where they built the ostrog of Verkhne-Kamchatsk and collected iasak from the natives. The other members of the expedition, exhausted, prevailed upon Atlasov to return to Anadyrsk where the party arrived on 2 July 1699.[16]

From Anadyrsk, Atlasov went to Iakutsk, arriving on 3 June 1700, and from there, in view of the importance of his exploration, the voevoda of Iakutsk sent him on to Moscow to report in person. There, on 10 February 1701, he gave the Siberian prikaz the information already related and data on the geography of the area he had visited. The winters were milder than in Moscow, without much snow, especially in the south. In summer there were heavy thunderstorms and heavy rains. He described the many volcanoes as high mountains shaped like hay stacks which smoked in the daytime and shot out sparks and gave off a red glow at night. When one climbed them, noise and thunder could be heard. His detachment had lived largely on the meat of their reindeer and on fish which they confiscated from the natives. Sometimes they themselves caught fish with nets brought along from Anadyrsk. The fish on Kamchatka were of a different kind than those in Russia. There were about seven new varieties. One kind of fish, he said, went up the river from the sea and did not return to the sea (salmon). The fish were abundant, and along the rivers there were sables, foxes, and otters which lived on fish. He noted the abundance of birds, especially wild ducks. There were lakes which did not freeze, where wild swans lived. There were a great many wild berries, some of an unfamiliar kind. Green berries of one type (*Trillium obovatum*) tasted like raspberry and were nearly the size of an egg. A certain type of grass had a sweet taste; the natives used it as a sweet; the Russians made a wine out of it and discovered that the juice killed head lice. There was also a variety of small cedar. There were whales and seals in the sea along the coast. The natives killed the seals by clubbing them while they were on shore.[17]

DISORDERS, AND THE END OF ATLASOV

After presenting his report in Moscow, Atlasov was promoted to the rank of golova and appointed to administer Kamchatka. He was authorized to enroll a hundred men from Tobolsk, Eniseisk, and Iakutsk for cossack service, and to draw a small cannon, muskets, lead, gunpowder, and other necessary equipment and supplies.[18]

Just when his prestige and prospects were at their highest, however, Atlasov yielded to the piratical side of his nature. On the way back to Kamchatka, in 1701, on the Lower Tunguska River, he and ten men accompanying him met a Russian merchant's boat laden with Chinese goods and plundered it. When the news reached Iakutsk, Atlasov and his men were arrested and thrown into prison.[19]

In the meantime, Potap Seriukov, who, with sixteen cossacks, had been left by Atlasov at Verkhne-Kamchatsk, had enjoyed relatively good relations with the local Kamchadals. Because of the smallness of his force, he merely traded with them and did not try to collect iasak. After waiting in vain for reinforcements, however, he started out in 1699 for Anadyrsk, but on the way he and his men were attacked and killed by Koriaks.[20] When the voevodas of Iakutsk learned of this, in 1700, they appointed the boyar-son, Timofei Kobelev, as prikashchik of the ostrogs of Kamchatka and sent him to punish the Koriaks guilty of the murder of Seriukov and his party. Kobelev and his men travelled by reindeer from Anadyrsk to the Gulf of Penzhina, then went southward by kochi, evidently built on the spot, along the Kamchatka coast. Finding the Koriaks he judged responsible for the death of Seriukov and his party, Kobelev destroyed their village. He then moved the zimov'e of Verkhne-Kamchatsk to a better location and established the zimov'e of Nizhne-Kamchatsk at the mouth of the Kamchatka river.

Upon the arrival of Mikhail Zinov'ev, sent from Iakutsk in 1702 to replace Atlasov, Kobelev returned with the iasak he had collected, arriving in Iakutsk in 1704. Zinov'ev instilled some order into iasak collection by initiating the use of iasak books, giving the natives some protection against demands for double payment and depriving those registered in the books of any possibility of evading payment.

Zinov'ev's successor, Vasilii Kolesov, successfully placed the whole peninsula under iasak, including the remaining Kurile tribesmen, who had previously been independent.[21] A group of his men led by Mikhail Nasedkin reached Cape Lopatka at the tip of the peninsula and reported seeing land in the sea beyond it, doubtless Shumshu, one of the Kurile islands.[22] Kolesov expanded the zimov'es of Verkhne-Kamchatsk and Nizhne-Kamchatsk into ostrogs, and on the Bol'shaia River erected the zimov'e of Bol'sheretsk, later the main administrative centre for the peninsula.

Kolesov would have been replaced in 1705, but first one replacement, sent out from Iakutsk for that purpose in 1704 and then another, sent out in 1705, were killed on the way by the Koriaks of the Oliutora River district. Finally, in April 1706, Kolesov set out for Iakutsk, travelling first in *baidars* (boats made of sealskin, stretched over a wooden framework) to Aklansk ostrog, at the head of the Penzhina Gulf. At Aklansk, friendly Koriaks put Kolesov on his guard against an attack by another Koriak tribe, and, after waiting fifteen weeks at Aklansk for the onset of winter, he and his party, bearing the iasak, made their way to Iakutsk.

Following Kolesov's departure, the cossacks lived unrestrained by authority, seizing native women and enslaving youths, and spending their time in drink and gambling. Exasperated by the harsh exactions of the Russians, and encouraged by news of the actions of the Koriaks on the Oliutora, the Kamchatka natives rebelled. They killed many iasak collectors and destroyed the zimov'e of Bol'sheretsk.[23] Seeking a man to maintain order in Kamchatka, the authorities in Iakutsk again turned to Atlasov. In 1707 he was released from jail and given complete charge of the region, with wide authority, including the right to flog the cossacks. He was warned to avoid extreme measures, especially mistreatment of the natives, but even on the journey his conduct so angered his men that nearly all joined in sending a protest to Iakutsk. Upon arrival in Kamchatka in July, Atlasov took over command of the ostrogs of Verkhne- and Nizhne-Kamchatsk and custody of the iasak that had been collected.

Atlasov pacified the natives, but because of his harsh rule, in December 1707 his own cossacks rebelled and imprisoned him. In justification they complained to Iakutsk that he had not distributed foodstuffs collected from the natives; that he had released native hostages for his own gain, thereby imperilling men collecting iasak; that he had struck down with his sword anyone who dared oppose him and had boasted that the Government would not punish him even if he killed them all; that he had appropriated trade goods for his own use; and, worst of all, that he had appropriated hundreds of sable, red fox, sea otter, and other choice skins which were Government property.[24]

It could be expected that Atlasov's hard-bitten subordinates put down this bill of particulars more in envy then self-righteousness, and their characteristic turbulence no doubt at least partly justified the harshness of his rule.

In any case, Atlasov was not yet through. He escaped from captivity at Verkhne-Kamchatsk, and fled down river to Nizhne-Kamchatsk, hoping to take command there. However, the local commander, Iarygin, refused to step aside, and Atlasov had to dwell there on sufferance.

When the authorities in Iakutsk received the complaints of Atlasov's men regarding his conduct on the way to Kamchatka, they wrote to Moscow for instructions and sent in place of Atlasov the boyar, Ivan Paniutin, with fifty-five men, and the boyar-son Petr Chirikov, with fifty men, along with two copper cannon and a hundred cannon balls, powder, and lead. Near Penzhina Bay, on 20 July 1709, the Oliutora Koriaks fell on them and killed Paniutin and ten of his men. Chirikov and the others escaped.

When, in January 1709, word reached Iakutsk of Atlasov's abuses and of his arrest by his men, the authorities there sent word to Chirikov to conduct an investigation and to send the resultant testimony to Iakutsk along with the iasak collected in 1707, 1708, and 1709. Chirikov, however, was having enough trouble keeping control of his men and protecting his command against hostile natives. When he sent a detachment of forty men to the Bol'shaia River, the Kamchadals attacked in force, killed eight cossacks, and besieged the others for a month until they broke free and fled to safety. Chirikov later led a punitive detachment to quell the natives. On another occasion he led fifty cossacks to Avacha Bay and rescued four shipwrecked Japanese held prisoner by the Kamchadals.[25]

In August 1709 Osip Mironov (or Lipin) arrived with forty cossacks to take charge at Verkhne-Kamchatsk.[26] Chirikov, at Nizhne-Kamchatsk, prepared to return to Iakutsk with the accumulated iasak. Both men had gained the dislike of the cossacks, however, and on 23 January 1711 while both were on the road between the two ostrogs the cossacks attacked and killed Mironov and captured Chirikov. Thirty-one of the mutineers then went to Nizhne-Kamchatsk to kill Atlasov. The main body concealed themselves near the ostrog and sent three of their number within the gates to seek out Atlasov, with the stratagem that they would give him a letter and kill him while he read it. But this proved unnecessary; the mutineers caught Atlasov in his quarters asleep, and there killed him.[27]

Thus died, rather ignominiously, the figure whom Pushkin has referred to as 'the Ermak of Kamchatka'. That comparison seems overdrawn, for, as F. A. Golder has observed, he cannot be called either the 'discoverer' or the 'conqueror' of Kamchatka, but rather 'it would be more just to call him the 'explorer' of Kamchatka, because in that particular field he was superior to any Siberian of his time. His description of the peninsula and its inhabitants is one of the best and shows him to have been a man endowed with a clear and observing mind.'[28] Those qualities, combined in a strange dualism with an amoral penchant for violence and brigandage, carried far with hardiness and intrepidity, made him representative *par excellence* of the breed which conquered Siberia.

ANTSYFEROV AND KOZYREVSKII RECONNOITRE THE KURILES (1711)

The mutineers, joined by the cossacks at Nizhne-Kamchatsk, were now seventy-five in number. They divided the property of the slain prikashchiks, met in a traditional cossack circle, and elected the ringleaders Danilo Antsyferov and Ivan Kozyrevskii as ataman and *esaul* (captain). They plundered supplies gathered by Atlasov for a boat journey across the Bay of Penzhina to the mainland and by Mironov in order to send Chirikov across with the iasak. They then transferred their headquarters to Verkhne-Kamchatsk, where on 20 March 1711 they threw Chirikov, still fettered, into the river.[29]

The mutineers prepared a petition to the Government explaining their deeds on the grounds that the officers had cheated them of part of their salaries, and that they had appropriated state goods for themselves.[30] To further redeem themselves they set out in the spring for the Bol'shaia river to subdue the rebellious natives. In one battle on 23 May they killed so many of the natives 'that their bodies dammed up the river', while the mutineers lost only three of their own number. After that the natives submitted and resumed paying iasak. In August, Antsyferov and Kozyrevskii crossed the strait from Cape Lopatka and became the first Russians to visit the Kuriles. They landed on the island of Shumshu and perhaps the next island, Paramushir. From the Ainu inhabitants they obtained information about the islands farther south, and returned to Bol'sheretsk 18 September 1711 with a tentative map of the whole Kurile chain.[31]

CONTINUED DISORDERS

Later in the same year, 1711, unaware of the fate of his three predecessors, the cossack desiatnik Vasilii Sevast'ianov (Shchepetkoi), arrived from Iakutsk to replace Mironov. Finding the latter had been killed by the mutineers, he nevertheless began the collection of iasak at the ostrogs of Verkhne- and Nizhne-Kamchatsk. The mutineer leader, Antsyferov, seeking forgiveness for his crimes, now voluntarily brought the iasak which had been collected at Bol'sheretsk ostrog and was sent back by Sevast'ianov to collect more. However, in February 1712, fate caught up with him on the Avacha River. The natives willingly gave Antsyferov and his men a large balagan to sleep in and gave him hostages, whom he placed in chains, and promised to pay him all the iasak he desired. That night, however, they prepared to set fire to the building in which the Russians and hostages slept. They got word to the hostages, but the latter could not free themselves and refused rescue, desiring only that the cossasks should not escape death. The natives set fire to the building and all the inmates perished.

Thus the law was deprived of punishing Antsyferov for his crimes. The historian Krasheninnikov observed that his death proved the truth of a proverb the mutineers had, that on Kamchatka one could live seven years as he wished, but would then have to live for seven years as God willed.[32]

Sevast'ianov, his life probably saved by the elimination of Antsyferov and many of his men, left Kamchatka in July 1712 for Anadyrsk, taking several years' accumulation of iasak. He and his men built boats at the mouth of the Kamchatka River and went along the coast to the Oliutora River. There, however, the party was forced to halt because of the shallowness and swiftness of the river at that season. To protect the iasak and themselves from the Oliutora natives, they built fortifications. Wood was scarce, so instead of an ostrog (palisade), they made dug-out dwellings.[33] Sevast'ianov and eighty-four men remained there until 9 January 1713, when help came from Anadyrsk in the form of sixty men and a number of reindeer to carry the iasak. In January 1714 Sevast'ianov finally arrived in Iakutsk. It was the first iasak to be delivered since 1707, other attempts having failed because of the attacks by the Koriaks or the cossack mutinies. From 1703 at least two hundred servicemen had lost their lives in this region.[34]

As soon as Sevast'ianov had departed, the *zakashchik* (foreman), Konstantin Kirgizov, mutinied at Verkhne-Kamchatsk, gathered the men of that ostrog, and went down the river to Nizhne-Kamchatsk, where they manhandled the zakashchik, Iarygin, and a priest, plundered their possessions, beat some of Iarygin's men, and forced Iarygin to resign his command and become a monk.

Retribution came to Kirgizov in the person of Vasilii Kolesov, formerly in Kamchatka as a cossack piatidesiatnik (1704–6), and now a nobleman (*dvorianin*). He had left Iakutsk to replace Sevast'ianov in 1711 and had arrived at Nizhne-Kamchatsk in September 1712 with authority to deal with the mutineers. Two men were executed; several had their ears cut off and their nostrils slit; others were branded. At Verkhne-Kamchatsk, Kirgizov held out for awhile, but eventually his men placed him under arrest, and Kolesov took command in 1713. Kirgizov and several of his closest associates were hanged, others were mutilated or fined.

Kozyrevskii and his men at Bol'sheretsk were beaten with the knout or were fined, and in April 1713 Kolesov sent Kozyrevskii with fifty-five servicemen and promyshlenniks and eleven Kamchadals to expiate their guilt by exploring 'the sea islands and the Japanese state'. They investigated only the first two islands, Shumshu and Paramushir, but returned with considerable information about the islands to the south, and also with Japanese swords, iron kettles, lacquered wooden ware, and paper and silk materials.[35]

In April 1713 the nobleman, Ivan Eniseiskii, arrived to replace Kolesov. Eniseiskii led an expedition of 120 Russians and 150 Kamchadals against the Avacha natives who had killed Danilo Antsyferov and his men the year before. The natives took refuge in such a strong ostrog that the cossacks besieged it for two weeks without result. Finally they set fire to it and killed all Kamchadals who fled the fortress. They dealt similarly with another settlement, sparing only those who submitted and promised to pay iasak.[36]

In 1714 Eniseiskii collected his iasak, and leaving Ivan Kozyrevskii temporarily in charge, departed with Kolesov, who had been unable to go the preceding year because of insufficient personnel.

The continued disorders in Kamchatka, culminating in the murder of the three prikashchiks, Mironov, Chirikov, and Atlasov, and the failure to receive iasak for several years finally forced authorities in Tobolsk to turn attention to the remote region. To put an end to the disorders, the Governor of Siberia, Prince Gagarin, enrolled the clerk, Petr Tatarinov, as captain in the Tobolsk dragoons and ordered him to take over the ostrog of Anadyrsk and command of Kamchatka.[37] Tatarinov set out in the summer of 1713 with fifty-eight dragoons and cossacks and 140 serving men, but because of lack of provisions had to leave most of them in zimov'es along the way, arriving at Anadyrsk on 27 April 1714 with only a few men.

Tatarinov found Afanasii Petrov, erstwhile commandant of Anadyrsk, engaged in action against the Koriaks on the River Oliutora, aimed at building an ostrog there which would guarantee safe arrival of iasak sent from Kamchatka by sea. With the aid of reinforcements and supplies sent by Tatarinov, Petrov built a fence around the principal Koriak settlement and on 6 August attacked. From behind shields, his men threw grenades and finally took the ostrog, killing all of the defenders.

Taking homage of the neighboring Koriaks, Petrov began building the ostrog of Oliutorsk. On 24 August boats arrived from Kamchatka bearing the prikashchiks, Kolesov and Eniseiskii, with iasak. Petrov appropriated reindeer from the Iukagirs on the Oliutora and set out with Kolesov and Eniseiskii with the iasak.[38]

This action proved to be the last straw for the Iukagirs. Petrov had taken them from Anadyrsk, with their families and herds, to campaign on the Oliutora. Many had been injured in the fighting. They had been forced to hunt down fugitive Koriaks, bringing back fingers of the slain as proof of their zeal: those returning without such trophies were hanged. Their reindeer were taken in such numbers that they and their families were on the verge of starvation; they were refused permission to return to their native tundra; and Petrov demanded payment for tobacco and other trade items they had consumed.[39]

On 2 December, as the party made its way to Aklansk, the Iukagirs struck. In a raging blizzard, Kolesov and Eniseiskii with several cossacks pushed on ahead, leaving Petrov and the main body in camp. Soon after they left, the natives fell on the encampment, killed most who were there, including Petrov, and seized all the iasak. Meanwhile, Kolesov and Eniseiskii, finding the going too rough, were forced to turn back to camp. One of the party pressed ahead, came on the bodies of the slain, and hastened back with the news. Eniseiskii, Kolesov, and the others then fled to Aklansk, the Iukagirs in close pursuit.

Eniseiskii sent word of what had happened to Tatarinov at Anadyrsk by a converted Koriak, stating that he had at Aklansk only eleven service men and some Koriaks of doubtful loyalty, and that the ostrog was surrounded by Iukagirs. Tatarinov tried to send powder and lead and gifts for the Koriaks, but the emissaries came upon a large body of Iukagirs and fled back to Anadyrsk, abandoning all their reindeer and supplies. Tatarinov, with only forty cossacks at Anadyrsk, could do little but sit tight and send requests for reinforcements to Iakutsk.[40] Finally, on 19 February 1715, a Koriak convert brought word from Sergeant Afanasii Surgutskii, a iasak collector, of the discovery in a Iukagir village of furs and other things evidently belonging to Russians. Heading for the protection of Oliutorsk, Surgutskii heard that the Aklansk Koriaks and the Iukagirs had killed Eniseiskii and Kolesov and most of their small force of serving men.

The Iukagirs and Koriaks next besieged Oliutorsk. The Iukagirs finally broke off and returned to their pastures on the upper Anadyr, but the Koriaks continued their siege. Driven by hunger, the garrison made up a party of twenty-nine, under Surgutskii, to go and get fish from the Koriaks on the River Pokhacha, who until then had been faithful to the Russians. While they were going through the mountains, the Koriaks attacked and killed Surgutskii and most of his party. Then, just when the remainder of the garrison, weakened by privation and illness, had lost all hope, smallpox broke out among the Koriaks. Thereupon the Koriak elders, thinking the epidemic the effect of conjuring by the Russians, ordered a retreat.

Tatarinov's requests for reinforcements and news of the killing of the prikashchiks and loss of the iasak reached Iakutsk on 15 March 1715. The authorities sent the nobleman, Stepan Trifanov, to Anadyrsk to restore order and recover the plundered iasak, and to send him to Iakutsk by a new route across the Sea of Okhotsk.[41] Trifanov took a slow, roundabout route, by way of the Aldan, the Indigirka, the Alazeia and the Kolyma. His advance party arrived in Anadyrsk on 19 January 1716, and Trifanov himself with the main body only on 8 May.

Tatarinov, meanwhile, finding the situation eased, had managed to retrieve most of the plundered iasak from the Iukagirs and send it to Iakutsk, as well as to send out parties to build a new ostrog at Aklansk and to repair the one at Oliutorsk.[42] After disputes over who would lead, Tatarinov and Trifanov took 120 cossacks to the River Penzhina in August 1716. Although they defeated the Koriaks at Aklansk, Tatarinov felt they lacked men for pursuit; they therefore returned to Anadyrsk, taking along some Koriak children as hostages. The arrival of reinforcements and supplies in the spring of 1717 enabled them to resume the offensive, however, and in April the Koriaks again submitted, buying their pardon by attacking their erstwhile Iukagir allies.[43]

The difficulty of communicating with Kamchatka, until then involving a six-month journey between Iakutsk and Anadyrsk alone, with consequent inability to supervise affairs there or to send aid in time of need, led to consideration of a sea route from Okhotsk. As mentioned before, as early as 1710 the cossack desiatnik, Vasilii Sevast'ianov, sent from Iakutsk to manage affairs in Kamchatka, was ordered to look into the possibilities of the route. In 1713 Peter I ordered shipbuilders and seamen sent to build a vessel with which to investigate the route. In compliance with the order, the serviceman, Kuz'ma Sokolov, formed a company in Iakutsk which made its way to Okhotsk to construct a vessel. They built a fifty-four foot open boat (*lodka*), and in June 1716 Sokolov, a seaman, Nikifor Treska, and several others took it on its maiden voyage to the mouth of the Tigil River. Thereafter this route, usually covered in about a week, was in general use.[44] Prikashchiks who were sent out from Iakutsk, took the sea route, and, if not arrested by their own men or killed by natives, each remained about a year before returning.

THE EL'CHIN EXPEDITION

Interest in St. Petersburg at this time was directed to more ambitious aims. In 1716 the voevoda of Iakutsk, Ia. A. El'chin, proposed a large expedition to study the coasts of Kamchatka and Chukotka. The Senate approved, authorized the so-called Great Kamchatka Command(*nariad*), and assigned extensive resources. In 1718, however, El'chin was summoned to St. Petersburg to answer certain charges, El'chin's second-in-command died, and the expedition was dissolved. It served mainly as a prototype for later efforts.[45]

EVREINOV AND LUZHIN MAP THE KURILES (1721)

In 1719, Peter I sent two topographers, Ivan Evreinov and Fedor Luzhin, to the region. Their instructions were 'to travel to Kamchatka and from there, as instructed, and to describe . . . whether Asia and America are joined by land. . . .'[46] This, however, appears to have been only a camouflage for other aims contained in secret instructions, the contents of which remain unknown. Probably they were to investigate whether there was silver ore on the Kurile Islands, as had been indicated in the report of Kozyrevskii, who wrote that the Japanese obtained silver from the sixth island. Whatever their true aim, Evreinov and Luzhin sailed in September 1720 from Okhotsk to Kamchatka, wintered there, and in May 1721 sailed to the Kurile Islands. They reached the sixth island, probably Simushir, and returned safely to Bol'sheretsk. They then sailed to Okhotsk and, without telling local authorities what they had done, hurried from there to European Russia. In 1722 they reported their findings directly to Peter and showed him the map they had made of the Kuriles,[47] which influenced later maps.

FURTHER DISORDER

Meanwhile, in spite of this official attention, affairs on Kamchatka had continued along their customary course. In 1715 the piatidesiatnik, Petrilovskii, rebuilt the ostrog of Oliutorsk and in the following year made his way from there to Kamchatka by sea. Taking over at Nizhne-Kamchatsk, he at once began to feather his nest, plundering not only natives but cossacks, using the knout, cudgel (*batog*), and torture. He took the property of the former mutineer, Kozyrevskii, and forced Kozyrevskii and Iakov Iarygin, in charge at Nizhne-Kamchatsk, to become monks. The cossacks, finally losing patience, arrested Petrilovskii, confiscated his goods, and entrusted the collection of iasak to the trader (*posadskii*), Koz'ma Vezhlivtsov. Petrilovskii was sent to Iakutsk in 1720 and there tried not only for his oppressive acts, but for necromancy, because of a manuscript found in his possession. Vezhlivtsov was succeeded by a service man, Kamkin, from Anadyrsk, and he in 1718 by Vasilii Kachanov, a member of the El'chin expedition.[48]

Kachanov, in an effort to win the loyalty of the Kamchadals, released two native leaders, Kivriu and Kupka, long held as hostages. These, learning of various depredations committed by the Russians, led their people in revolt. The Kamchadals killed several Russian iasak collectors before a punitive force restored them to order by burning certain of the offending villages and killing most of the inhabitants. Blaming Kachanov's conciliatory policy for the revolt, the cossacks sent a complaint to Iakutsk, confiscated Kachanov's goods, and would have arrested him had he not fled.[49]

In June 1719 the voevoda of Iakutsk, Rakitin, sent the nobleman, Ivan Kharitonov, to Kamchatka as prikashchik. Kharitonov had special orders to bring the Kurile Islands to submission, but never reached them. Hearing early in 1720 that the Palana River Kamchadals had refused to pay iasak, he led a force of sixty cossacks into their territory. The offending tribesmen willingly gave iasak and hostages, and, lulled to a sense of false security, Kharitonov and his cossacks settled down in a yurt for the night. As soon as the Russians were asleep, the Kamchadals fell on them with spears and knives, killing Kharitonov and nine of his men, and wounding fourteen others. The remaining cossacks, taking arms, counterattacked, and only left the village after not one Kamchadal remained alive. Not knowing Kharitonov's further plans, they returned to Bol'sheretsk, ravaging other Kamchadal villages on their way.[50]

A period of relative tranquility followed. Prikashchiks, now furnished with comprehensive written instructions, came and went annually. Priests were brought to the peninsula to provide spiritual guidance for the unruly cossacks and to convert the natives, attempts were made to regularize iasak collection and to prevent cheating either government or natives, and a census was taken of the natives and their property.

BERING'S FIRST EXPEDITION

In December 1724, Peter I, dreaming of an Arctic route to China and India, ordered what later became known as the First Kamchatka Expedition, to determine whether there was actually a strait separating Asia from America. Vitus Bering, a Dane in Russian service, was appointed to head the expedition.

Early in January 1725, Bering left St. Petersburg with Lieutenants Aleksei Chirikov and Martin Spanberg, and a train of geodesists, pilots, shipbuilders and other personnel. Still others joined along the way. Travelling by land, the unwieldy force arrived at Tobol'sk on 17 March 1725, waited for spring, set out again by boat down the Irtysh to the Ob, followed the Ob's right tributary, the Ket, as far as the ostrog of Makovsk, portaged a hundred miles to Eniseisk, continued by boat again up the Enisei, the Upper Tunguska (Angara), and the Ilim, and arrived at Ilimsk on 25 September. After wintering at Ilimsk, the party set out on 5 May 1726 by portage to the River Muka, then travelled by boat along the Muka and the Kut to the ostrog of Ust'-Kut on the river Lena, and thence downriver to Iakutsk, where they arrived in June 1726. From Iakutsk, Bering and others made the eight hundred mile journey to Okhotsk by land. Most of the provisions and light goods were borne by over six hundred packhorses, of which nearly half fell along the way. Bering arrived in Okhotsk on 1 October, and the supply parties straggled in for weeks afterward. Heavy goods were sent by water along the Lena, the Aldan, the Maia, and the Iudoma, and thence by land, under Spanberg. After great hardship and losses, these goods were brought into Okhotsk in the spring of 1727. And since Okhotsk at that time consisted of only a dozen houses, members of the expedition had to build their own dwellings and storehouses.

Already, in 1725, an advance party had begun building in Okhotsk a shitik, or decked boat, for the expedition. The vessel, named the *Fortuna*, was launched in June 1727. The plan was to build a larger vessel at Nizhne-Kamchatsk, but Bering, fearing to risk everything by rounding Kamchatka by water, decided to send goods to Bol'sheretsk on the western shore of the peninsula and then tranship it across to Nizhne-Kamchatsk. Spanberg accordingly sailed with the *Fortuna* on 30 July, unloaded cargo at Bol'sheretsk, and returned for Bering and other personnel. The cargo then had to be carried more than six hundred miles along the rivers Bystraia and Kamchatka on Kamchadal boats, and in winter on sledges drawn by dog teams.

This decision was ruinous for the Kamchadals. Men, dogs, and sledges were requisitioned from all villages for the operation. The Kamchadals lost valuable time that winter for trapping fur animals, essential for their own needs and to satisfy the inexorable demands of the iasak collectors; most of their dogs died, their sledges were lost, and they never received compensation. Bering ordered the exemption of those in service from iasak payment, but the collectors took it anyway for their own use.[51]

At Nizhne-Kamchatsk, Bering supervised construction of the vessel, *Sviatii Gavriil* (Saint Gabriel), and on 13 July 1728, nearly four years after leaving St. Petersburg, he and his party put to sea. Then followed the indecisive survey of the strait now bearing his name, after which Bering returned to Nizhne-Kamchatsk on 2 September 1728 and wintered there. On 5 June 1729 he set out again, this time hoping to reach undiscovered shores of North America. Instead, meeting strong winds and mist, he turned the vessel back on 8 June, rounded the southern tip of Kamchatka, landed in Bol'sheretsk on 2 July, and thence sailed to Okhotsk. From there he set out across Siberia, arriving in St. Petersburg on 1 March 1730 to report his limited achievements to an unenthusiastic Senate.

THE SHESTAKOV EXPEDITION

Even before the results of Bering's expedition were known, however, St. Petersburg had ordered another, under the cossask golova, Afanasii Shesta-kov, to study the whole northeastern region of Siberia and adjacent islands, to explore the coasts, and to conquer the Chukchi and Koriaks. Four hun-dred soldiers of the Tobol'sk infantry regiment under command of Captain Dmitrii Pavlutskii, to be assistant to Shestakov, were assigned to the expedition, along with pilot Iakov Gens, assistant pilot Ivan Fedorov, geodesist Mikhail Gvozdev, and other specialists. To further his work, the Senate made Shestakov 'commander-in-chief of the northeastern region' (*glavnyi komandir severo-vostochnogo kraia*). His expedition was to work independently of Bering's, but the two were to help each other when possible.[52] In 1729 parts of the expedition were arriving in Okhotsk just as Bering returned from his voyage. The members of the expedition built two vessels, the *Vostochnii Gavriil* (Eastern Gabriel) and the *Lev* (Lion), and acquired two others, the *Sv. Gavriil* and the *Fortuna*, from Bering.

In the autumn of 1729 Shestakov boarded the *Vostochnii Gavriil* and set out for the mouth of the Penzhina River, thence to go by land to the Anadyr River and Chukotka. He was accompanied by the *Lev,* which was to proceed from the Penzhina around Kamchatka to Anadyrsk. The *Fortuna,* commanded by Shestakov's son Vasilii, was to take cargo to Bol'sheretsk and investigate the Kurile Islands. The *Sv. Gavriil,* under his nephew Ivan, was to examine the Shantar and Kurile Islands and, if time permitted, go to 'the great Land' (America).

Only the last of these aims was carried out. The Koriaks fell on the crew of the *Lev* at the mouth of the River Iama, killed almost everyone aboard, and burned the vessel. Shestakov undertook an expedition into the Koriak land to pacify the natives but on 14 March 1730 he was killed in a skirmish on the Egach River between the Rivers Paren and Penzhina. The men on the *Sv. Gavriil* failed to find the Shantar Islands and returned to Okhotsk, whence, in September 1730, pilot Iakov Gens took the vessel to Kamchatka. With it sailed the *Vostochnii Gavriil,* commanded by Ivan Fedorov, but this vessel was wrecked near the mouth of the Bol'shaia River in a storm. Only in July 1732 did Fedorov and Gvozdev, on the *Sv. Gavriil,* chart the Diomede Islands in Bering Strait and stand briefly off Alaska, near Cape Prince of Wales, thus effectively demonstrating, as neither Dezhnev nor Bering had done before, the division between Asia and North America.[53]

THE KAMCHADAL REBELLION OF 1731

Meanwhile, in spite of this official attention, affairs in the northeastern regions had continued to be characterized by misrule and lawless behaviour on the part of officials and subordinates and by native rebellion. In the spring of 1729 a cossack piatidesiatnik, Andrei Shtinnikov, leading a party of Kamchadals, murdered fifteen shipwrecked Japanese for their few belongings.[54] According to testimony at a government inquiry held several years later, Ivan Novgorodov, in charge of iasak collection on Kamchatka in 1730, bought his appointment from the voevoda of Iakutsk, Ivan Poluektov, for seven hundred rubles. Under his rule the Kamchadals were forced to pay iasak twice and even three times a year. If they did not, their women and children were beaten mercilessly or enslaved. Novgorodov's successor, Mikhail Shekhurdin, confessed to similar misdeeds and revealed that he had received a large amount of furs as bribes for permitting individual cossacks to collect iasak, in turn giving a share of this to the same voevoda, Poluektov.[55]

Goaded to desperation by this rapacious and cruel behaviour, and encouraged by rumours that the Koriaks had wiped out the force led by Afanasii Shestakov, some of the Kamchadal leaders began to consider ways to rid their land of the Russians. As a people of simple culture, scarcely able to count beyond twenty, large combinations were foreign to them, but they had learned something of Russian military tactics and methods of defence, and a few had learned to use firearms, acquired by trade or theft. Prominent among the advocates of revolt was Fedor Kharchin, a Christian convert who had often served as an interpreter for the iasak collectors.

The Kamchadals around Nizhne-Kamchatsk waited until the numbers of the Russians would be at their lowest point. First, the prikashchik, Shekhurdin, left Kamchatka with the iasak from the preceding year. Then, on 20 July 1731, the *Sv. Gavriil* set sail for the Anadyr. At once the Kamchadal chieftains ordered their men to their boats. The natives killed whatever cossacks they met, took their wives and children as concubines and slaves, and burned their huts. That evening they reached the ostrog, set fire to a house, then killed the cossacks who ran to put out the flames. They killed nearly all of the settlement and seized the fort. A few survivors, however, bore the news to the ship, which had had to drop anchor because of headwinds and was still lying in the mouth of the Kamchatka. Hearing that the ship was still there and that a force had disembarked, Kharchin and his band occupied the ostrog, dismantled the church to build a second wall, and called on their compatriots for reinforcements. The next day they plundered the houses of the cossacks and danced and strutted about in their clothes, some in women's and others in priests' clothing.

From the ship, a Russian force of sixty men, led by the pilot, Iakov Gens, came and halted before the walls of the ostrog. They called to the Kamchadals that they could have the Tsar's mercy if they would submit, but were only answered by jeers and abuse. Gens then sent to the ship for cannon, and on 26 July his force opened fire and blew a hole in the wall. This caused such a panic among the defenders that the captive women were able to flee. Kharchin, seeing that the game was up, clad himself in women's clothing and also fled. He was pursued, but, as he could run like a deer, he escaped. Thirty men then surrendered, but others fought on, until a shot ignited the magazine, and the entire fort and all its rich content of furs blew up. Only four cossacks were killed in the struggle, but many were wounded, and the others were so enraged that they slaughtered all the prisoners.

Kharchin rallied his supporters and retreated to a height above the Kliuchevka River. On 29 August the pursuing cossacks drew up on the opposite bank. Negotiations began, but by a ruse the cossacks captured Kharchin and then easily dispersed and hunted down his followers. Some of the native leaders killed their families and committed suicide.

Meanwhile, word of the native capture of Nizhne-Kamchatsk had encouraged other Kamchadals to revolt. They killed all the cossacks who did not take refuge in Bol'sheretsk and Verkhne-Kamchatsk ostrogs. However, armed parties from both ostrogs, reinforced by a detachment from Nizhne-Kamchatsk, advanced on the natives, killed guilty and innocent alike, and captured women and children. By the summer of 1732 the peninsula was again at peace.[56]

PAVLUTSKII'S EXPEDITION AGAINST THE CHUKCHI

In the north, similar action was undertaken against the Chukchi by Captain Pavlutskii. Arriving in Anadyrsk on 3 September 1730, Pavlutskii was met by requests for aid from the Koriaks, who had suffered repeated raids from the Chukchi, in which hundreds of iasak-paying Koriaks were slain or forced to renew their earlier submission to the Chukchi, and in which entire reindeer herds were driven off. On 12 March 1731 Pavlutskii and a force of 215 Russians, 160 Koriaks, and 60 Iukagirs headed north into Chukchi country. According to his later report, which may be exaggerated, on 14 June he defeated seven hundred Chukchi, killing three hundred, with no Russian losses, and drove off forty thousand reindeer. On 30 June near Bering Strait, he met and put to flight a thousand Chukchi. After further campaigning, he and his men returned to Anadyrsk on 21 October.[57]

In the following year, on 10 February 1732, Pavlutskii set out with another party for the Gizhiga Bay area to punish the Koriaks responsible for the murder of the crew and the burning of the *Lev* in 1729. On his return to Anadyrsk, Pavlutskii received an order sent out from the Siberian Prikaz on 10 August 1731, telling him to take command over the Shestakov expedition, but enjoining him not to go against the Chukchi until ordered and to treat them well. From the Governor-General at Tobolsk he received word of his promotion to major.[58]

The authorities in far-away St. Petersburg now decided to tighten control over the turbulent easten maritime holdings. Convinced that the remoteness of Iakutsk made it difficult for the officials there to follow the deeds of persons sent to such remote places for iasak, St. Petersburg made Okhotsk the administrative centre for the whole northeastern region of Siberia, including Kamchatka.[59]

MAJOR MERLIN RESTORES ORDER (1733–1739)

Upon receiving a report of the rebellion on Kamchatka, the authorities at Tobolsk sent word to Iakutsk to send Major Vasilii Merlin to Kamchatka with a party to investigate the causes and to set up a Field Enquiry Office (*Pokhodnaia rozysknaia kantseliariia*). This party set out from Iakutsk on

6 July 1733 and arrived in Kamchatka on the *Sv. Gavriil* in September. Merlin at once assumed the protection of the Kamchadals from Russian oppression and ordered an elder in each native village to speak for his people. He set about investigating the causes of the revolt, the chronic state of disorder among the Russians, and the killing of the fifteen Japanese. He reported his findings, which eventually received approval, and in 1735 carried out sentences. In all, nine Kamchadal leaders, including Kharchin, were executed; forty-four others were beaten with the knout. Russian wrongdoers fared equally hard. For their great 'outrages and destruction', four were hanged, including Shtinnikov, who had slain the Japanese, and the former commissar, Novgorodov; fifty-seven, including the former commissar, Shekhurdin, were beaten with the knout, three others with the cudgel (*batog*); one soldier was made to run the gauntlet. When, in the autumn of 1739, Merlin departed for Okhotsk, he left affairs on the peninsula in better order than at any time since the Russians first appeared there.[60]

BERING'S SECOND EXPEDITION

Meanwhile, preparations had now begun on Kamchatka for Bering's second expedition, part of a grandiose complex today known collectively as the Great Northern Expedition, aimed at wholesale reconnaissance of the Arctic and Pacific coasts of Siberia. Ordered in April 1732, the enterprise was to consist of three detachments. One, under Bering, was to try to reach America; another, under Spanberg, was to explore the islands of Japan, and a third, actually several expeditions, was to explore the Arctic coast. Any one of these operations was of great scope and difficulty; Bering was charged with responsibility for all three. In the spring of 1733 the aging navigator set out from St. Petersburg with five hundred men. In Siberia he picked up five hundred soldiers, several hundred cossacks, and other personnel. The Academy of Sciences sent the naturalists, Johann Georg Gmelin and Georg Wilhelm Steller; the historian and geographer, Gerhard Friedrich Müller; the astronomer, Louis Delisle de la Croyère; the future historian of Siberia, Johann Eberhard Fischer; and the student, S. P. Krasheninnikov, future writer of the classic history and description of Kamchatka.

The expeditions to America and Japan were delayed for some time by the needs of the parties assigned to explore the northern coasts. Despite extreme hardships and a high cost in lives and resources, these groups achieved brilliant success. In 1734–35 Lieutenants Stepan Murav'ev and Mikhail Pavlov explored the Kara Sea coast and along the west coast of the Iamal Peninsula, reaching, respectively, latitudes 73°04′ and 73°11′

north, before being forced back by ice. In 1736–37 Lieutenants Stepan Malygin and Aleksei Skuratov rounded the Iamal Peninsula. In 1734–37 Lieutenant Dmitrii Ovtsyn sailed from the Ob to the mouth of the Enisei. In 1738–40 pilot Fedor Minin and Lieutenant Dmitrii Sterlegov penetrated from the Enisei eastward to the west coast of the Taimyr Peninsula. Lieutenant Vasilii Pronchishchev in 1735 and Lieutenant Khariton Laptev in 1739–40 explored the east coast of the peninsula. In 1736-43, Lieutenant Dmitrii Laptev managed, first, to follow the coast eastward from the Lena to the Indigirka, and then to continue as far eastward as Cape Bol'shoi Baranov, beyond the mouth of the Kolyma, before being stopped by ice. Other parts of the expedition made slow progress across Siberia, reaching Iakutsk in the fall of 1735 and covering the final, hardest stretch to Okhotsk in 1736. Then followed the painfully slow accumulation of needed supplies and the building and equipping of ships.

In the spring of 1738 Spanberg, in the three-masted brig *Arkhangel Mikhail,* accompanied by Lieutenant William Walton in the three-masted double sloop *Nadezhda* and Lieutenant Alexis Schelting in Bering's old vessel, the *Sv. Gavriil,* sailed from Okhotsk to Bol'sheretsk and thence southward to investigate the Kuriles and the islands of Japan. The vessels separated, Spanberg mapping most of the Kurile Islands as far as the Island of Urup, Walton reaching the Island of Hokkaido. In 1739 both Spanberg and Walton independently reached the main Japanese Island of Honshu.[61]

Bering finally launched his own part of the enterprise on 8 September 1740, putting to sea from Okhotsk in the two packet boats, *Sv. Petr* and *Sv. Pavel,* and a double sloop and a galiot carrying supplies. On 20 September they arrived at Bol'sheretsk. The water outside the river mouth was too shallow for the *Sv. Petr* and *Sv. Pavel,* so the two supply ships were left there, and the two larger vessels continued to Avacha Bay. There the members of the expedition built a zimov'e and named the harbour Petropavlovsk after the two vessels.

Again the Kamchadals and their dogs and sledges were drafted to bring the goods overland from Bol'sheretsk to Petropavlovsk. Frightened by the demand, some of the natives rebelled, killing twenty Russians and fleeing with their wives and children to the protection of some rocks at the mouth of the Utkoloki River. At Bering's order, a force of soldiers surrounded the rocks and drove the fugitives out with hand grenades. Bering, Chirikov, and others interrogated the prisoners and with the aid of the knout singled out seven for punishment as instigators of the mutiny.[62]

On 4 June 1741 the *Sv. Petr,* under Bering, and the *Sv. Pavel,* under Chirikov, set forth to seek new lands. After a vain hunt for a non-existent 'Gama Land', a brief visit to America, and sighting some of the Aleutians, Bering's vessel was wrecked on 4 November on what became known as

216

Bering Island, and the navigator and nineteen of his men died there. On 26 August 1742 the survivors built a small boat from the wreckage of the *Sv. Pavel* and managed to return to Petropavlovsk.[63] Chirikov also reached America, but the mysterious disappearance of two shore parties, probably slain by Indians, deprived him of his two small boats, and he returned to Kamchatka.[64] These were meagre results in view of the effort expended and the lives lost. The main result of the expedition was the reconnaissance of the Aleutian Islands and the return of Bering's party with furs, which started a rush of private traders to the islands.

THE PACIFICATION OF KAMCHATKA

Following the departure of surviving members of the Bering expedition, life in Kamchatka resumed a more normal course. As Krasheninnikov, who observed the region from 1737 to 1741, puts it, probably with irony, 'peace and tranquility' settled over the troubled peninsula. Indeed, measures taken during the reigns of Empresses Anna and Elizabeth did somewhat lighten the burden of iasak upon the Kamchadals; their arrears were cancelled, and those who accepted Christianity were freed from iasak payment for ten years. The first school in Kamchatka was established at Bol'sheretsk in 1741, and subsequently others were established in most of the ostrogs for the joint instruction of cossack and native children. From 1742 Russian priests began to convert the Kamchadals in wholesale numbers. Rough measures were used on those slow to see the light: by 1744 six thousand out of a population of ten thousand were converts.[65]

The Government nevertheless remained suspicious of Kamchadal motives and potentiality for rebellion. In 1743 the Senate ordered their villages kept under close surveillance. During the Koriak uprisings of 1745–49, much was made of an alleged plot by certain Kamchadal chieftains to aid the Koriaks.[66] Except for minor flare-ups in the 1740s, however, and the killing of nine Russians in 1756, the Kamchadals showed no heart for further resistance. Their numbers declined, suicides becoming so frequent that the Government ordered local officials to try to take preventive measures. Finally, in 1768–69, a disastrous smallpox epidemic swept the peninsula. By 1773 only 706 iasak-paying Kamchadal males were left,[67] or about twenty-five hundred of both sexes.

THE SUBJUGATION OF THE KORIAKS

Fate was similarly relentless toward the Koriaks. Angered by attempts at conversion and by Russian failure to defend them against the Chukchi, in November 1745 they wiped out two parties of Russians totalling twenty-four men, then laid siege to the ostrog of Aklansk until May 1746. After the Russian garrison evacuated the ostrog, the Koriaks plundered and burned it. In 1753 the Koriaks attacked the Russians near Izheginsk (Gizhiginsk, on the Gizhiga River), and on 15 September 1755 fell upon a shore party from a vessel in Penzhina Bay, killing two sailors. These outbreaks were followed by the usual punitive expeditions, until at last, in 1757, the Koriaks, having lost over half of their number, asked for peace. The smallpox epidemic of 1768–69 nearly annihilated the remainder.[68]

THE SUBJUGATION OF THE CHUKCHI

The Chukchi, described by an eighteenth century writer as 'the most savage, the most barbarous, the most untractable, the least civilized,, and the most rugged and cruel people of all Siberia',[69] held out longer than their neighbours. Their attacks on the Koriaks in 1737 and 1738 impelled the Senate to order Major Pavlutskii, after a short time of comparative ease as voevoda of Iakutsk, back into service against them.

Returning to Anadyrsk with several hundred soldiers, Pavlutskii undertook annual punitive expeditions, ravaging Chukchi settlements in an undisguised policy of extermination. Then, on 12 March 1747, the Chukchi invaded the area around Anadyrsk, attacked iasak-paying Koriaks, and drove off a large number of reindeer. That same night, Pavlutskii hastily gathered a force of ninety-seven cossasks and thirty-five Koriaks and set out against them, travelling with reindeer and dogteams. At dawn on the fourteenth, Pavlutskii sighted the Chukchi, nearly six hundred in number, on a mountainside, and without waiting for the rest to come up, attacked. But for once the doughty fighter had bitten off more than he could chew. The Chukchi killed fifty of the Russian party, including Pavlutskii himself, wounded twenty-eight, put the rest to flight, and took their arms, a cannon, and a flag and drum.[70] When news of the defeat reached St. Petersburg, the Siberian Prikaz authorized a force of five hundred dragoons, which set out from Irkutsk in 1748. These made annual forays into Chukchi territory throughout the 1750s.[71]

Ultimately, even the Chukchi had to give way. A large number came to Anadyrsk in 1756 saying that they wanted to live in peace and were willing to pay iasak of one fox skin per man per year, although they would not give hostages. The offer was accepted by the local commander, but other groups continued to attack the Koriaks. This led to Russian retaliation, although a final decision was never reached because of the expense and difficulty of operating in such a remote land.[72]

In 1788 a large group of Chukchi for the first time proposed to trade with the Russians, promising to be true subjects and not to attack the Koriaks. The authorities at Irkutsk authorized what became annual fairs on the River Aniui in the Kolyma region, and on 11 October 1789, by ukaz of the Empress Catherine II, the Chukchi were received as subjects.[73] In the same year, thirty cast iron plates bearing the Russian coat of arms were placed along the shore of Bering Strait, signifying that Chukotka belonged to Russia. But even then the Government accorded the Chukchi special privileges, written into the laws, which they retained until modern times.[74]

SUMMARY

The northeastern region was the last and in many ways the most difficult part of Siberia to conquer. The indigenous Iukagir, Chukchi, and Koriaks, although the most primitive of the Siberian peoples, proved also the most warlike and stubbornly resisted alien encroachment. The remoteness of the region and the severity of its climate taxed even the endurance and enterprise of the cossack frontiersmen.

Based on the ostrog of Anadyrsk, founded on the Anadyr River in 1656 following the explorations of Dezhnev and Stadukhin, and the ostrog of Aklansk, founded in 1669, the Russians imposed iasak on the Koriak reindeer hunters. Rumours of a land to the south—Kamchatka—caused Vladimir Atlasov, prikashchik at Anadyrsk, to send in 1696 an expedition which went down the Kamchatka coast as far as the River Tigil. In 1697 Atlasov himself led an expedition which went south nearly to the end of the peninsula, conquering the Kamchadals.

The region's isolation made it difficult to impose Government control, and for many years the region was in an almost constant turmoil, with mutiny, mistreatment of the natives, and native revolts. Order was not established among the Russians until the 1730s. Many of the Kamchadals and Koriaks died in vain attempts to revolt, and epidemics wiped out large numbers. The Chukchi held out until the second half of the eighteenth century.

Government expeditions, especially Bering's second expedition, of 1732–41, greatly advanced knowledge of the Siberian Arctic. The Bering expedition gave a new impetus to the search for furs by bringing back information about the islands of the northern Pacific and the abundance of sea otters to be found there. As they had from many a region before, eyes now turned from eastern Siberia toward yet another frontier, this time beyond the sea.

Chapter 13

Conclusions

The expansion of Russia poses problems in the reconstruction of events, the selection of significant agents, and generalization and analysis. The term 'expansion' is itself an oversimplification, for behind it lie movements of various kinds. Relations in the east and south, usually sparsely populated by more primitive populations, differed from those in the west, which involved contact with settled states.

DIVERSITY OF RUSSIAN EASTWARD EXPANSION

The early Kievan state produced three currents of expansion eventually leading to Asia. One of these was directed toward the southern steppes to ward off the attacks of the Pechenegs and Polovtsy, who raided the Russian settlements and drove the people into captivity. 'Defence lines' were developed, and various diplomatic means were employed to deal with the steppe peoples. The Russian princes tried to attract some of the nomads as allies, using one tribe against another, settling them to protect the frontier, or cementing ties by intermarriage.

A second current of expansion accompanied the decline of Kiev, in which, due in large part to the pressure of nomads and internal strife, some of the population moved away from Kiev into the less populated forest area along the Volga and Oka to the northeast. This movement was in fact a retreat in search of security, but it resulted in a great gain of territory. The movement was gradual and led to Russian infiltration among the scattered Finnish tribes, many of whom accepted Christianity and became assimilated. Together with the newcomers they formed what is known as the Great Russian branch of the Eastern Slavs. The princes followed the colonists; the strong Volga principalities came into existence; and more energetic and enterprising rulers encouraged further colonization in order to gain new subjects, soldiers, and taxpayers.

The rather peaceful expansion in the Volga–Oka area changed its character when the Russians came in contact with the numerous Finnic people of the Mordva, south of the River Oka, and with the Turkic people, the Bulgars, on the east bank of the Volga. In the first armed encounters, the advantage sometimes lay with the Bulgars and Mordva, but by the second half of the twelfth century the Volga princes led several successful expeditions into the lands of the Bulgars and Mordva, destroying their towns and villages and carrying away many prisoners. In 1221 the Russians founded a fortified town, Nizhnii Novgorod, at the confluence of the Oka and Volga, which for three centuries remained the Russian southern frontier terminal on the Volga.

A third current of expansion during the Kievan period started from the wealthy commercial city of Novgorod and went northeastward toward the Arctic Ocean and the Ural Mountains. The Novgorodians were interested in fish, salt, walrus ivory, and particularly in pelts of sables, ermine, foxes, and other animals, which were important items of their internal and external markets. Sailing along the northern rivers and their tributaries, they braved the hardships of difficult travel and obtained valuable furs and other articles from the natives by violence or by trade. Already, in the twelfth century, the Novgorodians reached the urals and before long they became active in the northwestern corner of Siberia.

The early activities of the Novgorodians in the northeast of European Russia were in the nature of raids, but gradually permanent colonies appeared there, and, at least in the valley of the Northern Dvina, a sort of colonial administration was developed. East of the Dvina there were a very few Russian settlements, mostly temporary, serving as stations for the collection of furs brought by the aborigines for trade and as tribute. For a long time the Novgorodians were not disturbed in their 'fur empire', but after the twelfth century they acquired competitors. The colonization of the Volga–Oka region began to overflow across the Volga and spread along its northern tributaries, which are separated by easily passable portages from the rivers descending into the Arctic Ocean—the Novgorodian northern trade routes. The Volga princes began to look enviously at the Novgorodian profits from the fur trade. With the aid of their own colonists north of the Volga and of rebellious Novgorodian colonists, they made a series of armed attempts to obtain a hold in the Novgorodian colonial possessions.

Novgorod was saved from these dangerous rivals by the Mongol invasion and for a time was able to exploit its northeastern territories without interference. Gradually, however, Mongol power declined, and the principality of Moscow rose not only to take the place of the earlier Volga principalities but to unify and liberate all of Russia. Novgorod resisted this renewed aggression from the Volga area until 1478, when she and her colonies were absorbed by Moscow.

Two of the currents of expansion noted earlier were thus joined. The third, toward the south, proceeded more slowly, in the face of the Tatar overlords. Profiting from strife within the Golden Horde and the secession of Kazan and the Crimea, Moscow itself gained liberation in 1480. Striving to prevent the fragments of the Horde from recombining, employing adroit diplomacy, encouraging defectors, and building defence lines in the steppe, the Moscow rulers gradually extended their sway, although it would not be until the eighteenth century, with the annexation of the Crimean khanate, that the struggle in that sector would finally be won.

In the northeast, Moscow remained largely within the limits of Novgorod's erstwhile possessions until 1552, when Ivan the Terrible conquered Kazan, removing the road block on the easiest route to Siberia. A few years later the merchant family of the Stroganovs established a private chartered colony west of the Ural Range and financed the raid of Ermak and his cossacks east of the Urals. The successful outcome of this raid showed the government that Siberia was accessible and vulnerable and that possibilities existed for an enormous increase of state revenues from the exploitation of the Siberian fur resources.

The ensuing advance was at first systematic, controlled by the government, but during the 'Time of Troubles' the initiative passed to local commanders, and thereafter the government usually lagged somewhat behind the forces of local commanders and private traders before finally establishing control. This lag was particularly noticeable in the Amur region and in Kamchatka. Even when they arrived on the scene, the government men were usually accompanied by frontier traders who augmented the fighting force of the expeditions and in turn benefited from the protection afforded by government troops. The valley of the Amur was conquered through the efforts of a frontier trader, Khabarov. He organized and financed the expedition himself, although assisted by the local administration. By the early eighteenth century, the Russians had explored Siberia and to a large degree exhausted its fabulous fur wealth. The Bering expedition gave a new impetus to the search for furs, causing merchants, fur traders, and cossacks to turn to the sea and eventually bring Russian dominion to the shores of North America.

CAUSES

Numerous attempts have been made to provide some comprehensive explanation of these movements and those of the eighteenth and nineteenth centuries which brought Russia to the Black Sea littoral, into the Caucasus, into Central Asia, and back to the Amur valley.

The interpretation put forward most persistently is that Russia expanded merely to satisfy an obsession for the acquisition of territory and a lust for power over other peoples. Such views have arisen whenever Russia has made new territorial gains or has aroused concern in other countries over her further intentions. But ideas of this sort are not borne out by the facts. With the exception of individual rulers, particularly Peter the Great and Catherine the Great, who had far-reaching ambitions, the several currents of expansion from Kievan times, the varied aims of trade and defence, the frequent exercise of private initiative, and pure chance create a record of diversity which refutes any theory based on mere megalomania on the part of those in power.

Others have claimed special qualities for the participants in the advance. Thus, Johann Fischer, concluding his *History of Siberia*, published in 1744 under the auspices of the Russian Imperial Academy of Sciences, exclaims that 'Greece, Rome, and the Old and New Worlds can take pride in their heroes and praise them as much as they please; I do not know if they would have dared to do what the Siberian heroes Buza, Perfil'ev, Nagiba, Khabarov, Stepanov, and many others did'.[1]

Frank A. Golder, on the other hand, denying such singularity, states that

entirely too much emphasis may be laid on the actors in the play at the expense of the play itself. The Siberians of the seventeenth and eighteenth centuries were part of a movement in which they were caught and carried along without leaving any impress of their personalities. They were men of more or less average ability, yet from the time of Müller to the present it has not been possible to speak of them with calmness. As soon as the banner bearing the magic word 'promyshlennik' is waved we are expected to fall on our knees and bow to heroes. As a matter of fact they were, at best, very ordinary men and some of them were vicious and depraved. . . . In every seaport town and in every frontier community one will find men who risk their lives and suffer hardships for the sake of pleasure and gain just as the Siberians did. There is nothing heroic about all this and if we stop to think it will be seen that it is very commonplace.[2]

Golder provides a needed antidote for the praise sometimes lavished on the promyshlenniks and cossacks, but he goes too far. The participants in the advance had many shortcomings, but it took more than 'average ability' to achieve what they did. From the 'very ordinary men' to be found in every seaport and frontier settlement might have come the rank-and-file—the followers—but the leaders, however reprehensible, were few and outstanding. They were brutal and ruthless, but they explored and took possession of a continent. Excluding any idea of hereditary traits shared by all the members of their group, one can still credit them with exceptional individual abilities, which were called to use by the challenge of their environment, and the good sense to make use of the fund of experience left by those who had gone before.

There is equally some foundation for explaining the Russian expansion in these sectors by factors of geographic determinism. That terrain, resources, and climate would help to set the direction of the various parts of this movement is inescapable. Thus, the flatness of the Russian plain has invited a search for defensible frontiers. The river system provided natural highways and had a centrifugal effect. Rough though they were, the participants in the advance can also be credited with some feeling for the great lands which they traversed. The lands ahead must have called them on, always to another river, another mountain range, in a supreme adventure which transcended mere hopes of personal gain.

Going beyond the undoubted effects of physical geography, however, many writers have attributed certain 'instincts' for expansion to the Russians. Thus, in the United States the view was put forth repeatedly by Robert J. Kerner, a leading figure in Slavic studies, of a Russian 'urge to the sea, a centuries-old national longing,' which dominated Russian history.[3] Other writers have made similar assertions, but though recurrent, this line of reasoning is inadequate as a comprehensive explanation of Russian expansion. It is obvious, for example, that an enormous landlocked country like Russia would at various times seek an outlet to the sea, but such an explanation can hardly be applied to all areas of expansion. As John A. Morrison has pointed out in a penetrating critique of this concept, the greatest amount of Russian territory was gained for other reasons.[4]

As we have seen, the early acquisitions of Novgorod and Moscow in northeastern European Russia, and the later expansion of Moscow across Siberia involved a quest for furs. The expansion in the southern part of Russia was for centuries a form of defence against the attacks of nomadic peoples. Ivan the Terrible's aspiration to maritime trade by way of the Baltic and White Seas and Peter the Great's drive for 'a window on Europe' bear out the hypothesis, but the Russian movement into central Asia grew out of the intention to establish a Russian land trade route to India and from the quest for secure frontiers. The reacquisition of the Amur valley in the nineteenth century was motivated in part by need of a good base for eastern Siberia and the Russian American colonies, and partly by fear that other powers might occupy the region. Georgia, in the Caucasus region, was acquired when the Russian government accepted that Christian country under a protectorate to defend it from Moslem Persia and Turkey. The conquest of the turbulent Caucasian tribes separating Georgia from Russia was undertaken in order to secure safe communications. The acquisition of the Black Sea coast did not become a goal until the eighteenth century, when the government for the first time became conscious of the possibility and desirability of reaching the Mediterranean trade. The effort to obtain a warm-water port in the Far East, from the 1890s, was a conscious aspiration of Russian leaders which foreigners chose to interpret as a late manifestation of an 'age-old longing.' It would seem, therefore, that although physical geography must be considered of great importance in Russian expansion, the variety of conditions at various periods makes it impossible to explain all the related movements by this single factor.

Another alleged cause of Russian eastward expansion, frequently suggested, has been the tendency of the Russian people toward migration and colonization. This tendency has been evident from early times, in the outward migration of peasants and in the formation of the various cossack groups. To the great Russian historian, S. M. Solov'ev, colonization was 'one of the dominant phenomena of early Russian life',[5] while, in the oft-quoted words of the illustrious V. O. Kliuchevskii, 'the history of Russia is the history of a country in the process of colonization, . . . migration and colonization have been the basic factor in our history'.[6]

The importance of this factor can be demonstrated readily enough, although here, too, earlier foreign writers frequently took the matter to an absurd degree, attributing the movements to instincts peculiar to the Russian people. But did this colonization in any case play any particular role in the phases of Russian eastward expansion considered here? It would seem that it did apply to the steppe, with the growth of cossack communities and the gradual movement of peasants into lands secured by the defence lines. It does not appear, however, to have played any particular role in the initial advance into Siberia, nor in the subsequent exploration and conquest. The conquest of Siberia did not in itself mark a renewal of the colonization process, it merely prepared the way for that renewal. Consquently, colonization must be rejected as an important factor in connection with the advance into the region.

An economic motive suggested for the Russian advance into Siberia is more easily demonstrated. The desire of the state for revenue and of individuals for personal enrichment centred on furs. Although stressing that the economic life of Russia took many other channels as well, Raymond H. Fisher, in his detailed study of the role of this commodity, shows furs to have been pre-eminent among the raw products traded by the Russians from early Kievan times. The exhaustion of fur resources of the forest regions of the Dnepr River basin was a cause of the decline of the Kievan state. The fur wealth of northeastern Russia led to the rise of Novgorod and its commercial empire and in time caused inroads by the rising state of Moscow which resulted in the loss of Novgorodian independence and the appropriation of its territories. The quest for furs then became an important motive behind Ermak's crossing of the Urals and a primary cause of much of the subsequent advance.

Finally, in this quest for causes of Russian eastward expansion, one may single out the psychology of superiority characteristic of all expansionist peoples, convinced of their right to dispossess inferior and barbaric foes, to establish the true faith, and to reap the economic benefits of dominion. In the Russian consciousness, this feeling dates back certainly to the acceptance of Christianity in 988, with all of the implied and expressed superiority of the believer over the unenlightened and the right to conquer and proselytize. The feeling intensified with the development of the 'Third Rome' concept in the fifteenth century. It appears in the cloak of piety which was laid upon the conquest of Kazan in 1552 and upon every Muscovite conquest that followed. Contemporary accounts picture Ermak and his followers as chosen by God to vanquish the unbelievers. It appears in the contests with the Turk, the Tatar, and the Pole. It comes out strongly in the openly expansionistic elements in Russia in the nineteenth and early twentieth centuries.

These sentiments, almost as old as Russia, unite the seventeenth-century promyshlennik with the twentieth-century empire builder, and both with the Roman legionary, the Spanish conquistador, or the North American 'Indian fighter'.

Summing up, one may ascribe the Russian eastward advance to four main factors: (1) the physical features, particularly rivers and plains, which facilitated movment; (2) the qualities of the participants who, without recourse to innate 'urge' or 'instinct', responded ably, if not always nobly, to the challenge of their environment; (3) the drive for furs; and (4) the national psychology which permitted the participants to disregard the rights of the primitive peoples in their path and to take the land for Russia.

EFFECTS

From consideration of the causes of Russian eastward expansion, one may turn to its effects. What influence did the advancing frontier exert upon Russia, upon those who pushed it forward, and upon the regions occupied?

The most comprehensive statement of any experience possibly analogous to that of Russia is F. J. Turner's famous hypothesis concerning the influence of the frontier upon the development of the United States.

Turner, it will be recalled, asserted in 1893 that 'the existence of an area of free land, its continuous recession and the advance of American settlement westward, explain American development'.[7] This development, he claimed, had been constantly conditioned by a succession of frontier zones. A social laboratory, the frontier had given rise to the doctrine of democracy and attitudes toward government, and from the common experience had emerged a distinctly American people.

This hypothesis, the most influential single contribution ever made to American history, has been discussed ever since, and although subjected to much criticism, still commands many adherants. Efforts also have been made to apply the hypothesis to other parts of the world with an advancing frontier. Thus, B. H. Sumner states that 'throughout Russian history one dominating theme has been the frontier; the theme of the struggle for the mastering of the natural resources of an untamed country, expanded into a continent by the ever-shifting movement of the Russian people and their conquest of and intermingling with other peoples'.[8]

Inasmuch as Russia's frontiers on the southern steppe and in Siberia, especially the latter, would seem in part analogous to the American frontier, some aspects of the Turner hypothesis might therefore seem applicable. Here, however, one must first make the distinction that Turner was talking mainly about the influence of the frontier upon the American colonies, or the societies into which they were transformed, rather than upon the motherland, England. Second, the limitation of the present study to the line of advance itself, rather than to the settlement and subsequent administrative, social, and economic development which occurred in its wake, excludes a number of possible similarities with the American West from discussion here. Only part of the hypothesis, that concerning the frontier as 'the outer edge of the wave, the meeting point between savagery and civilization', can be applied. In this light, one may consider some of the remaining similarities, real or apparent. Thus, Turner sees 'the American national character' developing as the frontier moved westward: 'To study this advance, the men who grew up under these conditions, and the political, economic, and social results of it, is to study the really American part of our history.' Assuming the existence in some degree of sets of qualities which distinguish one people from another, it would seem that the 'national character' of Russia may well have been affected by centuries of contact and conflict with steppe peoples, but could hardly have been shaped by the rapid and relatively late movement of a few men across Siberia, any more than England or France were shaped by their American colonists. One cannot start with the Russian crossing of the Urals as if it were the equivalent of the landing of the Pilgrims at Massachusetts Bay. If the origin of the majority of Russian characteristics is sought, one would have to examine as far as possible the earlier, largely prehistoric phase of Russian history, when the population lived for centuries under frontier conditions and worked out the considerable fund of culture already present by the ninth century, when Russian recorded history began. Involving a vastly greater period of time, the impact of that earlier frontier would have been more general and deeper than that of the later, shorter period of advance with which this study has been concerned.

Turner's assertion, with regard to the American people, that 'the frontier promoted the formation of a composite nationality', can certainly be applied to Russia, but again one must also turn to very early times, even antedating the movements from Kiev into the frontier in the Volga region that resulted in a mixture with Finnic tribesmen to form the Great Russian branch of the Eastern Slavs. Again, just as the 'isolation of the [American frontier] region increased its peculiarly American tendencies', so probably did the cultural isolation of early Russia help to shape the Russian character and to determine the nature of the later advance. On the other hand, it may have been the isolation of the frontier, rather than any 'unifying tendencies', which furthered the differentiation of the Eastern Slavs into Great Russians, Ukrainians, and Belorussians.

Turner stated further that American development exhibits 'not merely an advance along a single line, but a return to primitive conditions on a continually advancing frontier. . . . Social development has been continually beginning over again on the frontier.' This seems also applicable to Russia's successive Siberian frontiers. There, as in America, the experience gained on one frontier could be applied to the next.

This 'constant readjustment' on successive American frontiers, which adherants of the hypothesis believe formed a pattern of attitudes and methods which became standard as the advance continued, probably resembles the experience which was gained in early Russia and passed on through successive advances eastward or southward. Thus, from need developed frontier self-help and initiative, while poor communications, the nature of the men involved, and the lag in establishment of central control fostered the frontier lawlessness so characteristic of both countries.

One may conclude from these points, then, that certain of the more general aspects of the Turner thesis do seem applicable to Russia. However, other analogies must be sought for European Russia, in periods antedating those considered in this study or in the course of the settlement which followed the line of advance. Nevertheless, with due allowance for its shortcomings and dissimilar features, this thesis would seem of some use as an approach to the study of the Russian frontier.

ACHIEVEMENTS AND AIMS

Russian eastward expansion (and to that may be linked the earlier phases of southward expansion) thus followed many channels and stemmed from a variety of causes and motives. Is it possible to make any overall characterization of this enormous process, which resulted in the acquisition by Russia of the entire northern part of Asia?

In general, Russian historians have lauded this acquisition. After 1917 Pokrovskii, Bakhrushin, Ogorodnikov, and other Soviet historians for a time pointed out the misdeeds of the participants in the eastward advance, but in the 1930s official desires to lessen the resentment of minority peoples toward Russian dominance became expressed in a selective extolling of the men concerned as explorers and contributors to knowledge, with very little said about their clashes with the natives. Thus, the recent (1968–69) five-volume *Istoriia Sibiri* devotes barely twenty-five pages to the Russian takeover of Siberia and substitutes for the term 'conquest' (*zavoevanie*) the milder 'annexation' (*prisoedinenie*). It states that although there were cases of compulsion (for example, the conquest of the Siberian Khanate), there were other instances of passive or voluntary attitudes of the natives toward annexation. This variance in attitudes and circumstances existed, but using the rare instance of passivity to characterize the Russian takeover as something other than the generally forcible measure that it was would be like referring to Rome's 'annexation' of Gaul, or Spain's 'annexation' of Mexico and Peru on similar grounds.

Soviet historians now label this process, be it conquest or annexation, as 'progressive', in that it brought Siberia out of age-old isolation into contact with the rest of the world and prepared the way for civilization. However, neither 'progress' nor 'civilization' are as clear-cut as they once were. In human and economic terms, the advance into Siberia was enormously destructive. The societies of the natives were shattered, their leaders were removed or bought, their economies were wrecked, and their numbers diminished by the conqueror's diseases and alcohol. The wealth of furs was plundered by uncontrolled hunting methods, almost exterminating the most valuable animals over vast areas, forcing the hunters to go ever farther afield.

Certainly, given the time and circumstances, these results were to be expected. Being but few in number, inhabiting a large area with valuable natural resources, the natives in the path of the advancing Russians, like the inhabitants of frontiers in other parts of the world, were certain to suffer this fate, paying the penalty of backwardness. If the Russians had not penetrated and appropriated the region, other peoples would have done so, as the stronger and more advanced have done in every corner of the globe. Similarly, it must be noted that the plundering of natural resources by the seventeenth- and eighteenth-century Russians was nothing unique, but merely an expression of attitudes which prevailed everywhere until now, when ideas of conservation are beginning to gain acceptance.

Nevertheless, although we cannot now act as a court of posterity on these Russian pioneers, we may gain a better understanding of our own times, motives, and deeds by achieving a better knowledge of theirs. In spite of its detrimental aspects, the Russian advance preceded a great economic achievement which still unfolds. If the problems accompanying this growth can be solved, the lands which once made up Russia's open frontier, along with other Arctic territories, will become increasingly important in world history.

Appendix

A Note on the Ethnic Groups Mentioned in this Work (See map, end paper)

The many peoples of Russia are distinguished by language, culture, and physical characteristics. Language is the principal criterion. Although there is still controversy about certain relationships, several large groups may be discerned. The dominant group in Russia has been that of the *Eastern Slavs*, as distinguished from the Western Slavs (Poles, Czechs, Slovaks) and Southern Slavs (Croats, Serbs, Bulgarians). The languages of the Slavic peoples are part of the far-flung Indo-European group, comprising nearly all the tongues of Europe except for those of the Finns, Magyars, and Turks.

During the period of Mongol rule, three sub-groups appeared among the Eastern Slavs. The *Ukrainians,* sometimes known as the Little Russians, inhabit southern Russia. The *Belorussians,* or White Russians, live in the territories to the west, adjoining Poland and Lithuania. The *Great Russians* are descended from people who settled the upper Volga region, where they blended with the Finnic inhabitants and formed the strong principalities of Vladimir, Suzdal, and later Moscow.

To the north of the Slavs are the *Finnic peoples,* who occupied a large territory extending from northern Russia into the Ob basin east of the Urals. They included the earlier Ves', Chud', Iugra, and Pechorans (Komi*), and still comprise the Mordva, the Permians (Komi*), Zyrians (Komi*), the Cheremis (Mari*), Chuvash, Votiaks (Udmurts*), Ostiaks (Khanty*), and Voguls (Mansy*). Names in parentheses followed by an asterisk are those applied by Soviet historians and ethnologists in an effort to employ the respective peoples' own designations for themselves.

The struggle of the Slavic peoples with successive waves of nomads who invaded the southern steppes was a constant theme in the early history of Russia. The first were Indo-European in language (Cimmerians, Scythians, Sarmatians); then, as if the reservoir of these peoples was finally exhausted, they were followed by others of *Turkic* extraction (Huns, Bulgars, Khazars, Pechenegs, Polovtsy) and finally by tribes rolled up in the advance of the Mongols under Genghis Khan. This conglomerate of peoples, predominantly

Turkic, became known as *Tatars*. When the Mongol state of the Golden Horde broke up, there then appeared the Tatars of the Crimea, of Kazan, and of Astrakhan. Also prominent were the Nogais, the Bashkirs, the Kazakhs, and the Kirgiz. (One should here distinguish between the Kazakhs and the cossacks, the latter being descendants of predominantly Slavic fugitive serfs and others who established themselves in free communities in the river valleys of southern Russia, and who later became involved in the conquest of Siberia. The Iakuts, of the Lena River region in Siberia, are also of Turkic origin; their ancestors apparently fled northward during the turmoil incident to the rise of Mongol power.

The *Mongols*, of Mongolia, of similar culture but of a different language stock from that of the Turkic peoples, first came to prominence under Genghis Khan. The Buriats, of the Lake Baikal area, are of Mongol origin, but did not take part in the movements of the main group of the Mongols.

Northern Scandinavia and the Kola Peninsula of Russia have been inhabited since early times by the *Lapps*, whose reindeer-herding economy resembles that of other peoples all across northern Asia. East of the Lapps, in northern Russia and the Ob basin, are the *Samoyeds* (Nentsy*). Still farther east, in an enormous territory extending from the Arctic Ocean to Manchuria, are the *Tungus* (Evenki*), comprising many peoples. They include the Lamuts, bordering the Pacific, the Manchus, and the Duchers, Giliaks (Nivkhi*), Ol'chi and Natki of the Amur valley. The Daurians are said to be distantly related to the Mongols.

A wide area east of the Lena was occupied by the *Iukagirs* (Oduly*), and the extreme northeast of Siberia by the *Chukchi* (Luorovetlany*), *Koriak* (Nymylany*) and by *Eskimos*. The Kamchatka peninsula was inhabited by the *Kamchadals* (Itel'meny*), and the southern tip of the peninsula and the Kurile islands by the *Ainu* or *Kuriles*, the aborigines of the islands of Japan.

Notes

List of Abbreviations

A.A.E.	Akademiia Nauk. *Akty sobrannye v bibliotekakh i arkhivakh Rossiiskoi imperii Arkheograficheskoi ekspeditsieiu . . .*
A.I.	Russia. Arkheograficheskaia kommissiia. *Akty istoricheskie . . .*
Berg, *O.K.*	Berg. *Otkrytie Kamchatki i Kamchatskie ekspeditsii Beringa.*
Chteniia	*Chteniia u Imperatorskom obshchestve istorii i drevnostei rossiiskikh pri moskovskom universitete.*
D.A.I.	Russia. Arkheograficheskaia kommissiia. *Dopolneniia k aktam istoricheskim.*
D.R.V.	Novikov, N., compiler. *Drevniaia rossiiskaia vivliofika . . .*
P.D.R.V.	Novikov, N., compiler. *Prodolzheniia drevnei rossiiskoi vivliofiki.*
P.S.I.	Russia. Arkheograficheskaia kommissiia. *Pamiatniki sibirskoi istorii XVIII veka.*
P.S.R.L.	Russia. Arkheograficheskaia kommissiia. *Polnoe sobranie russkikh letopisei.*
R.I.B.	Russia. Arkheograficheskaia kommissiia. *Russkaia istoricheskaia biblioteka.*
R.K.O.	*Russko-kitaiskie otnosheniia v XVII veke.*
S.G.G.D.	Russia. Treaties, etc. *Sobranie gosudarstvennykh gramot i dogovorov khraniashchikhsia v gosudarstvennoi kollegii inostrannykh del.*
Sib. let.	Russia. Arkheograficheskaia kommissiia. *Sibirskie letopisi.*

CHAPTER 1

Russian Expansion in Kievan Times

1. From George V. Lantzeff, 'Russian Eastward Expansion Before the Mongol Invasion', read at the meeting of the Pacific Coast branch of the American Historical Association at Claremont, California, 4 January 1947, and published in the *American Slavic and East European Review*, VI, Nos. 18–19 (December 1947), 1–10.
2. Robert J. Kerner, *The Urge to the Sea. The Course of Russian History. The Role of Rivers, Portages, Monasteries and Furs.* (Berkeley, 1946), p. 26.
3. Raymond H. Fisher, *The Russian Fur Trade, 1550–1700.* (Berkeley, 1943), pp. 3–5.
4. Arkheofraficheskaia Kommissiia, *Polnoe sobranie russkikh letopisei*, 24 vols. (St. Petersburg, 1841–1914, cited hereafter as *P.S.R.L.*) IX, 79.
5. E. K. Ogorodnikov, 'Priberezh'ia Ledovitago i Belago morei s ikh pritokami po Knige Bol'shogo Chertezha', *Zapiski Imperatorskago russkago geograficheskago obshchestva. Otdelenie etnografii.* (St. Petersburg, 1877) VII, 32–34.

6. *P.S.R.L.*, II, 3. See also Kerner, p. 26.
7. *P.S.R.L.*, I, 107; M. D. Priselkov, *Istoriia russkago letopisaniia* (Leningrad, 1940), p. 44, suggests that the story was inserted in the chronicle in 1118.
8. N. M. Karamzin, *Istoriia gosudarstva rossiiskago*, 12 vols., 2nd ed., (St. Petersburg, 1818–29) II, 180; notes, 148.
9. *P.S.R.L.*, I, 107; II: 5; Ogorodnikov, 'Priberezh'ia . . .', p. 10.
10. Karamzin, II, notes, 155–56.
11. Ogorodnikov, 'Priberezh'ia . . .', pp. 15, 52, 119, 139, 163, 166.
12. The charter mentions the amount of salt to be delivered to the Bishop from the sea coast. The Novgorodian salt works were situated near the mouth of the Northern Dvina. Karamzin, II, notes, 156.
13. Quoted by Ogorodnikov, 'Priberezh'ia . . .', p. 107.
14. 'Letopisets Dvinskii', *Drevniaia rossiiskaia vivliofika*, 2nd ed., 20 vols. (Moscow, 1788–91), XVIII, 3.
15. Kerner, pp. 31–32, 118–24.
16. Rurik assigned them as fiefs to his warriors. *P.S.R.L.*, I, 9; V. S. Ikonnikov, *Opyt russkoi istoriografii*, 2 vols. in 4 (Kiev, 1891–1908), II:1, 614–15, 855–56.
17. A. E. Presniakov, *Obrazovanie velikorusskago gosudarstva* . . . (Petrograd, 1918), pp. 32, 36.
18. S. M. Solov'ev, *Istoriia Rossii s drevneishikh vremen*, 29 vols. in 15 (Moscow, 1959–66) I, 436, 438; Presniakov, p. 36.
19. *P.S.R.L.*, II, 39.
20. Solov'ev, I, 424–25, 457–58.
21. Presniakov, p. 37.
22. *P.S.R.L.*, II, 88.
23. *Ibid.*, III, 13–14; Solov'ev, I, 516–17, 529–37; Presniakov, p. 37.
24. *P.S.R.L.*, III, 14–15; IV, 12; V, 9–10; Solov'ev, I, 595; D. I. Ilovaiskii, *Istoriia Rossii* 5 vols. (Moscow, 1876–1905), I:1, 254–55.
25. Kerner, pp. 124–25.
26. Solov'ev, I, 254; S. V. Bakhrushin, *Ocherki po istorii kolonizatsii Sibiri v XVI i XVII vv.* (Moscow, 1927), p. 88.
27. *P.S.R.L.*, I, 128; VII, 24.
28. *Ibid.*, I, 150–51, 155; II, 115.
29. *Ibid.*, I, 164–65, 169; II, 125–26.
30. *Ibid.*, III, 17–19, 23, 31.
31. Presniakov, pp. 37–38.
32. *P.S.R.L.*, III, 19; IV, 17.
33. *Ibid.*, V, 169–70; Ilovaiskii, I:2, 196–97.
34. Bakhrushin, *Ocherki* . . . , p. 65.
35. *P.S.R.L.*, V, 169.
36. *Ibid.*, III, 23.
37. *P.S.R.L.*, I, 211–15.
38. Presniakov, p. 40.
39. The origin of Ustiug, at the junction of the Sukhona and Iug rivers, where they form the Northern Dvina river, is uncertain, but during the struggle between Novgorod and Rostov-Suzdal it leaned generally toward the latter and accepted the ecclesiastical jurisdiction of Rostov bishops.
40. *P.S.R.L.*, I, 215; IV, 26; V, 172; VII, 126.
41. *Ibid.*, VII, 126–27.
42. *Ibid.*, VII, 128.
43. In its subsequent history, Nizhnii Novgorod justified these expectations and even superseded Novgorod the Great.
44. *P.S.R.L.*, VII, 134–35, 138.

CHAPTER 2

Russian Expansion under Mongol Rule

1. Presniakov, p. 37.
2. *P.S.R.L.*, III, 50–54.

Notes

3. *Ibid.*, III, 56–57.
4. *Ibid.*, I, 202.
5. *Ocherki istorii SSSR*, 8 vols. (Moscow, 1953–1957), III:1 (*period feodalizma IX–XV vv.*), 773–74.
6. Presniakov, p. 72.
7. *Sobranie gosudarstvennykh gramot i dogovorov khraniashchikhsia v gosudarstvennoi kollegii inostrannykh del* (cited hereafter as *S.G.G.D.*) 5 vols. (Moscow, 1813–94), I, 1–4.
8. Akademiia nauk, *Akty sobrannye v bibliotekakh i arkhivakh Rossiiskoi imperii arkheograficheskoiu ekspeditsieiu* . . . (cited hereafter as *A.A.E.*), 4 vols. (St. Petersburg, 1836; Index, 1838), I, 1.
9. *P.S.R.L.*, III, 63.
10. *Ibid.*, III, 64.
11. V. S. Borzakovskii, *Istoriia tverskogo kniazhestva*, (St. Petersburg, 1876), pp. 18–19; Presniakov, p. 111; G. Peretiatkovich, *Povolzh'e v XV i XVI vekakh, ocherki iz kraia i ego kolonizatsii* (Moscow, 1877), pp. 72–73; *Ocherki istorii SSSR* . . . , II, 136; *P.S.R.L.*, I, 184; III, 33.
12. Peretiatkovich, p. 72; *P.S.R.L.*, VII, 245.
13. *P.S.R.L.*, II, 29; I, 185.
14. *S.G.G.D.*, I, 5.
15. Solov'ev, II, 198.
16. *Ibid.*, II, 198, 216.
17. *P.S.R.L.*, III, 70–73; IV, 48; *S.G.G.D.*, I, 6–18; Solov'ev, II, 218–20.
18. *P.S.R.L.*, III, 72; IV, 49; Solov'ev, II, 221–24.
19. *P.S.R.L.*, III, 72–73; Solov'ev, II, 229.
20. Kerner, pp. 26, 28.
21. *P.S.R.L.*, V, 9;
22. *P.S.R.L.*, IV, 185.
23. *Ibid.*, VII, 127.
24. *Ibid.*, III, 72–73.
25. *Ibid.*, III, 74–78; M. N. Pokrovskii, *Russkaia istoriia s drevneishikh vremen*, 2nd ed. (Moscow, 1913–14), I, 184; Message of Grand Prince Ivan, 1328–40, *A.A.E.*, I, 1–2.
26. S. F. Platonov, *Lektsii po russkoi istorii*, 6th ed. (St. Petersburg, 1909), p. 144.
27. *P.S.R.L.*, III, 79.
28. Platonov, p. 144.
29. *A.A.E.*, I, 3.
30. *P.S.R.L.*, III, 86–87.
31. *Ibid.*, IV, 63; V, 229; VII, 7.
32. *Ibid.*, III, 88; IV, 65–67, 71–72, Solov'ev, II, 295–96.
33. *Ibid.*, IV, 65–66, 93–94; V, 241; Solov'ev, II, 295, 297
34. Solov'ev, II, 555, 561, III, 73; Ilovaiskii, II, 403–6; Bakhrushin, *Ocherki* . . ., pp. 65–66; *P.S.R.L.*, VIII, 61; *Ocherki istorii SSSR*, III:2 (period feodalizma IX–XV vv.), 456–57.
35. Pokrovskii, I, 206.
36. *P.S.R.L.*, III, 81–82.
37. *Ibid.*, IV, 64–65.
38. Pokrovskii, I, 230.
39. *Atlas istorii SSSR*, 3 vols. (Moscow, 1949–50), I, map 15.
40. *P.S.R.L.*, VIII, 61, Solov'ev, II, 363.
41. *P.S.R.L.*, IV, 99.
42. *Ibid.*, III, 96; IV, 100; VIII, 63; Solov'ev, II, 358.
43. *Ibid.*, IV, 100; VI, 123; VIII, 63.
44. *Ibid.*, IV, 100; VIII, 63.
45. *Ibid.*, III, 98.
46. *A.A.E.*, I, 8–9. See also translation of this document in George Vernadsky, *Medieval Russian Laws* (New York, 1947), pp. 57–60.
47. *P.S.R.L.*, III, 81, 99.
48. *Ibid.*, III, 99–100.
49. *Ibid.*, IV, 103.
50. *Ibid.*, III, 101–2.
51. *Ibid.*, XXV, 239, 244; Solov'ev, II, 361.
52. *P.S.R.L.*, III, 106–7.

53. *Ibid.*, III, 110.
54. Solov'ev, II, 422–23.
55. *P.S.R.L.*, III, 111–13; Solov'ev, II, 423.
56. *P.S.R.L.*, IV, 124.
57. *Ibid.*, IV, 217; VIII, 147; Treaty, Novgorod with Ivan III, 1456, *A.A.E.*, I, 43–45; Presniakov, p. 412; Ilovaiskii, II, 335.
58, Karamzin, VI, 192–93; Ilovaiskii, I, 198–99; II, 406; Solov'ev, II, 426.
59. *P.S.R.L.*, V, 271; Solov'ev, III, 73–74; Bakhrushin, *Ocherki . . .*, pp. 51–56; Ilovaiskii, II, 406.
60. *A.A.E.*, I, 66–69.
61. Presniakov, p. 436.
62. *P.S.R.L.*, IV, 128; Solov'ev, III, 21; Karamzin, VI, 43.
63. Solov'ev, III, 73; Karamzin, VI, 51.
64. *Ibid.*
65. Karamzin, VI, 12–21; Solov'ev, III, 34–35.
66. Solov'ev, III, 69.
67. *Ibid.*, III, 35–36.
68. *Ibid.*, III, 74; Bakhrushin, *Ocherki . . .*, 66–67; I. V. Shcheglov, *Khronologicheskii perechen' vazhneishikh dannykh iz istorii Sibiri, 1032–1882* (Irkutsk, 1883), 10; Karamzin, VI, 284–85, fn. 460, 461; *S.G.G.D.*, II, p. 4. 'Drinking water from the gold' was a custom of drinking water which had been run over a gold object such as a plate, cup, piece of jewelry, etc.
69. *P.S.R.L.*, XII, 249; XXVI, 291; XXVIII, 332; Solov'ev, III, 74; Shcheglov, p. 12; Karamzin, VI, 285–286, fn. 462, 463; *Razriadnaia kniga 1475–1598 gg.* (Moscow, 1966), p. 29. G. F. Müller, *Istoriia Sibiri* (Moscow-Leningrad, 1937–1941, 2 vols.) I, 204–5, quotes the chronicles and the cited entry in the records of the *Razriad* (a military affairs department in the Moscow government).
70. See 'O chelovetskikh neznaemykh na vostochnoi strane i o iazytsekh roznykh', in A. Titov, *Sibir' v XVII veke* (Moscow, 1890), pp. 1–6. Discussed by D. N. Anuchin, *K istorii oznakomleniia s Sibir'iu do Ermaka*, in 'Drevnosti', *Trudy Moskovskogo arkheologicheskogo obshchestva*, XIV (Moscow, 1890), cited by V. A. Aleksandrov, 'Nachalo khoziaistvennogo osvoeniia i prisoedinenie k Rossii severnoi chasti Eniseiskogo kraia', *Sibir' XVII–XVIII vv.*, (*Materialy po istorii Sibiri. Sibir' perioda foedalizma*, I), 9, and by M. I. Belov, *Arkticheskoe moreplavanie s drevneishikh vremen do serediny XIX veka* (*Istoriia otkrytiia i osvoeniia Severnogo morskogo puti*, I), 39. 'Molgomzaya' also appears on Jenkinson's map of Russia of 1562.

CHAPTER 3

Liberation and Advance

1. The scope and complexity of the events described in this chapter has largely precluded the use of primary materials. For important secondary accounts providing guidance to such materials, see S. M. Solov'ev, *Istoriia Rossii s drevneishikh vremen;* Henry H. Howorth, *History of the Mongols from the 9th to the 19th Century,* 4 vols. in 5 (London, 1876–1927), chiefly II:1; A. A. Novosel'skii, *Bor'ba moskovskogo gosudarstva s Tatarami v pervoi polovine XVII veka* (Moscow-Leningrad, 1948); Boris Nolde, *La formation de l'Empire Russe: études, notes et documents* 2 vols. (Paris, 1952–53); George Vernadsky, *The Mongols and Russia* (New Haven and London, 1953), *Russia at the Dawn of the Modern Age* (New Haven and London, 1959), *The Tsardom of Moscow, 1547–1682* (New Haven and London, 1969); J. L. I. Fennell, *Ivan the Great of Moscow* (London, 1961); L. V. Cherepnin, *Obrazovanie russkogo tsentralizovannogo gosudarstva v XIV–XV vekakh* (Moscow, 1960); I. I. Smirnov, *Ocherki politicheskoi istorii russkogo gosudarstva 30–50kh godov XVI veka* (Moscow-Leningrad, 1958); K. V. Bazilevich, *Vneshniaia politika russkogo tsentralizovannogo gosudarstva vtoraia polovina XV veka* (Moscow, 1952); Bertold Spuler, *Die Goldene Horde, Die Mongolen in Russland, 1223–1502*, 2d ed., Wiesbaden, 1965.
2. Vernadsky, *The Mongols and Russia,* pp. 290–91; Howorth, II:1, 1022.
3. *Istoriia SSSR,* 2nd ed. (Moscow, 1947) I:248.
4. Vernadsky, *The Mongols and Russia,* p. 290; *Istoriia SSSR,* I:247–48.
5. *Istoriia SSSR,* I, 248.

6. Vernadsky, *The Mongols and Russia*, p. 331. For an extensive account of the Kasimov khanate see V. V. Vel'iaminov-Zernov, *Izsledovanie o kasimovskikh tsariakh i tsarevichakh*, 4 vols. St. Petersburg, 1863–66.
7. S. V. Bakhrushin, 'Sibirskie sluzhilye Tatary v XVII v.,' *Istoricheskie zapiski*, (1937), I:7–8; Bazilevich, pp. 57–58.
8. *Istoriia SSSR*, I, 248.
9. *P.S.R.L.*, VIII, 152; Bazilevich, pp. 64–65.
10. See Chap. 2.
11. Bazilevich, pp. 67–71; Howorth, II:1, 373.
12. Bazilevich, pp. 99–100.
13. *Ibid.*, pp. 99–101.
14. Text, *S.G.G.D.*, V, 1–2; G. F. Karpov, *Pamiatniki diplomaticheskikh snoshenii moskovskago gosudarstva s krymskoiu i nagaiskoiu ordami i s Turtsiei*, I: S 1474 po 1505 god, epokha sverzheniia mongol'skago iga v Rossii. (*Sbornik Imperatorskago Russkago istoricheskago obshchestva* (St. Petersburg, 1884), XLI, 9–13.
15. Bazilevich, p. 110.
16. Text, *S.G.G.D.*, V, 2; Karpov, pp. 14–24.
17. Bazilevich, pp. 118–19.
18. *Ibid.*, p. 159.
19. *Ibid.*, pp. 161–63.
20. *Ibid.*, p. 167; Howorth, II:1, 326.
21. *Ibid.*
22. Nolde, I, 16–17.
23. *Ibid.*, I, 19; cf. Howorth, II:1, 377–78.
24. Nolde, I, 18–19; Howorth, II:1, 381.
25. *Istoriia SSSR*, I, 291.
26. Howorth, II:1, 476.
27. *Ibid.*, 287.
28. *Ibid.*, 288.
29. Karamzin, VII, 149; Howorth, II:1, 478–79.
30. Karamzin, VII, 151–54.
31. *Ibid.*, VII, 161–63; Howorth, II:1, 480.
32. *Ibid.*, 486.
33. Peretiatkovich, p. 199.
34. Howorth, II:1, 418.
35. *Ibid.*, 420.
36. Solov'ev, III, 472.
37. Nolde, I, 36.
38. Shcheglov, pp. 33–34, 41.
39. *Ibid.*
40. *Ibid.*, p. 47; Peretiatkovich, p. 232.
41. *P.S.R.L.*, XIII, 516; Karamzin, pp. 185, 188–89; Nolde, I, 37.
42. Nolde, I, 71.
43. *P.S.R.L.*, XIII, 528.
44. Nolde, I, 50.
45. G. Vernadskii, *Nachertaniia russkoi istorii . . .* (Prague, 1927), I, 127.
46. Peretiatkovich, p. 240; Nolde, I, 39–40.
47. Nolde, I, 48–49.
48. Vernadskii, *Nachertaniia . . .*, I, 127.
49. Howorth, II:1, 354.
50. *Ibid.*, 354–57.
51. *Ibid.*, II:2, 1039; see also Chap. 4.
52. *Ibid.*, II:2, 1040–41; Grekov, *Istoriia SSSR*, I, 320.
53. Grekov, *Istoriia SSSR*, I, 321.
54. Novosel'skii, p. 17.
55. Nolde, I, 54.
56. Vernadskii, *Nachertaniia . . .*, p. 251.
57. Karamzin, VIII, n. 66.
58. *Ibid.*, VIII, n. 246.
59. Kerner, p. 55.

60. Peretiatkovich, p. 241, n. 1.
61. Vernadskii, *Nachertaniia . . .*, p. 145.
62. Solov'ev, IV, 23–24.
63. Nolde, I, 50–51.

CHAPTER 4

The Rise of the Cossack Hosts

1. For an extensive analysis of the origins of the cossacks, see Gunter Stökl, *Die Entstehung des Kosakentums* (Munich, 1953).
2. Solov'ev, III, 314.
3. Stökl, pp. 19, 123 ff.
4. Solov'ev, III, 385, n. 407; V. O. Kliuchevskii, *Kurs russkoi istorii*, 8 vols. (in *Sochineniia*, Moscow, 1956–59), III, 104–5, and in *A Course in Russian History. The Seventeenth Century* (Chicago, 1968), translation by N. Duddington, pp. 110–11; Stökl. pp. 19–20.
5. Stökl, pp. 23–26.
6. Vernadsky, *Kievan Russia*, p. 78.
7. Solov'ev, III, 316.
8. Stökl, pp. 39–40, 43–44.
9. Stökl, pp. 44, 53–56, 108. Kliuchevskii, *Seventeenth Century*, p. 111, assumes these to have been Russians.
10. Stökl, pp. 61–62.
11. Stökl, p. 62, from *P.S.R.L.* VI, 9, and XX/1, 290.
12. Karamzin, VI, n. 495; Stökl, pp. 86–87.
13. Karamzin, VII, n. 136, n. 236.
14. Stökl, p. 95, from *Sbornik*, XCV, 49 ff., and *S.G.G.D.*, II, 30.
15. *P.D.R.V.*, VII, 226, 247.
16. *Ibid.*, VIII, 72–73.
17. Stökl, pp. 107–8.
18. *Ibid.*, pp. 118, 143.
19. Solov'ev, III, 316.
20. Arkheograficheskaia kommissiia, *Dopolneniia k aktam istoricheskim* (cited hereafter as *D.A.I.*), 2 vols. (St. Petersburg, 1846–72), I, 24; *A.A.E.*, I, 179, 303–4, 426.
21. Karamzin, VI, n. 17.
22. Karamzin, quoting Dela Nogaiskie of 1549, VIII, n. 254; Solov'ev, III, 694.
23. Karamzin, *Ibid.*; Solov'ev, III, 695.
24. Solov'ev, III, 481–482.
25. *Cambridge History of Poland (to 1696)* (Cambridge, 1950) pp. 503–5.
26. G. Peretiatkovich, *Povol'zhe v XV i XVI vekakh. Ocherki iz istorii kraia i ego kolonizatsii* (Moscow, 1877) p. 277.
27. R. Hakluyt, *The Principal Navigations, Voyages, Traffiques and Discoveries of the English Nation . . .* 10 vols. (London, Toronto, and New York, 1927) I, 441; H. H. Howorth, *History of the Mongols* (London, 1876, 2 parts in 3 vols.) II:2, 1036.
28. Solov'ev, III, 696.
29. Peretiatkovich, p. 305.
30. *Ibid.*
31. Karamzin, IX, 416.
32. Karamzin, quoting *Bol'shoi chertezh* and the letter of Prince Urus of the Nogais to Tsar Fedor, 1586, X, n. 138; Pekarskii, 241.
33. Karamzin, *loc. cit.*

CHAPTER 5

The Stroganovs and Their Frontier Mark

1. [Isaak Massa]. *Beschryvinghe van der Samoyeden Landt in Tartarien . . .*, published by (and sometimes erroneously attributed to) Hessel Gerritszoon, (Amsterdam, 1612). Two chapters, 'A Description of the Countries of Siberia, Samoiedia, and Tingoesia . . .', and 'A Brief Description of the Ways and Rivers, Leading out of Moscovia Toward

the East and Northeast into Siberia, Samoedia, and Tingoesia . . .', the latter dealing in part with the Stroganovs, are provided in Samuel Purchas, *Hakluytus Posthumus or Purchas His Pilgrimes*, vol. 13 (Glasgow, 1906), 170–93. The second chapter, retranslated, with commentary, appears in John F. Baddeley, *Russia, Mongolia, China* . . ., II, 3–20. The relevant passage appears in Nicolaes Witsen, *Noord en Oost Tartarye* . . ., 2nd ed., revised and enlarged (2 vols., Amsterdam, 1705), II, 826–829, and in Russian translation in A. A. Vvedenskii, *Torgovyi Dom XVI-XVII vekov* (Leningrad, 1924), pp. 160–63.

2. G. F. Müller, *Istoriia Sibiri*, 2 vols. (Moscow and Leningrad, 1937-41), I, 478–79; Arkheograficheskaia kommissiia, *Sibirskiia letopisi* (cited hereafter as *Sib. let.*) (St. Petersburg, 1907), p. 369.

3. A. A. Vvedenskii, *Torgovyi dom XVI i XVII vekov* (Leningrad, 1924), pp. 168–69; A. A. Vvedenskii, *Dom Stroganovykh v XVI–XVII vekakh* (Moscow, 1962), p. 15.

4. 'Remember how in old times you (the Stroganovs) ransomed Grand Prince Vasilii Vasil'evich from captivity and received great honours.' Message of Tsar Vasilii Shuiskii to the Stroganovs, 1611, quoted by S. M. Solov'ev, *Istoriia Rossii s drevneishikh vremen*, 29 vols. in 15 (Moscow, 1959–66), III, 688.

5. 'The Three Surveys of the Dvina Land, 1471', Akademiia nauk, *Akty arkheograficheskoi ekspeditsiei* (hereafter cited as *A.A.E.*), 4 vols. (St. Petersburg, 1836), I, 74.

6. A. A. Vvedenskii, 'Anika Stroganov v svoem Sol'vychegodskom khoziastve', *Sbornik statei po russkoi istorii posviashchennykh S. F. Platonovu* (St. Petersburg, 1922), p. 91.

7. *A.A.E.*, I, 132–33.

8. Vvedenskii, 'Anika . . .', p. 92.

9. *Ibid.*, p. 99.

10. *Ibid.*, p. 112.

11. *Ibid.*, pp. 91, 94, 109–12; S. V. Bakhrushin, *Ivan Groznyi* (Moscow, 1945), p. 97.

12. Vvedenskii, 'Anika . . .', pp. 91–97; Vvedenskii, *Torgovyi Dom*, pp. 19–20.

13. Vvedenskii, 'Anika . . .', p. 97; Vvedenskii, *Torgovyi Dom*, p. 25.

14. Vvedenskii, 'Anika . . .', p. 101. Vvedenskii, *Torgovyi Dom*, p. 29, states 1566.

15. S. F. Platonov, 'Stroganovy, Ermak i Mangazeia', in his *Proshloe russkago severa. Ocherki po kolonizatsii Pomor'ia* (Petrograd, 1923), p. 75. Mangazeia is first mentioned in an ethnographic list compiled at the end of the fifteenth century. See 'O chelovetskikh neznaemykh na vostochnoi strane i o iazytsekh roznykh', in A. Titov, *Sibir' v XVII veke* (Moscow, 1890), pp. 1–6. Discussed by D. N. Anuchin *K istorii oznakomleniia s Sibir'iu do Ermaka* in 'Drevnosti', *Trudy Moskovskogo arkheologicheskogo obshchestva*, XIV, (Moscow, 1890), cited by V. A. Aleksandrov, 'Nachalo khoziaistvennogo osvoeniia i prisoedinenie k Rossii severnoi chasti Eniseiskogo kraia', Sibir' XVII–XVIII vv., *Materialy po istorii Sibiri. Sibir' perioda feodalizma*, I, 9, and by M. I. Belov, *Arkticheskoe moreplavanie s drevneishikh vremen do serediny XIX veka*, 3 vols. (*Istoriia otkrytiia i osvoeniia Severnogo morskogo puti*) I, 39. Mangazeia also appears on Jenkinson's map of Russia of 1562. See A. V. Efimov, *Atlas geograficheskikh otkrytii v Sibiri i v Severo-Zapadnoi Amerike XVII–XVIII vv.* (Moscow, 1964), map 22. For popular accounts of recent excavations, see M. I. Belov, *Mangazeia* (Leningrad, 1969), and *Raskopki 'zlatokipiashchei' Mangazei* (Leningrad, 1970); and Vanda Beletskaia, 'Mangazeia zlatokipiashchia', *Ogonëk*, 1970:40, 24–25.

16 Platonov, 'Stroganovy', p. 75.

17. One Russian verst in the sixteenth century was equal to 1,000 sazhen or 7,000 feet.

18. Charter granted to Grigorii Stroganov, 4 April 1558, text in Müller, I, 332–35; and in Vasilii Shishonko *Permskaia letopis' s 1263–1881*, 8 vols. (Perm 1889–1900, I, 48–49.

19. *Sibirskie letopisi* (cited hereafter as *Sib.let.*), 2; Solov'ev, III, 691.

20. *A.A.E.*, I, 227.

21. Solov'ev, II, 310; Charter to the Stroganovs, 1564, Arkheograficheskaia kommissiia, *Dopolneniia k aktam istoricheskim* (cited hereafter as *D.A.I.*), 12 vols. (St. Petersburg, 1846–1872), I, 170; *A.A.E.*, I, 277; Shishonko, I, 51–54; Vvedenskii, *Dom Stroganovykh*, 76–77.

22. *D.A.I.*, I, 170–71; *Sib. let.*, 3; S. V. Bakhrushin, *Ocherki po istorii kolonizatsii Sibiri v XVI i XVII vv.* (Moscow, 1927), p. 96.

23. *D.A.I.*, I, 171.

24. Message of Metropolitan Afanasii to Grigorii Stroganov, 4 May 1565, Vvedenskii, *Torgovyi dom*, p. 153.

25. Charter to Iakov Stroganov, 1568, Müller, I, 335–37; *Sib. let.*, 4; *D.A.I.*, I, 172–75.
26. *Sib. let.*, 4–5.
27. Bakhrushin, *Ocherki* . . ., p. 97.
28. *Ibid.*, p. 94; *A.A.E.*, III, 166; *A.I.*, III, 165–67.
29. Bakhrushin, *Ocherki* . . ., p. 94; *D.A.I.*, I, 182–83.
30. Bakhrushin, *Ocherki* . . ., p. 95.
31, *Ibid.*, pp. 90, 91, n. 5.
32. Charter of 1572, Müller, I, 338; *D.A.I.*, I, 175–76.
33. *Sib. let.*, 5.
34. Bakhrushin, *Ocherki* . . ., p. 149.
35. Charter of 1572, Müller, I, 338–39; Shishonko, I: 68–69.
36. *Ibid.*, p. 91, n. 3; *D.A.I.*, I, *loc. cit.*; Müller, I, 211.
37. Bakhrushin, *Ocherki* . . ., p. 95.
38. V. V. Vel'iaminov-Zernov, *Izsledovanie o kasimovskikh tsariakh i tsarevichakh* 4 vols. (St. Petersburg, 1863–66), III, 48–51; Howorth, II:2, 985.
39. Charter of 1574, Müller, I, 339; Bakhrushin, Ocherki . . ., p. 91.
40. V. I. Ogorodnikov, *Ocherki istorii Sibiri* (Vladivostok, 1924), pt. I, 22; Bakhrushin, Ocherki . . ., pp. 91, 95.
41. Charter to Iakov and Grigorii Stroganov, 1574, Müller, I, 339–41; Shishonko, I, 70–73; Vvedenskii, *Dom Stroganovykh*, p. 82.
42. According to Bakhrushin, *Ocherki* . . ., p. 150, n. 1, the territory along the Tura River, later called Epanchin Iurt.
43. Charter of 30 May 1574, to Iakov and Grigorii Stroganov, Müller, I, 340.
44. Solov'ev, III, 687.
45. Platonov, 'Stroganovy', p. 77; Vvedenskii, *Dom Stroganovykh*, pp. 55–56; Vvedenskii, *Torgovy: Dom,* 102–3.

CHAPTER 6

Expedition of Ermak

1. S. V. Bakhrushin et al, 'Primechaniia k tekstu 'Istorii Sibiri' i k prilozheniiam', in Müller, *Istoriia Sibiri*, I, 469–508.
2. Message of Tsar Ivan Vasil'evich . . . 1582, Müller, *Istoriia Sibiri*, I, 342–43.
3. Bakhrushin, 'Primechaniia k tekstu . . .', *ibid.*, 483–85.
4. Vvedenskii, *Dom Stroganovykh*, 96–97, states that up to the 1890s a harquebus, which has since vanished, was kept in the Stroganov family home in St. Petersburg, with the inscription 'Given to Ataman Ermak by Maksim Iakovlev Stroganov in the town of Kergegan on the river Kama in the summer of 1582'.
5. *Sib. let.*, 10–11, 59, 98, 263, 314–16.
6. *Ibid.*, 11, 59, 276, 297, 314; Müller, *Istoriia Sibiri*, I, 220.
7. Müller, *Istoriia Sibiri*, I, 220.
8. *Sib. let.*, 314, 317; Müller, *Istoriia Sibiri*, I, 221.
9. *Sib. let.*, 318; Bakhrushin, 'Primechaniia k tekstu . . .', Müller, *Istoriia Sibiri*, I, 485.
10. *Sib. let.*, 321–22.
11. *Ibid.*, 322; Bakhrushin, 'Primechaniia k tekstu . . .', Müller, *Istoriia Sibiri*, I, 224.
12. *Sib. let.*, 16–17, 65, 99, 126, 194–95, 263, 297.
13. *Ibid.*, 323–24.
14. *Ibid.*, 67, 277, 327; Müller, *Istoriia Sibiri*, I, 225–27.
15. Bakhrushin, 'Primechaniia k tekstu . . .', Müller, *Istoriia Sibiri*, I, 487.
16. *Sib. let.*, 17, 65, 127, 327–29. Müller, *Istoriia Sibiri*, I, 227–28.
17. *Sib. let.*, 329–31, 23–24, 69–70, 130–31.
18. *Ibid.*, 331.
19. Müller, *Istoriia Sibiri*, I, 232–33; Grekov, et al., *Istoriia SSSR*, I, 252.
20. Müller, *Istoriia Sibiri*, I, 230.
21. *Ibid.*, I, 198–200; Bakhrushin, 'Sibirskie sluzhilye Tatary . . .', 59, 69; *Sib. let.*, 339; Howorth, II:2, 1061–65.
22. *Sib. let.*, 332–33.
23. *Ibid.*, 337; Müller, *Istoriia Sibiri*, I, 236.

24. Messages of Tsar Ivan Vasil'evich, 1581, Müller, *Istoriia Sibiri*, I, I, 341–42; *D.A.I.*, I, 182–83; and Vvedenskii, *Torgovyi dom*, pp. 62–64.
25. Message of Tsar Ivan Vasil'evich, 1582, Müller, *Istoriia Sibiri*, I, 342–43; *D.A.I.*, I, 184–85.
26. Müller, *Istoriia Sibiri*, I, 238; *Sib. let.*, 200–9, 250, 337–38.
27. Message of Patriarch Filaret, 1622, *S.G.G.D.*, III, 246–47.
28. Müller, *Istoriia Sibiri*, I, 239.
29. *Sib. let.*, 29, 74–75.
30. Message of Tsar Ivan Vasil'evich, 1584, Müller, *Istoriia Sibiri*, I, 343–44.
31. *Sib. let.*, 333.
32. *Ibid.*, 336–37.
33. *Ibid.*, 338–39.
34. 19 March 1584.
35. *Sib. let.*, 334.
36. *Ibid.*, 333–36; G. E. Katanaev, 'Eshche ob Ermake . . .', *Zapiski zapadnosibirskago otdela . . . russkago geograficheskago obshchestva*, XV, pt. II, (Omsk, 1893), pp. 28–29.
37. *Sib. let*, 28, 325–26, 339; Katanaev, 30.
38. *Sib. let.*, 340, 79.
39. *Idem.*
40. *Sib. let.*, 31–32, 284, 288. In general, the chronicles mention 'many warriors', whereas the Remezov Chronicle gives the exact number of five hundred. *Ibid.*, 339.
41. *Ibid.*, 340.
42. *Ibid.*, 341–44.
43. *Ibid.*, 344.
44. *Ibid.*, 284, 288.
45. *Ibid.*, 344; Müller, *Istoriia Sibiri* I, 265–66.
46. *Sib. let.*, 348–49.

CHAPTER 7

Frontier Policies of Boris Godunov

1. G. N. Anpilogov, *Novye dokumenty o Rossii kontsa XVI-nachala XVII v.* (Moscow, 1967), pp. 9–10, citing K. A. Nevolin, *Polnoe sobranie sochineniia*, (St. Petersburg, 1859), pp. 41–94, describes the effort of the Posol'skii Prikaz (Ambassadors' Office, or Foreign Office) to portray to foreigners the great services of Godunov to the Tsar Fedor, including the building of stone fortifications in Moscow and Astrakhan, and of many new towns which helped to secure the frontiers.
2. A. A. Novosel'skii, pp. 44, 443 (map); D. I. Bagalei, 'Ocherki iz istorii kolonizatsii i byta stepnoi okrainy moskovskogo gosudarstva', *Chteniia v imperatorskom obshchestve istorii i drevnostei rossiiskikh pri moskovskom universitete* (cited hereafter as *Chteniia*) 1886; 2, 39; Kerner, p. 57 (map).
3. *P.S.R.L.*, XIV, 45.
4. *Ibid.*, Novosel'skii, p. 44; Kerner, p. 59.
5. *P.S.R.L.*, XIV, 36.
6. Novosel'skii, p. 34.
7. *P.D.R.V.*, IX, 190, 210, 215–16; Peretiatkovich, pp. 286, 313, 321; V. N. Vitevskii, *I. I. Nepliuev i orenburgskii krai v prezhnem ego sostave do 1758 g.*, 4 vols. (Kazan, 1889—97), I, 127; *P.S.R.L.*, XIV, 52; Novosel'skii, p. 39.
8. Izmail, who had asked for the construction of these forts, was dead by this time.
9. Pekarskii, pp. 239, 258.
10. Instructions to I. Strakhov, September, 1586, quoted by Pekarskii, pp. 250–51.
11. Peretiatkovich, pp. 312–3; G. Katanaev, 'Eshche ob Ermake . . .', p. 7.
12. Vvedenskii, *Torgovyi dom* . . ., p. 162; Karamzin, IX, n. 618; X, n. 24, n. 418, Fisher, p. 25.
13. Pekarskii, p. 251; Nolde, I, 147; Bakhrushin, *Ocherki* . . ., p. 107.
14. Bakhrushin, *Ocherki* . . ., p. 107; Pekarskii, pp. 259–60; Müller, I, 359.
15. Ogorodnikov, *Ocherki* . . ., II:1, *Zavoevanie russkimi Sibiri* (Vladivostok, 1924), p. 33.
16. *Sib. let.*, 228–231; Lantzeff, p. 94; Müller, I, 276.
17. Bakhrushin, *Ocherki* . . ., p. 154,

18. Müller, I, 278, 290.
19. Instruction for the building of Tara, 1593–94, Müller, I, 354–61.
20. Müller, I, 355.
21. Instructions to the voevodas of Tara, February, 1595, and the message of Tsar Fedor to Tara, June, 1595, Müller, I, 363–68.
22. G. E. Katanaev, 'Kirgizskiia stepi, Sredniaia Aziia i severnyi Kitai v XVII i XVIII stoletiiakh . . .', *Zapiski zapadno-sibirskago otdela imperatorskago russkago geograficheskago obshchestva*, XIV, pt. 1 (1893), pp. 25–26.
23. Message of Tsar Fedor to Tara . . ., June 1595, Müller, I, 366–67.
24. Message of Tsar Fedor to Tara . . ., August, 1595, Müller, I, 368–70.
25. Petition of Zhigat Murzas, 1597, *S.G.G.D.*, II, 128, also known as Chat, or Dzhagat Murzas, Müller, I, 507.
26. Message of Khan Kuchum, *S.G.G.D.*, II, 130.
27. Letter of Abdul-Khair, 1597, *S.G.G.D.*, II, 131–32.
28. Message of Tsar Fedor, 1597, *S.G.G.D.*, II, 132–34.
29. Report from the voevoda of Tara, 1598, *A.I.*, II, 1–2.
30 *Ibid.*, 2–3.
31. Report of the voevodas of Tara, September, 1598, *A.I.*, II, 6.
32. Report of the voevodas of Tara, October, 1598, *A.I.*, II, 7.
33. Müller, I, 502; *Sib. let.*, 80; Report of the voevoda of Ufa, 1601, Arkheograficheskaia kommissiia, *Russkaia istoricheskaia biblioteka* (cited hereafter as *R.I.B.*), 39 vols. (St. Petersburg, 1875–1927), II, 283.
34. Ogorodnikov, *Ocherki . . .*, II, 35.
35. Bakhrushin, *Ocherki . . .*, pp. 90, 100–1; *Drevniaia rossiiskaia vivliofika*, III, 115.
36. Müller, I, 276–77; Ogorodnikov, *Ocherki . . .*, II:1, 35; Bakhrushin, *Ocherki . . .*, p. 89.
37. Ogorodnikov, *Ocherki . . .*, II:1, 35.
38. Müller, I, 281; Bakhrushin, *Ocherki . . .*, p. 156; Bakhrushin, 'Istoricheskii ocherk . . .', p. 30.
39. Müller, I, 351.
40. Instructions to Pelym, *R.I.B.*, II, 108–9; for translation see Lantzeff, pp. 94–95, n. 39.
41. Charter, Tsar Fedor to Prince Igichei Alachev, 1594, *S.G.G.D.*, II, 127; Bakhrushin, 'Istoricheskii ocherk . . .', p. 30.
42. Müller, I, 379.
43. Bakhrushin, *Ocherki . . .*, pp. 102–9; *Idem*, 'Istoricheskii ocherk . . .', p. 30.
44. Lantzeff, p. 158.
45. *Ibid.*, p. 159.
46. Müller, I, 408.
47. Ogorodnikov, *Ocherki . . .*, II:1, 35.
48. Bakhrushin, 'Istoricheskii ocherk . . .', p. 31.
49. Müller, I, 284.
50. *Ibid.*, 209.
51. *Ibid.*, 285.
52. *Ibid.*
53. *Ibid.*
54. *Ibid.*, 286.
55. *Ibid.*; Bakhrushin, 'Istoricheskii ocherk . . .', p. 31.
56. Ogorodnikov, *Ocherki, II:1, 37–38.
57. Müller, I: 312, 394–404; Bakhrushin, *Ocherki . . .*, p. 158; *R.I.B.*, II, 814–15; Belov, *Mangazeia*, pp. 32–38. See also n. 15, ch. 5.
58. Müller, I, 287.
59. Ogorodnikov, *Ocherki . . .*, II:1, 38.
60. Bakhrushin, 'Istoricheskii ocherk . . .', p. 32.
61. Ogorodnikov, *Ocherki . . .*, II:1, 39.
62. Müller, I, 451–55. For related materials see *Russko-mongol'skie otnosheniia, 1607–36. Sbornik dokumentov* (Moscow, 1959).

Notes

CHAPTER 8

From the Ob to the Pacific

1. Lantzeff, *op. cit.*, p. 161, n.
2. Bakhrushin, 'Istoricheskii ocherk . . .', p. 34; Müller, *op. cit.*, II, 177.
3. Müller, *op. cit.*, II, 232–33, 261, 314–15.
4. *Ibid.*, II, 232.
5. *Ibid.*, II, 23; J. E. Fischer, *Sibirskaia istoriia s samogo otkrytiia Sibiri do zavoevaniia sei zemli rossiiskim oruzhiem* . . . (St. Petersburg, 1774), p. 233; Kerner, *op. cit.*, p. 71.
6. Fischer, *op. cit.*, pp. 271–72.
7. *Ibid.*, pp. 273–74.
8. *Ibid.*, p. 274.
9. *Ibid.*, p. 274–75.
10. *Ibid.*, pp. 233–34; Müller, *op. cit.*, II, 23, 215, 216–17 (1609–1610); 219–220 (1611); 222–23 (1611); 231–42 (1617).
11. Message of the voevoda of Ketsk to the voevoda of Tomsk, 1605, Müller, *op. cit.*, I, 414–15.
12. *Ibid.*
13. *Ibid.*, II, 202, 205, 214; see also *R.I.B.*, II, 170.
14. A. M. Gnevushev, *Akty vremeni pravleniia tsaria Vasiliia Shuiskago|(1606 g. 19 maia—17 iiulia 1610 g.)* (Moscow, 1914), pp. 72–73, 374–76.
15. V. I. Ogorodnikov, 'Russkaia gosudarstvennaia vlast' i sibirskie inorodtsy v XVI–XVIII vv.', *Sbornik trudov professorov gosudarstvennogo Irkutskogo universiteta*, (Irkutsk, 1921) otd. 1, vyp. 1, (II:3 of his *Ocherki* . . .) pp. 100–102.
16. Müller, *op. cit.*, II, 243.
17. Fischer, *op. cit.*, pp. 275–76; Müller, *op. cit.*, II, 248–51.
18. Müller, *op. cit.*, II, 254.
19. *Ibid.*; Fischer, *op. cit.*, pp. 276–77.
20. Müller, *op. cit.*, II, 250.
21. Fischer, *op. cit.*, pp. 278–79.
22. Andrievich, I: 64; Fischer, *op. cit.*, p. 261; Ogorodnikov, *Ocherki* . . ., II:1, 47.
23. Fischer, p. 279.
24. *Iakutiia v XVII veke*, p. 12; Ogorodnikov, *Ocherki* . . ., II:1, 47.
25. Fischer, *op. cit.*, p. 360.
26. *Ibid.*, p. 361; Ogorodnikov, *op. cit.*, II:1, 48. See extended account in A. P. Okladnikov, 'Penda—zabytyi russkii zemleprokhodets XVII veka', *Letopis' severa*, 1949, I, 94–102.
27. Ogorodnikov, *Ocherki* . . ., II:1, 48.
28. *Ibid.*, 49; *Iakutiia v XVII v.*, p. 16.
29. Ogorodnikov, *Ocherki* . . ., II:1, 49; Tokarev, *Ocherki istorii Iakutskago naroda*, p. 40–41. For biography of Bugor, see N. N. Ogloblin, 'Vostochnosibirskie poliarnye morekhody', *Zhurnal Ministerstvo narodnogo prosveshcheniia*, 1903, ch. 347, May, section 2, pp. 46–49.
30. Fischer, *op. cit.*, pp. 353–55; *D.A.I.*, III, 303–4.
31. *Sibirskaia sovetskaia entsiklopediia*, 3 vols. (Moscow, 1929–   ), II, col. 1110.
32. Fischer, *op. cit.*, pp. 356–57.
33. *Ibid.*, p. 358.
34. Tokarev, *op. cit.*, p. 41.
35. *Ibid.*, pp. 41–44.
36. Fischer, *op. cit.*, p. 365; O. V. Ionova, *Iz istorii iakutskogo naroda (pervaia polovina XVII veka)* (Iakutsk, 1945), p. 29.
37. Fischer, *op. cit.*, p. 366.
38. Ionova, *op. cit.*, p. 28.
39. Tokarev, *Ocherki istorii iakutskago naroda*, pp. 46–47; Fischer, *op. cit.*, pp. 367–68.
40. Ogorodnikov, *Ocherki* . . ., II:1, 52.
41. Fischer, *op. cit.*, pp. 369–70; Ionova, *op. cit.*, pp. 30–31.
42. Fischer, *op. cit.*, pp. 371–72.
43. *Ibid.*, p. 379; Ogorodnikov, *Ocherki* . . ., II:1, 51; L. S. Berg, *Ocherki po istorii russkikh geograficheskikh otkrytii* (Moscow–Leningrad, 1949 ed.) p. 144.
44. Ogorodnikov, *Ocherki* . . ., II:1, 50–51.
45. Ionova, *op. cit.*, pp. 32–33; Tokarev, *Ocherki istorii iakutskago naroda*, p. 49.
46. Ogorodnikov, *Ocherki* . . ., II:1, 52–53.

47. Tokarev, *Ocherki istorii iakutskago naroda*, p. 51.
48. Quoted by Ogorodnikov, *Ocherki . . .*, II:1, 51–52.
49. Fischer, *op. cit.*, p. 528.
50. Tokarev, *Ocherki istorii iakutskago naroda*, pp. 51–53.
51. *Ibid.*, p. 51; S. A. Tokarev, *Obshchestvennyi stroi iakutov XVII–XVIII vv.* (Iakutsk, 1945), p. 279.
52. Tokarev, *Obshchestvennyi stroi . . .*, pp. 279–80.
53. *Ibid.*, p. 281.

CHAPTER 9

Buriatia and Transbaikalia

1. Ogorodnikov, *Ocherki . . .*, I:1, 62.
2. A. P. Okladnikov, *Ocherki iz istorii zapadnykh Buriat-Mongolov* (XVII–XVIII vv.), (Leningrad, 1937), p. 29. The best secondary source for this period, derived from archival materials. See also the older but still useful compilation, V. K. Andrievich, *Kratkii ocherk istorii Zabaikal'ia ot drevneishikh vremen do 1762 goda* (St. Petersburg, 1887).
3. Okladnikov, *Ocherki . . .*, p. 27.
4. *Ibid.*, p. 32; Müller, II, 307; Fischer, p. 279.
5. Andrievich, *Kratkii ocherk . . .*, p. 12.
6. Fischer, p. 340.
7. Okladnikov, *Ocherki . . .*, p. 31, mentions also Ataman Pozdei Firsov as a leader of the expedition.
8. Fischer, pp. 340–41.
9. Okladnikov, p. 32.
10. Fischer, p. 341.
11. Okladnikov, pp. 32–33.
12. Ogorodnikov, *Ocherki . . .*, II:1, 62.
13. Okladnikov, pp. 33–34.
14. *Ibid.*, pp. 34–35; Fischer, pp. 342–43.
15. Fischer, pp. 271–72, 281–82.
16. *Ibid.*, p. 282; Müller, II, 49.
17. Fischer, p. 282.
18. *Ibid.*, p. 282; Müller, II, 51–52.
19. Müller, II, 51: Instructions to Krasnoiarsk, 1629, *ibid.*, II, 347–51.
20. Shcheglov, p. 84; Fischer, pp. 400–1; Ogorodnikov, *Ocherki . . .*, II:1, 45; Müller, II, 344–46; Kerner, p. 74, map.
21. Ogorodnikov, *Ocherki . . .*, II:1, 45.
22. Müller, II, 351; S. B. Okun', 'K istorii Buriatii v XVII v.', *Krasnyi Arkhiv*, no. 3 (76) 1936, 174–75.
23. Okladnikov, pp. 35–36.
24. *Ibid.*, pp. 45–46.
25. *Ibid.*, 46–47; Ogorodnikov, *Ocherki . . .*, II:1, 64.
26. Okladnikov, pp. 47–48.
27. *Ibid.*, pp. 51–52.
28. *Ibid.*, p. 54: Fischer, p. 547.
29. Okladnikov, pp. 55–59.
30. *Ibid.*, p. 59.
31. V. K. Andrievich, *Istoricheskii ocherk Sibiri po dannym predstavliaemym Polnym sobraniem zakonov*, 6 vols. in 8 (St. Petersburg, 1886–1889), I, 72.
32. Ogorodnikov, *Ocherki . . .*, II:1, 64–65; Okladnikov, p. 60.
33. Okladnikov, pp. 64–65.
34. *Ibid.*, pp. 71–72; Fischer, p. 352.
35. Okladnikov, pp. 74–75.
36. *Ibid.*, pp. 76, 79.
37. Ogorodnikov, *Ocherki . . .*, II:1, 64.
38. Okladnikov, p. 80.
39. Fischer, 381–84; Ogorodnikov, *Ocherki . . .*, II:1, 67–68.
40. Fischer, p. 547.

41. *Ibid.*, 548; Ogorodnikov, *Ocherki* . . ., II:1, 66; account of Kurbat Ivanov, in S. Okun', 'K istorii Buriatii v XVII v.', *Krasnyi Arkhiv*, no. 3 (76) 1936, 174–75.
42. Fischer, p. 548.
43. Ogorodnikov, *Ocherki* . . ., II:1, 69; *D.A.I.*, III, 108—11; Fischer, pp. 550–51; account, Konstantin Ivanov, of embassy to Turukai Tabun, 29 June 1647, *Russko-kitaiskie otnosheniia v XVII veke* (cited hereafter as *R.K.O.*) (Moscow, 1969), I, 122–24.
44. Okladnikov, p. 83.
45. Ogorodnikov, *Ocherki* . . ., II:1, 69.
46. Okladnikov, p. 84; Fischer, p. 552.
47. Fischer p. 552.
48. Account by I. Pokhabov of embassy to Tsetsen Khan and attempt to go to China, 20 October 1648, *R.K.O.*, I, 124–26. Howorth, I, 485–87, 690; Fischer, p. 553. The envoys of Tsetsen Khan made the journey to Moscow, and returned to Eniseisk in 1650, accompanied by the boyar-son Erofei Zabolotskii, his son, and seven cossacks. Zabolotskii, with his party, was supposed to go to Tsetsen Khan as an envoy to Moscow. He joined the expedition of Kolesnikov (q.v.), but after crossing Lake Baikal became separated from him, was attacked by Buriats or Mongols and killed (Fischer, pp. 556,560). The Mongol envoys and the Russian interpreter, who had remained in the boat, escaped the fate of the others and the interpreter completed the mission. See N. N. Ogloblin, 'Sibirskie diplomaty XVII veka' (Posol'skie 'stateinye spiski'), *Istoricheskii vestnik*, XLVI:158–71, 1891:10.
49. Okladnikov, pp. 84–85.
50. Ogorodnikov, *Ocherki* . . ., II:1, 70.
51. Fischer, pp. 555–56.
52. Ogorodnikov, *Ocherki* . . ., II:1, 71.
53. Fischer, p. 557.
54. Andrievich, *Istoricheskii ocherk* . . ., I, 80.
55. *Ibid.*, I:113.
56. Okun,' p. 134.
57. Okladnikov, pp. 98, 118.
58. *Ibid.*, p. 126.
59. Andrievich, *Istoricheskii ocherk* . . ., I, 80–81; Fischer, p. 557. Fischer, followed by Andrievich, apparently errs in ascribing to Ivan Pokhabov the founding of Irkutsk in 1661. *D.A.I.*, IV, 249–50 indicates that this was done by Iakov Ivanov Pokhabov, perhaps a son.
60. *D.A.I.*, IV, 199–200; Okladnikov. pp. 128–30.
61. Fischer, pp. 563, 567, 572, 569.

CHAPTER 10

Seizure and Loss of the Amur

1. V. G. Shcheben'kov, *Russko-kitaiskie otnosheniia v XVII v.* (Moscow, 1960), p. 123.
2. Fischer, pp. 380–81; L. S. Berg, *Ocherki* . . ., p. 144.
3. Ogorodnikov, *Ocherki* . . ., II:1, 79.
4. 'Instruktsiia pis'mianomu golove Poiarkovu, 16 July 1643', *Chteniia*, 1861:1, 1–16; Shcheben'kov, p. 124.
5. Poiarkov's report, 12 June 1646, *D.A.I.*, III, 50–51; Poiarkov and Vizhevtsov reports, 27 May 1647, *Ibid.*, 102–4; Fischer, pp. 571–72; Ogorodnikov, *Ocherki* . . ., II:1, 75–76.
6. *D.A.I.*, III, 52–54; Berg, *Ocherki* . . ., p. 145; Fischer, pp. 574–75; Ogorodnikov, *Ocherki* . . ., II:1, 76–77.
7. *D.A.I.*, III, 55–56 Ogorodnikov, *Ocherki* . . ., II:1, 78–80.
8. Berg, *Ocherki* . . ., pp. 147–48.
9. *D.A.I.*, III, 56.
10. Report of Grigorii Vizhevtsov, 27 May 1647, *D.A.I.*, III, 102–4.
11. Fischer, pp. 388, 585; Ogorodnikov, *Ocherki* . . ., II:1, 83–84; D. N. Sadovnikov, *Nashi zemleprokhodtsy (razskazy o zaselenii Sibiri [1581–1712 gg.])*, (Moscow, 1898), pp. 81–83.
12. Report of Frantsbekov, 26 May 1650, *D.A.I.*, III, 258–61; report of Frantsbekov, 29 May 1651, *A.I.*, IV, 68, 76; Golder, p. 39.

Eastward to Empire

13. Report of Frantsbekov, 26 May 1650, *D.A.I.*, III, 258–61; Ogorodnikov, *Ocherki . . .*, II:1, 84–86.
14. *D.A.I.*, III, 367; Report of Frantsbekov, 29 May 1651, *A.I.*, IV, 74–75; Ogorodnikov, *Ocherki . . .*, II:1, 86–88; instructions, 9 July 1650, to E. P. Khabarov regarding expedition to Dauria, *R.K.O.*, I, 126–28. Letter, ca. 9 July 1650, Frantsbekov to Chinese Emperor, inviting him to become a Russian subject, *ibid.*, 129–30.
15. Instructions, July and 24 October 1652, *A.I.*, IV, 168–72; Ogorodnikov, *Ocherki . . .*, II:1, 89.
16. *D.A.I.*, III, 360–65; Ogorodnikov, *Ocherki . . .*, II:1, 89–90.
17. Hsüan-Ming Liu, 'Russo-Chinese relations up to the Treaty of Nerchinsk', *The Chinese Social and Political Science Review*, January–March 1940, XXIII:4, 395.
18. Ogorodnikov, *Ocherki . . .*, II:1, 90–91; N. N. Firsov, *Chteniia po istorii Sibiri . . .* (Vol. I–II, Moscow, 1920–21), I, 30—31; Khabarov to Frantsbekov, not before 1 August 1652, *R.K.O.*, 134–38; *D.A.I.*, III 365–68; Fischer, p. 395.
19. *D.A.I.*, III, 368; letter, to Khabarov, on sending T. E. Chechigin, *R.K.O.*, 130–34; Fischer, p. 597; Ogorodnikov, *Ocherki . . .*, II:1, 91. Nagiba went down the Amur and somehow passed Khabarov. Near the mouth of the Amur, the party was surrounded by a Giliak flotilla, and had to spend two weeks anchored in the middle of the river, besieged by the Giliaks. Finally the hungry cossacks broke through the cordon and stole some supplies of dried fish from the next village. At the mouth of the Amur, they built a vessel, and when threatened anew by the boats of the Giliaks, they sank one with forty men. They went to sea, but were soon shipwrecked. They continued along the coast, living on the carcasses of dead walruses and seals, which had drifted ashore. They finally reached the river Tungir, where the cossack Ivan Uvarov and a few men were left to build a zimov'e while the remainder of the party crossed the Stanovoi range and returned to the Lena by way of the Maia and Aldan rivers. They reached Iakutsk after completing almost the same itinerary as Poiarkov before them. *D.A.I.*, III, 354; E. G. Ravenstein, *The Russians on the Amur . . .* (London, 1861), pp. 22–23; Ogorodnikov, *Ocherki . . .*, II:1, pp. 92–93; Firsov, I, 32.
20. *D.A.I.*, III, 369–71, 397–98; Ogorodnikov, *Ocherki . . .*, II:1, 92–93; Firsov, I, 32.
21. *D.A.I.*, IV, 33; Ogorodnikov, *Ocherki . . .*, II:1, 94.
22. Fischer, p. 611.
23. Ogorodnikov, *Ocherki . . .*, II:1, 94; Fischer, 611; *D.A.I.*, IV, 85, 89; N. N. Ogloblin, 'Bunt i pobeg na Amur 'vorovskago polka' M. Sorokina. (Ocherk iz zhizni XVII veka)', *Russkaia starina*, LXXXV, 1896:1, January, 205–24.
24. Fischer, pp. 609–10, 612.
25. Report, 17 June 1653, *A.I.*, IV, 184.
26. See Baddeley, II, 139–66, N. N. Bantysh-Kamenskii, *Diplomaticheskoe sobranie del mezhdu Rossiiskim i Kitaiskim gosudarstvami s 1619 po 1792-i god . . .* (Kazan, 1882), 8–11, for description of the Baikov journey. For discussion and documents see N. F. Demidova and V. S. Miasnikov, *Pervye russkie diplomaty v Kitae* ('Rospis' I Petlina i stateinyi spisok F. I. Baikova)* (Moscow, 1966), *R.K.O.* and Mark Mancall, *Russia and China, Their Diplomatic Relations to 1728* (Cambridge, Mass., 1971), pp. 44–53. Ablin led trading missions to Peking in 1658–62 and 1668–73.
27. Report of Onufrii Stepanov to voevoda of Iakutsk, August 1654, *D.A.I.*, III, 523–28, and *R.K.O.*, 192–96.
28. Report, Stepanov to voevoda, after 4 April 1655, *D.A.I.*, IV, 27–31, and *R.K.O.*, 205–8. cf. Mancall, pp. 30–31.
29. Report, Stepanov to voevoda, 7 June 1655, *D.A.I.*, IV, 35–37, and *R.K.O.*, 209–11; Ogorodnikov, *Ocherki . . .*, II:1, 97–99; Hsüan-Ming Liu, 396.
30. Report, Stepanov to voevoda, 22 July 1656, *D.A.I.*, IV, 80–83, and *R.K.O.*, 211–14; Ogorodnikov, *Ocherki . . .*, II:1, 89–99; V. I. Ogorodnikov, *Tuzemnoe i russkoe zemledelie na Amure v XVII v.* (Vladivostok, 1927), p. 50.
31. *D.A.I.*, IV, 40–41, 53, 55–56; Ogorodnikov, *Ocherki . . .*, II:1, 99–100; *R.K.O.*, 199–203.
32. Pashkov, report to Siberian Prikaz on defeat of Stepanov, summer 1658, *R.K.O.*, 234–35; Pashkov, report on same subject, December 1661, *D.A.I.*, IV, 260–62; Ogorodnikov, *Ocherki . . .*, II:1, 100; Hsüan-Ming Liu, p. 396.
33. Letter of voevoda of Iakutsk, February (?) 1671, *D.A.I.*, VI, 153; Andrievich, *Istoricheskii ocherk . . .*, II, 34; Bakhrushin, *Ocherki . . .*, 167.
34. Case summary, 19 April 1680, *D.A.I.*, VIII, 275–76; report of voevoda of Nerchinsk

246

on rewards given men serving in Dauria, December, 1681, *D.A.I.*, VIII, 347–48; Andrievich, *Istoricheskii ocherk* . . ., II, 34.

35. Bakhrushin, *Ocherki* . . ., p. 167; Andrievich, *Istoricheskii ocherk* . . ., II, 34.
36. *D.A.I.*, VI, 41–46; V. G. Kurts, *Russko-kitaiskie snosheniia v XVI, XVII i XVIII stoletiiakh* (Kharkov, 1929), p. 37.
37. N. N. Ogloblin, *Obozrenie stolbtsov i knig sibirskogo prikaza (1592–1768 gg.)*, in *Chteniia*, Kn. I (1902), p. 102.
38. *D.A.I.*, VI, 41; Andrievich, *Istoricheskii ocherk* . . ., II, 42.
39. Bantysh-Kamenskii, p. 14.
40. M. N. Pavlovsky, *Chinese-Russian Relations* (New York, 1949), pp. 131–36; Bantysh-Kamenskii, pp. 14, 17–18; Kurts, p. 37; Hsüan-Ming Liu, p. 397. See *R.K.O.* for many documents on the Spafarii mission, including (346–458) an abridgement of Spafarii's report (*stateinyi spisok*), 1676; the same, in Baddeley, II, 242–446, including the report, abridged, 286–422.
41. Pavlovsky, p. 117, from Fu-Kuang Ch'en, 'Sino-Russian Diplomatic Relations Since 1689', *The Chinese Social and Political Science Review*, April 1926, X:2. For a theory as to why Spafarii's mission failed, see M. N. Pavlovsky, 'Concerning a Strange Document', in his *Chinese-Russian Relations*, pp. 127–44. Pavlovsky speculates that during Spafarii's visit the Chinese found in their archives an arrogant letter delivered by an earlier mission which had not been read at the time. Others have speculated that it was because Spafarii failed to perform the kow-tow; P. T. Iakovleva, *Pervyi russko-kitaiskii dogovor 1689 goda* (Moscow, 1958), p. 111, states that it was because the Chinese had opened military operations on the Amur; Shcheben'kov, p. 179, attributes it to the Russian failure to return the fugitive Gantimur. For a detailed account of the embassy, see Mancall, pp. 65–110.
42. Pavlovsky, p. 122, from Ravenstein, pp. 41–44; Kerner, p. 80 (map); Bakhrushin, *Ocherki* . . ., pp. 135–36. By the end of 1682, Russian possessions in the region included Albazin and four villages surrounding the fortress, namely Novozeisk, Selymzhinsk, Dolonskoi on the Zeia, and Dukikamsk on the Amgun. In addition there were Tugursk and Udsk near the Sea of Okhotsk.
43. Hsüan-Ming Liu, pp. 398–99; Bakhrushin, *Ocherki* . . ., p. 168.
44. Hsüan-Ming Liu, p. 398, n. For Lang Tan's report, see Iakovleva, p. 115.
45. Hsüan-Ming Liu, p. 399, n.
46. Bakhrushin, *Ocherki* . . ., p. 136; Shcheben'kov, p. 191.
47. Hsüan-Ming Liu, pp. 400–1, n. 21; Bantysh-Kamenskii, pp. 36–37; Firsov, p. 34; Bakhrushin, *Ocherki* . . ., p. 168.
48. Hsüan-Ming Liu, pp. 399, 401, n. 23; Bantysh-Kamenskii, p. 38; Shcheben'kov, p. 192.
49. Bantysh-Kamenskii, p. 38.
50. Bantysh-Kamenskii, p. 38; *D.A.I.*, X,252; Hsüan-Ming Liu, pp. 401–2; Ravenstein, pp. 47–48; Shcheben'kov, pp. 192–93; Pavlovsky, pp. 145–64; Mancall, pp. 132–33.
51. Bantysh-Kamenskii, p. 39; *D.A.I.*, X, 252–54, 258–60.
52. Bantysh-Kamenskii, pp. 39–40; Mancall, pp. 135–39.
53. Bantysh-Kamenskii, pp. 40-43; *D.A.I.*, X, 259–60; Kurts, p. 48; Firsov, p. 34. The Mongol role at this time is stressed in an important new study by V. A. Aleksandrov, *Rossiia na dal'nevostochnykh rubezhakh (vtoraia polovina XVII v.)*, (Moscow, 1969), reviewed by Joseph Fletcher in *Kritika* (Cambridge, Mass.) Spring 1971. VII:3, pp. 138–70.
54. Bantysh-Kamenskii, p. 51.
55. *Ibid.*, p. 52; Pavlovskii, p. 15.
56. Bantysh-Kamenskii, pp. 51–52, 54; Pavlovsky, p. 16; Howorth, I, 627–28; Mancall, pp. 146–49.
57. Bantysh-Kamenskii, p. 59; treaty text (12 March 1689) *S.G.G.D.*, IV, 596–99; Mancall, pp. 149–52.
58. Fu-Kuang Ch'en, p. 500.
59. Iakovleva, pp. 131–34.
60. For details regarding the negotiations, and a comparison of the three treaty texts, see Hsüan-Ming Liu, pp. 416–22. See also Bantysh-Kamenskii, pp. 61–63; Fu-Kuang Ch'en, pp. 500–4; Father François Gerbillon in Jean Baptiste Du Halde, S. J., *Description . . . de la Chine . . .*, 4 vols. (Paris, 1735) IV, 228–41; Joseph Sebes, S. J., *The Jesuits and the Sino-Russian Treaty of Nerchinsk (1689), The Diary of Thomas Pereira, S.J.* (Rome,

1961); Iakovleva, pp. 127–219; Shcheben'kov, pp. 185–219; C. Bickford O'Brien, *Russia Under Two Tsars, 1682–1689, The Regency of Sophia Alekseevna* (Berkeley-Los Angeles, 1952, University of California Publications in History), XLII, 105–22. Mancall, pp. 141–62 sums up Chinese and Russian source materials and relates the treaty to the overall problem of Sino-Russian relations.

61. Bantysh-Kamenskii, p. 63; Kurts, p. 50. For treaty text see Fu-Kuang Ch'en, pp. 504–6; Hsüan-Ming Liu, pp. 423–27 (comparison of Latin, Russian, and Manchu texts, in English). The treaty reflected the ignorance of both parties concerning the geography of the regions under discussion, but particularly that of the Chinese. V. S. Frank asserts that the Russians may have deliberately fostered certain ambiguities in order to avoid an exact demarcation. V. S. Frank, 'The Territorial Aims of the Sino-Russian Treaty of Nerchinsk, 1689', *Pacific Historical Review*, 264–70. XVI:3 (August 1947).

62. Ogorodnikov, *Ocherki . . .*, II:1, 100–2.

63. Pavlovsky, p. 123.

64. G. Vernadskii [*George Vernadsky*], 'Protiv solntsa. Rasprostranenie russkago gosudarstva k vostoku', *Russkaia mysl'*, kn. 1, January 1914, 71, 76; O'Brien, pp. 119–21; Golder, pp. 64–66; Robert J. Kerner, 'The Russian Eastward Movement: Some Observations on its Historical Significance', *Pacific Historical Review*, XVII:2, (May 1948), 135–48. James R. Gibson, in 'Russia on the Pacific: the Role of the Amur', *Canadian Geographer*, XII:1, 1968, 15–27; and in *Feeding the Russian Fur Trade. Provisionment of the Okhotsk Seaboard and the Kamchatka Peninsula, 1639–1856* (Madison, Milwaukee, and London, 1969) discusses the problem of the Amur at length.

65. See Andrew Malozemoff, *Russian Far Eastern Policy, 1881–1904, with Special Emphasis on the Causes of the Russo-Japanese War* (Berkeley and Los Angeles, 1958), pp. 1–19, for the difficulties of colonization and agriculture in the Amur region after the 1850s.

CHAPTER 11

To Arctic Shores

1. M. I. Belov, *Semen Dezhnev* 2nd ed. (Moscow, 1955) pp. 46–47. For additional information on early Arctic shipping, see S. V. Mikhailov, 'Drevnerusskoe sudostroenie na severe', *Letopis' severa*, 1949, I, p. 103–6.

2. N. N. Zubov, *Otechestvennye moreplavateli—issledovateli morei i okeanov* (Moscow, 1954), p. 34; A. P. Okladnikov, *Russkie poliarnye morekhody XVII veka u beregov Taimyra* (Moscow-Leningrad, 1948), p. 94.

3. Zubov, pp. 34–35.

4. See Chap. 8. P. N. Butsinskii, *Mangazeia i mangazeiskii uezd (1601–1645 gg.)* (Kharkov, 1893), pp. 37–39.

5. A. V. Efimov (comp.), *Otkrytiia russkikh zemleprokhodtsev i poliarnykh morekhodov XVII veka na severo-vostoke Azii. Sbornik dokumentov.* (Moscow, 1951), p. 153; N. N. Ogloblin, 'Vostochnosibirskie . . .', p. 45; Belov, *Semen Dezhnev*, p. 21.

6. Ogloblin, 'Vostochnosibirskie . . .', pp. 45–46; V. A. Samoilov, *Semen Dezhnev i ego vremia* (Moscow, 1945), p. 43; Belov, *Semen Dezhnev*, p. 21.

7. Petition of Elisei Buza for back pay, ca. 1 September 1638, in Efimov, *Otkrytiia . . .*, p. 96; V. I. Ogorodnikov, *Ocherki . . .*, II:1, 54; II:2, 60.

8. Efimov, *Otkrytiia . . .*, p. 96.

9. Belov, *Semen Dezhnev*, p. 21.

10. Samoilov, p. 43.

11. Statement of Prokopii Lazarev Kozlov, 17 September 1640, *D.A.I.*, II, 240, 242–43; Efimov, *Otkrytiia . . .*, p. 97.

12. Belov, *Semen Dezhnev*, p. 21.

13. Fischer, pp. 372–74; D. M. Lebedev, *Geografiia v Rossii XVII veka (dopetrovskoi epokhi)*, *Ocherki po istorii geograficheskikh znanii)* (Moscow, 1949), p. 52 n.; Ogloblin, 'Vostochnosi-birskie . . .', pp. 50–51; V. Iu. Vize, *Moria sovetskoi Arktiki; ocherki po istorii issledovaniia*, 2nd enl. ed., (Leningrad, 1936), p. 62. A personal glimpse of Buza is supplied in the complaint submitted about this time by one Prokofii Bragin, who tells of meeting Buza at sea, and how Buza beat him and made off with his Iakut mistress and interpreter. (Ogloblin, 'Vostochno-Sibirskie . . .', p. 57.

14. Druganko narrative, M. I. Belov (comp.), *Russkie morekhody k Ledovitom i Tikhom okeanakh.*

Sbornik dokumentov o velikikh russkikh geograficheskikh otkrytiiakh na severo-vostoke Azii v XVII veke (Leningrad-Moscow, 1952), pp. 40–41 n.

15. Samoilov, p. 43.
16. Belov, *Russkie morekhody* . . ., p. 41 n.
17. Samoilov, p. 44.
18. Fischer, p. 374.
19. Document of ca. August, 1640, report of Iakutsk voevodas, Belov, *Russkie morekhody* . . ., pp. 35–39.
20. *Ibid.*, p. 41 n.
21. *Ibid.*; Belov, *Semen Dezhnev*, p. 54.
22. *D.A.I.*, II, 262, instructions to Elisei Buza sending him to Indigirka region to seek the river Neroga, 1642; Belov, *Russkie morekhody* . . ., p. 41 n.
23. Belov, *Semen Dezhnev*, p. 23.
24. Belov, *Russkie morekhody* . . ., p. 39 n.
25. *Ibid.*
26. *Ibid.*, p. 40; cf. *Ibid.*, p. 48 n.
27. Belov, *Semen Dezhnev*, p. 54.
28. Ogorodnikov, *Ocherki* . . ., II:1, 54; *D.A.I.*, II, 241–43; Efimov, *Otkrytiia* . . ., pp. 100–1.
29. Belov, *Russkie morekhody* . . ., p. 57; Ogorodnikov, *Ocherki* . . ., II:1, 63.
30. Belov, *Russkie morekhody* . . ., p. 57.
31. Ogorodnikov, *Ocherki* . . ., II:2, 55.
32. *D.A.I.*, II, 88; Fischer, *op. cit.*, pp. 385–87.
33. Belov, *Russkie morekhody* . . ., p. 57.
34. Ogloblin, *Vostochno-Sibirskie* . . ., p. 59.
35. Ogorodnikov, *Ocherki* . . ., II:1, 55, Belov, *Russkie morekhody* . . ., p. 57.
36. Ogorodnikov, *Ocherki* . . ., II:1, 55; Efimov, *Otkrytiia* . . ., pp. 132–35; Ogloblin, *Vostochno-Sibirskie* . . ., p. 59.
37. Belov, *Russkie morekhody* . . ., pp. 56–58, Belov, *Semen Dezhnev*, pp. 40–41.
38. Belov, *Russkie morekhody* . . ., p. 58.
39. Ogorodnikov, *Ocherki* . . ., II:1, 64. Belov, *Russkie morekhody* . . ., p. 46 n., mentions that Moscow had to import silver coin at this time and was therefore eager to find its own sources.
40. Ogloblin, 'Vostochno-Sibirskie . . .', p. 41.
41. Ogorodnikov, *Ocherki* . . ., II:1, 68.
42. *D.A.I.* III, 24; Belov, *Russkie morekhody* . . ., pp. 59–60, 61 n.; Belov, *Semen Dezhnev*, p. 45.
43. Belov, *Semen Dezhnev*, p. 43; Belov, *Russkie morekhody* . . ., p. 61 n.; *D.A.I.*, III, 98; Ogorodnikov, *Ocherki* . . ., II:1, 56; Ogorodnikov, *Ocherki* . . ., II:2, 72.
44. Belov, *Semen Dezhnev*, pp. 39, 55.
45. Ogorodnikov, *Ocherki* . . ., II:1, 56; Ogorodnikov, *Ocherki* . . ., II:2, 72; Belov, *Semen Dezhnev*, p. 57.
46. *D.A.I.*, 25; see Efimov, *Otkrytiia* . . ., pp. 169, 174, 192.
47. Ogorodnikov, *Ocherki* . . ., II:2, 72–4; N. N. Ogloblin, 'Semen Dezhnev (1638–71)', *Zhurnal Ministerstvo narodnago prosveshcheniia*, 1890, no. 272, pp. 5–6; G. F. Müller, *Voyages et decouvertes* . . . (Amsterdam, 1766), pp. 7–8; Belov, *Russkie morekhody* . . ., pp. 110–11; Belov, *Semen Dezhnev*, p. 64.
48. Ogorodnikov, *Ocherki* . . ., II:1, 57.
49. Ogorodnikov, *Ocherki* . . ., II:1, 58; II:2, 74; *D.A.I.*, IV, 24–27; L. S. Berg, *Otkrytie Kamchatki i kamchatskie ekspeditsii Beringa*, cited hereafter as Berg, *OK* (3rd ed., Moscow, 1946), pp. 28–40; Samoilov, p. 68; Belov, *Semen Dezhnev*, pp. 74–75.
50. Samoilov, p. 68.
51. Ogorodnikov, *Ocherki* . . ., II:1, 58.
52. *D.A.I.*, IV, 27.
53. Ogorodnikov, *Ocherki* . . ., II:1, 59; Müller, *Voyages et decouvertes* . . ., p. 13.
54. Ogorodnikov, *Ocherki* . . ., II:1, 59.
55. Quoted from Berg, *OK*, p. 28.
56. Ogorodnikov, *Ocherki* . . ., II:1, 59.
57. *Ibid.*, II:2, 76–77.
58. *Ibid.*, pp. 77–78.

59. Belov, *Russkie morekhody* . . ., p. 66 n.
60. Samoilov, pp. 72–73.
61. Ogorodnikov, *Ocherki* . . ., II:2, 81–82.
62. Frank A. Golder, in *Russian Expansion on the Pacific, 1641–1850* . . . (Cleveland, 1914), denied the claim that Dezhnev passed through Bering Strait. However, it is generally accepted that Golder misread the principal evidence and ignored or overlooked supporting data. See Raymond J. Fisher, 'Semen Dezhnev and Professor Golder', *Pacific Historical Review*, XXV:3 (August 1956) 281–92.

CHAPTER 12
The Conquest of Kamchatka and Chukotka

1. S. P. Krasheninnikov, *Opisanie zemli Kamchatki* (Moscow, 1949), pp. 14–16, 473–74; Berg, *OK*, p. 61.
2. E. Isbrants Ides, *Three Years Travels from Moscow Over-land to China* . . ., London, 1706 (trans. from the Dutch), p. 104.
3. Krasheninnikov, p. 475; Berg, *OK*, p. 62; Lebedev, p. 38.
4. Report by Atlasov at Iakutsk, 3 June 1700, in Ia. P. Al'kor and L. K. Drezen, *Kolonial'naia politika tsarizma na Kamchatke i Chukotke v XVIII veke. Sbornik arkhivnykh materialov.* (Leningrad, 1935), pp. 25–29.
5. Report by Atlasov at Moscow, 10 February 1701, *Ibid.*, 29–33; Berg, *OK*, pp. 77–78; Ogorodnikov, *Ocherki* . . ., II:1, 105.
6. As Krasheninnikov, 361–62 points out, they called themselves 'Itel'men', meaning 'inhabitants', but 'Kamchadal', of Koriak derivation, became the term by which they were known until recent times.
7. Al'kor, p. 27; Ogorodnikov, *Ocherki* . . ., II:1, 105; Berg, *OK*, p. 80.
8. Al'kor, p. 67; Berg, *OK*, p. 80.
9. From Atlasov's Moscow report.
10. Krasheninnikov, p. 380; Berg, *OK*, pp. 84–85.
11. Krasheninnikov, p. 428. Known as *mukhomor*, this mushroom was used in European Russia to kill flies.
12. The most extensive early accounts of the Kamchadals are those given by Krasheninnikov and Steller. For another description, see the account of the Japanese castaway Denbei, in Berg, *OK*, pp. 162–64. For a modern summation of materials on this now almost extinct people, see Chester S. Chard, *Kamchadal Culture and its Relationships in the Old and New worlds*, Madison, Wisconsin, 1961 (Archives of Archeology, no. 15).
13. Al'kor, p. 27. It was probably these Koriaks that Ogorodnikov refers to as fighting on sledges, one man driving the reindeer, another shooting, recalling the use of chariots by the Romans. Ogorodnikov, II:1, 280.
14. Al'kor, p. 27; Berg, *OK*, pp. 68–69, 160–61. Peter promised to send Denbei back to Japan, but this was never done. He was baptised under the name of Gabriel and lived out his days in St. Petersburg, the first Japanese in Russia. See N. N. Ogloblin, 'Pervyi iaponets v Rossii, 1701–1705', *Russkaia starina*, October, 1891, LXXII:10, 11–24.
15. Al'kor, p. 28; Berg, *OK*, pp. 69–70.
16. Al'kor, p. 28; Berg, *OK*, p. 70; Ogorodnikov, II:2, 106.
17. Al'kor, pp. 25–33; Berg, *OK*, pp. 71–76. For a map, believed by some to have been prepared with Atlasov's assistance by the cartographer Remezov in 1700, see A. V. Efimov, *Iz istorii russkikh ekspeditsii na Tikhom Okeane*, 74–5; A. V. Efimov, *Atlas geograficheskikh otkrytii* . . . *Amerike*, map 48, and p. 33; and Krasheninnikov, 773–74, 779. This map bears several features not mentioned by Atlasov in his reports, but of which he may have heard, notably a long 'island' off Chukotka labelled as 'a land newly visited', and the term 'Kynyntsy', a Chukchi word for the inhabitants of Alaska. For further discussion of use of Atlasov's data, see L. A. Gol'denberg, *Semen Ul'ianovich Remezov, Sibirskii kartograf i geograf, 1642–posle 1720 gg.* (Moscow, 1965).
18. Krasheninnikov, p. 476; Shcheglov, pp. 146–48.
19. Shcheglov, p. 149; Krasheninnikov, p. 476; A. Sgibnev, 'Istoricheskii ocherk glavneishikh sobytii v Kamchatke, 1650–1856 g., pt. I, *Morskoi sbornik*, 1869, CI:4, 76.
20. Krasheninnikov, p. 476; cf. P. A. Slovtsov, *Istoricheskoe oborzrenie Sibiri* (St. Petersburg, 1886, 2 vols. in one), kn. 1, 136; V. K. Andrievich, *Istoricheskii ocherk Sibiri* . . ., II, 106.

21. Sgibnev, pt. I; 77; Shcheglov, p. 154.
22. Berg, *OK*, pp. 136–37; Lebedev, p. 52.
23. Krasheninnikov, p. 478; Sgibnev, p. 78.
24. Krasheninnikov, p. 480.
25. Sgibnev, pt. I, 80.
26. See Russia. Arkheograficheskaia komissiia. *Pamiatniki sibirskoi istorii XVIII veka* (cited as *P.S.I.*) 2 vols. (St. Petersburg, 1882–85), I: 428–31, for Mironov's account of 27 September 1710 of his difficulties enroute.
27. Krasheninnikov, p. 482. See *P.S.I.*, I: 438–40, for account by mutineers petitioning for pardon, 23 May 1711, and 451–53 for account of thirty others, denying complicity, 30 April 1711.
28. Golder, p. 98.
29. Krasheninnikov, p. 483.
30. *P.S.I.*, I, 441–51.
31. Petition to Peter I, 26 September 1711, *P.S.I.*, I, 459–64; Krasheninnikov, p. 484; Berg, *O.K.*, pp. 91–92; Lebedev, p. 53.
32. Krasheninnikov, p. 484; Shcheglov, p. 158 n.
33. Krasheninnikov, p. 484; Account by Sevast'ianov of events on Kamchatka from 1710, 29 December 1712, *P.S.I.*, I, 495–508.
34. Krasheninnikov, p. 485; Sgibnev, p. 83.
35. Krasheninnikov, pp. 486–87; Sgibnev, pt. I, 84–85; Berg, *O.K.*, p. 142; Lebedev, p. 54. For accounts of Kozyrevskii's colourful career, see report by Kolesov to voevoda of Iakutsk, June 1713, *P.S.I.*, I, 527–51; Shcheglov, pp. 158–59; Berg, *O.K.*, pp. 114–16. For an account of the modern discovery of Kozyrevskii's map of his second visit to the Kuriles, see A. V. Efimov, *Iz istorii russkikh ekspeditsii na Tikhom Okeane*, p. 86; and his *Iz istorii velikikh russkikh geograficheskikh otkrytii*, p. 48. The latter includes a copy of the map.
36. Sgibnev, pt. I, 85; Krasheninnikov, p. 488.
37. Ukaz, 17 February 1713, in *P.S.I.*, I, 508–10.
38. Tatarinov's report to Iakutsk commandant, 13 October 1714, *P.S.I.*, I, 43–47.
39. Sgibnev, pt. I, 87–88.
40. Tatarinov to Iakutsk, late December 1714, *P.S.I.*, II, 53–58; ditto, 16 June 1715, 73–76.
41. Orders to Trifanov, 1 August 1715, *P.S.I.*, II, 76–83.
42. Sgibnev, pt. I, 98.
43. *Ibid.*, 95.
44. Berg, *O.K.*, pp. 93–94; Sgibnev, pt. I:97; Golder, p. 108; *P.S.I.*, II, 37.
45. Efimov, *Iz istorii russkikh ekspeditsii na Tikhom Okeane*, pp. 132–34; A. Sgibnev, 'Bol'shoi Kamchatskii nariad (Ekspeditsiia El'china)', *Morskoi sbornik*, No. 12, December, 1868; *P.S.I.*, II, 109.
46. Lebedev, pp. 143–44; *Polnoe sobranie zakonov . . .*, V, Law 3,266.
47. Berg, *O.K.*, pp. 151–52.
48. Sgibnev, pt. I, 99–100.
49. *Ibid.*, 101.
50. *Ibid.*, 102; Krasheninnikov, p. 491; Report, written after May 1720, *P.S.I.*, II, 270–74.
51. Al'kor, pp. 47–50, with order of Bering, 11 July 1728; statements of soldier Zmiev, 15 April 1731; statement of Kamchadal, 27 September 1731; and report of Senate to Empress Anna, 9 May 1733.
52. Efimov, *Iz istorii russkikh ekspeditsii na Tikhom Okeane*, pp. 156–58.
53. *Ibid.*, 158–75, 236–49; Golder, pp. 151–63. Hubert Howe Bancroft, *History of Alaska, 1730–1885* (San Francisco, 1886, New York, 1960), pp. 37–40, 44.
54. Two Japanese, one a boy of eleven, were spared and taken by Shtinnikov to Verkhne-Kamchatsk as slaves. They were later sent to St. Petersburg, educated, converted to the Orthodox faith, and employed by the government to teach Japanese. Krasheninnikov, pp. 490–92.
55. *Ibid.*, 498–99; Sgibnev, pt. I, 117–18.
56. Al'kor, pp. 47–81 gives documents on reasons for the revolt and reports of it, including testimony of Iakov Gens, Fedor Kharchin, and others.
57. Sgibnev, pt. I, 127; Al'kor, pp. 158–60, report, 1763.
58. Sgibnev, pt. I, 129–30.
59. *Ibid.*, 130.

60. Krasheninnikov, pp. 498–99; Golder, pp. 163–64.
61. A. V. Efimov, *Atlas geograficheskikh otkrytii v Sibiri i v severo-zapadnoi Amerike XVII–XVIII vv.* (Moscow, 1964), Maps 103–6; Efimov, *Iz istorii russkikh ekspeditsii na Tikhom okeane,* 170–71; Map, facing page 168.
62. Sven Waxell, *The American Expedition,* 98–99; Siberian Prikaz to Senate, 8 February 1742, Al'kor, pp. 81–82.
63. For some of the many accounts of the voyages of Bering and Chirikov, see Bancroft, pp. 75–98; N. N. Zubov, *Otechestvennye moreplavateli-issledovateli morei i okeanov* (Moscow, 1954), pp. 94–101; V. I. Grekov, *Ocherki iz istorii russkikh geograficheskikh issledovanii v 1725–1765 gg.* (Moscow, 1960), pp. 109–30. For documents, see F. A. Golder, *Bering's voyages. An Account of the Efforts of the Russians to Determine the Relation of Asia and America,* 2 vols. (New York, 1922–25); D. M. Lebedev, *Plavanie A. I. Chirikova na paketbote 'Sv. Pavel' k poberezh'iam Ameriki. S prilozheniem sudovogo zhurnala 1741 g.* (Moscow, 1951); L. S. Berg, *Otkrytie Kamchatki i ekspeditsii Beringa, 1725–1741* 3rd ed., (Moscow-Leningrad, 1946). Raymond H. Fisher, 'Kerner, Bering, and the Amur: A Refutation', *Jahrbücher für Geschichte Osteuropas,* (September 1969) XVII:3, 397–407 disposes of an attempt to link Bering's voyages with the Amur problem.
64. As late as 1825, reports persisted in Alaska of a settlement of descendants of Chirikov's lost crewmen.
65. Krasheninnikov, pp. 499–500; for documents regarding proselytization, see *P.S.I.,* II, 139–49.
66. Al'kor, pp. 30, 83, 85–86.
67. *Ibid.,* 83, 96.
68. Krasheninnikov, p. 499, note; Al'kor, pp. 122–32; Sgibnev, pt II, *Morskoi sbornik,* 1869, CII:5, 73; Part III, CII:6, 46–47.
69. I. G. Georgii, *Russia, or a Compleat Historical Account of all the Nations which Comprise that Empire* 4 vols., (London, 1780), III, 176.
70. Report of sotnik Kotkovskii to Irkutsk provincial chancery, 3 April 1747, Al'kor, pp. 172–74; Sgibnev, pt. II, 59.
71. Reports, Capt. Shatilov to Irkutsk provincial chancery, 11 March, 22 October 1752, Al'kor, 174, 176–79; Sgibnev, Part II, 60.
72. Secret reports of Irkutsk chancery to War College, 26 and 29 November 1756, Al'kor, pp. 179–80.
73. Report, Zashiversk zemskii ispravnik Ivan Banner to Iakutsk commandant, 8 February 1791, Al'kor, pp. 188–89; Sgibnev, pt. IV, *Morskoi sbornik,* 1869, CIII:7, 30–31.
74. Shcheglov, p. 243; *Svod zakonov rossiiskoi imperii,* 1912 ed., V, 'Statute of Direct Taxes', sec. 681, n. 4, states: 'The Chukchi . . . pay tribute on their own volition in both quantity and quality, on the basis of special rules.' II, "Statute of aliens', sec. 4, states: 'The Chukchi . . . constitute special cases.'

CHAPTER 13

Conclusions

1. Fischer, pp. 630–31.
2. Golder, pp. 14–15.
3. Kerner, p. 103.
4. John A. Morrison, 'Russia and Warm Water: a Fallacious Generalization and its Consequences', U.S. Naval Institute, *Proceedings,* November, 1952, LXXVIII, 1169–79.
5. Solov'ev, III, 314.
6. Kliuchevskii, I, 31–32.
7. Frederick J. Turner, *The Frontier in American History,* New York, 1920.
8. B. H. Sumner, *A Short History of Russia,* New York, 1943, p. 1. Later reprints bear title *Survey of Russian History.*

Glossary

Accents indicate the syllable on which stress is to fall

Atamán. Cossack military commander.
Boyár. Noble of high rank.
Boyar sons (syny boiarskie, deti boiarskie). Lesser nobility, probably originally impoverished or younger sons of boyar families.
Desiátnik. Petty officer in charge of ten soldiers; a corporal.
D'iák. Secretary in Muscovite bureaucratic apparatus.
Esaúl. Cossack captain or lieutenant.
Golová. Senior officer.
Górod. Town; earlier a fortified settlement or citadel.
Gorodók. Fortification; a small town.
Grámota. A document; order; charter.
Iám. Post station.
Iamshchík. Post-driver.
Iasák. Tax in furs paid by Ural and Siberian tribesmen.
Iurt, iurtá. Earlier, a village or state; later, a felt tent on a dome-shaped wooden framework.
Koch', kocha (pl. *kochi*). A decked boat.
Murzá. A member of the Tatar gentry class.
Naméstnik. In Muscovy of the fourteenth to sixteenth centuries, a local administrator, governor or judge appointed by the Grand Prince.
Okhóchaia rat'. A volunteer force (ca. fourteenth century).
Okól'nichii. An official rank next to boyar in importance.
Ostróg. A fort or blockhouse.
Ostrózhek. A small ostrog.
Peredóvshchik. Foreman.
Piatidesiátnik. Commander of a unit of fifty soldiers.
Písmennyi golová. An official capable of preparing reports; an officer serving as assistant to a voevoda in seventeenth century Siberia.
Pod'iáchei. Clerk.
Poméshchik. Petty noble; landholder.
Posádnik. In Kievan times, a prince's lieutenant, appointed to govern a town and surrounding province.
Posádskii. Small retail trader; artisan.
Posól'skii prikaz. Ambassadorial Office; the central office for foreign affairs.
Prikáshchik. Administrator of a village or a rural district.
Promýshlennik. Private trader or hunter in Siberia.
Razriád. Military affairs department of Muscovite government.
Slobodá. A settlement or group of settlements exempt from ordinary taxes and work obligations.
Slobódchik. In Russia an elected village head; in Siberia a minor official who founded and later administered new villages.

Sluzhílye liudi. Men in government service.

Sluzhílye Tatary. Tatars in state service.

Sótnia (pl. *sotni*). A troop of a hundred cossacks.

Sótnik. A commander of a sotnia.

Stanítsa. A cossack settlement.

Streléts (pl. *streltsy*). Muscovite regular troops, organized in Ivan IVs reign.

Strelétskii prikaz. The government department or bureau concerned with the streltsy.

Taigá. Forest zone.

Tatars. The predominantly Turkic peoples in the Mongol armies in Russia.

Ushkúinik. A Novgorodian freebooter.

Úlus. A tatar settlement; realm or domain of a Tatar sovereign.

Voevóda. A general; later a military governor.

Vólost. District.

Volostél. Chief of a volost.

Zakáshchik. Agent.

Zimóv'e. Winter quarters.

Bibliography

Akademiia nauk. *Akty arkheograficheskoi ekspeditsiei,* cited as *A.A.E.*—a generally accepted abbreviation of *Akty, sobrannye v bibliotekakh i arkhivakh rossiiskoi imperii arkheograficheskoi ekspeditsiei imperatorskoi akademii nauk.* 4 vols. St. Petersburg, 1836; Index, 1838.

Aleksandrov, V. A. 'Nachalo khoziaistvennogo osvoeniia i prisoedinenie k Rossii severnoi chasti Eniseiskogo kraia', *Sibir' XVII–XVIII vv. Materialy po istorii Sibiri,* Vyp. 1, *Sibir' perioda feodalizma.* Novosibirsk, 1962. 7–29.

Al'kor Ia. P., and Drezen, L. K., compilers. *Kolonial'naia politika tsarizma na Kamchatke i Chukotke v XVIII veke. Sbornik arkhivnykh materialov.* Leningrad, 1935.

Al'kor, Ia. P., and Grekov, B. D., compilers. *Kolonial'naia politika moskovskogo gosudarstva v Iakutii. Sbornik dokumentov.* Leningrad, 1935–36. 2 vols. vol. 1, XVII v.; vol. 2, XVIII v.

Andrievich, V. K. *Istoricheskii ocherk Sibiri po dannym predstavliaemym Polnym sobraniem zakonov.* 6 vols. in 8. St. Petersburg, 1886–9.

———. *Kratkii ocherk istorii Zabaikal'ia ot drevneishikh vremen do 1762 goda.* St. Petersburg, 1887.

Arkheograficheskaia kommissiia. See Russia.

Atlas istorii SSSR. 3 vols. Moscow, 1949–50.

Baddeley, John F. *Russia, Mongolia and China, Being Some Record of the Relations Between Them from the Beginning of the XVIIth Century to the death of the Tsar Alexei Mikhailovich, A.D. 1602–1676 . . .* 2 vols. London, 1919.

Bagalei, D. I. 'Ocherki iz istorii kolonizatsii i byta stepnoi okrainy moskovskogo gosudarstva', *Chteniia v imperatorskom obshehestve istorii i drevnosti rossiiskikh pri moskovskom universitete,* cited as *Chteniia,* 1886:2, 1–264.

Bakhrushin, S. V. *Ivan Groznyi,* Moscow, 1945.

———. *Ocherki po istorii kolonizatsii Sibiri v XVI i XVII vv.* Moscow, 1927. (Also in S. V. Bakhrushin, *Nauchnye trudy,* III, Moscow, 1955, 13–160.)

———. 'Sibirskie sluzhilye Tatary v XVII v.', *Istoricheskie zapiski,* I (1937), 55–80.

Bancroft, Hubert Howe. *History of Alaska, 1730–1885.* San Francisco, 1886; New York, 1960.

Bantysh-Kamenskii, N. N. *Diplomaticheskoe sobranie del mezhdu Rossiiskim i Kitaiskim gosudarstvami s 1619 po 1792-i god, sostavlennoe po dokumentam khraniashchimsia v Moskovskom arkhive Gosudarstvennoi kollegii inostrannykh del, v 1792–1803 godu . . .* Kazan, 1882.

Bazilevich, K. V. *Vneshniaia politika russkogo tsentralizovannogo gosudarstva vtoraia polovina XV veka.* Moscow, 1952.

Beletskaia, Vanda. 'Mangazeia zlatokipiashchaia', *Ogenëk,* 1970:40, 24–25.

Belov, M. I. *Arkticheskoe moreplavanie s drevneishikh vremen do serediny XIX veka.* Leningrad, 1956. vol. I of *Istoriia otkrytiia i osvoeniia Severnogo morskogo puti,* 3 vols., 1956–59.

———. *Mangazeia* Leningrad, 1969.

———. *Raskopki 'zlatokipiashchei' Mangazei,* Leningrad, 1970.

———. *Russkie morekhody k Ledovitom i Tikhom okeanakh. Sbornik dokumentov o velikikh russkikh geograficheskikh otkrytiiakh na severo-vostoke Azii v XVII veke.* Leningrad-Moscow, 1952.

———. *Semen Dezhnev.* Moscow, 1955. 2nd ed.

Berg. L. S. *Ocherki po istorii russkikh geograficheskikh otkrytii.* 2nd ed., Moscow-Leningrad, 1949.

———. *Otkrytie Kamchatki i kamchatskie ekspeditsii Beringa.* 3rd ed., Leningrad-Moscow, 1946.

Borzakovskii, V. S. *Istorii tverskogo kniazhestva.* St. Petersburg, 1876.

Butsinskii, P. N. *Mangazeia i mangazeiskii uezd. 1601–45 gg.* Khar'kov, 1893. From *Zapiski Khar'kovskogo universiteta,* I, 1893.

The Cambridge History of Poland (to 1696). Cambridge, 1950.

Chard, Chester S. *Kamchadal culture and its relationships in the Old and New worlds*. Madison, Wisconsin, 1961. (Archives of Archeology, no. 15).

Ch'en Fu-kuang. 'Sino-Russian Diplomatic Relations since 1689', *Chinese Social and Political Science Review*, vol. X:1 (Jan. 1926), 120-44; X:2 (April, 1926), 476–508.

Cherepnin, L. V. *Obrazovanie russkogo tsentralizovannogo gosudarstva v XIV–XV vekakh* (Moscow, 1960).

Dopolneniia k aktam istoricheskim. See Russia. Arkheogaficheskaia . . .

Efimov, A. V., ed. *Atlas geograficheskikh otkrytii v Sibiri i v Severo-Zapadnoi Amerike XVII–XVIII vv. Moscow, 1964.*

_____. *Iz istorii russkikh ekspeditsii na Tikhom okeane*. Chast' 1, Pervaia polovina XVIII veka. Moscow, 1948.

_____. *Otkrytiia russkikh zemleprokhodtsev i poliarnykh morekhodov XVII veka na severo-vostoke Azii. Sbornik dokumentov*. Moscow, 1953.

_____. *Iz istorii velikikh russkikh geograficheskikh otkrytii v Severnom Ledovitom i Tikhom okeanakh; XVIIi-pervaia polovina XVIII v*. Moscow, 1950.

Fennell, J. L. I. *Ivan the Great of Moscow*. London, 1961.

Firsov, N. N. *Chteniia po istorii Sibiri* . . . 2 vols. in 1. Moscow, 1920–21.

Fischer, J. E. *Sibirskaia istoriia s samogo otkrytiia Sibiri do zavoevaniia sei zemli rossiiskim oruzhiem* . . . St. Petersburg, 1774.

Fisher, Raymond H. *The Russian Fur Trade, 1550–1700*. University of California publications in History, vol. 31. Berkeley, 1943.

_____. 'Kerner, Bering, and the Amur: A Refutation', *Jahrbücher für Geschichte Osteuropas*, XVII:3, September, 1969, 397–407.

_____. 'Semen Dezhnev and Professor Golder', *The Pacific Historical Review*, Berkeley, Calif., XXV:3 (August, 1956), 281–92.

Frank, V. S. 'The Territorial Aims of the Sino-Russian Treaty of Nerchinsk, 1689', *Pacific Historical Review*, 1947:3, August, XVI, 264–70.

Georgii, I. G. *Russia, or a Compleat Historical Account of All the Nations which Comprise that Empire* (4 vols., London, 1780).

Gnevushev, A. M., compiler. *Akty vremeni pravleniia tsaria Vasiliia Shuiskago (1606 g. 19 maia-17 iiulia 1610 g.)*. Moscow, 1914, and *Chteniia*, CCLIII (1915), Bk. 2, sec. 1, i-xix, 1–422.

Golder, Frank A. *Bering's Voyages. An Account of the Efforts of the Russians to Determine the Relation of Asia and America*, 2 vols. New York, 1922–1925.

_____. *Russian Expansion on the Pacific, 1651–1850; an Account of the Earliest and Later Expeditions Made by the Russians Along the Pacific Coast of Asia and North America; Including some Related Expeditions to the Arctic Regions*. Cleveland, 1914.

Grekov, V. I. *Ocherki iz istorii russkikh geograficheskikh issledovanii v 1725–65 gg*. Moscow, 1960.

Hakluyt, R. *The Principal Navigations, Voyages, Traffiques and Discoveries of the English Nation* . . . London, Toronto and New York, 1927–28. 10 vols.

Halde, Jean Baptiste du, S. J. *Description, geographique, historique, chronologique, politique et physique de la Chine et de la Tartarie chinoise*. 4 vols. Paris, 1735.

Howorth, Henry H. *History of the Mongols from the 9th to the 19th Century*. 4 vols. in 5. London, 1876–1927.

Hsüan Ming Liu. 'Russo-Chinese Relations up to the Treaty of Nerchinsk', *The Chinese Social and Political Science Review*, XXIII:4 (1940), 391–440.

Iakovleva, P. T. *Pervyi russko-kitaiskii dogovor 1689 goda*. Moscow, 1958.

Iakutiia v XVII veke (Ocherki), S. V. Bakhrushin and S. A. Tokarev, eds. Iakutsk, 1953.

Ikonnikov, V. S. *Opyt russkoi istoriografii*. 2 vols. in 4. Kiev, 1891–1908.

Ilovaiskii, D. I. *Istoriia Rossii*. 5 vols. Moscow, 1876–1905.

'Instruktsiia pis'mianomu golove Poiarkovu', *Chteniia*, 1861:1, January–March, Bk. 1, pt. 5, 1–14.

Ionova, O. V. *Iz istorii iakutskogo naroda (pervaia polovina XVII veka)*. Iakutsk, 1945.

Istoriia SSSR, I 2nd ed., (Moscow, 1947). B. D. Grekov, S. V. Bakhrushin, V. I. Lebedev, eds.

Karamzin, N. M. *Istoriia gosudarstva rossiiskago*. 12 vols. 2nd ed. St. Petersburg, 1818–29.

Karpov, G. F. *Pamiatniki diplomaticheskikh snoshenii moskovskago gosudarstva s krymskoiu i nagaiskoiu ordami i s Turtsiei*, I (s 1474 po 1505 god, epokha sverzheniia mongol'skago iga v Rossii), *Sbornik Imperatorskago Russkago istoricheskago obshchestva*, St. Petersburg, 1884, XLI.

Katanaev, G. E. 'Eshche ob Ermake i ego sibirskom pokhode (Novyia variatsii na staruiu temu)', *Zapiski zapadnosibirskago otdela Imperatorskago Russkago geograficheskago obshchestva,* XV, pt. 2 (1893), 1–36.

————. 'Kirgizskiia stepi, Sredniaia Aziia i severnyi Kitai v XVII i XVIII stoletiiakh, po pokazaniiam razvedkam, doezhim zapisiam, otchetam i izsledovaniiam zapadno-sibirskikh kazakhov i prochikh sluzhilykh sibirskikh liudei', *Zapiski zapadnosibirskago otdela Imperatorskago Russago geograficheskago obshchestva,* XIV:1 (1893), 1–72.

Kerner, Robert J. *The Urge to the Sea: The Course of Russian History. The Role of Rivers, Portages, Ostrogs, Monasteries, and Furs.* Berkeley, 1946.

Krasheninnikov, S. P. *Opisanie zemli Kamchatki, s prilozheniem raportov, donesenii i drugikh neopublikovannykh materialov.* Moscow, 1949.

Kurts, B. G. *Russko-kitaiskie snosheniia v XVI, XVII i XVIII stoletiiakh.* Kharkov, 1929.

Lantzeff, George V. 'Russian Eastward Expansion Before the Mongol Invasion', *The American Slavic and East European Review,* VI:18–19, 1–10.

————. *Siberia in the 17th Century, a Study of the Colonial Administration.* Berkeley, 1943.

Lebedev, D. M. *Geografiia v Rossi XVII veka (dopetrovskoi epokhi). Ocherki po istorii geograficheskikh znanii.* Moscow-Leningrad, 1949.

————. *Plavanie A. I. Chirikova na paketbote 'Sv. Pavel' k poberezh'iam Ameriki.* Moscow, 1951.

'Letopisets Dvinskii', *Drevniaia rossiiskaia vivliofika* 20 vols., (Moscow, 1788–91), XVIII, 1791.

Mikhailov, S. V. 'Drevnerusskoe sudostroenie na severe', *Letopis' severa,* vyp. 1, 1949, 103–6.

Müller, G. F. *Istoriia Sibiri,* 2 vols., 1937–41, Moscow–Leningrad, of a projected 3 vols. Vol. I was originally published as *Opisanie Sibirskago Tsarstva* (1750). A German edition of the first volume appeared in 1761 in the series *Sammlung Russischer Geschichte,* and the second volume in the same series in 1763.

————. *Opisanie sibirskago tsarstva i vsekh proisshedshikh v nem del ot nachala a osoblivo ot pokoreniia ego rossiiskoi derzhave po sii vremena.* 2nd ed. St. Petersburg, 1787.

————. *Voyages et decouvertes faites par les Russes le long des cotes de la mer Glaciale et sur l'ocean Oriental, tant vers le Japon que vers l'Amerique. On y a joint l'Histoire du fleuve Amur et des pays adjacens, depuis la conquete des Russes . . .* Translated from the original German. Amsterdam, 1766,

Nolde, Boris. *La formation de l'Empire Russe: Etudes, Notes et Documents.* 2 vols. Paris, 1952–53.

Novikov, N., compiler. *Drevniaia rossiiskaia vivliofika, soderzhashchaia v sebe: sobranie drevnostei rossiiskikh, do istorii, geografii i geneologii rossiiskiia kasaiushchikhsia,* cited as *D.R.V.* 20 vols. 2nd ed., Moscow, 1788–91.

————. *Prodolzhenie drevniei rossiiskoi vivliofiki,* cited as *P.D.R.V.* 11 vols. St. Petersburg, 1786–1801.

Novosel'skii, A. A. *Bor'ba moskovskogo gosudarstva s tatarami v pervoi polovine XVII veka.* Moscow-Leningrad, 1948.

O'Brien, C. Bickford. *Russia Under Two Tsars, 1682–1689, the Regency of Sophia Alekseevna.* Berkeley-Los Angeles, 1952. University of California Publications in History, XLII, 105–22.

Ocherki istorii SSSR. 8 (?) vols. Moscow, 1953–57 (?).

Ogloblin, N. N. 'Sibirskie diplomaty XVII veka (posol'skie stateinye spiski)', *Istoricheskii vestnik,* 1891, XLVI:10, 158–71.

————. 'Bunt i pobeg na Amur 'vorovskago polka' M. Sorokina (Ocherk iz zhizni XVII veka)', *Russkaia starina,* LXXXV, 1896:1, Jan., 205–24.

————. *Obozrenie stolbtsov i knig Sibirskago prikaza (1592–1768 gg.),* in *Chteniia,* 1895, Bk. 1, part 4, 1–421; 1898, Bk. 1, part 3, pp. 1–162; 1900, Bk. 3, part 3, 1–394; 1902, Bk. 1, part 3, 1–288.

————. 'Pervyi iaponets v Rossii, 1701–1705', *Russkaia starina,* October 1891, LXXII:10,

————. 'Semeon Dezhnev (1638–71)', *Zhurnal Ministerstvo narodnago prosveshcheniia,* 1890, no. 272.

————. 'Vostochnosibirskie poliarnye morekhody', *Zhurnal Ministerstvo narodnago prosvescheniia,* 1903, no. 347, May, sec. 2, 38–62.

Ogorodnikov, E. K. 'Priberezh'ia ledovitago i belago morei s ikh pritokami po knige bol'shago chertezha', *Zapiski imperatorskago russkago geograficheskago obshchestva po otdeleniiu etnografii,* VII (1877), 1–265.

Ogorodnikov, V. I. *Ocherki istorii Sibiri do nachala XIX st.* Chast' 1, *Vvedenie. Istoriia do-russkoi Sibiri,* Irkutsk, 1920. Chast' 2, Vyp. 1, *Zavoevanie russkimi Sibiri,* Vladivostok, 1924. Chast' 2, Vyp. 2, *Iz istorii pokoreniia Sibiri. Pokorenie iukagirskoi zemli,* Chita, 1922. This part also in *Trudy Gosudarstvennogo instituta narodnogo obrazovaniia v Chite*, Kn. 1, Chita, 1922. Chast' 2, Vyp. 3, *Russkaia gosudarstvennaia vlast' i Sibirskie inorodtsy v XVI–XVIII vv.* Irkutsk, 1920. Also in *Sbornik trudov professorov gosudarstvennogo Irkutskogo universiteta*, otd. 1, nauki i gumanitarnye, vyp. 1 (1921), 69–113. Chast' 2, Vyp. 3, *Prilozhenie.* Irkutsk, 1920.

―――――. *Tuzemnoe i russkoe zemledelie na Amure v XVII v.* Vladivostok, 1927, and in *Trudy Gosudarstvennogo Dal'nevostochnogo universiteta*, Series 3, no. 4.

Okladnikov, A. P. *Ocherki iz istorii zapadnykh Buriat-Mongolov (XVII–XVIII vv.).* Leningrad, 1937.

―――――. 'Penda—zabytyi russkii zemleprokhodets XVII veka', *Letopis' severa*, I, 1949, 94–102.

―――――. *Russkie poliarnye morekhody XVII veka u beregov Taimyra.* Moscow, 1948.

Okun', S. B. 'K istorii Buriatii v XVII v.', *Krasnyi Arkhiv*, no. 3 (76) 1936. 153–91.

Pavlovskii, Michel N. *Chinese-Russian Relations.* New York, 1949.

Pekarskii, P. P. 'Kogda i dlia chego osnovany goroda Ufa i Samara?' *Zapiski imperatorskoi akademii nauk*, XXI (1872), 232–60.

Peretiatkovich, G. I. *Povol'zhe v XV i XVI vekakh (ocherki iz kraia i ego kolonizatsiia).* Moscow, 1877.

―――――. *Povol'zhe v XVII i nachale XVIII veka (ocherki iz istorii kolonizatsii kraia).* Odessa, 1882.

Platonov, S. F. *Lektsii po russkoi istorii.* 6th ed. St. Petersburg, 1909.

―――――. 'Stroganovy, Ermak i Mangazeia', in his *Proshloe russkago severa. Ocherki po kolonizatsii Pomor'ia.* Petrograd, 1923, 72–79.

Pokrovskii, M. N. *Russkaia istoriia s drevneishikh vremen.* 2nd ed., Moscow, 1913–14.

Polnoe sobranie russkikh letopisei. See Russia. Arkheograficheskaia kommissiia.

Presniakov, A. E. *Obrazovanie velikorusskago gosudarstva, ocherki po istorii XIII–XV stoletii.* Petrograd, 1918.

Priselkov, M. D. *Istoriia russkago letopisaniia XI–XV vv.* Leningrad, 1940.

Ravenstein, E. G. *The Russians on the Amur; Its Discovery, Conquest, and Colonisation, with a Description of the Country, its Inhabitants, Productions, and Commercial Capabilities; and Personal Accounts of Russian Travellers.* London, 1861.

Razriadnaia kniga, 1475–1598 gg. Moscow, 1966.

Russia. Arkheograficheskaia kommissiia. *Akty istoricheskie*, cited as *A.I.* 5 vols. St. Petersburg, 1841–42; Index, 1843.

―――――. *Dopolneniia k aktam istoricheskim*, cited as *D.A.I.* 12 vols. St. Petersburg, 1846–72; Index, 1875.

―――――. *Pamiatniki sibirskoi istorii XVIII veka.* 2 vols. (Book 1:1700–13; Book 2: 1713–24). St. Petersburg, 1882–85.

―――――. *Polnoe sobranie russkikh letopisei*, cited as *P.S.R.L.* 24 vols. St. Petersburg, 1841–1914.

―――――. *Russkaia istoricheskaia biblioteka*, cited as *R.I.B.* 39 vols. St. Petersburg, 1875–1927.

―――――. *Sibirskiia letopisi.* St. Petersburg, 1907.

Russia. Sobstvennaia ego imperatorskago velichestva kantseliariia. *Polnoe sobranie zakonov Rossiiskoi imperii, s 1649 goda.* St. Petersburg, 1830–1916. 239 vols.

―――――. *Svod zakonov Rossiiskoi imperii . . . (Neoffitsial'noe izdanie).* 16 vols. in 5, with Index.

Russia. Treaties, etc. *Sobranie gosudarstvennykh gramot i dogovorov khraniashchikhsia v gosudarstvennoi kollegii inostrannykh del*, cited as *S.G.G.D.* 5 vols. Moscow, 1813–28, 1894.

Russko-kitaiskie otnosheniia v XVII veke. Materialy i dokumenty. I, Moscow, 1969.

Russko-Mongol'skie otnosheniia, 1607–36. Sbornik dokumentov. Moscow, 1959.

Sadovnikov, D. N. *Nashi zemleprokhodtsy (razskazy o zaselenii Sibiri, 1581–1712 gg.)* 2nd ed. Moscow, 1898.

Samoilov, V. A. *Semen Dezhnev i ego vremia.* Moscow, 1945.

Sebes, Joseph, S. J. *The Jesuits and the Sino-Russian Treaty of Nerchinsk (1689). The Diary of Thomas Pereira, S. J.* Vol. XVIII of Bibliotheca Instituti Historici S. I. Rome, 1961.

Sgibnev, A. 'Bol'shoi Kamchatskii nariad (Edspeditsiia El'china)', *Morskoi sbornik*, no. 12, December, 1868.

_____. 'Istoricheskii ocherk glavneishikh sobytii v Kamchatke, 1650–1856 g.,' *Morskoi sbornik*, 1869, numbers 4–8, April–August, Also published separately, St. Petersburg, 1869.

Shchenben'kov, V. G. *Russko-kitaiskie otnosheniia v XVII v.* Moscow, 1960.

Shcheglov, I. V. *Khronologicheskii perechen'vazhneishikh dannykh iz istorii Sibiri, 1032–1882.* Irkutsk, 1883.

Shishonko, Vasilii. *Permskaia letopis's 1263–1881g.* Perm, 1881–89. 7 vols.

Sibirskaia Sovetskaia Entsiklopediia. 3 vols. (to 'N'). Moscow, 1929.

Slovtsov, P. A. *Istoricheskoe obozrenie Sibiri.* St. Petersburg, 1886. 2 vols. in 1.

Smirnov, I. I. *Ocherki politicheskoi istorii russkogo gosudarstva 30–5oth godov XVI veka.* Moscow-Leningrad, 1958.

Sobranie gosudarstvennykh gramot i dogovorov. See Russia. Treaties, etc.

Solov'ev, S. M. *Istoriia Rossii s drevneishikh vremen.* 29 vols. in 7. St. Petersburg, 1894?–95?.

Titov, A. *Sibir' v XVII veke.* Moscow, 1890.

Tokarev, S. A. *Ocherk istorii iakutskogo naroda.* Moscow, 1940.

_____. *Obshchestvennyi stroi iakutov XVII–XVIII vv.* Iakutsk, 1945.

Vel'iaminov-Zernov, V. V. *Izsledovanie o kasimovskikh tsariakh i tsarevichakh.* 4 vols. St. Petersburg, 1863–66. Reprint from *Trudy imperatorskago arkheologicheskago obshchestva. Vostochnoe otdelenie,* Parts 9–11.

Vernadsky, George. 'Protiv solntsa. Rasprostranenie russkago gosudarstva k vostoku', *Russkaia mysl'*, XXXV:1, Jan. 1914, 56–79.

_____. *Nachertaniia russkoi istorii.* Chast' 1. Prague, 1927.

_____. 'The expansion of Russia', *Transactions of the Connecticut Academy of Arts and Sciences,* XXXI (1933) July, 393–425.

_____. *A history of Russia*, comprising: *Ancient Russia,* New Haven, 1943; *Kievan Russia,* New Haven, 1948; *The Mongols and Russia,* New Haven, 1953; *Russia at the Dawn of the Modern Age.* New Haven, 1959; *The Tsardom of Moscow, 1547–1682,* in 2 parts, New Haven, 1969.

Vitevskii, V. N. *I. I. Nepliuev i orenburgskii krai v prezhnem ego sostave do 1758 g.; istoricheskaia monografiia.* 4 vols. Kazan, 1889–97.

Vize, V. Iu. *Moria sovetskoi Arktiki; ocherki po istorii issledovaniia.* 2nd enl. edition. Leningrad, 1939.

Vvedenskii, A. A. 'Anika Stroganov v svoem Sol'vychegodskom khoziaistve', *Sbornik statei po russkoi istorii posviashchennykh S. F. Platonovu.* St. Petersburg, 1922.

_____. *Torgovyi dom XVI i XVII vekov.* Leningrad, 1924.

_____. *Dom Stroganovykh v XVI–XVII vekakh.* Moscow, 1962.

Waxell, Sven L. *The American expedition.* London, 1952. (Translation of the Danish version of the original German manuscript, now in Saltykov-Shchedrin Public Library, Leningrad.

Witsen, Nicolaes Corneliszoon. *Noord en Oost Tartarye . . .* 2nd revised and enl. ed., 2 vols. Amsterdam, 1705.

Zubov, N. N. *Otechestvennye moreplavateli—issledovateli morei i okeanov.* Moscow, 1954.

Index

Abalak, Lake, 102–103

Abdul Kerim, Prince of Pelym, defeated (1594), 120

Abdul-Khair, son of Kuchum: captured (1591), 114, 115; appeal, 117–18

Abdul-Latif, granted Kashira by Ivan III, 55; Khan of Kazan (1497–1501), 60, 74

Ablai, Siberian Tatar prince, captured (1586), 111

Ablin, Seitkul, envoy to China (1656), 167, 172

Abreu, Antonio de, Portuguese navigator, 137

Achansk (1651), 163; evacuated by Russians (1652), 164

Adashev, Daniil, leader of expedition against Crimea (1559), 70

Afanasii, Metropolitan, authorizes baptism of Tatars and Voguls (1565), 86

Agriculture: along Northern Dvina, 38, 40; in Ob region, 127, 137–38; on Enisei, 159; in Baikal region, 142, 153; on Amur, 137–38, 153, 161, 166–67; on Ilim and upper Lena, 160

Aigun, Chinese supply base and fort, 174

Ainu. See Kuriles

Akhmat, Khan of Golden Horde, raids Moscow (1472), 57–58; (1480), 59

Aklan (Oklan) River, 195

Aklansk: (1669), 195, 201; rebuilt (1715), 206–7; besieged by Koriaks (1746), 218

Alachev, Igichei, Ostiak chief, Russian ally (ca. 1594), 121–22

Alaid (now Atlasov) Island (Kurile chain), 199

Alatyr, 68, 71

Alazeia River, 188–89, 207

Albaza, Prince of Dauria (ca. 1650), 162

Albazin, Daur town on Amur: seized by Khabarov (1650), 162, 166, 174, 175; abandoned (1653); restored by Chernigovskii (1665), 171–73; conquered by Chinese (1685), 175; reoccupied by Russians, again attacked (1686–87), 176–77; renounced by Russia (1689), 180

'Albazinians,' special force of Russian prisoners at Peking, 176

Alberdov, Andrei, Moscow boyar, envoy to Northern Dvina region (1397), 41

Albychev, Peter, founder of Makovsk (1618) and Eniseisk (1619), 131–32

Aldan River, 136, 156, 207, 210; route to Amur, 155–56, 158, 159

Alekseev, Vasilii. See Tiumenets

Aleksin, frontier town, 57

Aleutian Islands, 216

Alexander Iaroslavich (Nevskii), Prince of Novgorod (1236–52), Grand Prince, Vladimir (1252–63), 31

Ali, son of Kuchum: reoccupies Isker, ousted by Seid Akhmat (1585), 106; opposes Russians (1594), 115–16

Altyn Khans, Mongol rulers, 124

Amazar River, 160

Amga River, 135

Amur River, 137, 148, 155

Anadyr River, 189, 191, 192

Anadyrsk, zimov'e (1649); ostrog (1656), 192, 195, 200, 207, 214, 218

Anauls, East Siberian tribe, 191, 193

Andreev, Afanasii, detachment leader in expedition to Anadyr (1648), 190

Andrei Aleksandrovich, Prince of Novgorod, Grand Prince, Vladimir (1294–1304), 32, 33

Andrei Iur'evich (Bogoliubskii), Grand Prince, Vladimir (1169–75): assumes protectorate of Dvina region (1169), 25, 26, 28; attacks Bulgars, 27; wins Dvina region, 34–35

Angara (Upper Tunguska) River, 146, 147, 178

Aniui Range, 192

Aniui River, 219. See also Bol'shoi and Malyi Aniui rivers

Ankudinov, Gerasim, detachment leader in expedition to Anadyr (1648), 190

Anna, Empress (1730–40), 217

Anna Ignat'eva, Ostiak princess of Koda, rebel (1607, 1608), 130

Antsyferov, Danilo, mutineer on Kamchatka (1711); explores Kuriles, killed by Kamchadals, 205

Argun River, 159, 171, 175, 180

Argunsk (1689), 180

Arins, Turkic tribe in upper Enisei, first encounter with Russians (1608), 128, 141, 143, 144, 146

Arkhangel Mikhail, three masted brig, used in Great Northern Expedition, 216

Arkhangel'sk: early monastery site, port (1584), 24, 83, 190, 124; sea route to

Mangazeia from, 127

Arkhangel'sk Chronicle, 74

Arshinskii, Danila, voevoda at Nerchinsk (*1669*), 172

Arsk, fort (ca. *1555*), 68

Astaf'ev, Besson, on expedition to Anadyr (*1648*), 190

Astrakhan, Khanate of: origin, 53, 59; annexed by Moscow (*1556*), 69

Asyka, Vogul prince, 120

Atlasov, Vladimir: expedition to Kamchatka (*1697-99*), 195-96 ff.; to Iakutsk and Moscow (*1700*), 200; return to Kamchatka (*1707*), 202; death (*1711*), 203, 206

Avacha Bay (Kamchatka), 216

Avacha River (Kamchatka), 204

Azov (Don) cossacks, 75, 76

Babinov, Artemii, discoverer of shorter route across Urals (*1597*), 121

Babinov Road, 121

Baibakhta, Ob Ostiak chief, conspirator (*1604*), 129

Baikal, Lake, 134, 148-49, 178

Baikov, Fedor Isakovich, envoy to China (*1653*), 167, 172

Bakhrushin, Sergei Vladimirovich (*1882-1950*), 94, 229

Bakhteiarov, Enalei, explorer of Vitim route to Amur, 155

Balagansk (*1653*), 149, 152

Balboa, Vasco Nuñez de, Spanish explorer (ca. *1513*), 137

Bantysh-Kamenskii, Nikolai Nikolaevich, historian (*1737-1814*), 175

Bardak, Ostiak princeling, 123

Barguzin (*1648*), 149, 151, 152

Barguzin River, 151, 154

Basandai, Tomsk Tatar chief, conspirator (*1604*), 129

Bashkiria, 68, 111, 113

Bashkirs, 67, 87, 114

Batur, Mongol leader (seventeenth century), 178

Bauntovskii, ostrog on Vitim River (*1652*), 152

Beiton, cossack golova: restores Albazin (*1685*), 176-77; destroys Albazin (*1689*), 180

Beketov, Peter: in Buriatia (*1628*), 144-45; conquest of Iakuts of Lena region (*1631-33*), 134-35; fights Buriats, founds Tutursk (*1631*), 169; commandant at Bratsk (*1648*), 153; sent to Amur (*1652*), joins Stepanov (*1654*), 168; founds Nerchinsk (*1654*); returns to Eniseisk (*1660*), 153

Belaia (Belaia Volozhka) River, 68, 112

Belgorod (*1593*), 110

Belobotskii, Andrei, Pole in Russian service, at Nerchinsk (*1689*), 179

Belogorsk Ostiaks, 130

Beloozero, Novgorodian colony: sought by Suzdal (twelfth century), 24-25, 34-35; devastated by Novgorod (*1340*), 36; under Moscow, 39; devastated by Novgorod (*1393*, *1398*), 40, 42

Belskii, Posnik, prikashchik of Ketsk (*1602*), 130

Berezov (*1593*), 121-22, 130

Berezovyi Iar, battle site (ca. *1582*) on Tobol River, 97

Bering, Vitus (*1680-1741*), navigator: first Kamchatka Expedition (*1725-30*), 210-11; second Kamchatka (Great Northern) Expedition (*1733-43*), 215

Bering Island, 217

Bering Sea, 191

Bering Strait, 219

Bezhetskii Verkh, Novgorodian territory, 41

Bezhitsky, portage on Volga, 44

Bezzubtsov, Konstantin Aleksandrovich, voevoda, (fifteenth century), 54

Biriusa River, 141

Birsk, fort (*1554*), 68

Blagoveshchensk (*1858*), 165

Boats: *ushkui*, 36; *koch*, 183 ff., 201; *lodka*, 208; *shitik* (decked boat), 210; of Koriaks, 196

'Bogdoi Khan,' Russian name for Chinese emperor, 168

Boiar, Ostiak chief, 100

Bolkhovskoi, Prince Semeon, voevoda, death in Siberia (*1584*), 102

Bol'shaia River, 203

Bol'shaia Kokshaga River, 110

Bol'sheretsk (*1704*), 201, 202, 204, 211, 212, 216

Bol'shoe Eravnoe, Lake, 150

Bol'shoi Aniui River, 192

Bol'shoi Baranov, Cape, 216

Bol'shoi Begichev Island, 184

Bol'shoi Kamennyi Nos (now Cape Dezhnev), 190

Botama River, 133

Botoga, Daur princeling (ca. *1640*), 148

Bratsk: (*1631*), 146; destroyed by Buriats (*1634*), restored (*1635*), 147, 154

Briakhimov (Bulgar the Great), Volga Bulgar centre, 27

Brianta River, 156

Briazga, Bogdan, lieutenant of Ermak, 103

Brünnel, Oliver, Flemish employee of Stroganovs (ca. *1570-85*), 90-91

Bugor, Vasilii, explorer of upper Lena (*1628-30*), 133; seeks 'Pogycha' River under Stadukhin (*1647*); joins Dezhnev on the Anadyr (*1650*), 192

Bukhara, 64, 118

Bukharan merchants, 105, 116, 118

Bulgakov, Prince Ivan, voevoda in Perm (*1572*), 87

Bulgar the Great. *See* Briakhimov
Bulgaria, 21
Bulgars (of Volga), 21, 26, 27; loot Ustiug (*1218*), 29, 221
Buriat steppe, 133, 143
Buriats, 129; plunder Arins (*1612*), 141, 143, 151, 178; resist Beketov (*1628*), 144–45 (*1631*), 169; revolt, flight to Mongolia (*1657*), 152–53; claimed by Mongols (*1688*), 178
Butal'sk (*1636*), 137
Buza, Elisei, explores Olenek, Omoloi, and Iana rivers (*1636–42*), 193, 224
Bystraia Sosna River, 110
Bystraia River, Kamchatka, 211
Byzantine Empire, 21

Campaign of the Host of Igor, epic poem of expedition against Steppe nomads (*1184*), 22
Cape Prince of Wales, Alaska, 212
Catherine II (the Great), Empress (*1762–96*), 219
Chagir, Ostiak chief, death (*1573*), 88
Chaun Bay, 189
Cheboksary (*1555*), 68
Chebukov, Tret'iak, Moscow envoy (*1573*), 118
Chechigin, Tret'iak Ermolaev, sent to Amur to aid Khabarov (*1651*), killed by Duchers while setting out on mission to China (*1654*), 164
Cherdyn, Permian town, taken by Russians (*1472*), 48, 87, 101
Cheremis (Mari), tribe subject to Kazan: plundered by Russians (*1468*), 56; refuse to pay tribute to Moscow (*1552*), 67, 68; rebellions (*1567, 1570, 1571*), 70; attack merchants on the Kama (*1572*), 87, 110
Cherkess (Circassians), 70
Chernigov, 60
Chernigovskii, Nikifor, Polish mutineer at Ilimsk (*1665*), 171; restores Albazin, 171
Chilikul, Lake, Russians attack encampment of Kuchum at (*1591*), 114
Chin Murza, Siberian Tatar chieftain (sixteenth century), 117, 118
China: trade with Buriats, 141; trade with Mongols, 150; relations with Amur peoples, 156, 161; relations with Russians on Amur, 161 ff., 225; and Treaty of Nerchinsk (*1689*), 179–82
Chirikov, Aleksei, Lieutenant (*1703–48*): on First Kamchatka Expedition, 206, 210; in command of *Sv. Pavel* on Second Kamchatka Expedition, 216
Chirikov, Peter: sent to Kamchatka (*1709*), 202; killed (*1711*), 203
Chona River, 133, 141
Chondon River, 186, 193
Chud, Lake, site of 'Ice Massacre' (*1242*), 31

Chukchi, East Siberian tribe: first seen (*1641*), 188, 190, 191; raids on Koriaks, punished by Russians, 214, 218; decline, 218
Christianity, conversion to: Finnic peoples, 22; Zyrians, 37; Tatar princelings (fifteenth century), 54; Siberian Tatars and Voguls (*1565*), 86; Buriats (*1657*), 152; Kamchadals, 217, 227
Chulkov, Danilo, founder of Tobolsk (*1587*), 113
Chumei, Ostiak rebel (*1608*), 130
Chusovaia River, 84, 95, 119; early route to Siberia, 119
Chuvashes, Ural tribe, 67, 68, 110
Colonization: of Volga–Oka region (twelfth century), 22; by Novgorod in northeastern Russia, 23–24; of Kazan lands, 69; by cossacks, 76, 78; in Perm lands, 86; by exiles (from *1593*), 120; failure on Amur, 180; as expansion motive, 226
Copper and lead ores, reported above Amur River, 155, 156
Cossacks: origins, 73; on Terek River, 70; of Smolensk, 75; of Volga, 75, 79; of Zaporog, 76; in Polish Ukraine, 76; first known use in Moscow forces (*1468*), 56, 74; in Stroganov territory (ca. *1578*), 89; expedition to Siberia (*1581*), 93 ff.
Crimea, Khanate of: secedes from Golden Horde (ca. *1427*), 53; friction with Moscow (after *1502*), 60 ff.; defeat of Golden Horde (*1502*), 60; raids on Russian territory (*1507, 1521*), 60; (*1527, 1533*), 62–63; (*1540*), 64; (*1552*), 66; (from *1558*), 70; (*1571*), 71; later raids, 72; on Astrakhan (*1549*), 69; Russian defense lines, 70–71; invasion routes, 110

Daniel (Daniil) Aleksandrovich (*1261–1303*), Prince of Moscow, 33
Daurs, tribe on Amur River, 148, 152, 156, 159, 160–62, 166
Dankov (Donkovo) (*1571*), 71
Dedilov (*1571*), 71
Defence lines, of Oka of 1571, 70–71
Delisle de la Croyère, Louis (d. *1741*), astronomer on Great Northern Expedition, 215
Dem'ianka River, 100
Dervish Khan, Khan of Astrakhan (ca. *1538; 1554–56*), 69
Devlet–Girei, Khan of Crimea (*1551–77*), raids (*1552*), 66; (*1571*), 69
Dezhnev, Semeon Ivanovich: on Alazeia River with Stadukhin and Zyrian (*1641–46*), 188, 190, 191; expedition to Anadyr (*1648–51*), 193, 195, 212
Dmitrii Konstantinovich of Suzdal, Grand Prince (*1360–62*), 36
Dmitrii Aleksandrovich of Pereiaslavl', Prince

of Novgorod (*1263*), Grand Prince,
Vladimir (*1277–94*), 32; invades Novgorod
(*1281*), 32
Dmitrii Ivanovich (Donskoi), Grand Prince,
Moscow (*1362–89*), 36, 37; defeats Tatars
(*1378, 1380*), 51
Dmitrii Mikhailovich of Tver, Grand Prince,
Vladimir (*1322–26*), 35
Dolonskii, Russian ostrog on Zeia River,
evacuated (*1682*), 174
Domozhirov, Boris, cossack officer,
campaigner against Kuchum (*1594*),
116–17
Don River, 75, 110
Don cossacks, 75, 76, 78, 110
Dubenskii, Andrei, founder of Krasnoiarsk
(*1627*), 143–44, 146
Duchers, Amur tribe, 157, 163, 167; flee
Russians, 170
Dutch: in Russian north, 90; seek sea route
to the Enisei and Orient (*1609*), 127, 131
Dvina River. *See* Northern Dvina River
Dvina Chronicle, 24
Dvina colonies: refusal to pay tribute to
Novgorod (*1169*), 28, 42; accept Moscow
rule (*1471*), 46–47
Dzhan–Ali, Khan of Kazan (*1532–35*), 63
Dzhani–bek, Khan of Golden Horde
(*1342–57*), 51
Dzhungars, western Mongol tribe, 178
Dzhugdzhur Mountains, 137, 158

Edigei, Khan of Golden Horde (*1399–1407*),
52, 53
Ediger (Iadiar Muhammed), Nogai prince,
Khan of Kazan (*1553*), 66–67
Ediger, Khan of Sibir (ca.*1553*–ca.*1563*),
vassal of Moscow (*1555*), 70, 89, 117
Egach River, 212
Ekaterinburg (*1721*), 121
El'chin, Ia. A., voevoda of Iakutsk, planner
of Great Kamchatka Command (*1716*),
208
Elets (*1592*), fortified town on Bystraia Sosna
River, 110
Eletskii, Prince Fedor, builder of Tara
(*1593*), 114
Elizabeth, Empress (*1740–62*), 217
Emtsa River, 23
English: in Russian north, 90; seek northern
sea route to Orient, 127–28
Enisei River, 124, 127, 128; Turukhansk
founded on (*1607*), 128, 130, 131
Eniseisk: (*1619*), 132, 135, 142, 143, 152,
154; expedition to Trans–Baikal region
(*1638–40*), 148
Eniseiskii, Ivan, commander in Kamchatka
(*1713–14*), 205; death, 206.
Epancha, Tatar prince: resists Ermak (ca.
1582), 96, 121; Turinsk founded on side
of his village (*1600*), 121

Epifan (*1571*), 71
Ermak, conqueror of Khanate of Sibir
(*1581*), 79, 90, 94, 102; death (*1585*),
105–106; 223, 226
Evreinov, Ivan, topographer on Kurile
expedition (*1719–22*), 208
Exiles, first sent to Siberia (*1593*), 120
Expansion of Russia, causes, 223

Faddeia Island, 184
Favorov, Ivan, envoy to China (*1686*), 176,
177
Fedor Aleksandrovich, Prince of Rostov: sent
to Dvina region by Grand Prince Vasilii I
(*1398*), 41; ousted by Novgorod, 42
Fedor I Ivanovich, Tsar (*1584–98*), 109, 110,
117, 176
Fedor II Alekseevich, Tsar (*1676–82*), 176
Fedorov, Ivan, assistant pilot of Shestakov
expedition, explorer of Bering Strait
region (*1732*), 211
Filofei, Bishop of Perm (*1480s*), 48
Finnic tribes, 21; Russian intermarriage with,
22
Fischer, Johann Eberhard, historian
(*1697–1771*), 165, 215, 224
Fortuna, vessel built in Okhotsk for first
Kamchatka Expedition (*1725–27*), 210,
211
Fort construction: Tara (*1593–94*), 114–15;
Kumarsk (*1654–55*), 168–69; of
Kamchadals, 198
Frantsbekov, Dmitrii, voevoda of Iakutsk (ca.
1649), 160
Frolov, Roman, associate of Stroganovs (ca.
1517), 82
Fur trade: of Novgorod, 23, 34; of
Stroganovs, 83; as expansion motive, 226

Gagarin, Prince Matvei Petrovich, Siberian
governor (executed *1721*), 206
Galdan Bosugtu Khan, Dzhungar Mongol
overlord (reign *1676–97*), 178–79
Galich, town on Volga: acquired by Moscow
(*1363*), 36; raided by Novgorod (*1398*),
42; raided by Kazan (*1467*), 56
Galkin, Ivan: campaign on Lena (*1633*), 134;
expedition to Transbaikalia (*1648–50*),
151, 152
'Gama Land,' mythical Pacific island, 216
Gantimur, Tungus chief, conquered by
Khabarov (*1651*), serves Chinese, defects
to Russians (*1667*), 171, 172, 175, 178
Genghis Khan (*1206–27*), 54
Gens, Iakov, pilot on Shestakov expedition
(*1729*), 211, 212; helps quell Kamchadal
uprising (*1731*), 213
Gerasim, monk, renegade Novgorodian
(*1401*), 42
Gerbillon, Jean–François, Father

(*1631–1707*), Jesuit missionary in China, negotiator at Nerchinsk (*1689*), 179

Giliaks, Amur tribe, 158

Gizhiga Bay, 214

Gizhiga River, 192, 218

Gleb Ol'govich, Prince of Novgorod (*1137–38*), 23

Gleb Sviatoslavich of Pereiaslav, Prince of Novgorod, killed on expedition to Zavoloch'e (*1079*), 23

Glebov, Matvei, voevoda of Iakutsk (*1638*), 139

Glukhov, Ivan, evacuates Sibir (*1585*), 106

Gmelin, Johann Georg (*1709–55*), naturalist on Great Northern Expedition, 215

Godunov, Boris, advisor to Ivan IV: regent for Tsar Feodor (*1584–98*), 109; namestnik of Kazan (*1586*), 112; Tsar (*1598–1605*), 127; as frontier guardian, 109 ff.

Godunov, Petr Ivanovich (d. *1670*), voevoda of Tobolsk (ca. *1667*), 195

Gold, sought among Ostiaks, 103

Golden Horde: tribute to, 32, 44; Khans of, bestow patent of Russian Grand Prince, 33, 34, 35, 36, 44; decline of, 51–53; Moscow liberated from (*1480*), 57–59; extinction (*1502*), 60

Golder, Frank A., historian (*1877–1929*), 203, 224

Gol'dy ('Natki', now Nanaitsy), tribe on Amur, 158, 163

Golovin, Fedor Alekseevich (d. *1706*), envoy, negotiator of Nerchinsk treaty (*1685–89*), 176, 179

Golovin, Petr, voevoda of Iakutsk (ca. *1638*), 139

Golygina River, Kamchatka, 199

Gonam River, 156

Gorbaty–Shuiskii, Prince Aleksandr Borisovich, raids Kazan (*1547*), 65

Gorbitsa River, 180

Gorodets–Meshcherskii (Kasimov), 74

Grain: supply to Novgorod cut off, 24; (*1170*), 26; (*1196*), 28, 33; (*1397*), 41; trade, Volga to Dvina (fourteenth century), 39; tillage, in Siberia. *See* Agriculture

Great Bulgar. *See* Briakhimov

Great Horde, fragment of Golden Horde (from *1481*), 59

Great Kamchatka Command (*1716–18*), 208

Greben (Terek) cossack host, 78

Grey Horde, of Ostiaks, 123

Grigor'ev, Litvin who served with Kuchum, 119

Guliashchie liudi (vagabonds), in Khripunov's 'regiment,' 145

Gusel'nikov, Vasilii, merchant (early seventeenth century), 190

Gvozdev, Ivan, geodesist, assistant pilot on Shestakov expedition (*1729–32*), 211

Hai Se, Chinese military leader, 163

Haji-Girei, Khan of Crimea (ca. *1440–66*), 57–58

Hokkaido Island, Japan, 216

Honshu Island, Japan, 216

Hostages, 156, 204, 207

Iablonovyi Range, 141, 159, 160

Iaik (Ural River), 76, 78, 90, 92

Iaiva River, 86

Iakub, Prince, Tatar defector to Moscow (*1446*), 61

Iakub, Prince, Tatar defector to Moscow (*1446*), 61

Iakuts: discovered by Mangazeia men (ca. *1620*), 132; conquered by Beketov (*1631–32*), 134–35; rebellion (*1642*), 139

Iakutsk (*1632, 1642*), 133, 135, 138

Iam, postal station, 121

Iama River, Kamchatka, 212

Iamal Peninsula, 183

Iamshchik, driver, 121

Iamgurchi, Khan of Astrakhan (ca. *1549–54*), 69

Iana River, 136, 186, 187, 193

Iarensk, fortified (*1597*), 109

Iaroslav (the Wise) Vladimirovich, Grand Prince, Kiev (*1019–54*), 21

Iaroslav (II) Vsevolodovich: Prince of Novgorod (ca. *1196*), 28; Grand Prince, Kiev (*1238–46*), 29

Iaroslav (III) Iaroslavich, Prince of Tver and Grand Prince, Vladimir (*1263–72*), 33

Iaroslavl', Volga town: looted by Novgorod–Kievan army (*1149*), 25; plundered by ushkuiniki (*1371*), 37

Iarygin, Iakov: commander at Nizhne–Kamchatsk, 202; deposed (*1712*), 205; forced to become monk (*1715*), 208

Iasak, 68

Iasyr', Grisha, cossack officer (sixteenth century), 116

Iazhelbitsy, Treaty of, Moscow–Novgorod (*1456*), 45, 46

Ibak (Ivak), Khan of Sibir (ca. *1443–ca. 1481*), 59, 117

Ibrahim, Khan of Kazan (ca. *1460–82*), 59

Icha River, Kamchatka, 199

Ides, Isbrandt, envoy to China (*1693–95*), 195

Idirma River, 133

Idirma–Kut portage, 168

Ignat'ev, Isai (Mezenets), at Chaun Bay (*1646*), 189

Igor of Novgorod–Seversk, Prince, expedition against nomads (*The Campaign of the Host of Igor*) (*1184*), 22

Ilham (Ali–Khan), Khan of Kazan (*1482–87*), 59

Ilim River, 134, 149, 210

Ilim–Lena portage, 148
Ilimsk (*1630, 1631*), 134, 153, 210
Ilovaiskii, Dmitrii Ivanovich, historian
  (*1832–1920*), 45
Indigirka River, 187, 188, 189, 193, 207, 216
Indigirsk (Uiandinsk) (*1640*), 188
Ingoda River, 197–98
Intermarriage, of Russian and nomad
  princely families, 22, 54; of Russians with
  Finnish tribes, 22, 221
In'va River, 86
Iona, Bishop of Perm (from *1455*), 46
Iren' River, 86
Irgen', Lake, 152
Irgensk (*1653*), 153
Irgiz River, 111
Irkut River, 152
Irkutsk (*1650, 1661*), 152, 245
Iron, 83, 88
'Iron Gates,' Northern Ural region, 23
Irtysh River, 98, 103, 104, 114, 117, 121,
  123, 127
Ishberdei, Siberian Tatar chief, 100
Ishim River, 114
Isker (Kashlyk or Sibir), capital of Khanate
  of Sibir, 53, 93, 98–99, 105, 113
Islam–Girei, Crimean commander, raids
  Moscow (*1527*), 62
Istlen'ev, voevoda of Pelym (*1612*), 131
Iudoma River, 137, 210
Iug River, 34
Iugra, Finnish tribe, 23, 27, 48, 89
Iugra, Land of, 28, 44; Novgorod
  expeditions to (*1096, 1114*), 23; (*1187,
  1193*), 28; (*1363*), 38; (*1446*), 44; Moscow
  expedition to (*1465*), 45–46
Iugra River, 'Battle' of (*1480*), 58–59
Iukagirs, first met by Russians on Iana River
  (ca. *1635*), 185, 186, 187, 188, 189, 191,
  192, 193; rebellion on Anadyr (*1697*), 197,
  206, 207, 214
Iumshan, Vogul prince, raid on Perm
  (*1481*), surrender to Moscow (*1484*), 48,
  120
Iur'ev, granted to Abdul–Letif, Moscow
  vassal (after *1501*), 60
Iurii (I) Vladimirovich, 'Dolgoruki,' Prince of
  Kiev (*1149–57*), 25, 27
Iurii (II) Vsevolodovich, Grand Prince,
  Vladimir (*1219–36*), raids Bulgar land,
  builds Nizhnii Novgorod (*1221*), 29
Iurii (III) Danilovich, Prince of Moscow;
  Grand Prince, Vladimir (*1319–26*), 33, 35
Iusuf, Nogai chieftain, ally of Khan
  Iamgurchi of Astrakhan (*1554*), 69
Ivan (I) Danilovich, 'Kalita,' Grand Prince,
  Moscow (*1328–40*), 32, 35, 36
Ivan (II) Ivanovich, Grand Prince, Moscow
  (*1353–59*), 36
Ivan (III) Vasil'evich (the Great), Grand
  Prince and Tsar, Moscow (*1462–1505*), 45,

46, 49, 56, 74, 77
Ivan (IV) Vasil'evich (the Terrible), Grand
  Prince and Tsar (*1533–84*), 63, 65, 66–67,
  75, 77, 78, 81, 83; grant to Stroganovs
  (*1558*), 84, 225; (*1564*), 85, 87; (*1574*),
  89, 225
Ivanov, Kurbat, discoverer of Lake Baikal
  (*1643*), 148–49
Ivanov, Posnik (Gubar'), first to cross the
  Verkhoiansk range (*1636–37*), 187, 193
Izheginsk (Gizhiginsk), 218
Iziaslav Mstislavich of Kiev, Prince of
  Novgorod (ca. *1147–54*), 25
Izmail, Murza, Nogai prince (ca. *1551–63*),
  76, 77, 110–11

Japan, 199
Japanese: shipwrecked on Kamchatka, 196;
  (*1697*), 199; (*1710*), 203; (*1729*), 212, 215
Jassaktu Khan, protege of Galdan, 178
Jenkinson, Anthony, official of Muscovy
  Company (sixteenth century), 77

Kacha River, 144
Kacha Tatars, attack Krasnoiarsk (*1628*),
  144, 146
Kachanov, Vasilii, member of Il'chin
  expedition, prikashchik in Kamchatka
  (*1718*), 209
Kaffa, Crimea, 58
Kalmuks, Mongol tribe, 118, 124
Kama River: Bulgar state on, 27, 29, 36, 47;
  Kazan Khanate, 52–53, 56, 59, 60, 61, 62;
  Ivan IV's conquest of region, 64–67;
  increase in trade on, 87; colonization, 88
Kamchadals: first known contact with
  Russians (*1697*), 197; described by Atlasov,
  197–98; revolts (*1706*), 202; (*1718*), 209;
  (*1731–32*), 212–14; (*1740*), 216; decline,
  217
Kamchatka: early references to, 195–96;
  described by Atlasov, 200
Kamchatka Expeditions: First (*1724–29*),
  210, 211; Second (*1732–42*), 215–17
Kamchatka River, 197, 200
Kamkin, prikashchik in Kamchatka, 209
Kamskoe Usol'e–Solikamsk, 85
Kan River, 141, 144
K'ang Hsi, Emperor of China (*1662–1722*),
  172, 173, 175
Kankor (ca. *1558*), Stroganov fort, 85, 87
Kansk (*1628, 1640*), 144
Karacha, chief counsellor of Kuchum, 98,
  104, 105; captured (*1588*), 114
Karacha–Kul, Lake, 98
Karamzin, Nikolai Mikhailovich, historian
  (*1766–1826*), 23, 73
Kas River, 128
Kashira, granted exiled Khan of Kazan
  (*1497*), 54–55
Kashlyk. *See* Isker

Kasim, Tatar prince, defector to Moscow (*1440*), invited to rule Kazan (*1467*), 54

Kasmir IV, King of Poland (*1447–92*) and Grand Duke of Lithuania, treaty with Novgorod (*1471*), 46

Kasimov, Tatar Khanate and Russian protectorate (ca. *1452*), 54, 65, 74

Katorzhnyi, early cossack leader on Don, 76

Kazan: seized by ushkuiniki (*1392*), 39; Khanate of, separation from Golden Horde (ca. *1440s*), 52–53; Moscow expedition against (*1468*), 55–56; (*1485*), 47; invades Viatka (*1478*), 47; Moscow expeditions against (*1524–31*), raids Moscow (*1539, 1540*), 64; conquered (*1552*), 223–27

Kazakh Horde, 118

Kazyi, Khan of Sibir, of Toibuga house (ca. *1560s*), 117

Kazym River, 123

Kemchik (Khemchik) River (or Upper Enisei), 124

Kergedan (*1558*), 85, 87

Kerner, Robert J., historian (*1887–1956*), 34; 'urge to the sea' hypothesis, 225

Ket' River, 124

Ketsk (*1602*), 124, 127, 128, 129, 131, 144

Khabarov, Erofei Pavlovich: early career, 159; to Iakutsk (*1633*), 135; first Amur expedition (*1649–50*), 159–61; second (*1650–53*), 162–67, 224

Khadzhi–Girei, Khan of Crimea (ca. *1427–66*), 53

Kharchin, Fedor, Kamchadal rebel, 213, 215

Kharitonov, Ivan, prikashchik in Kamchatka, death (*1720*), 209

Khatanga Bay, 184

Khazars, Turkic tribe, 21

Khilok River, 152

Khodyrev, Parfen, in Lena region (*1639*), 138

Kholmogory, White Sea port, 43, 47, 183, 190

Khotun, granted exiled Khan of Kazan (*1497*), 54–55

Khovanskii, Prince Andrei, campaign against Cheremis (*1573*), 87

Khripun, Prince Fedor, campaign against Kazan Tatars (*1468*), 56

Khripunov, Danila, founder of Mangazeia ostrog (ca. *1600*), 123

Khripunov, Ignatii, first Russian exile to Siberia (*1593*), 120

Khripunov, Iakov: first voevoda of Eniseisk (*1623*), 141; expedition to Buriatia (*1629*), 145–46

Khutuktu, Mongol religous leader, 178, 179

Kiev, 21, 25; population shift from, to upper Volga region, 221

Kirenga River, 133

Kirgiz, 124, 128, 130, 143–44

Kirgizov, Konstantin, mutineer on Kamchatka (*1712*), 205

Kirin, 174

Kivriu, Kamchadal leader, 209

Klichen Gorodok, captured by Novgorod (*1393*), 40

Kliuchevka River, Kamchatka, 213

Kliuchevskii, Vasilii Osipovich, historian (*1841–1911*), 73, 226

Kobelev, Timofei, prikashchik of Kamchatka (*1700*), 200

Koda region, 121, 130

Koda tribes, 48

Kokshaisk, fort on Volga River, 110

Kola Peninsula, 90

Kolesnikov, Vasilii: discoverer of Barguzin–Nercha route to Amur (*1650*), 149; expedition to Trans–Baikal region (*1644*), 149, 152; takes command at Barguzin (*1650–52*), 149

Kolesov, Vasilii, prikashchik in Kamchatka (*1703–1706*), 201, 205, 206; (*1712–13*), 205; death, 206

Kolov, Ostafii, Litvin in charge of Mangazeians on Lower Tunguska (*1633*), 136–37

Kol'tso, Ivan: sent to Moscow by Ermak, 100; killed, 104

Kol'tsov, Iakov, ataman, killed by Krasnoiarsk mutineers (*1629*), 146

Kol'tsov–Masal'skii, Vladimir Vasil'evich, voevoda in pursuit of Kuchum (*1590*), 114

Kolyma River, reached by Stadukhin (*1644*), 189, 192, 207, 216

Konda River, 122

Konstantin of Suzdal (thirteenth century), 36

Kopor'e, fort, taken from Swedes (*1241*), 31

Kopylov, Dmitrii, explorer from Tomsk (ca. *1636*), 137

Koriaks: met by Stadukhin (*1651*), 192; to be controlled by Aklansk ostrog (*1669*), 195; Atlasov meets (*1697*), 196, 198, 199, 201, 202, 207; burn vessel *Lev* (*1729*), 212; rebellion (*1745–49*), 217–18

Korovin, Stepan, envoy to China, 178

Korytov, Stepan, leader of Mangazeian party on lower Lena (*1633*), arrested by Eniseisk men, 136–37

Kostroma (twelfth century): acquired by Ivan Kalita (ca. *1337*), 36; captured by ushkuiniki (*1371, 1375*), 37, 55

Kotel'nich, 59; taken by Moscow (*1469*), 59

Kotel'nyi Island, 184

Kotuga, Tungus chief, captured by Kolesnikov (*1645*), 149

Kozel'sk, raided by Tatar cossacks (*1497*), 74

Kozlov, Zhdan, envoy to Buriats (*1623*), 141

Koz'modem'iansk, fort on Volga (*1583*), 110

Kozyrevskii, Ivan: mutineer on Kamchatka (*1711*), 203, 205, 208, 209; visits Kurile Islands (*1713*), 205, 208; forced to become

a monk (*1715*), 209
Krasheninnikov, Stepan Petrovich, historian (*1711–55*), 195, 197, 204, 215, 217
Krasnoirask: (*1628*), 144; mutiny and famine (*1629*), 146, 147
Krizhanich, Iurii (*1617–83*), Croatian priest, exile in Siberia (*1661–76*), 173
Kromy, fortified town on Oka (*1595*), 110
Kuchum, Khan of Sibir (ca. *1563* to ca. *1582*): seizes power (*1563*), 85; expedition of Ermak (ca. *1581*), 93, ff.; evacuates capital, 99; raids Tatars near Tobolsk (*1590*), 114; sought by Russians, 116; appeal to Tara voevodas, 117; death (ca. *1598*), 119
Kulikovo, Battle of (*1380*), 51
Kuma River, North Caucasus, 78
Kumara River, 165
Kumarsk (*1652*), 165, 168; attacked by Manchus (*1655*), fortification, 171, 173
Kungur (*1647*), 121
Kupka, Kamchadal leader, 209
Kurakin, Prince Ivan Semenovich, voevoda of Tobolsk (ca. *1620*), 131
Kurakin, Prince Andrei Petrovich, campaign against Cheremis (*1573*), 87
Kurbskii, Prince Fedor, expedition to Siberia (*1483*), 48
Kurbskii, Prince Semeon Fedorovich, expedition to Siberia (*1499*), 49
Kuriles (Ainu) tribe, 199, 204
Kurile Islands: first sighted, 204, 208; visited (*1711*), 204; (*1713*), 276
Kurochkin, Kondratii: Dvina merchant at Mangazeia (ca. *1610*), 128; reaches Piasina River, 184
Kursk, refortified (*1587*), 110
Kuta (Kut) River, 133, 134
Kuznetsk (*1618*), 124
Kvashnin, Ivan, promyshlennik on Amur (*1650*), 160

Laishev (*1555*), fort, 68
'Lama' River, 186
Lamuts, tribe, Tungus sub-group: report Amur (*1639*), 137, 155, 158; of upper Indigirka, 187
Lang Tan, Chinese general on the Amur (*1681*), 173, 175; at Nerchinsk (*1689*), 179
Laptev, Lieutenant Dmitrii Iakovlevich, explorer (*1736–43*) of Arctic coast from Lena to Kolyma rivers, 216
Laptev, Lieutenant Khariton Prokof'evich, explorer (*1739–40*) of east coast of Taimyr Peninsula, 216
Lavkai, Daur princeling: heard of by Perfil'ev (*1640*), 148; by Poiarkov (*1643*), 156, 159; met by Khabarov (*1650*), 160–61, 162
Lena River, 128, 132, 133, 139, 185, 210
Lenskii Volok (later Ilimsk) (*1630*), 134
Lev, vessel built at Okhotsk for Shestakov

expedition (*1729*), destroyed by Koriaks, 211, 212
Liao River, Manchuria, 173
Lipitsa, Battle of (*1216*), 29
Lithuania, secession of Russians from (fifteenth century), 57, 60, 62
Lithuanians, 29
Little Khingan River, 164
'Litvins,' Lithuanian war prisoners, 114, 142
Livny (*1586*), fortified town on Bystraia Sosna River, 109
Livonian Knights, invade Moscow territory (*1480*), 58
Livonian War (*1558–82*), 70, 71, 101
Lobanov–Rostovskii, Prince Fedor Mikhailovich, head of proposed expedition to Amur, cancelled (*1653*), 163, 166, 167
Lopatka, Cape, Kamchatka, 201
Lower (Nizhniaia) Tunguska, 132, 133, 141, 200
Loz'va River, 119
Loz'vinsk (*1590*), 119; dismantled (after *1597*), 121
Lugui, Ostiak prince, 122
Luzhin, Fedor, topographer, maps Kuriles (*1719–22*), 208

Maia River, 137, 210
Makarii, Metropolitan, 86
Makhmet, aide of Kuchum, 118
Makovsk (*1618*), 131, 210
Malaia Kokshaga River, 110
Maloe Eravnoe, Lake, 150
Malyi Aniui River, 189
Malygin, Lieutenant Stepan, explorer of Iamal Peninsula (*1736–37*), 216
Mamai, Mongol general (fourteenth century), 41, 42
Mamet–Kul, nephew of Kuchum: raids Stroganov holdings (*1573*), 88; resists Ermak (*1582*), 97–98; capture (*1584*), 99, 102–103; in Moscow service, 117, 118
Mamruk, Ostiak chief, rebel (*1608*), 130
Manchus, 163, 164
Mangazeia (*1600*), 49, 84, 123, 128, 143, 154, 157, 159, 163, 164, 167, 177, 179–80, 183, 189, 201
Mansurov, Ivan, voevoda, esablishes fort at mouth of Irtysh River, 106, 123
Manuk, Ostiak chief, rebel (*1608*), 130
Manuk, Nogai prince, Khan of Kazan (*1496–97*), 60
Manych River, 78
Massa, Isaak, Dutch traveller in Russia (ca. *1598–1618*), 81, 84
Mekhmet, Khan of Sibir (*1560s*), 117
Mengli–Girei, Khan of Crimea (*1469–73, 1478–1517*), 54; non-aggression pact with Moscow (*1575*), 58, 74
Mercator, Gerhard, cosmographer (*1512–94*), 90
Meria, Finnic people, 22

Merlin, Major Vasilii, sent to Kamchatka (*1733*), 214, 215
Mezen, 189
Miasnoi, Ivan, voevoda, builder of fort at Tiumen (*1586*), 113
Michael, Permian chief, defeated (*1472*), 47
Michael Iaroslavich, Prince of Tver, Grand Prince (*1304–19*), 33, 34
Michael, Tsar (*1613–45*), 184
Mikhailov (*1551*), 71
Mikitin, Anfal, Novgorodian renegade: invades Dvina region (*1401*), 42; invades Bulgar land (*1409*); slain (*1418*), 43
Mikitin, Elistrat, ataman at Tara (*1597*), 118
Mikitin, Ivan and Konon, Novgorodian voevodas, renegades (ca. *1397*), 41, 42
Milovanov, commandant of Argunsk (ca. *1689*), 180
Minin, Fedor, pilot, explorer of coast from Enisei to Taimyr Peninsula (*1738–40*), 216
Mining: Iron ore, sought by Stroganovs (*1550s*), 83; silver, copper and lead sought in Amur region (*1644*), 156. *See* Silver
Mironov (Lipin), Osip: sent to take over Verkhne–Kamchatsk (*1709*), killed (*1711*), 203
Mogula, Ostiak chief, conspirator (*1604*), 129
Moldikichid, Daur town, 156
Molodo River, 186
Mologa River, 41
Monasteries: Perm, 37–38; Solovetskii, 83
Mongol invasion of Russia (*1227, 1238–40*), spares Novgorod, 31–32
Mongols, of Mongolia: Advance northward (ca. *1640*), 144; Pokhabov visits Eastern Khalkas (*1647*), 151; Turukai, the Tsetsen Khan of the Eastern Khalkas, sends embassy to Moscow (*1650*), 151, 245; Veniukov and Favorov visit (*1686*), 176; Korovin visits (*1687–88*), besiege Selenginsk and Udinsk (*1688*), 178; Galdan, leader of Oirat (Dzhungar) tribe, seeks Russian alliance, 178–79
Mordva, Russian raids upon: (*1184*), 27; (*1229*), 29; (*1232*), 30; (*1369*), 37, 67, 221
Morozko, Luka, explorer of Kamchatka (*1696*), 196, 197
Morrison, John A., historian (*1903–   *), 225
Moscow: first mention (*1147*), 33; liberation from Golden Horde (*1480*), 223; war with Lithuania (*1500–1503*), 60; Kazan campaign (*1506*), 60; war with Poland–Lithuania (*1507–1508, 1512–22*), 60; threatened by Crimea (*1521*), 61–62; Kazan campaigns (*1524*), 62; (*1530*), 63; (*1547, 1549–50, 1552*), 65–66
Moskva River, 19
Moskvitin, Ivan, discovers Pacific (*1639*), 137
Motora, Semeon, leads party to Anadyr (*1650*), 192, 193

Mstislav Andreevich, Prince, invades Novgorod (*1169*), 22
Mstislav Iur'evich, Prince, Novgorod (*1169*), 25
Mstislav (II) Iziaslavich, Grand Prince, Vladimir (*1167–69*), 26
Mtsensk, 71
Müller, Gerhard Friedrich, historian (*1705–83*), 94, 95, 195, 215
Muhammed–Amin, Khan of Kazan (*1487–96, 1501–18*), 55, 59, 61
Muhammed–Girei, Khan of Crimea (*1515–23*), invades Moscow (*1521*), 61
Muhammed–Girei (II), the Fat, Khan of Crimea (*1577–84*), incites Nogais to raid Kama region (*1583*), 78
Murav'ev, Lieutenant Stepan, explorer of Kara Sea coast (*1734–35*), 215
Murom: army joins attack on Bulgars (*1184*), 27; fortified against Kazan Tatars (*1467*), 56
Muroma, Finnic people, 22
Murtaza, Tatar prince in Russian service (ca. *1474*), 74
Myl'nikov, Grigorii, captured by Manchus near Aigun (*1682*), 174

Nadezhda, three-masted double sloop used by Great Northern Expedition, 216
Nagiba, Ivan Antonov, explorer of lower Amur (*1652*), 164, 224, 246
Namak, Ostiak chief (ca. *1612*), 129, 131
Narei, Buriat chief, 151
Nasedkin, Mikhail, reaches tip of Kamchatka Peninsula (*1705*), 201
Narym (*1598*), 124, 129; plundered by mutineers (*1629*), 145
Navatskii, Samson, explorer of Viliui region (*1628–29*), 133
Nemcha, Kirgiz chief, conspirator (*1604*), 129
Nercha River, 153, 171
Nerchinsk (*1654, 1658*), 171, 172, 176; negotiations at (*1689*), 179–80; treaty of, 180, 248
'Neroga' River. *See* 'Pogycha' River, 186
Neuna, prince of Surgut Ostiaks, rebel (*1608*), 130
New (Novaia) Mangazeia. *See* Turukhansk
Niudoma River, 137
Niugzi River. *See* Niukzha
Niuiamka River, 156
Niukzha, 159, 160
Nizhne–Kamchatsk, zimov'e (*1701*), ostrog (*1703*), 201, 205, 209, 211, 212; seized by Kamchadals (*1731*), 213
Nizhne–Kolymsk (*1644*), 189, 192
Nizhniaia Tunguska River. *See* Lower Tunguska River

Nizhnii Novgorod (*1221*): attacked by Mordva (*1229*), 29; plundered by ushkuiniki (*1366, 1375*), 37, 39; fortified against Kazan Tatars (*1467*), 56; besieged by Kazan Tatars (*1505*), 61; fortified (*1508*), 71

Nogai, Khan of Golden Horde (ca. *1279–1300*), 53

Nogai Horde: secedes from Golden Horde (after *1411*), 53, 55, 59, 65, 68; break-up of (mid-sixteenth century), 70, 75, 77, 83, 89, 91–92; policy of Boris Godunov toward, 110, 118

Nonni River, Manchuria, 171

Northern (Severniaia) Dvina River, 23, 24, 32, 222; colonists attempt secession from Novgorod (*1169*), 26, 28, 38; Stroganovs on, 90

Northern sea route to Orient, sought by Brunnel (*1570s*), 90, 210

Novaia Zemlia, 128

Novgorod: expedition to "Iron Gates" (*1032*), Zavoloch'e (*1079*), "Pechora tribute" to Prince of Kiev, 23; colonies, 24–26; raid on Rostov–Suzdal (*1149*), 25; expeditions to Iugra (*1169, 1187, 1194, 1446*), 28, 44; and Mongols, 32–33; under Prince Alexander Nevskii, 31; and princely rule, 34; relations with Moscow, 35, 40; expedition to lower Ob region, Siberia (*1364*), 38–39, 121; war with Moscow (*1393*), 40, 42; reconquest and loss of Dvina region (*1398, 1401*), 42; during Moscow civil war, 44, 45; invasion by Moscow (*1441*), 45; defeat (*1456*), 45; subjugation (*1478*), 47, 222

Novgorodov, Ivan, in command in Kamchatka (*1730*), misdeeds of, 212, 215

Novosil', 71

Novyi Torg. *See* Torzhok

Nur Daulet, Tatar prince, 54; Khan of Crimea (*1467–69, 1473?–74*), 57

Oaths of allegiance, 46, 47, 49, 68

Ob River: Novgorod expedition to (*1364*), 38–39, 121; Moscow expedition to (*1499*), 49; Stroganovs' trade with Samoyeds on (*1550s*), 84; Ermak on (*1584*), 104; Kuchum on (*1598*), 119, 121; rebellion of natives on (*1607, 1608, 1612*), 130–31

Obdora region, 122

Ogorodnikov, E. K., historian, 23

Ogorodnikov, Vladimir Ivanovich, historian, 229

Oimiakon River, 189

Oka River (Volga), 24, 27, 62, 144, 147, 221

Oka River (Angara), 144, 145, 146, 147

Okhota River, 158

Okhotsk Sea: discovered by Russians (*1639*), 137; Poiarkov's coastal voyage (*1645*), 158; Nagiba's voyage (*1652*), 164, 246;

Stadukhin on north coast of (*1651*), 192; route to Kamchatka opened (*1716*), 208

Okun, Buriat princeling (ca. *1626*), 145

Ol'chy, Tungus tribe, 158, 163

Olekma River, route to Amur, 148, 155, 159, 160, 166

Olekminsk ostrog (*1635*), 148

Olenek River, 185, 186, 190, 193

Oliutora River, 195, 204, 206

Oliutorsk ostrog (*1714*), 206; besieged by Iukagirs and Koriaks (*1715*), 207; rebuilt, 209

Olkhon Island, in Lake Baikal, Russian and Buriat battle site (*1643*), 149

Om River, 117

Omoloi River, 186, 193

Onega, Lake, 23

Onitsifor Lukavich, Novgorod posadnik (*1350–54*), 38

Oprichnina, participation of Boris Godunov in, 83

Opuka River, eastern Siberia, 196

Orel, 71

Orlets, fort (*1342*), 38, 41; captured by Novgorod (*1398*), 42

Osa, fort on middle Kama River (*1557*), 68

Oshanin, Andrei, voevoda of Eniseisk (ca. *1625*), 142, 143

Oshel, Bulgar town, destroyed in Russian raid (*1220*), 29

Oskol (*1593*), 110

Oskol River, 110

Ostaf'ev, founder of Kansk (*1628*), 144

Ostiaks (Mansi), 99, 100, 103, 121; of Obdora and Koda region, 122; of Berezov region, rebellion attempts (*1595*), 122; (*1612*), 131; of Belogorsk, 130.

Ovtsyn, Lieutenant Dmitrii, explorer of coast from Ob to Enisei (*1734–37*), 216

Padun Rapids, Angara River, 144

Palana River, Kamchatka, 197, 209

Paletskii, Prince, 87, leader of expedition against Cheremis (*1573*), 87

Paniutin, Ivan, commandant in Kamchatka, killed by Koriaks (*1709*), 202

Paramushir Island, Kuriles, 204, 205

Paren River, Bay of Penzhina, 211

Pashkov, Afanasii, voevoda of Eniseisk, restores Nerchinsk (*1658*), 170

Pavlov, Lieutenant Mikhail, explorer of Kara Sea coast (*1734–35*), 215

Pavlutskii, Captain Dmitrii: assigned to Shestakov expedition (*1729*), 211; campaigns atainst Chuckchi (*1731, 1732*), 214; death (*1747*), 218

Pechenegs (Patzinaks), Turkic tribe (eleventh century), 21

Pechora River, 23; massacre of Novgorod tribute takers on (*1187*), 28; revenues from, 32, 90, 193

Pelym, Vogul centre, 120; Russian fort at
(*1593*), 120; native rebellion plot at, 131
Penda, explorer of Lena River (*1620–23*),
133, 140
P'eng Ch'un, Chinese general, scouts
approaches to Albazin (*1681*), 173
Penzhina River, 192, 211
Penzhina Bay, 158, 218
Pereira, Father Thomas, Jesuit missionary in
China, negotiator at Nerchinsk (*1689*), 179
Perfil'ev, Maksim, cossack ataman at Eniseisk
(*1624*): leads exploration of Upper
Tunguska (*1627–28*), 142, 143;
subdues Buriats, founds Bratsk (*1631*),
146–47; explores Transbaikal region
(*1638–40*), 148, 159; hears of Daurs on
Shilka and Amur, 155; administers Bratsk
region (*1645–46*), 150
Perfir'ev, Il'ia, explores Iana River (*1633*),
184, 185, 193
Perm region, 27; St. Stephen bishop of
(*1383–96*), 37–38, 45; Bishop Pitirim killed
by Voguls (*1455*), 46; conquered by
Moscow (*1472*), 47, 48, 52, 56; Stroganovs
active in, 83, 84, 85; Ermak departs for
Siberia from, 94, 101, 105
Persia, struggle with Turkey and Crimea, 70
Pestrii, Fedor, voevoda at Perm (*1472*), 47
Peter I, the Great: orders investigation of sea
route, Okhotsk to Kamchatka (*1713*),
208–209; sends Evreinov and Luzhin to
explore Kuriles (*1719*), 208–9; orders first
Kamchatka expedition (*1724*), 210
Petrilovskii, rebuilds Oliutorsk (*1715*),
arrested by subordinates, 209
Petropavlovsk harbour, mapped (*1740*), 216
Petrov, Afanasii, comandant of Anadyrsk,
slain by Iukagirs (*1714*), 206
Petrov, Iurii, with Poiarkov on Amur (*1644*),
156–57
Piasina River, 128, 184
Pinega River, 23
Pit River, 142
Pitirim, Bishop of Perm, killed by Voguls
(*1455*), 46
Podkamennaia Tunguska River. *See* Stony
Tunguska
Poganoe, Lake, 104
Pogodin, Mikhail Petrovich (*1800–75*),
historian, 73
'Pogycha' (or 'Pogicha'—the Anadyr?) River,
186, 188, 189, 192, 193
Poiarkov, Vasilii, first Russian explorer of
Amur (*1643–46*), 155–59
Pokhabov, Ivan: to Transbaikalia (*1644–45,
1646–48*), 150, 151; harsh rule, at
Barguzin (*1652*), at Balagansk (*1657*),
152. Explores region north of Vitim river,
founds Bauntovskii ostrog, 152
Pokhacha River, Kamchatka, 207
Pokrovskii, Mikhail Nikolaevich, historian

(*1868–1932*), 39, 229
Poland–Lithuania, negotiations with
Novgorod (*1471*), 46, 54, 57, 59;
friendship with Crimea (ca. *1502*), 60; war
with Moscow (*1507–1508*), 60–61,
(*1534–36*), 63
Polotsk, 26
Polovtsy (Kumans or Kypchaks), 22
Poluektov, Ivan, voevoda of Iakutsk (ca.
1730), 212
Pomor'e, cradle of Russian arctic seafaring,
127, 183–84
Popov, Fedot Alekseev, expedition to Anadyr
(*1648*), 190–91, 195
Preobrazheniia Island, 184
Prisoners of war: employed by Stroganovs,
94; 'Litvins' (Lithuanians), 114, 142
Promyshlenniks, 127; forbidden use of sea
route (*1619*), 128, 224
Pronchishchev, Lieutenant Vasilii, explores
east coast of Taimyr Peninsula (*1735*), 216
Pronsk, fort (*1536*), 71
Pskov, recaptured from Livonian Knights
(*1242*), 31
Pur River, 123
Putivl, 71
Pyskorskii Mys, Kama River, 85

Radom, 71
Radukovskii, leader of expedition against
Buriats (*1635*), 147
Rakitin, voevoda of Iakutsk (ca. *1719*), 209
Rebellion, native: of Kazan region (*1553*),
68; Cheremis (*1567, 1570, 1571*), 70;
Siberian Tatars against Ermak (ca. *1584*),
104; Ostiaks (*1595*), 122; Ostiaks, Tatars,
Kirgiz (*1604*), 129; Buriats (*1629*), 145,
146; Iakuts (*1642*), 139; Iukagirs (ca.
1697), 197; Kamchadals (*1731*), 214;
(*1741*), 216; Koriaks (*1714*), 206–207;
(*1745–49, 1755*), 217, 218
Rebrov, Ivan, to Olenek River (*1633*), to
Indigirka River (*1638*), 184, 185, 193
Reindeer, 196, 197, 198–99, 201, 206, 214,
218
Riazan, 51; Tatar attack (*1444*), 74; Crimean
Tatars plunder region (*1533*), 63
Riazhsk, 71
Rostislav Iur'evich, Prince of Kiev (twelfth
century), 25
Rostov monastery, 37
Rostov, early Novgorod dependency, 24–25
Rostov–Suzdal principality, 22, 24, 25;
aggression against Novgorod, 26, 28;
against Bulgars, 27; against Mordva, 29
Rukin, Cherkas, founder of Makovsk (*1618*),
and Eniseisk (*1619*), 131, 132
Runo, Ivan, leader of Russian army against
Kazan (*1468, 1469*), 74
Rurik (*862?–70*), 24

Rybnoi, later Rybnyi, now Rybnoe (*1628*), ostrozhek at confluence of Uda and Angara, 144, 178
Ryl'sk, 71

Safa–Girei, Khan of Kazan (*1524–31, 1535–40*), 62, 63, 65
Sahib–Girei, Khan of Kazan (*1521–24*), 61, 62; ravages Riazan area (*1533*), 63
Saian Range, 149
Saidat–Girei, Khan of Crimea (*1523*), 62
Salt, 83, 85, 87, 222, 234
Samar, village at mouth of Irtysh River, 130
Samar, Ostiak prince, killed (ca. *1582*), 104
Samara (*1586*), 111, 112, 124
Samarov, Tair, Ostiak prince, rebel (*1608*), 130
Samoyeds (Nentsy), 23, 49, 123; subdued (*1595*), 123, 128; in conspiracy (*1608*), 163
Sanchursk (*1585*), 110
Saraichik, Nogai town on Iaik River (ca. *1577*), cossacks attack (*1581*), 78
Saratov (*1590*), 111
Sary Azman (Osman), Don cossack leader, 76
Savvin, Vikhor: sent to Upper Tunguska (*1624*), 142; killed by Buriats (*1628*), 146
Schelting, Lieutenant Alexis, commander *Sv. Gavriil,* with Spanberg expedition to Japan (*1738*), 216
Seid Akhmat, prince of Toibuga house: rival of Kuchum for Sibir khanate, 100; return to Sibir (*1584*), 104; seizes Isker, captured by Russians (*1588*), 113–14
Seim River, 110
Seit Tul Mamet, Moslem ecclesiastic, 119
Selemdzha River, 156
Selenga River, main source of Lake Baikal, 151, 152
Selenginsk (*1665*), 177, 178, 179
Seliverstov, Iurii, on Anadyr River (ca. *1654*), 193
Semeon Ivanovich, 'the Proud,' Grand Prince, Moscow (*1341–53*), 36
Semeonov, N., explorer of Upper Aniui (*1649*), 192
Serebrianyi, Prince, expedition against Cheremis (*1573*), 87
Seredennyi Range, Kamchatka, 196
Seriukov, Potap: founds Verkhne–Kamchatsk (*1699*), killed by Koriaks, 199, 201
Serpukhov: granted exiled Khan of Kazan (*1497*), 54–55; fortified (*1556*), 71
Sevast'ianov (Shchepetkoi), Vasilii, in command on Kamchatka (*1711–12*), 204, 205, 208
Severskii Donets River, 110
Shah-Ali, Khan of Kasimov, Khan of Kazan (*1518–21*), 61; (*1546*), 64; (*1551–52*), 65–66
Shakhov, Voin, in Lena region (*1633*), 136

Shakhovskoi, Prince Miron, cossack officer, founder of Mangazeia ostrog (ca. *1600*), 123
Shamagirs, 139. *See also* Tungus
Shaman Rapids, Angara River, 144, 149
Shantar Islands, 212
Shatsk, 71
Sheibanids, dynasty of Siberian khanate, 85, 100, 104
Shekhurdin, Mikhail, commander on Kamchatka (*1731*), 212, 213, 215
Sheksna River, 24
Shelagskii Nos, 192
Shelon River, 31
Shelon, Treaty of (Moscow–Novgorod, *1471*), 46
Shemiaka, Dmitrii, of Novgorod (d. *1453*), 44
Shestakov, Afanasii: expedition, northeast Siberia (*1729*), killed by Koriaks, 211–12
Shilka River, 152, 155, 160, 180
Shtinnikov, Andrei, murders Japanese shipwrecked on Kamchatka (*1629*), 212, 215
Shubin, Lev Ivanov, crosses Iamal Peninsula to Mangazeia (*1602*), 183
Shumshu Island, Kuriles, 201, 204, 205
Shun–chih, Emperor of China (*1644–61*), orders attack on Achansk (*1652*), 163
Siberia: Novgorod expeditions to, (*1364*), 38–39, 121; (*1446*), 44; Moscow expeditions to, (*1483*), 48; (*1499*), 49; raids on Stroganov territory, 88 ff.; Ermak expedition (ca. *1581*), 93 ff.
Siberia–Moscow road (from *1763*), 121
Siberian Chronicle, 87
Siberian Prikaz, 167, 214, 218
Sibir (Ibir), Khanate of: breaks away from Golden Horde (fifteenth century), 53; tributary of Moscow (*1555*), 70, 89, 117; Ermak conquest (from ca. *1581*), 93 ff.; Russians re-enter (*1586*), 112–13
Sibir, town. *See* Isker
Sigismund I, King of Poland (*1506–48*), 75
Silk, trade item on Amur, 159
Silver: exacted from Novgorod by Moscow (*1332*), 35; sought by Stroganovs, 85; discovered on Tura River, 88; sought on Angara River, 145; among Daurs, 148; sought in Transbaikalia, 149, 150; presence in Amur region denied, 156; further rumors of on Amur, 159; Khabarov directed to search for, 162; reported among 'Natty,' 186–87; among Iukagirs, 188; among Buriats, 143, 150; sought on Kurile Islands (*1719*), 208
Sims Bay, 184
Simushir, 208
'Siviriui' River, 186
Sokolov, Kuz'ma, first voyage, Okhotsk to Kamchatka (*1716*), 208

ikorokhodov, founds Barguzin (*1643*), 149

ikriaba, Vasilii, of Ustiug, leader of Moscow expedition to Iugra (*1465*), 45, 46

ikuratov, Lieutenant Aleksei, explorer of Iamal Peninsula (*1736–37*), 216

ilaves: Russian, 22, 27, 55–56, 62–63, 65, 69, 75–76; natives, 142, 152, 202; Japanese, 251

imolensk, 60; fortified (*1595–99*), 109

iobach'ia River. *See* Indigirka

iolikamsk, terminal of Babinov road across Urals (*1597*), 85

iolovetskii (Solovki) monastery, 83

iolov'ev, Sergei Mikhailovich, historian (*1820–79*), 73, 226

iol'vychegodsk, 83, 159

iophia, Regent (*1682–89*), 179

iorokin brothers, Mikhail and Iakov, lead mutiny at Ilimsk and Verkholensk, flee to Dauria (*1655*), 232

ios'va River, 122

ipafarii (Spatharii), Nikolai Milescu, Russian envoy to China (*1676*), 172, 173, 247

ipanberg, Lieutenant Martin: on first Bering expedition (*1728*), 210, 215, 216; on second Bering expedition, to Japan (*1738–39*), 215, 216

ipitzbergen, 183

itadukhin, Mikhail: to Kolyma (*1644*), 158, 188–89; reaches Anadyr (*1650*), 192, 195

itanovoi Range, 152, 156, 159, 180

iteller, Georg Wilhelm (*1709–46*), naturalist on second Bering expedition, 215

itepanov, Onufrii: on Amur (*1653–58*), 167 ff.; slain in battle with Chinese, 170

itephen of Perm (*1345–96*), Saint, Bishop (*1383*), 37, 38, 45

iterlegov, Lieutenant Dmitrii, explores coast from mouth of Enisei to Taimyr Peninsula (*1738–40*), 216

itony (Podkamennaia) Tunguska River, 132

itrel'tsy (Moscow regular troops), 64–65, 75, 105

itreletskii Prikaz, 75

itroganov family: origins, 81; Spiridon (d. fourteenth century), 81; Anika Fedorovich (*1497–1570*), 82–84; Grigorii and Iakov, receive charter to Kama lands (*1558, 1564*); Iakov, charter to Chusovaia lands (*1568*), 86; Iakov and Grigorii, charter authorizing war on Siberian Khanate (*1574*), 89; aid to Ermak (ca. *1581*), 93 ff.

itroganov Chronicle, 102

iugdaia (Sudak), 73

iukhona River, 23, 37

iukin, Vasilii, voevoda, builder of fort at Tiumen (*1586*), 113

iuklem, Siberian Tatar chief (ca. *1582*), 100

iuleiman I the Magnificent (*1520–66*), Turkish sultan, 69, 76

iumner, Benedict Humphrey, historian

(*1893–1951*), 227

Sungari River, 157, 163, 167, 168, 173

Surgutskii, Afanasii, killed by Koriaks (*1715*), 207

Suzdal: campaigns against Novgorod (twelfth century), 25–26; invasion of land of Bulgars (*1120, 1164, 1172, 1184, 1186*), 27; continued aggression against Novgorod (late twelfth century), 27–28; devastation by Mongol invasion (*1237–38*), 31

Sviatii Gavriil: vessel built at Nizhne–Kamchatsk (*1727–28*) for first Bering expedition, 211; used by Fedorov and Gvozdev expedition (*1730*), 212; in suppression of Kamchadal revolt (*1731*), 213, 215; in Great Northern Expedition (*1738*), 216

Sviatii Pavel, packet boat used by Bering (*1740*), 216

Sviatii Petr, packet boat used by Bering (*1740*), wrecked on Bering Island, 216

Sviatoslav Igorevich, Grand Prince of Kiev (*962–72*), 21

Sviatoslav Rostislavich, Prince (twelfth century), Novgorod, 25

Sviiaga River, 65

Sviiazhsk, advance base against Kazan (*1550*), 65

Svoezemtsev, Novgorodian purchaser of Vaga River valley (*1315*), 38

Sylva River, 87

Sym River, 128

Tagil portage, 87

Tagil River, 119

Taimyr Peninsula: rounded (early seventeenth century), 184; explored (*1730s*), 216

Takhcheia, district on Tura River, 89, 93

Tara, fort (*1594*), 97, 114–16, 124

Tartars: in Russian service, 54–55, 66, 67, 69, 76; colonists on Oka River (sixteenth century), 71; on upper Irtysh, 114; of Tom River country, 124, 129

Tatarinov, Petr, in command at Anadyrsk (*1714*), 206–7

Taui River, 137

Tavda River, 104, 119, 121; early route to Siberia, 119, 121

Taz River, 84, 123, 128, 132, 183

Temnikov, fort (*1571*), 71

Tenkei, Prince, Siberia (ca. *1586*), 111

Ter, on Kola peninsula, 32

Terek River, 76,

Terek (Greben) cossacks, 76, 78

Tersk (*1567*), 70

Tetiushi, fort (*1570*), 71

Tigil River, Kamchatka, 197, 208

Time of Troubles (*1598–1613*), 127, 223

Timur (Tamerlane) (*1333?–1405*), 52

Tin Akhmet, Nogai prince (sixteenth

century), 78

Tiumen: residence of Khans of Sibir, 53, 96, 113; rebuilt (*1586*), 116, 121

Tiumenents, Vasilii Alekseev, ascends Upper Tunguska (*1625*), 142

Tobol River, 93, 113, 119, 131

Tobolsk (*1587*), 114, 116, 145, 163, 210

Toian, Tatar prince, Tom region, Russian ally (*1604*), 124

Toibuga family, rival of Sheibanids for Siberian khanate, 104

Tokhtamysh, Khan of White Horde, invades Moscow (*1382*), 52

Tokmakov, Iurii, prince (sixteenth century), 83

Tolbuzin, Aleksei, voevoda of Albazin (*1683*), 175; killed in Chinese attack (*1686*), 177

Tom River, 124

Tomsk (*1604*), 124, 136

Torzhok (Novyi Torg): seized by Iurii Dolgorukii to block Novgorod supply route, 25; plundered by Vsevolod Iur'evich (*1178, 1181*), 27–28; seized by Iaroslav Vsevolodovich (*1196*), 28

Tot'ma, 82

Trade routes: Novgorod supplies cut off by Volga princes, 24 ff.; Astrakhan annexation (*1556*) secures Baltic–Volga–Caspian route, 69. Central Asia–Sibir–Urals–Kama–Volga route, 53

Trans–Baikalia (Za Baikal'e), 148, 151

Ter (Tre), Kola peninsula, 32

Treska, Nikifor, mariner, first to sail from Okhotsk to Kamchatka (*1716*), 208

Tribute: to Novgorod, 21, 23, 24, 26, 28; Novgorod to Golden Horde, 32; Novgorod to Moscow (*1332*), 35, 40, 41; Moscow to Kazan, 55; Moscow to Crimea (*1521*), 62; (*1533*), 63; Moscow to Golden Horde, 57; Siberian Tatars to Moscow (from *1555*), 70, 89, 117. *See* Iasak

Trifanov, Stepan, in command at Anadyrsk (*1716*), 207

Tsarevo–Borisov (*1600*), 110

Tsaritsyn (Stalingrad, Volgograd) (*1589*), 69, 111

Tsetsen Khan, Mongol prince (ca. *1647*), 151

Tsipa River, 148, 155

Tsivil'sk, fort (*1584*), 110

Tula, fort (*1530*), 71

Tungir (Tugir) River, 160

Tungus: attack Ketsk Ostiaks (*1608*), 128–29; besiege Makovsk (*1619*), 131; report Lena (ca. *1620*), 132, 134, 136; attack Tiumenets on Uda River (*1624*), 142; rebel on Viliui River (*1633*), 137; kill Russians on Lena (*1639–41*), 139; operations against Tungus of Vitim, 151; of Olenek, 185; iasak imposed on Tungus of Oimiakon (*1642*), 189. *See* Lamuts

Tura River, 88, 96, 97, 113, 119

Turgenev, Iakov, arrests Pokhabov (*1658*), 152

Turinsk (ca. *1600*), 96, 121

Turkey: makes Crimea a vassal (*1478*), 58; intervenes in Astrakhan (*1551, 1554*), 69; and Southern Russian (sixteenth century), 76

Turner, Frederick Jackson, historian (*1861–1932*), applicability of 'frontier hypothesis' to Russia, 227–29

Turkukai Tabun, Mongol prince, 150, 151

Turukhan River, 128

Turukhansk (*1607*), 133, 138

Tushetu Khan, head of Eastern Khalka Mongols, 176, 178; surrender to Chinese, 179

Tuskor River, 110

Tutura River, 134

Tutursk (*1631*), 134

Tver (*1209*), relations with Moscow and Novgorod, 33

Tvertsa River, 33

Ub Lake, 118

Uchur River, 156

Uda River, 137, 180

Uda (Taseeva, Chuna) River, 137, 141, 142, 144, 147, 180

Uda River, 154

Udinsk (*1665*) (later Verkhneudinsk, now Ulan-Ude, on Uda River, east of Lake Baikal, 178; besieged by Mongols (*1688*), 178

Ufa (*1586*), 111, 113, 116, 124

Ufa River, 111

Uiandina River, 188

Uiandinsk (Indigirsk) (*1640*), 188

Ukraine, 60, 63

Ul'ia River, 137, 158

Umlekan River, 156

Umymak, Iakut chief, 135–36

Unzha River, 29

Upper (Verkhniaia) Tunguska (Angara) River, 129, 133, 134, 144, 145, 148, 210

Ural (Iaik) cossack host, 77

Ural Mountains, 23, 27

Ural'sk (*1584*), 78

Urasov, cossack with Beketov, founds Nerchinsk (*1653*), 153

Urga, Mongol capital, 151, 178

Urka River, 160, 166

Urnuk, Ostiak chief, 129

Urup Island, Kuriles, 216

Urzhum, fort (*1584*), 110

Usa River, 112

Ushakov, Fedor, voevoda of Selenginsk, 180

Ushkuiniki, 36; seize Kazan (*1392*), 190

Usov, Aleksei, Moscow merchant, sponsor of Anadyr expedition (*1647*), 190

Ussuri River, 157, 163

Ustiug: origin, 34, 234; looted by Bulgars (*1218*), 29; preys on Novgorod trade, 35; birthplace of Stephen of Perm, 37; base for Moscow raids on Dvina region, 46; devastated by Novgorod (*1398*), 42, (*1417*), 43, (*1425*), 43; menaced by Kazan (fifteenth century), 55

Ustiuzhna, captured by Novgorodians (*1393*), 40

Ust'–Kut (*1631*), 134, 160, 210

Ust'–Prorva, established by Beketov (*1653*), 153

Ust'–Strelochnyi, at Shilka and Argun confluence (*1650*), 162

Ust'–Ul'insk, established by Poiarkov (*1645*), 158

Ust'–Viliuskoe (*1629*), 133

Ust'–Vychegodsk, town in Stroganov domain, 85

Ust'–Vymsk (fourteenth century), 37, 49

Uzbek, Khan of Golden Horde (*1313–40*), 35, 51

Vaga River, 23, 43

Vagai River, 105

Vaigach Island, 91

Valuiki (*1593*), 110

Varfolomeev, Luka, Novgorodian boyar, founder of Orlets (*1342*), 38, 41

Vasilii, Iaroslavich, Prince of Kostroma, Grand Prince, Vladimir (*1272–76*), devastates Vologda (*1274*), 32

Vasilii (I) Dmitrievich, Grand Prince, Moscow (*1389–1425*), 39, 41, 43, 52

Vasilii (II) Vasil'evich (the Blind), Grand Prince, Moscow (*1425–62*), Treaty with Novgorod (*1435*), 44; expedition to Novgorod (*1456*), 45, 81

Vasilii (III) Ivanovich, Grand Prince, Moscow (*1505–33*), relations with Kazan and Crimea, 61–63, 117, 184

Vasilii, Ostiak prince of Obdora, conspirator (*1607*), 130

Vasil'sursk, Moscow advance post against Kazan (*1523*), 62

Veche, Novgorod town meeting, 45, 47

Velikie Luki, town, burned (*1167*), 25

Veniukov, Nikifor, Russian envoy to China (*1686*), 176–77

Verbiest, Father Ferdinand, Jesuit missionary in Peking, meets Spafarii (*1676*), 173

Verkhne–Angarsk (*1646*), 149

Verkhne–Kamchatsk ostrog (*1699*), 200, 205, 214

Verkhne–Tagilsk (late 1580s), 119

Verkhneudinsk (earlier Udinsk; now Ulan-Ude) (*1655*), 154

Verkhniaia (Upper) Angara, 149

Verkhniaia Tunguska River. *See* Upper Tunguska

Verkhoiansk (*1638*), 187

Verkhoiansk Range, 187, 193

Verkholensk (*1641*), 133, 148, 149

Verkhotur'e (*1598*), 121, 163

Ves', Finnic tribe, 22

Vetluga River, 110

Vezhlivtsov, Koz'ma, trader, Kamchatka (*1716*), 209

Viatka (Khlynov) (late twelfth century), looted by ushkuiniki (*1374*), 37; captured by Moscow (*1459*), 45, 47; base for Moscow invasion of Novgorod (*1471*), 46; invaded by Kazan (*1478*), 47; invades Ustiug territory (*1486*), 47; surrender to Moscow (*1489*), 47–48

Viatka River, 45

Viliui River, 135

Vishera River, 119

Viten (Vytenis; Russian, Vitovt), Grand Duke of Lithuania (*1392–1430*), 43–44; defeat by Tatars at Vorskla River (*1399*), 52

Vitim River, 133, 148, 152; route to Amur, 159

Vizhevtsov, Grigorii, discoverer of Olekma route to Amur (ca. *1647*), 159

Vladimir Vsevolodovich (Monomakh), Prince of Kiev (*1113–25*), 24

Vladimir (I) Sviatoslavich, Grand Prince, Kiev (*980–1015*), 21

Vlass'ev, Russian agent on Sos'va River (*1608*), 130

Vlasov, I., voevoda at Nerchinsk (ca. *1685*), 176

Voguls (Mansi): invade Vychegda region (*1455*), 46; invade Perm region, Moscow counterattacks, 48; raid Stroganov holdings, 87, 101; oppose Ermak, 86, 99, 100, 104, 120; oppressed by Ostiaks (*1600*), 122; rebel (*1612*), 131

Voieikov, Andrei, voevoda of Tara (ca. *1598*), 118

Voieikov, Fedor, voevoda of Nerchinsk (ca. *1676*), 173, 174

Volga cossacks, 75, 79

Volga River: new Russian population centre on, 22; new political centre on, at Vladimir (*1169*), 26; Moscow blocks Novgorod use of (twelfth century), 28; becomes all-Russian route (*1550s*), 69

Volga–Oka quadrilateral, 22, 24, 26, 32–33, 221

Vologda: devastated by Vasilii of Kostroma (*1274*), 32; seized by Vasilii (*1397*), 41; devastated by Novgorod (*1398*), 42

Volok Lamskii, looted by Prince Vsevolod Iur'evich of Moscow (*1178*), 28

Vonia, Ostiak prince of Grey horde, submission of (*1598*), 123–24

Voronezh (*1586*), 110

Voronezh River, 110

Vorotynskii, Prince Mikhail Ivanovich (sixteenth century), burns steppe to halt

Crimean Tatars (*1571*), 71
Vorskla River, Battle of (*1399*), defeat of
 Prince Viten by Edigei, 52
Vostochnyi Gavriil, vessel built at Okhotsk for
 Shestakov expedition (*1729*), sinks at
 mouth of Kamchatka River, 211
Votiaks (Udmurts), 67, 68
Vsevolod (III) Iur'evich ('Big Nest'), Prince
 of Suzdal (*1176–1212*), Grand Prince,
 Vladimir: and Bulgars, 27; and Novgorod,
 28
Vvedenskii, Andrei Aleksandrovich,
 historian, 112
Vychegda River, 45, 83, 87, 122
Vychegodskii posad, 85
Vym River, 37, 45, 122

Walrus ivory, 23, 189; found by Dezhnev,
 193
Walton, Lieutenant William, with Great
 Northern (second Bering) expedition,
 explores Kuriles and Japan, 216
Witsen, Nicolaas (*1641–1717*), Dutch
 authority on Russia, 81, 100, 112, 195

Zabolotskii, Erofei, Moscow envoy to
 Mongols, killed enroute (*1650*), 245
Zaraisk (*1531*), Crimeans repulsed at (*1533*)
 63, 70
Zavoloch'e (the 'Country beyond the
 Portage'), 23, 28, 38, 40, 42, 43
Zeia River, 137, 155, 156, 164, 167
Zhigansk (*1632?*), 135, 184
Zhigat Murzas, allies of Kuchum, submit, 11'
Zhiguli Bend, Volga River, 112
Zhukotin, Bulgar town on Kama, seized by
 ushkuiniki (*1360*), 36; (*1392*), 39
Zinov'ev, Dmitrii Ivanovich, on Amur to aid
 Khabarov (*1652–53*), 166, 168
Zinov'ev, Mikhail, prikashchik on Kamchatka
 (*1702*), 201
Zmeev, cossack golova, operates out of
 Berezov against Voguls on Konda River
 (*1593*), 122
Zvenigorod, given Prince Kasim (*1446*), 54
Zyrian, Dmitrii to Indigirka River (*1640*),
 188; death (*1646*), 189
Zyrians (Komi), 37, 197